GW00838560

MODERN LEGAL STUDIES

EMERGENCY POWERS IN PEACETIME

General Editor of the Series
Professor J. P. W. B. McAuslan

Editorial Board
H. Beale
Professor W. R. Cornish
Professor T. C. Daintith
Professor R. P. Grime
B. Hoggett
Professor J. D. McClean
Professor C. Palley

AUSTRALIA AND NEW ZEALAND
The Law Book Company Ltd.
Sydney : Melbourne : Perth

CANADA AND U.S.A.
The Carswell Company Ltd.
Agincourt, Ontario

INDIA
N. M. Tripathi Private Ltd.
Bombay
and
Eastern Law House Private Ltd.
Calcutta and Delhi
M.P.P. House
Bangalore

ISRAEL
Steimatzky's Agency Ltd.
Jerusalem : Tel Aviv : Haifa

MALAYSIA : SINGAPORE : BRUNEI
Malayan Law Journal (Pte.) Ltd.
Singapore

PAKISTAN
Pakistan Law House
Karachi

MODERN LEGAL STUDIES

EMERGENCY POWERS IN PEACETIME

by

DAVID BONNER, LL.M.
Lecturer in Law
University of Leicester

LONDON
SWEET & MAXWELL
1985

Published in 1985 by
Sweet & Maxwell Limited of
11 New Fetter Lane, London.
Printed in Great Britain by
Page Bros. (Norwich) Limited.

British Library Cataloguing in Publication Data

Bonner, David
Emergency powers in peacetime. — (Modern legal studies)
1. War and emergency powers—Great Britain
I. Title II. Series
344.102′8 KD4440

ISBN 0–421–31070–7
ISBN 0–421–31080–4 Pbk

All rights reserved.
No part of this publication may be reproduced or transmitted, in any form or by any means, electronic, mechanical, photocopying, recording or otherwise, or stored in any retrieval system of any nature without the written permission of the copyright holder and the publisher, application for which shall be made to the publisher.

©
David Bonner
1985

PREFACE

This book is about peacetime emergency powers available in the United Kingdom. These are the extraordinary powers which the constitutional and legal order permits to government to enable it to deal with those exceptional circumstances threatening the well-being of the nation, with which normal powers cannot cope. The pristine modern examples of such powers dealt with here are emergency powers to combat terrorism, particularly terrorism connected with Northern Irish affairs, and powers to assist in the maintenance of supplies and services essential to the community. The book examines the nature and use of these powers, decision-making with respect to them, and mechanisms which endeavour to ensure control and accountability of decision makers and to prevent abuse of the powers. It represents a case-study of an area of public law inevitably incompletely dealt with in existing textbooks on constitutional law.

The powers examined are mainly statutory and found in the Northern Ireland (Emergency Provisions) Act 1978, the Prevention of Terrorism (Temporary Provisions) Act 1984, the Emergency Powers Act 1920 (and its Northern Ireland counterpart), the Emergency Powers Act 1964, the Energy Act 1976, and the Drought Act 1976. Most apply throughout the United Kingdom. The Northern Ireland (Emergency Provisions) Act 1978 is confined in its operation to the Province, and the Drought Act 1976 to England and Wales. Insofar as consideration of the powers inevitably invites contrast with "normal powers", the existence of three legal jurisdictions in the United Kingdom has proved problematic, given constraints of space and the author's legal training in one jurisdiction. Accordingly, apart from the chapter on combating terrorism in Northern Ireland, the comparison is with normal powers applicable in England and Wales. Scottish readers will no doubt be better able than the author to make appropriate comparison with "normal" powers applicable there.

Many of the emergency powers are politically controversial. This work is not, however, designed as a polemic. The aim is to present a clear legal analysis of the powers themselves together with as wide a range of views on their rationale, operation and reform, as space would permit. Some attempt has been made to set them in historical, political and social context and where appropriate comparisons have been made with powers in other jurisdictions. Hopefully this presentation will enable the reader to make informed judgments on the propriety, adequacy and effectiveness of the powers and of the mechanisms of control and accountability with respect to their use. The subject area has proved volatile during the book's preparation, subject to change, development and ongoing debate. Earlier versions of Chapters Three and Four formed evidence to two Reviews of anti-terrorism powers during that period. The Jellicoe Review of the Prevention of Terrorism (Temporary Provisions) Act 1976 threw increased light on the operation of that legislation and its proposals for change were the basis of the Prevention of Terrorism (Temporary Provisions) Act 1984, which received the Royal Assent in March 1984. The issues of "supergrass" evidence and the use of lethal force by the security forces in the Province increased concern over powers there which provide, for serious offences, a system of non-jury trial by judge alone, heavily reliant on confession evidence as the only or main evidence against the accused. Those powers were reviewed by the late Sir George Baker who reported in April 1984. The Government has expressed itself in broad agreement with the tone of his report and with most of its recommendations and conclusions, and will bring forward legislative proposals at an opportune moment. His proposals are fully dealt with in Chapter Three. Events in the first half of 1984 (the miners' strike, the docks' strike, and the drought) threw into topical focus emergency powers to assist in the maintenance of essential supplies and services, and the publication in London in 1983 by Routledge & Kegan Paul plc of Jeffery and Hennessy's *States of Emergency*, cast new light on decision-making with respect to the use of the Emergency Powers Acts 1920 and 1964. Taking due account of all this has made for a longish work with extensive footnotes. Most are reference only, or designed to lead the reader to extra sources. Inclusion of section numbers in the text ought to reduce the need to oscillate between text and footnotes. I have tried to state the law in accordance with sources available to me on January 1, 1985, by updating at proof stage main points in a text to date to August 31, 1984.

While much of the research is based on original sources (statutes, cases, official publications and those of pressure groups and political parties), writers in this area owe much to the research work of Boyle, Hadden, Hillyard and Walsh on Northern Ireland powers, and of Gillian Morris and Jeffery and Hennessy with respect to essential supplies and services' powers. The debt this work owes to theirs is, hopefully, fully documented in text and footnotes. My thanks must also go to Routledge & Kegan Paul plc for permission to quote several lengthy extracts from Jeffery and Hennessy.

I am indebted to the patience and encouragement of the editorial staff at Sweet and Maxwell. I must thank helpful library staff at Leicester, particularly in Official Publications and Inter-Library loans. The Research Board at Leicester provided funds for some of the research on anti-terrorist powers. Officials at the Northern Ireland Office and the Department of the Environment courteously answered my questions and supplied required information where possible. I express thanks to and continued amazement at the ability of those who deciphered and typed my untidy manuscript: Anne Folwell, Barbara Goodman, Barbara Harris, Gladys Hurst and Anne De Ville. The Department of Common Law at Queens University, Belfast were kind enough to invite me to give a staff seminar and lecture there in April 1983. I thank all of them for their hospitality and their assistance, but in particular, Desmond Greer, Paul Maguire and Brice Dickson. Conversations with John Coyle proved invaluable. David Allen, David Pollard and David Newell read and commented on all or part of an earlier draft. Responsibility for views and errors, regrettably, must remain mine.

My greatest debt is to my wife, Barbara, whose patience, love and forebearance during the preparation of this book in a sense combine to make it as much hers as mine. I dedicate it to her.

University of Leicester DAVID BONNER
May 23, 1985

STOP PRESS

GOVERNMENT PROPOSALS ON REFORM OF THE NORTHERN IRELAND (EMERGENCY PROVISIONS) ACT 1978 ("NIEPA 1978")

The Baker proposals for change in respect of emergency powers to combat terrorism in Northern Ireland are discussed in Chapter 3. On June 26, 1985, the Secretary of State for Northern Ireland, Mr. Douglas Hurd, outlined the Government's response to those proposals (H.C. Deb., Vol. 81, cols. 1034–1037). The Government's reform proposals will be incorporated in a Bill to be brought forward when the parliamentary timetable permits, but certainly within the lifetime of the present Parliament. The main points of Mr. Hurd's statement are summarised below:

(1) The power speedily to re-invoke detention without trial will be retained to protect citizens in times of grave crisis when the reintroduction of detention through legislation might not prove quick enough (*e.g.* during a parliamentary recess).

(2) The Attorney General's power to "certify out" scheduled offences, to declare them capable of jury trial, will be extended to increase the number of jury trials of such offences, although the specific list of situations in which this will be possible will not precisely coincide with Baker's. Nor will the power be exercisable by the DPP (NI). Where a scheduled offence is tried by jury, the judge will not be given power to discharge the jury in the event of intimidation and to continue the trial sitting alone. Ordering a retrial was thought more appropriate.

(3) The police power of arrest and extended detention without charge (NIEPA 1978, s.11) will be repealed, leaving the police to rely on section 12 of the PTA 1984.

(4) An Army power of arrest will be retained, although no final decision has been taken on the need for, or form of, any modifications to the extant power (NIEPA 1978, s.14).

(5) The power to grant bail (NIEPA 1978, s.2) will be reformulated to move the onus towards the prosecution, in line with the current practice of the courts. Section 2(5) will be widened to include the RUC and its Reserve.

(6) Section 8 of NIEPA 1978 will be reformulated to reflect judicial practice on its interpretation and use with respect to the admission of inculpatory statements by the accused.

(7) The Bill will provide for annual renewal and quinquennial re-enactment of the emergency legislation, as with the PTA 1984.

(8) Thought is being given in respect of scheduled cases

(a) to setting a maximum on the period between committal and trial;
(b) to reducing delays between first remand and trial; and
(c) to increasing the maximum period a court may remand in custody to 28 or 30 days, even where the accused does not consent.

Mr. Hurd had already made clear that it was thought inappropriate to enact an extra-ordinary provision ruling out uncorroborated accomplice evidence, preferring to leave it to a court to assess the weight of any such evidence proffered (H.C. Deb., Vol. 80, col. 1009).

CONTENTS

OTHER BOOKS IN THE SERIES

Anatomy of International Law (Second Edition), by J. G. Merrills
Compensation and Government Torts, by C. Harlow
Constructive Trusts, by A. J. Oakley
Council Housing (Second Edition), by D. C. Hoath
Court of Justice of the European Communities (Second Edition), by L. N. Brown and F. G. Jacobs
Development Control, by J. Alder
Economic Torts (Second Edition), by J. D. Heydon
Exclusion Clauses in Contracts (Second Edition), by David Yates
The Family Home, by W. T. Murphy and H. Clark
Grievances, Remedies and the State, by Patrick Birkinshaw
Homelessness, by David Hoath
Human Rights and Europe (Second Edition), by Ralph Beddard
Immigration Law (Second Edition), by John Evans
International Dispute Settlement, by J. G. Merrills
Law of the Common Agricultural Policy, by Francis G. Snyder
Mortgages (Second Edition), by Paul B. Fairest
Natural Justice (Second Edition), by Paul Jackson
Registered Land (Third Edition), by David J. Hayton
Remedies for Breach of Contract, by Hugh Beale
Small Businesses (Second Edition), by Michael Chesterman
Squatting, by A. Prichard
Strict and Vicarious Liability, by L. H. Leigh
Taxation and Trusts, by G. W. Thomas

SHORT TITLES OF BOOKS, OFFICIAL REPORTS AND REVIEWS

Review of the Operation of the Northern Ireland (Emergency Provisions) Act 1978 by the Rt. Honourable Sir George Baker, O.B.E., Cmnd. 9222 (1984)

=Baker

Report of the Committee of Inquiry into Police Interrogation Procedures in Northern Ireland, Cmnd. 7497 (1979)

=Bennett

Report of the Commission to consider legal procedures to deal with terrorist activities in Northern Ireland, Cmnd. 5185 (1972)

=Diplock

Report of a Committee to consider, in the context of civil liberties and human rights, measures to deal with terrorism in Northern Ireland, Cmnd. 5847 (1975)

=Gardiner

K. Jeffery and P. Hennessy: *States of Emergency: British Governments and Strike breaking since 1919* (1983)

=Jeffery and Hennessy

Review of the Operation of the Prevention of Terrorism (Temporary Provisions) Act 1976 by the Rt. Hon. Earl Jellicoe, D.S.C., M.C., Cmnd. 8803 (1983)

=Jellicoe

Keesing's Contemporary Archives (1948 onwards)

=Keesing

Second Report of the Commission of Inquiry Concerning Certain Activities of the Royal Canadian Mounted Police: Freedom and Security under the Law (Vol. 2), 1981

=McDonald Report

Review of the Operation of the Prevention of Terrorism (Temporary Provisions) Acts 1974 and 1976 by the Rt. Hon. Lord Shackleton, K.G., O.B.E., Cmnd. 7324 (1978)

=Shackleton

Report of the Tribunal appointed to inquire into the events on Sunday, 30th January 1972, which led to the loss of life in connection with the procession in Londonderry on that day, by the Rt. Hon. Lord Widgery, O.B.E., T.O., M.C. 220 (1971–72)

=Widgery

TABLE OF CASES

TABLE OF STATUTES

TABLE OF STATUTORY INSTRUMENTS

Chapter 1

INTRODUCTION

1. An Overview

This book is concerned with peacetime emergency powers—those extraordinary powers permitted to government to deal with threats to the nation that cannot adequately be met by ordinary powers—which are currently available in the United Kingdom. It eschews detailed consideration of emergency powers applied in the United Kingdom during the two World Wars which are well covered elsewhere.[1] Nevertheless that wartime context cannot wholly be ignored; it has done much to shape the modern approach to emergency powers, particularly in the sphere of legislative and judicial oversight of their use by government. While the principal focus is on the United Kingdom, comparative material—particularly from the common law world—will be deployed at suitable points to illuminate advantages and deficiencies in the United Kingdom approach, to encourage a critical, in the sense of questioning, attitude to study. The book is, hopefully, not unduly insular. Although primarily a legal study some attempt will be made to set the powers analysed in the historical, political and social contexts which have shaped them and which continue to mould them.

The study concentrates in detail on emergency powers in two broad areas: first, powers to combat terrorism, particularly terrorism connected with Northern Ireland (see Chapters 3 and 4); and, secondly, powers to assist in the maintenance of supplies and services essential to the community (see Chapter 5). That the emphasis is more on anti-terrorism powers reflects their currently more widespread use. Chapter 2 deals with the process of decision-making with respect to the invocation, formulation and use of emergency powers; with issues of accountability; and with mechanisms and institutions which aspire to legitimate, regulate

[1] See, *e.g.* C.K. Allen *Law and Orders* (1st ed., 1945; 2nd ed., 1956; 3rd ed., 1965); C.P. Cotter, "Constitutionalizing Emergency Powers: The British Experience" (1953) 5 Stan.L.Rev. 382, and "Emergency Detention in Wartime: The British Experience" (1954) 6 Stan.L.Rev. 238.

and control resort to, and use of, such powers. Chapter 6, the final chapter of the study, looks to enhancing control and accountability; might a Bill of Rights improve matters; might it be beneficial to enact a statutory code of emergency powers, invocable in whole or in part by government in times of acute crisis; and, if so, what might such a code appropriately contain?

This chapter explores the nature of emergencies and emergency powers. An examination is made of the constitutional provisions of certain states other than the United Kingdom. This enables a clearer conception of emergency powers to emerge. It also provides a perspective on United Kingdom mechanisms and those provisions constitute "models" which might usefully shape an Emergency Powers Code for future use in the United Kingdom. The chapter next considers the incidence of resort to emergency powers. An examination is then made of the problems which emergencies and the use of emergency powers can pose to the system of values of and the process of government of a liberal democracy. Finally, the chapter puts forward a series of basic principles which ought to regulate resort to emergency powers in a liberal democratic state.

2. Emergencies and Emergency Powers

The political rationale underlying resort to emergency powers was summed up by Abraham Lincoln:

> "Every man thinks he has a right to live and every government thinks it has a right to live. Every man when driven to the wall by a murderous assailant will override all laws to protect himself, and this is called the great right of self-defence. So every government when driven to the wall by a rebellion will trample down a constitution before it will allow itself to be destroyed. This may not be constitutional law but it is a fact."[2]

This underlying rationale of self-defence, resting on the concept of necessity, is often expressed in the maxim *salus populi, suprema lex esto* (the safety of the people is the highest law).

Emergencies, which *may* require extraordinary powers to overcome them, are of many types. A United Nations' study of 36 constitutions in the early 1960s lists a wide range of threats to the

[2] Cited in M.P. O'Boyle, "Emergency Situations and the Protection of Human Rights: a Model Derogation Provision for a Northern Ireland Bill of Rights" (1977) 28 N.I.L.Q. 160, at p. 161.

well-being of the polity which those constitutions recognised as permitting the taking of emergency measures: international conflict, war, invasion, defence or security of the state or part thereof; civil war, rebellion, insurrection, subversion or the harmful activities of counter-revolutionary elements; disturbance of the peace, public order or safety; danger to the constitutional authorities; natural or public calamity or disaster; danger to the economic life of the country or parts thereof; the maintenance of essential supplies and services for the community.[3] On this basis, in terms of the United Kingdom, leaving aside armed conflict between states, one might identify the following as potential candidates for the use of emergency powers, at least in some circumstances: the activities of domestic nationalist terrorist groupings, particularly of Republican and Loyalist paramilitaries, but more recent of the Scottish National Liberation Army and extreme Welsh Nationalists; the threat posed by international terrorism, particularly in the capital, seat of government, financial and commercial centre, host to foreign embassies and exiled, dissident political groups; riots and violent political demonstrations; the problems posed by organised crime; the activities of foreign agents; the havoc wrought by extreme weather conditions or industrial action; the nightmare horrors of major accidents at chemical or nuclear installations; the fear of runaway inflation and chronic unemployment.

Most organised societies throughout history have made provision for emergency government. The Roman Dictator was appointed by the Consuls on the proposal of the Senate when that body had determined that a grave emergency existed and that ordinary methods would not be able to secure the safety of the Republic. The Dictator's function was to conclude a war or quell a rebellion.[4] Modern international human rights' conventions recognise the need for the State to override certain human rights in times of crisis. Article 4(1) of the United Nations' Covenant on Civil and Political Rights, 1966, provides:

> "In time of public emergency which threatens the life of the nation and the existence of which is officially proclaimed, the State Parties to the present Covenant may take measures derogating from their obligations under the present Covenant to the extent strictly required by the exigencies of the

[3] United Nations Department of Economic and Social Affairs, *Study of the Right of Everyone to be free from Arbitrary Arrest, Detention and Exile*, U.N. Doc. E/CN4/826 Rev. 1 (1965), at p. 184.

[4] O'Boyle, *loc. cit.* n. 2, at pp. 160-161.

> situation, provided that such measures are not inconsistent with their other obligations under international law and do not involve discrimination solely on the ground of race, colour, sex, language, religion or social origin."[5]

Similar provision is made in Article 15(1) of the European Convention on Human Rights 1950[6] (*infra*, pp. 83-90) and in Article 27(1) of the American Convention on Human Rights 1969.[7] All three international Bills of Rights, however, recognise certain human rights as non-derogable (*e.g.* the right to life, freedom from *ex post facto* laws, freedom from torture, inhuman or degrading treatment or punishment). Most modern constitutions contain some facility for the taking of emergency measures.[8]

The terminology, inevitably, varies between constitutions. Some refer to a "state of siege" (France, Belgium, Argentina), others to a "state of war" (Italy, Netherlands) and yet others to a "state of emergency" (Ireland, Zimbabwe, South Africa). The West German Constitution refers to a "state of defence," rather than of war, and a "state of tension." In the Eastern bloc countries, resort is typically had to a "state of martial law." In some constitutions (Australia, Canada and the United States) the power to take emergency measures is implied from more general powers in the Constitution (the "defence" power, the "war" power, the power to make laws for peace, order and good government).[9] In others (Zimbabwe, Kenya) specific power is granted but "public emergency" is left undefined.

Some systems specify in detail the circumstances in which emergency measures may be taken. Thus, the Jamaican Constitution defines "period of public emergency" as

> "any period during which–
> (a) Jamaica is engaged in any war; or
> (b) there is in force a proclamation by the Governor-General declaring that a state of public emergency exists; or

[5] I. Brownlie (Ed.), *Basic Documents on Human Rights* (2nd ed., 1981), pp. 129-130.

[6] *Ibid.* p. 247.

[7] *Ibid.* pp. 401-402.

[8] See A.P. Blaustein and G.H. Flanz, *Constitutions of the Countries of the World* (1971 and supplements) from which collection the provisions cited in the text have been taken.

[9] W.S. Tarnopolsky, "Emergency Powers and Civil Liberties" (1972) 15 Can.Pub.Admin. 194, at p. 197.

(c) there is in force a resolution of each House supported by the votes of a majority of all the members of that House declaring that democratic institutions are threatened by subversion."

A proclamation by the Governor-General, who acts on ministerial advice, will, however, only be effective if it declares

"that the Governor-General is satisfied—

(a) that a public emergency has arisen as a result of the imminence of a state of war between Jamaica and a foreign state or as a result of the occurrence of any earthquake, hurricane, flood, fire, outbreak of pestilence, outbreak of infectious disease or other calamity whether similar to the foregoing or not; or

(b) that action has been taken or is immediately threatened by any person or body of persons of such a nature and on so extensive a scale as to be likely to endanger the public safety or to deprive the community or any substantial proportion of the community of supplies and services essential to life."

Article 16 of the Constitution of the Fifth French Republic gives the President power to take such measures as are demanded by the circumstances

"when the institutions of the Republic, the independence of the nation, the integrity of its territory or the fulfilment of its international commitments are threatened in a grave and immediate manner, and when the regular functioning of the constitutional public authorities is interrupted."

Under the Constitution of the Republic of Ireland, suspension of ordinary constitutional safeguards is possible in time of war or armed rebellion. Legislation enacted for the purpose of securing the public safety and preservation of the state at such times is immune from "judicial control on the ordinary constitutional criteria."[10] Armed conflicts in which the State is not a party may nonetheless fall within the phrase "time of war" if both Houses of the Oireachtas (Parliament) resolve that a national emergency affecting the vital interests of the State exists as a result of that armed conflict. Military tribunals may be set up to deal with such states. Article 38.1 permits the establishment by law of special criminal courts where it is resolved in accordance with that law

[10] J.M. Kelly, *The Irish Constitution* (1980), p. 133.

"that the ordinary courts are inadequate to secure the effective administration of justice and the preservation of public peace and order."

It is difficult to discern any universal pattern amongst these constitutional mechanisms. Typically, in Western Europe and those "New Commonwealth" states whose independence constitutions were forged in Whitehall (*e.g.* Zimbabwe, Jamaica), such constitutional provisions permit a concentration of power in, and an expansion of the power of, the executive. They sanction derogation from various basic human rights and freedoms. They represent a drastic departure, albeit envisaged as temporary, from established constitutional norms and procedures. In most cases, however, "there is some formal control over the declaration of a state of emergency by the executive either by legislative or judicial organs."[11] For example, both Jamaica and Zimbabwe envisage prompt legislative scrutiny of the executive's proclamation, repeated at intervals during the currency of the emergency, with power to revoke it or order its revocation at any time. In France, the President may only take the measures contemplated by Article 16 after official consultation with the Prime Minister, the Presidents of the two Houses and the Constitutional Council. A Presidential message to the nation is required; Parliament convenes as of right; the National Assembly (Legislature) cannot be dissolved during the period of exercise of the emergency powers. The Conseil d'Etat exercises a certain degree of review of the measures taken pursuant to Article 16. The decision to invoke that Article, however, escapes scrutiny as an "act of government." Moreover measures taken which would otherwise fall within the domain prescribed by Article 34 of the Constitution for *la loi* (legislation) also escape its scrutiny.[12] Professor Finer notes that "the German Constitution goes to most elaborate lengths to ensure that the legislature shall meet and above all that the Constitutional Court shall continue to sit and carry out its functions."[13] Statutes authorising executive proclamations to bring emergency measures into effect in Canada and in the Republic of Ireland provide for a degree of legislative oversight.[14]

[11] W.L. Twining, *Emergency Powers: a Fresh Start*, Fabian Tract 416 (1972), p. 16.

[12] Claude-Albert Colliard, *libertés publiques* (6th ed., 1982), pp. 135-136.

[13] S.E. Finer, *Five Constitutions: Contrasts and Comparisons* (1979), p. 74.

[14] On Canada, see *Second Report of the Commission of Inquiry Concerning Certain Activities of the Royal Canadian Mounted Police: Freedom and Security Under the Law* (1981) (MacDonald Report), p. 921; on the Republic of Ireland see Kelly, *op. cit.* n. 10, p. 312.

The nature of emergencies which may threaten the life of any nation is by now sufficiently plain. But what are "emergency powers"? In those states with written "higher law" constitutions enabling special measures to be taken in time of emergency, it might be appropriate to confine consideration to those powers whose constitutional validity depends on those particular provisions of the constitution, although in common law countries, at least, plenary coverage might necessitate consideration of inherent common law powers of the executive and the doctrine of martial law. The flexible, unwritten "non-higher law" nature of the United Kingdom constitution renders such a formalistic definition of little help in identifying relevant powers. It might be suggested that emergency powers are those legal powers that the state can deploy to deal with the emergency. Such a definition would, however, be overinclusive and obscure the relationship between ordinary and emergency powers. One must distinguish between, on the one hand, those provisions of the law equally applicable to normal times (*e.g.* serious criminal offences, the Public Order Act 1936) which may be deployed effectively to cope with abnormal situations of crisis for example, the riots of 1981 or organised crime and, on the other hand, those special powers, granted to cope with such crises, which would not normally be available to the government. The powers applicable on an everyday basis represent the context in which the special powers (the emergency powers) operate. It is often the inadequacy of those ordinary powers to deal with the threat that provides a justification for resort to special powers. An example may help. In Northern Ireland, in the face of high levels of terrorist violence, the substantive criminal law has remained, by and large, little altered, but the mode of trial, the rules of criminal evidence and the means provided for gathering evidence have been drastically changed because it was considered that the ordinary criminal process could not ensure that sufficient terrorists were brought to justice (*infra,* pp. 100-101). The international norms and constitutional experience discussed above suggest to the present writer that emergency powers have three principal characteristics:

(a) those who operate the constitution conceive of them as extraordinary in scope, as powers which would not be available to government but for the emergency;

(b) they tend to confer wide discretionary authority and enhanced powers on government, untrammelled by the normal constitutional fetters;

(c) they are envisaged as being temporary in that the power only arises at the time of crisis, or, if statutory, will lapse on the occurrence of a particular event (*e.g.* the termination of the present war) or on a set date or after a set period of time unless its renewal is sanctioned by the legislature, the clear implication being that renewal will only be sanctioned if the need for the powers continues to exist.

In the United Kingdom, emergency powers in the sense defined above, have several legal sources: the royal prerogative; common law; the doctrine of martial law; and legislation. The principal source today is statutory.

At common law the Crown possesses powers of uncertain scope to deal with emergencies. Some are unique to the Crown and may properly be categorised as prerogative powers. Others are shared with subjects. In some instances, it is uncertain on which side of that line the power falls. Its existence and extent are the important practical points. The majority of the powers seem relevant only to wartime. The Crown has prerogative power to intern enemy aliens in wartime.[15] During sudden invasion or insurrection it appears that the Monarch might demand personal service within the realm.[16] The right of angary gives the Crown power to appropriate the property of neutrals within the realm in wartime,[17] and it has a right to requisition British ships during time of war or urgent national necessity, at least where the vessel is in territorial waters.[18] The *Case of the King's Prerogative in Saltpetre* recognised a right in Crown and subject to invade another's land to erect fortifications for the defence of the realm.[19] The Crown can destroy property to prevent its falling into enemy hands.[20] Many such exercises of power, albeit lawful, import a duty to pay compensation.[21] To turn to a context most relevant to this work, Professor Bradley suggests that

[15] *R.* v *Bottrill, ex p. Keuchenmeister* [1947] K.B. 41.

[16] Chitty, *Prerogatives of the Crown* (1820), p. 49.

[17] *Commercial and Estates Co. of Egypt* v. *Board of Trade* [1925] 1 K.B. 271.

[18] *The Broadmayne* [1916] P. 64, at p. 67; *Crown of Leon* v. *Admiralty Commissioners* [1921] 1 K.B. 595; Holdsworth (1919) 35 L.Q.R. 12.

[19] (1607) 12 Co.Rep. 12.

[20] *Burmah Oil* v. *Lord Advocate* [1965] A.C. 75.

[21] Wade and Phillips, *Constitutional and Administrative Law* (9th ed., 1977, edited by A.W. Bradley), p. 238.

"If . . . an emergency arose in which it was necessary for the Armed Forces to take immediate action against terrorist action in the United Kingdom, it is possible both that private property needed for this purpose could be occupied under the prerogative and that compensation would at common law be payable to the owners."[22]

At common law, all citizens have a duty to aid in the suppression of a riot, although the principal duty will fall on the police and special constables aided, in exceptional situations, by the military whom the law regards in this context as citizens in uniform armed in a particular manner.[23] Section 3 of the Criminal Law Act 1967, and its equivalent in Northern Ireland,[24] replacing the common law on the point, permit the use of such force to prevent crime as is reasonable in the circumstances. This is, of course, a permanent provision in the law and does not fall squarely within the conception of emergency power referred to above. It becomes highly relevant, however, since it prescribes the amount of force which may be used in the exercise of emergency powers, and to the emergency situation where troops are deployed in aid of the civil power during civil disturbances or in industrial disputes, arguably under the authority of the prerogative, but possibly pursuant to a more general common law rule requiring citizens (including soldiers) to assist the civil authority to quell disturbances, although it may be that troops can only be used to perform non-military tasks during industrial disputes under the authority of statute.[24a] The controversial issue of the use of force, particularly lethal force, by the security forces in Northern Ireland is discussed in Chapter 3 (*infra*, pp. 162-166).

The term "martial law" may be used to describe the right of the Crown and its officers to use the amount of force necessary to restore order when there exists a state of actual war, or of insurrection, riot or rebellion amounting to war.[25] It is unclear whether it is a prerogative right.[26] Martial law has not been

[22] *Ibid.*

[23] M. Supperstone, *Brownlie's Law of Public Order and National Security* (2nd ed., 1981), p. 210.

[24] Criminal Law Act (N.I.) 1967.

[24a] The legal basis for the use of troops is somewhat confused. For differing views see Supperstone, *op. cit.*, n. 23, pp. 210-211; S. Greer "Military Intervention in Civil Disturbances: The Legal Basis Reconsidered" [1983] P.L. 573; S. Peak, *Troops in Strikes* (1984), esp. pp. 51-62.

[25] 8 *Halsbury's Laws of England* (4th ed.), para. 982.

invoked in Great Britain since 1800. It was deployed in Ireland before and after the emergence of the Irish Free State in 1922. It has been "employed in recent times in certain commonwealth countries."[27] Robin Evelegh has argued that it existed in Northern Ireland in the early and mid 1970s.[28] No government, however, has sought to support its actions in that Province by relying on a legal doctrine which would imply that it had lost control of the situation, attract further international opprobrium and the uncertainties of which do not give a secure enough legal base to the actions of the security forces.[29] Martial law could, however, prove particularly relevant to the aftermath of a nuclear war.[30] Martial law is well covered in other works[31] and is not pursued further in any detail in this book.

The uncertainties as to the extent, scope and, in some cases, the very existence of the powers noted above may constitute a formidable obstacle to their invocation in modern times, although imprecision in powers, by discouraging challenge to them, may occasionally work to the advantage of government. It may also be true to say that it would be constitutionally unacceptable today that extraordinary powers of the military should arise by process of common law.[32] Common law powers are not suitable for dealing with internal emergencies not founded on violence.[33] Reliance instead tends to be placed on statutory provisions conferring on the executive enhanced powers, broad discretion to act and respond to the changing exigencies of the situation and ability to legislate further. A statutory code, recently revised, covers civil defence.[34] The Government is reportedly polishing up

[26] Supperstone, *op. cit.* n. 23, p. 214.

[27] *Ibid.*

[28] R. Evelegh, *Peace-keeping in a Democratic Society: The Lessons of Northern Ireland* (1978), pp. 32-34.

[29] Supperstone, *op. cit.* n. 23, p. 214; D.R. Lowry, "Terrorism and Human Rights: Counter-Insurgency and Necessity at Common Law" (1977) 53 *Notre Dame Law* 49, at p. 53.

[30] Lowry, *loc. cit.* n. 29, at p. 53; H. Marx, "The Emergency Power and Civil Liberties in Canada" (1970) 16 McGill L.J. 39, at p. 47.

[31] As well as the standard constitutional law texts see C. Fairman, *The Law of Martial Rule* (2nd ed., 1943).

[32] Supperstone, *op. cit.* n. 23, p. 214.

[33] G.S. Morris, "The Emergency Powers Act 1920" [1979] P.L. 317.

[34] Civil Defence Act 1948; Civil Defence (General Local Authority Functions) Regulations 1983 (S.I. 1983 No. 1634); *The Times*, June 21, 1983, p. 1; and for critical comment see D. Campbell, *War Plan UK: The Truth about Civil Defence in Britain* (1982).

draft enabling legislation and subordinate legislation of the type used in the Second World War to meet future wartime contingencies.[35] This renders unlikely the prospect of future clarification of the scope of pertinent common law powers. It should be noted, however, that, emulating the Emergency Powers (Defence) Act 1939,[36] the current emergency legislation in Northern Ireland provides that, while other rules of law or enactments cannot detract from the extensive scope of the powers it confers, neither do those powers conferred derogate from the prerogative or from other common law or statutory powers.[37] Residual common law powers might, therefore, be relied on to supply an omission of the legislature should it prove necessary. Indeed, a curfew, imposed by the Army in the Falls Road area of Belfast from July 3-5, 1970, was upheld on the basis that "by a novel extension of the common law, citizens, the army for this purpose being regarded as citizens, may prevent violent crime and take all reasonable steps to prevent crime and suppress a riot."[38] Nor do the other statutory powers to be considered expressly abrogate common law or prerogative powers.[39]

In terms of statute, the pristine example of emergency powers is the legislation of the two World Wars which enabled the executive to regulate almost every facet of life.[40] For reasons stated earlier, these powers are not dealt with here. The areas to be dealt with in this work are combating terrorism and assisting in the maintenance of essential supplies and services. Consideration of these areas highlights problems which would also arise, perhaps in more acute form, with wartime emergency powers, and constitutes ample illustration of the fundamental dilemmas posed for democracies by emergency powers. Before proceeding further it will be useful to provide a more precise "pen-portrait" of the powers on which this book concentrates.

Emergency powers to combat terrorism are contained in two principal statutes: the Northern Ireland (Emergency Provisions) Act 1978 (hereinafter "NIEPA 1978") and the Prevention of

[35] *The Times*, June 21, 1983, p. 1.

[36] s.9.

[37] Northern Ireland (Emergency Provisions) Act 1978, s.35(1).

[38] C. Palley, "The Evolution, Disintegration and Possible Reconstruction of the Northern Ireland Constitution" (1972) 1 Anglo-Am.L.Rev. 368, at p. 413, n. 214.

[39] This might raise issues similar to those in *Att.-Gen.* v. *De Keysers' Royal Hotel* [1920] A.C. 508 were reliance sought to be placed on prerogative powers.

[40] See, generally, Allen, *op. cit.* n. 1, *passim.*

Terrorism (Temporary Provisions) Act 1984 (hereinafter "PTA 1984"). The former, applicable only in Northern Ireland, has widened the scope of the criminal law, gives executive power to proscribe organisations, and furnishes the security forces with wider powers of stop and search, search and seizure, and arrest and detention. It provides for the non-jury trial, pursuant to modified rules of evidence, of those serious criminal offences commonly committed by terrorists. The PTA 1984, which, for the most part, applies throughout the United Kingdom, permits the executive proscription of organisations, creates a number of new criminal offences related to terrorist activity, provides wider police powers, and enables the executive, by means of an administrative process, to exclude terrorist suspects from Great Britain, from Northern Ireland or from the United Kingdom as a whole. The criminal offences, and powers of proscription and exclusion, however, relate only to terrorism connected with Northern Ireland affairs.

Emergency powers to assist in the maintenance of essential supplies and services are primarily embodied in the Emergency Powers Act 1920 (hereinafter "EPA 1920") (and its Northern Ireland equivalent)[41] which enable the executive to proclaim a state of emergency

> "if at any time it appears . . . that there have occurred, or are about to occur, events of such a nature as to be calculated, by interfering with the supply and distribution of food, water, fuel or light, or with the means of locomotion, to deprive the community, or any substantial portion of the community, of the essentials of life. . . ."[42]

[41] The legislation is the Emergency Powers Act (N.I.) 1926, as amended by the Emergency Powers (Amendment) Act (N.I.) 1964. In addition the powers under s.2 of the Emergency Powers Act 1964 to use troops on agricultural or other urgent work of national importance (*infra*, pp. 229-233) apply to the Province. In substance, there is no real difference between the Northern Ireland legislation and its mainland counterpart. However, the proclamation of emergency continues in force, without time limit or periodic Parliamentary scrutiny, until revoked by the Secretary of State, and there was never any special provision for the Northern Ireland Parliament to take action in respect of regulations made under the 1926 Act. Nor, with Direct Rule, is there any provision for the Westminster Parliament to take such action in respect of them. Under s.2 of the Northern Ireland Act 1982, the Secretary of State *may* refer any regulations for consideration by the Northern Ireland Assembly, and, if he does so, any report of that Assembly must be laid before Parliament.

[42] EPA 1920, s.1(1).

Parliament must be informed of the occasion of the proclamation.[43] The executive then has power to make regulations "for securing the essentials of life to the community . . . and for any other purposes essential to the public safety and the life of the community."[44] The regulations require prompt parliamentary approval to continue in force.[45] A new proclamation and set of regulations must be issued at monthly intervals during the currency of the emergency, subject to the same procedure for legislative oversight.[46] Emergency powers to regulate or prohibit the production, supply, and consumption of energy are contained in the Energy Act 1976.[47] The Drought Act 1976 provides emergency powers to help meet deficiencies in water supplies caused by exceptional shortage of rain.[48]

3. The Incidence of Use of Emergency Powers

If, as in a recently published study by the International Commission of Jurists,[49] one defines states of emergency to cover not merely formally proclaimed states of exception in accordance with constitutional provisions, but extends the term to embrace "regimes of exception" (regimes which have overthrown the existing constitutional order and taken powers similar to those permissible under a formal proclamation of emergency), it is clear that the use of emergency powers is a common phenomenon of our times. "It is probably no exaggeration to say that at any given time in recent history a considerable part of humanity has been living under a state of emergency."[50] It is a phenomenon which reaches into every region of the globe.[51]

In Great Britain, states of emergency under the EPA 1920 have been proclaimed on "12 separate occasions, including nine since 1945 and five in the period 1970-74."[52] There have been several such proclamations under equivalent Northern Ireland

43 EPA 1920, s.1(3).
44 EPA 1920, s.2(1).
45 EPA 1920, s.2(2).
46 EPA 1920, ss.1(1), 2(2).
47 ss.1-4.
48 ss.1, 2.
49 *States of Emergency: Their Impact on Human Rights* (1983).
50 *Ibid.* p. 413.
51 *Ibid.*
52 G.S. Morris, *loc. cit.* n. 33, at p. 318.

legislation.[53] Emergency powers have been a common response to problems posed by violence connected with the issue of the status of Northern Ireland as part of the United Kingdom. Within the Province, such powers were invoked on several occasions from 1920,[54] and have been in continuous use since 1969. On this side of the water, the Prevention of Violence (Temporary Provisions) Act 1939 (hereinafter "PVA 1939") was a response to the IRA bombing campaign which began in January of that year and ended, for all practical effect, in 1940.[55] The spread of IRA violence to the mainland in 1972 eventually prompted the passage of the Prevention of Terrorism (Temporary Provisions) Act 1974 (hereinafter "PTA 1974"), the essential features of which were continued in the Prevention of Terrorism (Temporary Provisions) Act 1976 (hereinafter "PTA 1976") and are repeated in the PTA 1984. The oil crisis of 1973-74 led to emergency restrictions on production, supply and consumption of fuel.[56] Restrictions on the use of water in particular localities have been a feature of several summers since 1976, although problems in that year and in 1984 were particularly acute.[57]

4. The Dilemma Posed by Emergency Powers

A liberal democracy has several important facets.[58] Government is derived from, and must remain accountable to, public opinion through periodic elections. Government is also limited, in part through the provision of formal checks and balances, by a separation of powers within and between the organs and different levels of government. Thus, in the United Kingdom, the executive is accountable to a representative legislature and to the law as interpreted and applied by an independent judiciary whose judgments are generally respected by the executive. In such a democracy, government is responsive to public opinion, expressed in a free press and through organised pressure groups. It is also limited by the rule of law, by which is here understood not only

[53] Palley, *loc. cit.* n. 38, at p. 404; R. Fisk, *The Point of No Return* (1975).

[54] Twining, *op. cit.* n. 11, pp. 5-8.

[55] T.P. Coogan, *The I.R.A.* (1980), pp. 150-172.

[56] Fuel and Electricity Control Act 1973. See, *e.g.* Fuel Control (Modification of Enactments) (Speed Limits) Order 1973 (S.I. 1973 No. 2051). Earlier restrictions had been made pursuant to a proclamation of emergency under the EPA 1920 (see Morris, *loc. cit.* n. 33, at p. 343).

[57] *Infra*, pp. 217-220.

[58] See, in general, S.E. Finer, *Comparative Government* (1970), Chaps. 2, 5-7.

the notion that authority must act according to law, but also the idea that the law which governs its actions, and its actions themselves, must be consonant with respect for generally accepted concepts of the inherent dignity and rights and freedoms of the individual, whether embodied in international obligations, domestic constitutional arrangements or as values considered fundamental by the polity.[59] Government, for example, is expected to respect the right of the individual to be free from torture or cruel punishment, to freedom from arbitrary arrest, to due process of law, to trial by jury. The onus is squarely placed on government to justify interference with accepted rights and freedoms. Such a democracy is pluralistic, respects the rights of minorities and tolerates rights of dissent, of free expression and association so vital to the promotion of peaceful change in society and to the formulation of public opinion essential to genuine accountability of government. The emphasis, in such a democracy, is firmly on change through peaceful persuasion rather than through violence (or, to adopt current political jargon, is committed to change through the ballot-box not the bullet or the bomb).

The use of emergency powers can constitute a threat to that system. Legal power becomes concentrated in the government. At the extreme, it may result in the installation of an authoritarian government. This has been a typical Latin American experience. Western Europe has, however, witnessed the installation of such a regime in Greece (1967-73) and, more recently, in Turkey. It was arguably the result, albeit temporarily, of the Indian emergency proclaimed in 1975. In such situations, gross abuse of human rights may occur.[60] But, even if a democratic base is maintained, emergency powers typically involve interference with civil liberties in terms of detention without trial, house arrest, internal exile, restrictions on movement, the requisition of property, discrimination against racial or political groupings, interference with freedom of expression, freedom of association and the right to strike. An attitude that the end justifies the means may prevail, that to uphold the law one must, if necessary, break it. Ill-treatment of detainees is common.[61]

59 International Commission of Jurists, *The Rule of Law and Human Rights: Principles and Definitions* (1966), *passim.*

60 Niall McDermott, Introduction to ICJ Study, *op. cit.* n. 49, pp. i-iii.

61 D. O'Donnell, "Observations and Conclusions" in ICJ Study, *op. cit.* n. 49, pp. 413-458.

It is, of course, tempting to think that all this can only happen elsewhere. Current emergency powers to combat terrorism in the United Kingdom are, however, very wide and effect many restrictions on accepted civil liberties. Allegations of ill-treatment have been upheld and variously characterised as torture or inhuman and degrading treatment by responsible, independent international bodies.[62] Resort to the EPA 1920 to combat the effects of industrial disputes in essential industries inevitably has an impact on the practical effectiveness of the right to strike.[63] The Act itself has been denounced as "a constant menace to our civil rights" which permits the executive "to weight the scales heavily against those who may be in active opposition to the government of the day."[64]

Resort to emergency powers may become a habit. Michael O'Boyle suggests that

> "frequent use of emergency powers to cope with crises, coupled with the success of these powers acclimatises administrators to their use, and makes recourse to them in the future, all the easier. The danger is, that succeeding generations of administrators inherit these powers as being efficient and unobjectionable, and, in a particular emergency, do not give proper consideration to the possibility of less drastic measures being used."[65]

The example he cites is the frequent resort to internment without trial in Northern Ireland as a response to Republican violence. Frequent use may de-sensitise the populace to the problems of human rights involved.[66] The effect of emergency powers may be to increase authoritarian tendencies in law and society. What was once extraordinary, can, for varying reasons, become permanent and accepted. Professor Dugard has noted such a process at work in South Africa. In 1960, after police at Sharpeville had shot dead

[62] As torture by the European Commission on Human Rights (see M.P. O'Boyle, "Torture and Emergency Powers under the European Convention on Human Rights: *Ireland* v. *The U.K.*" (1977) 71 A.J.I.L. 674) and as inhuman and degrading treatment by the European Court of Human Rights (see D. Bonner, "Ireland v U.K." (1978) 27 I.C.L.Q. 897); *infra*, pp. 120-121.

[63] K. Jeffery and P. Hennessy, *States of Emergency: British Governments and Strikebreaking since 1919* (1983), p. 263.

[64] R. Kidd, *British Liberty in Danger* (1940), pp. 48, 51.

[65] O'Boyle, *loc. cit.* n. 2, at p. 164.

[66] *Ibid.*

Africans protesting at the pass-laws, the Government resorted to emergency powers. Their use was highly successful in terms of suppressing political opposition

> "but from an economic point of view [the proclamation of emergency] was disastrous, as foreign investors lost faith in the country's political stability. The Government therefore sought a new method that would permit it to combat radical political opposition effectively without endangering the economic stability of the country. Initially the solution took the form of the enactment of temporary measures, such as the 90-day detention law, which required annual renewal by Parliament; but, as foreign investors became more convinced of the ability of the security forces to counter political change and white opposition became more timid, the Government became bolder and enacted severe emergency-type measures that have become a permanent part of the South African legal system."[67]

The draconian Civil Authorities (Special Powers) Act 1922 in Northern Ireland was originally a measure subject to annual, and later quinquennial, renewal. In 1933, it was made permanent so that "in a sense Northern Ireland [was] treated as being in a permanent state of emergency."[68] Concern has been expressed that the current anti-terrorist measures are in danger of becoming *de facto* permanent features.[69] A common complaint about emergency powers is their retention for longer than necessary. The PVA 1939 was renewed annually and remained in force on the statute book until 1954. It has also been suggested that

> "[t]he danger of abolishing traditional safeguards in an emergency is that ultimately the new procedures will become the norm for criminal procedure. . . . [that] the dividing line between 'emergency' powers and powers used in ordinary criminal cases will become correspondingly difficult to draw."[70]

Commentators have not been slow in drawing critical parallels

[67] J. Dugard, *Human Rights and the South African Legal Order* (1978), p. 112.

[68] Twining, *op. cit.* n. 11, p. 4.

[69] See, *e.g.* C. Scorer and P. Hewitt, *The Prevention of Terrorism Act: The case for repeal* (NCCL, 1981), pp. 10, 13.

[70] C. Scorer, *The Prevention of Terrorism Acts 1974 and 1976: A Report on the Operation of the Law* (NCCL, 1976), p. 2.

between powers in the anti-terrorist legislation and the proposals for widening police powers of arrest and detention embodied in the Report of the Royal Commission on Criminal Procedure[71] and their enshrinement in the Police and Criminal Evidence Act 1984.[72] There is a related danger that emergency powers may be used to cope with ordinary crimes. Thomas Franck noted such a process in India and Ghana.[73] Mary Robinson has criticised the use of the Special Criminal Court in Dublin to deal with non-terrorist offences.[74] Concern has been expressed that offences not connected with paramilitary organisations or security forces' action against them are tried in Northern Ireland by a judge sitting alone without a jury and applying heavily modified evidentiary rules as to the admission of inculpatory statements made by the accused.[75]

The over-zealous use of emergency powers may prove counter-productive in the sense of exacerbating the problem they were designed to solve. In his recent *Review of the Operation of the Prevention of Terrorism (Temporary Provisions) Act 1976* Lord Jellicoe noted:

> "It has also been argued by many, including some who gave evidence to me, that this type of legislation represents a victory for the terrorist. Terrorist 'theoreticians' see it as a major aim to force governments to pass increasingly severe laws to counter the threat which they pose. This 'victory' will, it is argued, be enhanced if the legislation is operated in such a way as to alienate that part of the community which the terrorists claim to represent. If this happens, they will not only be likely to gain increased support from within the community; they will also be assisted to present themselves as its legitimate protectors. The support may simply be passive, in that members of the community refuse or are reluctant to assist the police, or it may be more active. . . . It is vital that

[71] Cmnd. 8092 (1981).

[72] See P. Hillyard, "From Belfast to Britain: Some Critical Comments on the Royal Commission on Criminal Procedure" *Power and Politics* (1981), p. 88; D. Walsh, "Arrest and Interrogation: Northern Ireland 1981" (1982) 9 B.J.L.S. 37, at pp. 53-57.

[73] T.M. Franck, *Comparative Constitutional Process: Cases and Materials* (1968), p. 236.

[74] M.T.W. Robinson, *The Special Criminal Court* (1974), pp. 35-36.

[75] D. Walsh, *The Use and Abuse of Emergency Legislation in Northern Ireland* (1983), pp. 80-82, 99. (*infra*, p. 106).

> such powers do not unnecessarily alienate—either in their essence or in their operation—any section of the law-abiding population in Great Britain or in Northern Ireland."[76]

It follows that, in questioning the operation of such powers, one should not be thought "soft on terrorism"; rather one is asking: how can terrorism best be fought? As the Shadow Home Secretary put it in a debate on the operation of the PTA 1976:

> " . . . both in Great Britain and Northern Ireland we shall have a lasting victory over terrorism only if we demonstrate our unqualified devotion to a genuinely free society . . . [W]e must be able to say to people questioning our commitment to a free society that, even in the face of a terrorist threat, we do all we can to ensure that it is preserved to the furthest degree that its preservation is possible. . . . [The Act] is manifestly a denial of civil liberties. It is essential that [one] does not review it lightly or as a matter of routine."[77]

The authors of a recent study on the use of the EPA 1920 and other powers to use troops to deal with the effects of industrial disputes point to the "dangerously seductive illusion" that emergency powers are a means of solving such a complex social and political phenomenon:

> "The post-war Attlee government reached a stage at which using troops became an almost automatic reaction to serious disputes. In the case of the docks, this not only exacerbated industrial unrest, but also blinded the government to the underlying causes of the trouble."[78]

It cannot be gainsaid that resort to emergency powers carries with it potential dangers. On the other hand, however, a government has a duty to protect its democracy and the lives and property of its citizens from terrorist attacks which are, by their very nature, fundamentally anti-democratic. Nor can it be expected to stand idly by and allow the populace to suffer in the wake of an industrial dispute affecting essential supplies and services. It may indeed be true to say that

> "*Now* we are a totally *inter*dependent society. No community, no industry and no public service lives to itself alone. We are all dependent on one another. More importantly we are now

[76] Cmnd. 8803 (1983), para. 10.
[77] Mr. R. Hattersley, MP, H.C. Deb., Vol. 1, col. 340 (March 18, 1981).
[78] Jeffery and Hennessy, *op. cit.* n. 63, pp. 264-265.

> so utterly reliant on some services that, without them, convenience, security, health and even life itself can be disastrously affected if any are disrupted or withdrawn from the community."[79]

The "politician's nightmare," sewage in the streets, would be "a vivid indication that the government has lost the capacity to govern."[80] Naturally, if the threats to the stability or well-being of the nation identified earlier in this chapter can be met adequately and effectively with "normal" powers, all well and good. But, if such powers prove unequal to the task, resort to emergency powers must be justifiable. Under-reaction may be just as dangerous to the polity as over-reaction. Clearly the problem of emergency powers has as much a political and social dimension as a legal one. In evaluating them much must depend on the nature of the powers, the purposes for which they are employed and one's view of the regime deploying them. The problem is one of striking the appropriate balance between competing values. As Michael O'Boyle has noted:

> " . . . the problem of emergency government is how a state can provide for the temporary abeyance of constitutional restraints without doing permanent damage to the norms and values underpinning constitutional government. More specifically, the problem concerns the way in which a government can deal effectively with an emergency situation, and, at the same time, endeavour to prevent the dangers of emergency government from occurring. From a legal standpoint this involves the creation of various checks and safeguards to take the place of the usual constitutional restraints that govern executive power but which have been temporarily relaxed to enable the state to defend itself."[81]

It is as well to remember that one's choice may be restricted to that of the lesser evil.

5. Some Governing Principles

In such a politically volatile area, sharp differences of opinion are only to be expected as to the necessity for and the appropriateness of particular emergency powers in any given situation. A

[79] Centre for Policy Studies, *The Right to Strike in a Free Society* (1983), p. 1.

[80] Jeffery and Hennessy, *op. cit.* n. 63, p. 249.

[81] O'Boyle, *loc. cit.* n. 2, at pp. 164-165.

statement of governing principles, being themselves "value-laden," cannot remove all differences: reasonable people may disagree on their content; or on the result of their application to particular contexts. Such a statement of principles at least indicates the author's stand-point, however, and ought to enable clearer identification of points of disagreement. In that spirit, it is suggested that the principles set out below ought to govern one's attitude to the invocation, formulation and use of emergency powers in a liberal democratic society. The principles are by no means novel.[82] They appear to the author to be inherent in the nature of the liberal democratic state, to be consonant with the Rule of Law as proclaimed by the International Commission of Jurists, to embody the spirit of the United Kingdom's international obligations under the European Convention on Human Rights and to reflect constitutional norms in the common law world. Their fundamental justification is that failure to respect them is likely to result in the arbitrary exercise of power.[83]

(1) There should only be resort to emergency powers in those situations where the Government can show it to be absolutely necessary. It must be abundantly clear, both in terms of the general situation and in respect of their application to individual cases, that existing powers are inadequate.

(2) The measures taken must not go beyond what the exigencies of the situation demand. There should be the minimum derogation possible from existing civil rights and freedoms in municipal and international law. In no circumstances should there be derogation from those rights and freedoms regarded as non-derogable under international obligations.

(3) Resort to emergency powers should not be prolonged further than is absolutely necessary.

(4) The measures taken must have a democratic aim and be subject to effective and periodic Parliamentary control of their invocation, use and continuation. There should be a measure of review by an independent judiciary.

(5) The measures should be clearly and precisely

[82] See, in particular: Twining, *op. cit.* n. 11, pp. 13-14; and, by the same author, "Emergency Powers and Criminal Process: The Diplock Report" [1973] Crim. L.R. 406, at pp. 407-409.

[83] Twining, *op. cit.* n. 11, p. 14.

formulated—preferably in statutory rules—so that all concerned are able to make an adequate assessment of their respective powers, rights and obligations.

(6) The introduction and exercise of each measure should be accompanied by adequate safeguards against its abuse. In circumstances where safeguards provided in existing law (*e.g.* habeas corpus) are likely to prove inadequate the measure itself ought to contain special remedies, procedures and provision for compensation to check abuse. Where there is doubt about whether sufficient safe-guards can be provided, careful consideration must be given to whether it is better to refuse to grant the power rather than run the risk of abuse, or whether the power is so vital that that risk must be run.

Chapter 2

DECISION-MAKING, CONTROL AND ACCOUNTABILITY

A. INTRODUCTION

Emergency powers are granted at the behest of, and/or invoked by, the Government which under the United Kingdom Constitution is politically and legally accountable. It is collectively responsible to Parliament in that the Government may fall if it or its policies cease to retain the confidence of the House of Commons. It is expected to inform Parliament about its policies and to explain and justify them there. Ministers are individually responsible to Parliament for the decisions of their departments. The Government, however, uses Parliament to confer emergency powers in wide terms. That Government is legally accountable (in that it must exercise power within the terms of statute and common law as interpreted and applied by the courts) might be thought important as a control factor, but the absence of an overriding Bill of Rights and of power of judicial review of the constitutionality of legislation predicates a limited role for the courts. As Anthony Lester has noted, this means that important

> "safeguards against the abuse of power by the government in Parliament are . . . not legally enforceable: they are constitutional understandings, conventions or principles of good administration, the observance of which depends upon the sense of fair play of Ministers and their civil servants; the vigilance of the opposition and individual Members of Parliament; the influence of the press, broadcasting and public opinion; and the periodic opportunity of changing the government through free and secret elections."[1]

[1] A. Lester, "Fundamental Rights in the United Kingdom" (1976-77) 125 Penn.L.Rev. 337, at p. 339. On modes of protecting human rights in the U.K. see further: Whitehall Inter-Departmental Working Group, *Legislation on Human Rights with particular reference to the European Convention: A Discussion Document* (1976), pp. 4-5; H. Street, *Freedom, The Individual and the Law* (5th ed., 1982), Chap. 14.

This chapter examines the roles of the executive, legislature and judiciary in the creation, invocation, operation and control of emergency powers. It further considers the importance of commissions, complaints and review agencies, pressure groups and media, in forming parliamentary and public opinion to which our governors may be responsive. An international legal dimension, particularly in terms of the European Convention on Human Rights, must be examined. The impact of Community law requires some consideration.

It will be seen that the executive is very much dominant, subject to surveillance, through a variety of mechanisms, by Parliament, and to a much straitened judicial review; that reviews and inquiries have been important in shaping emergency powers to combat terrorism; that wide leeway will be afforded governments under the European Convention; that the roles and influences of Community law and international labour law in this sphere are marginal.

Inevitably, because of the need to take prompt effective action and to be able to match the response to what might be quite rapid changes in the exigencies of the situation, executive dominance is likely to remain the keynote. It is submitted, however, that useful reforms could be made to the domestic system of control and accountability without preventing the executive from so acting in appropriate situations, and which would enhance accountability and promote good decision-making. Some reforms are examined in this chapter. More far reaching changes to enhance control and accountability are explored in Chapter 6 (*infra*, pp. 271-286).

B. THE DOMESTIC LAW CONTEXT

1. The Role of the Executive

The executive is very much in the driving seat over decisions to formulate new emergency powers and secure their enactment by Parliament, over decisions to invoke existing emergency powers, in planning possible responses to particular contingencies which may involve the use of such powers, and in operating and directing the operation of these powers when in force. The Cabinet and its committees are much to the fore in respect of the first three decisions, aided (and perhaps dominated) by advice from civil servants and other civilian officials, the police, the armed forces and the intelligence and security services. Cabinet, its committees and individual Ministers may play an important policy-making and supervisory role with respect to the fourth decision-making function. Day to day operation is in the hands of the permanent executive: civil servants, the police and the military. The collegiate and hierarchical nature of these decision-making processes may produce mechanisms which can work to limit the potential for abuse of power. The secrecy which surrounds executive decision-making in terms of current and to some extent also of past powers, however, renders it difficult to write in precise terms about its role. Subsequent chapters note specific reasons for the invocation of specific powers, gleaned from published official reviews and ministerial statements in Parliament. These give some insight into the processes but not a complete picture. Recently, in specific context, two studies have been published, based, in whole or in great part, on an analysis of relevant Cabinet papers. These studies throw some light on executive decision-making with respect to the enactment of the Emergency Powers Act 1920 ("EPA 1920") and its subsequent invocation in particular emergencies, and to the enactment of the Prevention of Violence (Temporary Provisions) Act 1939 ("PVA 1939") which, in many respects, may be regarded as a forerunner of the Prevention of Terrorism Acts. These studies are summarised below with the obvious caveat that their relevance to the modern process must be to some extent conjectural.

In a liberal democracy, one would expect careful decision-making by Cabinet and its committees to involve examination of such matters as: the precise nature of the crisis; whether ordinary powers can cope; whether extra-ordinary powers are needed, and why; what sorts of powers are needed, involving what nature and degree of interference with civil liberties; what protections should be inbuilt to maintain respect for such liberties; will the powers be effective or might they exacerbate the situation; at what point ought they to be invoked; the international repercussions; the likely response of Parliament and of public opinion. What do the specific studies tell us about the process?

Jeffery and Hennessy's study, *States of Emergency: British Governments and Strikebreaking since 1919,* [2] notes that in January 1920, the Cabinet's Supply and Transport Committee (STC), composed of ministers and senior civil servants, which dealt with

[2] K. Jeffery and P. Hennessy, *States of Emergency: British Governments and Strikebreaking since 1919* (1983). The points in the text are précised from pp. 50-57. Information on changes in the draft Bill (p. 27) comes from G.S. Morris, *A Study of the Protection of Public and Essential Services in Labour Disputes 1920-1976* (unpublished Ph.D. thesis, University of Cambridge, 1978), pp. 114-124.

disruptions in essential supplies and services on the basis of wartime powers, requested the Home and Scottish Offices to produce, after consultation with relevant departments, a Bill dealing with the subject, given that wartime powers would soon lapse and that continuing industrial unrest might be the tip of the revolutionary iceberg. The Bill was duly presented to the STC which deferred further action until departments indicated the precise powers they would require at each of three steadily worsening stages of a dispute: (a) from the beginning of the strike until the end of its fourth day; (b) after four days when the struggle became more intense; (c) when matters came close to attempts at revolution. The STC also saw the necessity to provide powers enabling use of servicemen in non-military capacities during an industrial dispute. When the matter of bringing a Bill forward was advanced in Cabinet, common agreement on the necessity for such a measure was tempered by problems of how best to present it and of the most propitious time to introduce it into Parliament. The matter was passed to the Cabinet's Home Affairs Committee (HAC), particularly for a perspective on the political problems. That Committee considered the matter in the context of a draft Bill prepared by the Home Office and of summaries of departmental desires as to powers to meet each of the three stages. Those summaries made it clear that there was no question of deferring action until stage three. Most of the drastic powers sought—to control, ration and requisition vital supplies and to enable the use of troops for essential non-military tasks—were wanted from the onset of the strike, although the Home Office were willing, in view of parliamentary considerations, to defer until stage two, powers such as bans on meetings, restrictions on the supply of alcohol, enhanced police powers and powers to sequester trades union funds. The HAC was torn between, on the one hand, the pressing need for action and the desirability of introducing the measure in a period of calm, and, on the other, the need to avoid stirring up labour passions, thus precipitating the very crisis such a measure was designed to obviate. The Cabinet decided to wait. Indeed, even during a period of concern over a possible miners' strike, opinion was divided between those who thought it right to proceed with the Bill to obtain necessary powers, and those who thought it better to rely on the prerogative and existing powers to do what was required and to seek indemnity from Parliament should issues of *ultra vires* arise. On October 16, 1920 the miners went on strike, but Cabinet still held back on the Bill for fear of provoking further labour unrest. Civil servants were inclined to take a harder line. The prospect of a railway-men's strike from October 25 in support of the miners led the Prime Minister to decide on the speedy introduction of the Bill which the Home Secretary presented to Parliament on Friday, October 22. Although the disputes were settled over the weekend the Cabinet decided to proceed with the Bill.

The draft Bill had been altered somewhat in the process of consideration within the executive. Earlier versions had more explicitly reflected the fear of revolution which, in part, gave rise to the legislation, setting out quite specifically a wide range of disruptive actions, together with the motives therefor, which could "trigger" the powers in the Bill. As thus formulated, it would have embraced most forms of challenge to the established order. Localised disputes were explicitly envisaged as capable of attracting use of the powers; one formulation, which would have enabled a proclamation of emergency where it appeared to the Crown that the safety of the realm or any part thereof was threatened, was not pursued. Much of what later went into subordinate regulations was at one time set out in the Bill itself. A provision empowering the revocation of the proclamation of emergency upon resolution of either House of Parliament that the proclamation was no longer necessary, was removed; a motion defeating the regulations made under the powers in the Bill was thought to have the same effect.

Owen Lomas' study of the preparation of the PVA 1939 reveals that it was formulated and decisions made through the interaction of the Home Office, the Cabinet and the HAC.[3] The study is based on the papers of the last two bodies; those of the first were closed for 150 years after the event.[4] On July 5, 1939, the Home Secretary presented a memorandum to Cabinet detailing the effects of the IRA campaign in Great Britain in the previous six months; an assessment of its extent; the degree of support and funding for it from groups in the United States; intelligence on plans to disrupt key installations and services; the increasing problems of gaining enough evidence to ensure conviction of members of an organisation increasingly conscious of its security; the insufficiency of existing powers under the Public Order Act 1936 and the Explosives Acts; and requests from the Metropolitan Police Commissioner and certain chief constables for enhanced

[3] O.G. Lomas, "The Executive and the Anti-Terrorist Legislation of 1939" [1980] P.L. 16. For details of the powers in the PVA 1939 see *infra*, pp. 167-169.

[4] *Ibid.* at note 1.

powers. It also set out policy options including internment and expulsion.[5] He sought and obtained Cabinet approval for a draft Bill to be drawn up by the Home Office.[6] This was then considered by the HAC without further prior reference to the parent body.[7] The Bill, little altered, was recommended to Cabinet and speedily approved.[8]

Throughout, the nature of the crisis was perceived purely in terms of security or law and order. No attempt was made to canvass the wider political issue of the status of Ulster which underpinned the campaign.[9] Calls for internment were rejected as unacceptable to Parliament and public opinion.[10] An exclusion policy was thought more acceptable, although its effects on relations with the Dominions, including Eire, were examined, as was the likely response of the Northern Ireland Government.[11] Little concern was expressed about the protection of the civil liberties of those affected by the Bill.[12] The issue of what Parliament would tolerate loomed large.[13] Lomas concludes that the roles of Cabinet and HAC were superficial and of relatively minor influence on the Bill which was made and decided upon in the Home Office. It was principally because of fear of parliamentary opposition that the merits of certain proposals were canvassed at all.[14]

To say that much the same is true of consideration of current emergency powers would be pure speculation. However, the strong influence of permanent officials and civil service committees on the decision-making process is a feature of the Crossman diaries.[15] It is also known that, although the Birmingham pub bombings predicated a speedy decision on the Prevention of Terrorism (Temporary Provisions) Act 1974 (hereinafter "PTA 1974") the Bill was the product of more than a

[5] *Ibid.* at pp. 20-22.

[6] *Ibid.* at p. 23.

[7] *Ibid.* at pp. 24-27.

[8] *Ibid.* at p. 27.

[9] *Ibid.* at pp. 18-19.

[10] *Ibid.* at pp. 20-21, 23, 32.

[11] *Ibid.* at pp. 21-22, 24.

[12] *Ibid.* at pp. 22-24.

[13] *Ibid.* at pp. 23, 25, 27-28, 32.

[14] *Ibid.* at p. 32.

[15] *Ibid.* at p. 30: R.H.S. Crossman, *The Diaries of a Cabinet Minister* (3 vols.) (1975, 1976, 1977).

year of Home Office contingency planning.[16] One MP, then a Home Office researcher, has suggested that the Bill was prompted more by a feeling that public outrage must be appeased by action than by the view that the powers in it would prevent such tragedies.[17] In a time of perceived crisis, it may be a natural, if not altogether desirable mode of decision-making in areas with acute political overtones, for politicians to fall back upon the existing work of the "experts" in the field, and put it before Parliament as soon as possible.[18]

The powers in the EPA 1920 have been invoked on twelve separate occasions, all concerned with industrial disputes in key undertakings (*infra*, pp. 223-228). The decision to invoke has typically been at Cabinet level founded on recommendations from an Emergencies Committee of the Cabinet, composed of ministers and senior officials from relevant departments, spawning sub-committees shadowed by official sub-committees closely monitoring the particular dispute. Advice has also been taken from the security services on the nature of the dispute. Recurring issues have been: the dilemma of if and when to invoke; the need to act quickly but to avoid provocative action; whether troops should be used; possible roles for civilian volunteers; which regulations should be prepared—regulations peculiar to that dispute or a more general code; whether subversive elements hide behind genuine industrial grievances and manipulate them for their own ends.[19] In terms of running the show, the present structure dates from 1972, when an internal review by Lord Jellicoe and the then Cabinet Office Deputy Secretary, John Hunt, led to "a refashioned, streamlined emergencies organisation, the Civil Contingencies Unit (CCU), located in the Cabinet Office and having the status of a standing Cabinet committee."[20] It is a mixture of ministers and officials, usually chaired by the Home Secretary when ministers are present.[21] Apparently, over the years

[16] C. Scorer, *The Prevention of Terrorism Acts 1974 and 1976: A Report on the Operation of the Law* (NCCL, 1976), p. 1; Mr. A. Lyon, MP, H.C. Deb. Vol. 1, col. 360 (March 18, 1981).

[17] Ms. C. Short, MP, H.C. Deb. Vol. 47, col. 91.

[18] *Cf.* Lomas, *loc. cit.* n. 3, at p. 30.

[19] Jeffery and Hennessy, *op. cit.* n. 2, *passim.*

[20] *Ibid.* at p. 237. Its Secretary has a responsibility to keep COBRA (Cabinet Office Briefing Room) "the Cabinet Office's 'doomsday' operations centre" in running order.

[21] *Ibid.* at p. 238. Currently, it is chaired by Lord Whitelaw, Lord President of the Council, the former Home Secretary, no doubt to reflect his experience. See P. Hennessy, "Whitehall's real power house" *The Times,* April 30, 1984, at

since 1920, officials and military men have by and large acted as a moderating influence on some of the "wilder notions" of their political masters in governments of varying political complexion. The CCU has a central role in planning the response to possible disputes and in so managing operations during them as to avoid, if possible, the necessity for resort to emergency powers or, if not, to be best able to judge when to invoke them. Jeffery and Hennessy have reconstructed the likely sort of planning meeting late in 1979 when an oil tanker drivers' strike was possible:

> "the meeting would be opened by Robert Wade-Gery, who succeeded Sir Clive Rose as chairman of the CCU in April 1979, with a summary of 'Operation Drumstick' (or whatever name the planners had chosen). The scheme is intended to maintain about 25 per cent of normal petrol and oil supplies, provided a state of emergency is declared, rationing introduced and the Royal Corps of Transport requisitions oil company vehicles since the army does not have enough of its own. Discussion would then be opened to the various government departments involved. The latest intelligence on the position inside the relevant section of the TGWU would be provided by the Department of Employment. The representative from Transport would explain their rationing scheme and the priority to be given to public transport and essential users. The Department of Energy would convey the oil companies' readiness to co-operate with the government through the medium of their Oil Industries' Emergencies Committee. From the Ministry of Defence would come logistical details. In any such emergency some 5,000 drivers and 10,000 general duties men would have to be trained to handle pumps and pipes at the army's West Moors petroleum centre in Dorset. At least eighteen days' notice is required to get men back from Germany and through West Moors. Both the Home Office and the Ministry of Defence would emphasise the importance of impressing upon Chief Constables their responsibility for securing the safe passage of men and vehicles as they are driven out of company depots to army barracks and emergency distribution centres. At this point the needs of special interest groups might have been raised. Agriculture might appeal for farmers to be given preferential treatment and essential feed manufacturers to be made a 'special case'; Industry might speak up for companies

p. 12, an article based on M. Cockerell, P. Hennessy and D. Walker, *Sources Close to the Prime Minister* (1984).

requiring oil to maintain continuous production processes. In summing up, Wade-Gery would stress the need for an urgent meeting of ministers to authorise the drafting of emergency regulations and the proclamation of a state of emergency. Before ministers gathered, a handful of officials would receive a special briefing from MI 5 on the origins of the strike, indicating whether a small group of extremists is manipulating the men, or whether it is a straight 'pay and conditions' affair. Invariably the evidence points to the latter, although the Security Service did see a conspiracy behind the 1966 Seamen's Strike. A joint-meeting of ministers and civil servants, under the Home Secretary's chairmanship, would then prepare recommendations for the full Cabinet."[22]

Once a dispute was under way, the process might operate much as during the transport workers' dispute during the "winter of discontent" (1978-79):

> "At Cabinet level the Prime Minister set up a secret *ad hoc* committee, known as 'GEN 158' and chaired by the Home Secretary. Of the officials in the central emergency organisation only Brigadier Bishop and Sir Clive Rose, a Deputy Secretary in the Cabinet Office and Chairman of the CCU, regularly attended this ministerial group. The CCU itself, with a mixture of ministers and officials, met two or three times each day at the Cabinet Office and its regional network swung into operation in a manner not seen since Heath's three day week of early 1974. Throughout England and Wales eleven Regional Emergencies Committees (RECs) were established. Based on the regional economic planning boards, with officials from the Departments of Environment, Trade, Transport, Energy, Employment and Agriculture, the RECs also included representatives of the local authorities, the police and the military. Beyond the RECs in any emergency there is a fallback in the home defence system, which comprises regional seats of government, designed to co-ordinate administration after a nuclear attack. If there is a severe breakdown of food distribution arising from an industrial dispute, the home defence emergency feeding depots, using strategic stockpiles of food, might be activated as a last resort. Short of such desperate circumstances, home defence's secure telephones and telexes are a useful adjunct to the often overloaded lines between RECs and London. The

[22] Jeffery and Hennnessy, *op. cit.* n. 2, pp. 256-257.

RECs can exercise executive functions if the government takes powers to limit energy consumption under the 1920 Act. In 1973-74, for example, regional offices were able to grant permits to local companies with standby generators to work longer hours than those prescribed by the three-day week.

The role of the RECs can be illustrated by showing how they fitted into the CCU's daily timetable during the 1979 dispute. At 8.30 each morning the regional committee chairmen would meet official representatives of the TGWU. They were not permitted to meet others, whether pickets or unofficial strikers, for fear of undermining the authority of the official union leadership. A representative of the Manpower Services Commission would attend to give the latest estimate of lay-offs resulting from the strike, based on figures from the Department of Employment's local offices. Next the chairmen would consult representatives of the Road Haulage Association and the Confederation of British Industry to gauge the general position in the region. Additional information would come from the RECs' reporting centres responsible for receiving evidence of alleged breaches of the TGWU's voluntary code on picketing. Then the full RECs would meet. By 11.30 a.m. telex reports from each region would be in the Department of Transport's emergency operations room in London. By 2.00 p.m. a summary of the national position would be with Brigadier Bishop in the Cabinet Office. An hour later he would have an agenda prepared for a full CCU meeting under the Home Secretary, Merlyn Rees, at which decisions would be taken on which definite cases of disruption of the voluntary code should be put before the TGWU. At that stage a most unusual meeting in constitutional terms would take place. Three senior civil servants from the CCU would call on the TGWU. They were Sir Clive Rose, Peter Lazarus from Transport and John Moss from Agriculture. For the TGWU, Alex Kitson would promise to do what he could. The next morning at 8.30 REC chairmen would see if Kitson had prevailed and the cycle would start again.

The RECs worked best where departmental and regional boundaries were coterminous, and where officials with experience of past winter crises knew how to avoid swamping the CCU with superfluous material. Some in the upper reaches of Whitehall preferred, in the end, to use the military network as the most reliable source of information.

> Soldiers have two advantages over civil servants in such circumstances: they are trained to ask direct questions ('how many ambulancemen have come out, how many army ambulances do you need to provide minimum cover?'); and they know how to grade crises. Indiscriminate use of the word 'crisis' weighed down many of the reports reaching the CCU. The major-generals in the military districts are a hidden source of strength. Most make a point of getting to know regional local authority chief executives, as well as leading trade unionists. Many of the weaknesses in the REC system arise from the difficulty of predicting danger points in advance. No two 'strike seasons' are the same."[23]

In April 1984 the Prime Minister established an ad hoc Cabinet Committee (Misc. 101) to receive reports from the Secretary of State for Energy in order effectively to monitor the coal strike. The Committee consisted also of representatives from interested departments (Trade and Industry, Employment, Transport, the Home Office and Scottish Office) with the services of the Attorney-General and representatives of armed forces' interests. The docks strike in July widened the group to take in the Prime Minister's Deputy (Lord Whitelaw) and the Chancellor. Reports on food-stocks were received from the minister from Agriculture.[24] Invoking the powers in the EPA 1920 requires the formal step of a royal proclamation.[25] Section 2 of the EPA 1964, however, permits the Defence Council to authorise the use of troops on agricultural or other urgent work of national importance without a proclamation of emergency. The Defence Council consists

> "of the Secretary of State for Defence as chairman, the Minister of State for Defence, the Minister of State for Defence Procurement, the Parliamentary Under-Secretaries of State for Defence, the Chief of the Defence Staff, the Chief of the Naval Staff and First Sea Lord, the Chief of the General Staff, the Chief of the Air Staff, the Chief of Personnel and Logistics of the Ministry of Defence, the Chief Scientific Adviser of the Ministry of Defence, the Chief Executive

[23] *Ibid.* pp. 244-246.

[24] *The Sunday Times*, April 15, 1984, p. 1; *The Times*, July 17, 1984, p. 2.

[25] On the nature and making of royal proclamations, see 8 *Halsbury's Laws of England* (4th ed.), paras. 1097-1098.

> (Procurement Executive) of the Ministry of Defence and the Permanent Under-Secretary of State of the Ministry of Defence."[26]

The requisite order may be signed by any two members of the Defence Council.[27]

The nature of powers and decision-making under the EPA 1920 and 1964 is such as to permit very direct ministerial or central government direction of operations. For example, in relation to disputes in the docks, a typical emergency regulation confers power on the Secretary of State, or on a committee acting on his behalf, to direct the running of the ports as best suits the national interest, over-riding proprietary interests in berths or storage accommodation.[28] Elsewhere the degree of central supervision varies according to context. Some of the anti-terrorist powers accord the Secretary of State, and therefore the hierarchy in the Ministry concerned, a very central role. Thus the appropriate Secretary of State must sanction exclusion orders,[29] extensions of detention beyond 48 hours under the PTA,[30] and interim custody and detention orders under the scheme of detention without trial (now in abeyance) in the Northern Ireland (Emergency Provisions) Act 1978 (hereinafter "NIEPA 1978").[31] He has the power to proscribe organisations,[32] and in Northern Ireland to characterise criminal offences as potentially warranting trial on indictment by judge alone.[33] In the context of Ulster, it would appear that Cabinet Committees have exercised an important role in directing overall security policy.[34] High level military

[26] *Ibid.* para. 1207.

[27] *Ibid.* para. 1207; C.J. Whelan, "Military Intervention in Industrial Disputes" [1979] I.L.J. 222 at p. 224; S. Peak, *Troops in Strikes* (1984), pp. 66-71.

[28] G.S. Morris, "The Emergency Powers Act 1920" [1979] P.L. 317, at p. 328. For a typical text of such a regulation see reg. 3, The Emergency (No. 2) Regulations 1973 (S.I. 1973 No. 2089). In practice the Committee would report to the Department of Transport: *The Times*, July 16, 1984, p. 2.

[29] PTA 1984, ss.3-7 (*infra.*, pp. 191-195).

[30] PTA 1984, s.12(4) (*infra.*, pp. 170-172).

[31] NIEPA 1978, s.12, Sched. 1, paras. 4, 8 (see further, pp. 152-161).

[32] PTA 1984, s.1(4); NIEPA 1978, s.21(4).

[33] NIEPA 1978, s.29(3). The powers of the Attorney General to certify a particular case out of the list (*i.e.* to declare it not to warrant trial by judge alone on indictment) or to proceed by way of summary trial for the particular offence are the real determinants of which cases end up in the modified criminal trial process (*infra*, pp. 103-107).

[34] E.C.S. Wade and G. Phillips, *Constitutional and Administrative Law* (9th ed.,

directives authorised interrogation in depth.[35] Policing must inevitably be left more in the hands of individual police forces. Powers of appointment, financial control and inspection, however, do enable the exertion of central government influence to encourage uniformity of practice through circulars and administrative directions, for example, on the proper use of powers under the PTAs[36] or on the use of force.[37] Some such directions or advice are not published for security reasons, although extracts have appeared in published reports, official[38] and unofficial,[39] and in the media.[40]

That internal supervision in forces like the police and army through directives and force orders backed up by disciplinary sanctions, can exercise a valuable control function with regard to the appropriate exercise of coercive powers is the central philosophy of the Bennett Report on Police Interrogation in Northern Ireland,[41] of Lord Jellicoe's Review of the PTA,[42] of the Royal Commission on Criminal Procedure and of the Police and

edited by A.W. Bradley, 1977), p. 247; Robin Evelegh has suggested that shifts in such policy during the 1970s were detrimental to the effectiveness of security forces' actions, see, *Peace Keeping in a Democratic Society: The Lessons of Northern Ireland* (1978), pp. 21-24. R. Fisk, *The Point of No Return: The Strike that broke the British in Ulster* (1975) contains useful information on relations between ministers, the Ministry of Defence and the security forces on the handling of the response to the Ulster Workers' Council strike which brought down the power-sharing Northern Ireland Executive in May 1974 (*infra*, p. 266).

35 *Ireland* v. *United Kingdom* (1978) 2 E.H.R.R. 25, at p. 60 (para. 97).

36 *Review of the Operation of the Prevention of Terrorism (Temporary Provisions) Act 1976 by the Rt. Honourable Earl Jellicoe, DSC, MC*, Cmnd. 8803 (1983) (hereinafter cited as "Jellicoe"), *e.g.* paras. 68, 75. See, *e.g.* Home Office Circular No. 26/1984.

37 *Report of the Tribunal appointed to inquire into events on Sunday, 30th January 1972, which led to the loss of life in connection with the procession in Londonderry on that day, by the Rt. Hon. Lord Widgery, OBE, TD*, H.C. 220 (1971-72) (hereinafter cited as "Widgery"), paras. 89-104, conclusion 9.

38 For example, Jellicoe and Widgery.

39 For example, some of the "Rules of Engagement for PVC Baton Rounds" issued to the British Army, can be found in T. Gifford, *Death on the Streets of Derry* (NCCL, 1982), p. 8.

40 For example, the Yellow Card, as issued at the date of the events into which Lord Widgery inquired (*supra*, n. 37), was reproduced in *The Times*, February 1, 1972, p. 1.

41 *Report of the Committee of Inquiry into Police Interrogation Procedures in Northern Ireland*, Cmnd. 7497 (1979) (hereinafter cited as "Bennett").

42 *Op. cit.* n. 36.

Evidence Act 1984.[43] The assumption is also implicit in the proposals put forward in the Baker Review of NIEPA 1978.[44] Emergency provisions may accord senior officers a supervisory role, replacing prior judicial authorisation altogether (*e.g.* the search of dwelling houses in Northern Ireland)[45] or in circumstances where urgent action is needed (*e.g.* search under a police superintendent's "warrant" under the PTA).[46] The creation of a central police unit, for example, to process applications for exclusion orders may well exercise a useful sifting role whereby, coupled with hierarchical review in the Ministry concerned, inappropriate cases are weeded out long before Secretary of State level.[47] Soldiers in Ulster carry a Yellow Card containing instructions on when they may open fire, breach of which could result in disciplinary action even though no breach of the civil law was involved.[48]

The extent to which such mechanisms and institutional constraints constitute an effective means of control must remain a matter of conjecture and controversy which it is beyond the scope of this work to resolve. Their directness and immediacy of operation, as compared with *ex post facto* judicial review, is an advantage, but much will depend on the attitudes and diligence of those in positions of control, and on the policy goals and approaches they set and support, for example, whether they are committed to an "ends justify means" approach or to operating solely according to the dictates of the law. This renders important the appointments' process.[49] To have such mechanisms and

[43] Royal Commission on Criminal Procedure, *Report*, Cmnd. 8092 (1981), paras. 3.24-3.34 (stop and search, and search of vehicles), 3.104-3.107 (length of detention after arrest); Police and Criminal Evidence Act 1984, ss.2, 3, 5, 33-42.

[44] *Review of the Operation of the Northern Ireland (Emergency Provisions) Act 1978 by the Rt. Honourable Sir George Baker OBE*, Cmnd. 9222 (1984) (hereinafter cited as "Baker"), *e.g.* para. 394.

[45] NIEPA 1978, s.15(2); Baker, paras. 355-369.

[46] PTA 1984, Sched. 3, para. 4(4).

[47] Jellicoe, para. 162. That some such sifting also takes place with respect to police applications to extend the detention of suspects held under PTA, s.12, is clear from paras. 40-44 and is implicit in Baker, para. 271. See also Home Office Circular No. 26/1984, para. 93.

[48] Widgery, *op. cit.* n. 37; Evelegh, *op. cit.* n. 34, pp. 85-86 where he bemoans the jurisdictional problems of the co-existence in the particular context of military and civil law.

[49] C. Palley, "The State of Emergency in Northern Ireland" in International Commission of Jurists, *States of Emergency: Their Impact on Human Rights* (1983), 217, at p. 240. The importance, in the analogous sphere of the

institutional constraints as the sole regulatory factors on executive action is no doubt undesirable because of issues of independence and accountability. To dismiss their role out of hand is equally inappropriate.

2. *The Role of the Legislature*

Parliament's role is not to govern, not to carry out or direct the carrying out of policies, but to scrutinise, influence and legitimise the Government, its measures and its actions; to provide a degree of critical oversight and to endeavour to ensure that executive powers are used wisely, effectively and properly; to strive to maintain the political responsibility to it of Government and of ministers. Its limitations in exercising its functions are well known.[50] The context of emergency powers exacerbates problems faced in its oversight of executive power in general. Parliamentary surveillance of emergency powers is effected in a number of ways, some traditional, others typically features of such emergency legislation.

Questions to ministers, emergency and adjournment debates, supply debates and debates on the Address are traditional mechanisms for ventilating policies, grievances and eliciting information. Where specific mechanisms are not provided they may be the only means of raising a matter in the legislature, for example, on the use of troops in industrial disputes without a proclamation of emergency, or in respect of exercises of prerogative emergency power. Northern Ireland security, for example, was chosen by the Opposition as a topic for a supply debate in session 1975-76, and Northern Ireland has been the subject of several adjournment debates.[51] Numerous questions, mainly eliciting written answers, have been posed concerning powers to combat terrorism and the security situation in general. For instance, in session 1978-79, there were questions in the Commons on *inter alia* the Diplock courts, paramilitary activity, political status for those convicted of terrorist crimes, exclusion

Canadian intelligence services, of the appointments process, direction by senior management and the policy goals and approaches they set is stressed at length in the *Second Report of the Commission of Inquiry Concerning Certain Activities of the Royal Canadian Mounted Police: Freedom and Security under the Law* (Vol. 2) (1981) (hereinafter cited as the "McDonald Report"), pp. 693-751.

[50] See, *e.g.* S.A. Walkland and M. Ryle (Eds.), *The Commons Today*, (revised ed., 1981), *passim;* P. Norton, *The Commons in Perspective* (1981), Chaps. 4-10.

[51] M. Ryle, "The Commons Today—A General Survey" in *The Commons Today*, *op. cit.* n. 50, pp. 17-18; Norton *op. cit.* n. 50, p. 172.

orders, interrogation procedures, troop levels in Northern Ireland and the problem of intimidation in the Province.[52] The written answer constitutes an established device for relaying statistics on security in Ulster.[53] It has also been used to make important statements on anti-terrorist policy, for example, on the use of "supergrasses."[54]

Consideration of legislative proposals gives Parliament the opportunity to influence the shape of emergency powers and to comment on the operation of existing powers. It is well known, however, that Parliament does not legislate as an autonomous entity; that legislation is made elsewhere and legitimated in Parliament; that successful amendment of key provisions in Government Bills is rare.[55] The general problems appear more acute with respect to the passage of emergency legislation proposed by the Government. Such legislation is often brought forward in a hurry, as a result of one crisis or another, albeit that its content may reflect much Whitehall contingency planning. Its speedy passage is often sought and granted in a tense or emotional atmosphere ill-suited to affording the careful consideration wide-ranging legislative proposals should receive (*supra*, p. 25). The Defence of the Realm Act 1914 gave the Government blanket power to make regulations "for securing the public safety and the defence of the realm." It was passed in August of that momentous year without Parliamentary debate.[56] The Emergency Powers (Defence) Bill 1939, the foundation for the sweeping powers vested in Government during the Second World War, passed its three readings in the Commons in the space of a few hours, was approved by the Lords the same day and received the Royal Assent in the evening.[57] The PVA 1939, enacted to deal with the IRA's mainland bombing campaign, was passed in four days, punctuated on July 26 by an explosion at the left-luggage office in Kings Cross Station which killed one man and severely injured

[52] See *Sessional Index* (1978-79), H.C. Deb., Vol. 966.

[53] R.J. Spjut, "Criminal Statistics and Statistics on Security in Northern Ireland" (unpublished paper kindly loaned to the author).

[54] For example, by the Attorney General, Sir Michael Havers: H.C. Deb., Vol. 47, cols. 3-5.

[55] S.A. De Smith, *Constitutional and Administrative Law* (4th ed., 1981, edited by H. Street and R. Brazier), p. 239; J.A.G. Griffith, *Parliamentary Scrutiny of Government Bills* (1973); Norton, *op. cit.* n. 50, Chap. 5; G. Drewry, "Legislation" in *The Commons Today, op. cit.* n. 50, pp. 87-117.

[56] J. Eaves, Jr., *Emergency Powers and the Parliamentary Watchdog: Parliament and the Executive in Great Britain, 1939-1951* (1957), pp. 8-9.

[57] *Ibid.* p. 15.

fifteen other people.[58] The catalyst for the passage of the PTA 1974 was the Birmingham pub bombing in November of that year in which 21 people died and more than 180 were injured, many seriously. The Bill passed all stages in the Commons during the night of November 28, the Lords the next morning and received the Royal Assent on November 29. Its approval was secured without a division as Parliament responded to an understandably outraged public opinion crying for something to be done.[59] One MP described the Commons as a panic-stricken mob.[60] It is clear, however, that its details were by no means as hastily conceived, but formed part of Home Office contingency plans drawn up and circulated to other departments under a Conservative Administration after the London bombings of March 1973.[61] The Fuel and Electricity Control Act 1973, passed to give government sweeping powers to control the use of energy when oil supplies were threatened because of the Middle East war and when there were industrial disputes affecting coal and electricity production, occupied both Houses in a little under 12 hours of debate.[62] The Drought Act 1976 required less than 10 hours of debate.[63]

But Parliament does not invariably grant emergency legislation as speedy a passage as the Government would wish. Nor is its scrutiny wholly without influence. The Government sought to have the Emergency Powers Bill 1920 passed in one sitting on October 22, 1920 by suspension of standing orders. It did not receive a second reading until October 25.[64] It was introduced during a miners' strike with the prospect of a railwaymen's strike in support, and at a time when a growth of revolutionary feeling among workers was feared; in short, "at the height of an industrial crisis, at precisely the time when Parliamentary and public opinion was least able dispassionately to weigh up either its short-term merits or long-term consequences."[65] It received the

[58] T.P. Coogan, *The I.R.A.* (revised ed. 1980), pp. 168-169. On whether the Home Secretary may have given a false impression of German involvement to the House of Commons, see Lomas, *loc. cit.* n. 3, at pp. 28-29.

[59] Scorer, *op. cit.* n. 16, p. 1: B. Rose-Smith, "Police Powers and Terrorism Legislation" in P. Hain (ed.), *Policing the Police* (Vol. 1) (1979), at p. 120.

[60] Scorer, *op. cit.* n. 16, p. 1.

[61] Sources cited *supra*, n. 16.

[62] For debates see: H.C. Deb., Vol. 865, cols. 34-154, 685-760; H.L. Deb., Vol. 347, cols. 316-333, 746-750, 839-841.

[63] For debates see: H.L. Deb., Vol. 373, cols. 152-153, 690-732, 952-958, 980-983, 1634-1649; H.C. Deb., Vol. 916, cols. 1744-1818, 2241-2282.

[64] Jeffery and Hennessy, *op. cit.* n. 2, p. 56.

[65] *Ibid.* p. 53.

Royal Assent on October 29 after only some 20 hours' debate. Criticism on Second Reading, however, led the Government to move amendments in Committee inserting limitations on the rule-making power to protect rights to strike, to persuade peacefully others to participate, and not to be subjected to compulsory military service or industrial conscription. A generic phrase "or other necessities," included after "the supply and distribution of food, water, fuel, or light," was deleted and the Government accepted the amendment.[66]

Emergency legislation designed to supersede and reform existing emergency powers has received a more considered passage through Parliament. The Energy Act 1976, which replaced the Fuel and Electricity Control Act 1973, is one such case.[67] The Prevention of Terrorism (Temporary Provisions) Act 1976 (hereinafter "PTA 1976") is another.[68] Indeed, the PTA 1976 was amended in response to backbench and minority party pressure to criminalise failure to disclose information about acts of terrorism and to permit the exclusion of terrorist suspects from Ulster to Great Britain.[69] The Prevention of Terrorism (Temporary Provisions) Act 1984 (hereinafter "PTA 1984"), which replaced the PTA 1976, was largely the product of the Jellicoe Review[70] which had already been endorsed and welcomed by Parliament in March 1983.[71] The Northern Ireland (Emergency Provisions) Act 1973 (hereinafter "NIEPA 1973") replacing the existing security powers in Northern Ireland embodied in the Civil Authorities (Special Powers) Acts 1922-1933 and its subordinate regulations, in part reflected an internal governmental review of those security powers,[72] but was also very much the product of the Diplock

[66] *Ibid.* p. 57; Morris, *Thesis, op. cit.* n. 2, p. 139.

[67] It received more than 40 hours of debate; see H.L. Deb., Vol. 368, col. 1411, Vol. 369, cols. 460-500, 1795-1835, 1884-1965, 2096-2139, Vol. 371, cols. 126-140, 153-192; H.C. Deb., Vol. 913, cols. 323-410; Official Report, Standing Committee J (1975-76), cols. 1-514; H.C. Deb., Vol. 917, cols. 1673-1732, 1793-1822, Vol. 919, col. 1521.

[68] For debates see: H.C. Deb. Vol. 901, cols. 182, 875-1004; Official Report, Standing Committee A (1975-76), cols. 1-158; H.C. Deb., Vol. 904, cols. 441-594, Vol. 908, cols. 157-167.

[69] H.C. Deb., Vol. 904, cols. 463-494.

[70] *Op. cit.* n. 36.

[71] H.C. Deb., Vol. 38, cols. 564-642: H.L. Deb., Vol. 440, cols. 476-518.

[72] H.C. Deb., Vol. 855, col. 277 (Mr. W. Whitelaw, MP, Secretary of State for Northern Ireland).

Commission Report.[73] It was subjected to probing scrutiny in Committee in the House of Commons by the Labour Opposition which secured the insertion there of an amendment providing trial by three judges rather than a single judge without a jury.[74] The Government, however, secured a return to the original proposal when the Bill returned to the floor of the House.[75] The Northern Ireland (Emergency Provisions) Amendment Act 1975 (hereinafter "NIEPA 1975") reflected the Report of the Gardiner Committee.[76] It was not contentious as between Government and Opposition and received a relatively quick and untroubled passage.[77] NIEPA 1978 was a consolidating measure subject to the special procedures applicable to such measures.

Emergency legislation is conceived of as temporary and extraordinary (*supra*, pp. 7-8). The Defence of the Realm Act 1914 provided powers for the duration of the present war,[78] the termination of which would, pursuant to other legislation, be signalled by an Order in Council.[79] Subsequent emergency legislation has made more specific provision for establishing its temporary nature, and at the same time increasing the opportunities for Parliamentary supervision. The Special Powers Act 1922 in Northern Ireland and the PVA 1939 were envisaged as lasting for twelve months[80] and two years respectively.[81] Both were in fact continued annually by little-debated Expiring Laws (Continuance) Acts, and the Special Powers Acts were rendered permanent in 1933.[82] The Emergency Powers (Defence) Act 1939 provided for annual renewal on an address to the Monarch from

[73] *Report of the Commission to consider legal procedures to deal with terrorist activities in Northern Ireland*, Cmnd. 5185 (1972) (hereinafter cited as "Diplock").

[74] Official Report, Standing Committee B (1972-73), Vol. 2, cols. 1-188.

[75] H.C. Deb., Vol. 859, cols. 735-796.

[76] *Report of a Committee to consider, in the context of civil liberties and human rights, measures to deal with terrorism in Northern Ireland*, Cmnd. 5847 (1975) (hereinafter cited as "Gardiner").

[77] H.C. Deb., Vol. 893, col. 1394, Vol. 894, cols. 886-980, Vol. 895, cols. 1191-1202; Official Report, Standing Committee J (1974-1975), cols. 1-44; H.L. Deb., Vol. 363, cols. 893-908, 918-955, 1601-1644.

[78] s.1.

[79] The Termination of the Present War (Definition) Act 1918.

[80] Civil Authorities (Special Powers) Act 1922, s.12.

[81] Prevention of Violence (Temporary Provisions) Act 1939, s.5(2).

[82] On the Special Powers Acts, see K. Boyle, T. Hadden and P. Hillyard, *Law and State: the case of Northern Ireland* (1975), p. 7: on the PVA 1939 see Expiring Laws Continuance Acts 1941-1953.

each House, thereby ensuring some opportunity for debate.[83] The Supplies and Services (Transitional Powers) Act 1945, continuing in force certain Defence Regulations to aid in post-war reconstruction, was, somewhat unusually since annual renewal had become something of a norm, to continue for five years but thereafter to be annually renewable by Order in Council after a prayer to that effect from each House.[84] The central provisions of the PTAs and the NIEPAs have required periodic renewal by executive order, made by way of statutory instrument, subject to the prior approval of each House through laying in draft subject to affirmative resolution. In cases of urgency, however, the orders may be made without a draft having been so approved, but the orders must then be laid before each House and will cease to have effect, without prejudice to anything done under them in the interim, unless approved by each House within the standard 40 day period.[85] The Northern Ireland legislation, initially renewable annually,[86] is now renewable for periods up to six months. The PTA 1974 required six-monthly approval. Its successors have been renewable for periods up to one year. In each case, the order may provide for renewal in whole or in part. An order may at any time provide that all or any of the temporary provisions shall cease to be in force.[87] The PTAs have always been renewed *in toto*. The provisions on detention without trial in NIEPA 1978 (s.12, and Sched. 1) were allowed to lapse in July 1980.[88] Provisions which have ceased to be in force, whether through non-renewal or specific order, may be brought back into force for up to the maximum renewal period in the Act in question, subject to the same procedures as apply to renewal orders.[89] The EPA 1920 is permanent legislation enabling recourse to a wide rule-making power during the currency of an executive proclamation of emergency.[90] A proclamation may not remain in force for more than one month, but another proclamation, likewise limited in duration, can be issued at or before the end of that period (s.1(1)).

[83] Eaves, *op. cit.* n. 56, pp. 18-19.

[84] s.8(1); Eaves, *op. cit.* n. 56, pp. 128-130; C.K. Allen, *Law and Orders* (3rd ed., 1965), p. 65.

[85] PTA 1984, ss.17, 14(10)-(12); NIEPA 1978, s.32.

[86] NIEPA 1973, s.30(2),(3)(*a*).

[87] PTA 1984, s.17(2); NIEPA 1978, s.33(2),(3).

[88] Baker, para. 231.

[89] PTA 1984, ss.17(2)(*c*), 14(10)-(12); NIEPA 1978, ss.33(3)(*c*),32.

[90] For the weaker controls in equivalent Northern Ireland legislation see Chap. One, n. 41.

The occasion of the proclamation must be communicated to Parliament forthwith. If Parliament is adjourned or prorogued and thus not due to meet within five days of the issue of the proclamation, it must be summoned to sit within five days (s.1(2)). There is no specific provision empowering Parliament to annul the proclamation. No doubt it could be made an issue of confidence. Regulations made during its currency must be laid before Parliament as soon as may be and would cease to have effect unless approved by both Houses within seven days of laying (s.2(2)). Unusually Parliament is given power, through resolution of both Houses, to add to, alter or revoke the regulations (s.2(4)). The debate on the motion to approve the regulations (a new set of which must be approved after each proclamation) thus provides quite wide-ranging scope for Parliamentary surveillance. The Energy Act 1976 contains reserve powers enabling the Government to give directions to undertakings as to their production supply and use of energy (a) when they are required by international obligations or (b) when "there exists, or is imminent in the United Kingdom an actual or threatened emergency affecting fuel or electricity supplies which makes it necessary in Her Majesty's opinion that the government should temporarily have at its disposal exceptional powers for controlling the sources and availability of energy" (s.3(1)). The reserve powers are brought into play by Order in Council which must be laid before Parliament. In situation (a), an Order is laid purely for information purposes. In situation (b), it is subject to affirmative resolution (s.3(2)), and may not remain in force for longer than 12 months unless before then both Houses resolve that it should be continued for a further 12 months (s.3(4)(5)).

The Defence of the Realm Act 1914 made no specific provision for Parliament to debate, annul or approve regulations made under its wide enabling power.[91] Subsequent legislation has tended to include the opportunity for parliamentary scrutiny afforded by a laying requirement, although many such Acts have relied primarily on the prayer of annulment procedure. Where, as in wartime, there is a likelihood of a massive panoply of regulations, this may be understandable,[92] but otherwise exceptional powers to interfere with the liberty of the subject should, if exercisable through executive order or subordinate legislation, be subject to the greater opportunity for surveillance afforded by the affirmative resolution procedure, which at least ensures that the

[91] Eaves, *op. cit.* n. 56, p. 9.
[92] *Ibid.* p. 19.

executive must find time to have the measure debated. This is the case with regulations under the EPA 1920. Under the PTAs and the NIEPAs crucial powers exercisable by order (renewal of the Acts, removal from force or the bringing back into force of provisions in them; proscription of organisations; the designation of offences as triable on indictment only in non-jury courts) are similarly subject to affirmative procedure, usually through prior approval of a draft but, where urgent, through subsequent approval of the order itself.[93] Oddly, the power under section 13 of the PTAs to establish a form of immigration/security control is subject only to annulment.[94] This is regrettable, since extraordinary powers of arrest, detention and interference with free-movement within the United Kingdom are involved (*infra*, pp. 170-172). The Drought Act 1976 contains no mechanism for parliamentary approval of orders made by the Secretary of State. They are sought by water authorities or companies, subject to planning-type procedures of notice and lodging of objections, with the possibility of public local inquiries and the consideration of objections by the Secretary of State (*infra*, pp. 217-220).

Parliamentary scrutiny may also be effected through select committees, enabling smaller groups of MPs, representative of the House as a whole, to undertake a study of some part of governmental activity in depth principally to be better informed but also to improve the degree of control exercised by the Commons over departments. In 1979 select committees were set up to monitor: agriculture; defence; education, science and arts; employment; energy; environment; foreign affairs; home affairs; industry and trade; social services; transport; Treasury and Civil Service. There were also established at the same time committees on Scottish and Welsh Affairs.[95] No single select committee monitors Northern Ireland affairs. Rather each of the above committees can look at the activities of the Secretary of State for Northern Ireland insofar as his responsibilities cover matters within their subject remit. Little has been done to make use of that power.[96] Nor have emergency powers, some of which would fall

[93] PTA 1984, ss.14, 17; NIEPA 1978, ss.32, 33.

[94] PTA 1984, s.14(9).

[95] See N. Johnson, "Select Committees as Tools of Parliamentary Reform: Some Further Reflections" in *The Commons Today*, *op. cit.* n. 50, pp. 230-232; Norton, *op. cit.* n. 50, pp. 127-137.

[96] B. Hadfield, "Committees of the House of Commons and Northern Ireland Affairs" (1981) 32 N.I.L.Q. 199.

within the terms of reference of Home Affairs, Energy, Trade and Industry, or Transport, been the subject of study by those committees. The select committee system, though not without its faults,[97] is said to have

> "considerably extended the range of the House's activity, strengthened its position relative to that of the Government and deepened the quality of its debates."[98]

Such manifold opportunities for scrutiny are, however, not enough. Effective operation as a critical forum also requires, as Michael Ryle has pointed out, "effective techniques for scrutinising government and calling Ministers to account. This involves not only debate but also techniques for informing Members—and people outside Parliament—about the policies and acts of government and also the background to such policy decisions."[99] There is some concern that scrutiny of emergency powers by the guardian of our liberties has been somewhat less incisive and concerned than such draconian powers merit. Gillian Morris records in respect of the EPA 1920 that

> "Opposition MPs divided the House of Commons on the motion to continue the emergency regulations on every occasion during the 1921 and 1926 emergencies, apart from the first motion of 1926, in each case on the general ground that the regulations were unnecessary and unfair to the working class."[1]

Since then, she notes, the Lords has been divided on one occasion, the Commons on four, by small groups of MPs on two occasions (1949 and July 1970) and by the Labour and Liberal Opposition in February 1972 and November 1973. On these last two occasions, opposition centred not on the need for emergency powers but rather on the responsibility for and the causes of the existence of the emergency.[2] There is a tendency to bring forward a complete set of regulations during each emergency.[3] Little use has been made of the power to amend regulations and certainly none since 1945. In 1921, however, the process of debate influenced the

97 Sources cited *supra*, n. 95.

98 First Report from the Liaison Committee, *The Select Committee System*, H.C. 92 (1982-83), para. 6.

99 *Op. cit.* n. 51 p. 16.

1 *Loc. cit.* n. 28, at p. 332.

2 *Ibid.* at pp. 332-333.

3 *Ibid.* at p. 325. See *infra*, pp. 267-268 for criticism.

content of the regulations: the Home Secretary omitted two regulations which were criticised and a part of a third.[4] Gillian Morris concludes

> "that, while the Emergency Powers Act appears to guarantee parliamentary control over the exercise of its power (when these powers are taken for any length of time), in practice the extent of this control is limited and compliance with the procedure is more a matter of form than an effective method of restraining the excesses of the executive. To some extent the blame must lie with Parliament itself. The Act does at least ensure that the Government provide some public justification for, and account of, its actions, and it would seem appropriate in a democracy for Parliament to adopt a more rigorous scrutiny of the powers taken."[5]

The bipartisan approach of Government and Opposition to Northern Ireland matters has to some extent blunted debate on anti-terrorist measures,[6] although in March 1983 Labour voted against renewal of the PTA 1976, having abstained the previous year.[7] Lord Jellicoe noted that the annual renewal debate on that legislation had two significant drawbacks:

> "First, there is no real possibility of amending the Act during renewal; in practice it has to be accepted or rejected in its entirety. Second, the renewal debates have not on the whole received the parliamentary time which they merit. There have been exceptions, but in the Commons they tend to be held late at night and to last no more than ninety minutes or so, and in the Lords they can be even briefer and more perfunctory."[8]

Renewal has always been supported by very clear majorities. A similar picture was painted by the Baker Review of renewal of the NIEPAs.[9] The reserve power mechanism for domestic emergencies under the Energy Act 1976 (*supra*, p. 43) has not yet been invoked.

[4] *Ibid.* at p. 333.

[5] *Ibid.* at pp. 333-334.

[6] Palley, *loc. cit.* n. 49, at p. 239.

[7] H.C. Deb., Vol. 38, cols. 569-574, 639-642. Opposition to the powers was maintained throughout the debates on the Prevention of Terrorism Bill 1983; see, *e.g.* Mr. R. Hattersley, H.C. Deb., Vol. 47, cols. 61-70.

[8] Jellicoe, para. 14.

[9] Baker, para. 443.

One problem concerning scrutiny may lie in a lack of detailed interest in MPs in topics that are not natural vote-winners. There is also the pervasive problem of other calls on limited parliamentary time. Another problem may lie in the gross imbalance of information between Ministers, on the one hand, and the rest of Parliament, on the other, with, as Professor Walkland has pointed out, "the Government usually holding all the cards."[10] He notes that

> "One aspect of this is the degree to which essential information about the background and provenance of government bills is difficult to come by. Both at second reading and in committee there is a tendency towards vagueness, generality and secrecy which is advantageous to the Government and disadvantageous to the Opposition. The view of groping backbenchers facing secretive departments is widely held in the case of legislative proceedings, and is largely justified."[11]

Those MPs who have chivvied the Government over the anti-terrorist legislation have had to rely on a variety of sources of information: on Parliamentary Questions (not always answered for security reasons or for reasons of disproportionate cost); on information provided by Ministers; on the very useful statistics published quarterly on the use of the PTAs (regrettably as yet none are published on use of NIEPA 1978 although Baker recommended they should); on information provided in the very influential Reports of Committees and Reviews of the operation of the legislation; and on briefing from pressure groups, in particular, the National Council for Civil Liberties. There has been no input from Parliamentary Select Committees. Nor do current emergency powers embody any specific reporting requirement such as that contained in the internment provisions of Regulation 18B in the Second World War, whereby the Home Secretary was obliged to report to Parliament at least once a month on action taken under the Regulation, including the number of persons detained and the number of cases in which he had not followed the recommendations of the Advisory Committee to which internees could make representations

[10] S.A. Walkland, "Whither the Commons?" in *The Commons Today, op. cit.* n. 50, p. 293.

[11] *Ibid.*

concerning release.[12] A similar requirement was embodied in the PVA 1939, section 1(7) of which required the Secretary of State to report to Parliament "at least once in every three months as to the number of occasions on which [expulsion, prohibition or registration] orders have been made by him and the number of persons with respect to whom such orders have been made." Such mechanisms are also a feature of legislation in Eire.[13]

It is submitted that there is urgent need to extend debate beyond such issues as the horrors of terrorism, praise for the security forces, condemning the latest atrocity and stressing the need for *some* emergency powers. There is a need to develop mechanisms to focus periodic debate on the key issues: are emergency powers needed at all; if so what type of powers, how wide, to whom granted, aimed at what target, with what purpose, subject to what safeguards? There is some feeling that the Bill procedure affords a good opportunity for such careful scrutiny by Parliament. Hence Roy Jenkins, as Home Secretary, declined constantly to renew the PTA 1974 by order, and instead brought forward a Bill to amend and re-enact it.[14] Similarly Lord Jellicoe proposed quinquennial re-enactment of future PTAs, a proposal now embodied in the PTA 1984,[15] in order to give Parliament "a genuine opportunity from time to time to consider cooly whether the legislation really needs to remain in force and, if so, whether it requires amendment in the light of changes in the terrorist" threat.[16] This is welcome. The Baker Review suggests it be extended to NIEPA 1978 or its successor.[17] It is not, however, readily adaptable to such skeleton legislation as the EPA 1920 or the reserve powers of the Energy Act 1976 since the "meat," the points of detailed concern, are contained in subordinate regulations and directions. There is, moreover, a need for more penetrating interim scrutiny, and there still remains the problem of imbalance of information. As to the former, periodic renewal debates under the anti-terrorist legislation provide one opportunity. More time should be afforded them. It would also be useful to extend the scope of

[12] Eaves, *op. cit.* n. 56, p. 39. See, *infra*, pp. 59-60 for the effect this had on judicial perception of their role in relation to such powers.

[13] C. Palley, "Internment: the need for proper safeguards" *The Times*, November 23, 1971; *Lawless* v. *Ireland* (1961) 1 E.H.R.R. 15, para. 37.

[14] Scorer, *op. cit.* n. 16, p. 4.

[15] s.17(3).

[16] Jellicoe, para. 14.

[17] Baker, para. 444.

control either by giving Parliament power to amend the renewal order so as to delete one part of the legislation (*e.g.* on exclusion orders, or the modified trial process) or by requiring the laying of separate orders to renew each part.[18] Monthly motions to continue regulations under proclamations of emergency pursuant to the EPA 1920, and debates on Orders to activate the reserve powers of the Energy Act 1976 provide other opportunities. The last Act might usefully be amended to provide for monthly scrutiny. Such mechanisms could be supplemented by periodic reporting requirements which would mandate the appropriate Minister to provide Parliament with details of the operation of the powers, and should be coupled with the opportunity of a short debate. Such a proposal would go some way to meeting the problem of information. Select Committee review should cover emergency powers. Lord Jellicoe and Baker properly suggested that quinquennial re-enactment of, respectively, the future PTA and NIEPA be preceded by a review of the legislation, its operation and consideration of proposed amendments, although Lord Jellicoe expressed no firm view on whether it should be carried out by an individual or group of individuals. Baker preferred parliamentary review.[19] However, Lord Jellicoe rejected review by a parliamentary select committee taking evidence in open session; any effective review of counter-terrorist legislation would necessitate assessment of information too sensitive to be made available outside a restricted circle.[20] This would be true of only part of the evidence, and would not necessarily apply to the same extent to other emergency legislation. Moreover, insofar as it is valid, it could be adequately met by provision for *in camera* hearings and non-publication of certain evidence (as distinct from conclusions drawn from it) in the report of the review body.[21] Committees of the legislature monitor governmental security and

[18] *Cf.* Lord Wigoder, H.L. Deb., Vol. 448, col. 943, Vol. 449, col. 413. The Government, of course, already has the power to renew the powers in the PTA 1984 and NIEPA 1978 piecemeal. All the Government was prepared to concede in respect of the PTA was "to lay an order . . . to renew . . . in ample time for [the Lords] to be able to debate it at a date which will permit the Government, if they are moved to do so by the debate, to withdraw the order and replace it with another drawn in the different terms in which [the Lords] have persuaded them to draw it."—Lord Elton, H.L. Deb., Vol. 448, col. 945. This seems cumbersome and impractical.

[19] Jellicoe, para. 17; Baker, para. 445.

[20] Jellicoe, para. 17.

[21] This is the position with the Ombudsman and sensitive material: Parliamentary Commissioner Act 1967, ss.8, 11.

intelligence agencies in the United States, in West Germany and in the Netherlands, and such a committee has been proposed for Canada.[22] It is submitted that a joint Lords-Commons Select Committee on Emergency Powers, able to call for witnesses, documents and go "on location," reporting to each House, could foster better informed debate on and surveillance of emergency powers by Parliament, enabling the legislature, as well as Government and civil servants who seem to do so already, to profit from the experience of provisions in operation and to make informed proposals for amendment. Its role in monitoring essential supplies and services' emergencies might in practice be more limited than in relation to the anti-terrorist context since such emergencies tend to be of relatively short duration (*infra*, pp. 225-226), but *ex post facto* review of them might highlight lessons to be learned for future emergencies. There is, of course, a need to equip any such body with expertise. An "Emergencies" Committee should be able to draw on members of Committees monitoring related areas (*e.g.* home affairs, energy, environment, transport, trade and industry). It ought to be backed up with adequate research staff, able to assist members to ask the right questions. The Government has merely announced, in respect of the PTA 1984, annual review by a Government appointed Commissioner, Sir Cyril Philips, chairman of the Police Complaints Board.[23]

3. The Role of the Judiciary

The rule of law requires that government be able to show legal justification for its actions. The ordinary courts, the traditional redressors of grievances, are sometimes perceived to stand between state and citizen, concerned to protect individual rights and freedoms when scrutinising administrative activity, keen to see that legal powers are not exceeded in terms of substance and procedure, and to apply principles of just administration.[24] However, their role in emergency powers situations may be more one of giving the seal of legal legitimacy to government action.

[22] McDonald Report, *op. cit.* n. 49 at pp. 896-905.

[23] Lord Elton, H.L. Deb., Vol. 449, cols. 404-407; *The Times*, January 16, 1985, p. 2.

[24] A.V. Dicey, *An Introduction to the Study of the Law of the Constitution* (10th ed., 1959), esp. Chap. IV: H.W.R. Wade, *Administrative Law* (5th ed., 1982), pp. 22-26.

Although this book is not the place for detailed discussion of remedial and substantive aspects of judicial review of administrative action, some indication must be given as to how disputes about emergency powers might arise in the courts, and as to the likely scope of judicial review of those powers.

Typically rights of appeal to the courts do not form part of such schemes, but the exercise of powers under them may be challenged by applications for habeas corpus by or on behalf of persons detained; through applications for judicial review; or through actions for damages, declarations or injunctive relief. Where purely public law rights are at issue, using actions rather than the application for judicial review may constitute an abuse of process,[25] but ordinary actions may legitimately be used to challenge exercises of power by public authorities which interfere with private rights (*e.g.* as a trespass to person or property).[26] Alternatively, collateral challenge may be used to establish that government has acted *ultra vires* by way of defence to criminal prosecution or civil action by the State at least where private law rights are at stake.[27] *Ultra vires* action would not usually result in the exclusion from criminal proceedings of relevant evidence obtained in consequence.

The scope of judicial review varies according to the source of the particular emergency power: prerogative; martial law; or statute. Although some prerogative powers are now reviewable on the same grounds as statutory ones, where the power concerns such matters as the defence of the realm, national security and, arguably, emergency powers, the courts may be limited to examining the existence of the power claimed, whether its ambit is sufficient to embrace the particular actions said to be based on it, and whether it has been exercised in the appropriate form, but cannot question in those areas the adequacy, propriety or reasonableness of the exercise of a prerogative discretion.[28] Once satisfied that a state of martial law exists, an issue on which the opinion of the military authorities is highly influential but not conclusive, the courts have no jurisdiction during its currency to

[25] *O'Reilly* v. *Mackman* [1983] A.C. 120; *Cocks* v. *Thanet U.D.C.* [1983] A.C. 286.

[26] *Davy* v. *Spelthorne District Council* [1984] A.C. 262; *An Bord Bainne Co-operative (Irish Dairy Board)* v. *Milk Marketing Board* [1984] 2 C.M.L.R. 584.

[27] *Wandsworth L.B.C.* v. *Winder* [1984] 3 W.L.R. 1254.

[28] *Council of Civil Service Unions* v. *Minister for the Civil Service* [1984] 3 W.L.R. 1174 (speeches of Lords Scarman, Diplock and Roskill).

call in question the actions of those authorities.[29] Once that state has terminated, however, they may review the legality of actions taken during it, but it appears that the test is one of bona fide belief in the necessity for the action rather than one of strict necessity.[30] Usually, matters will be covered by an Act of Indemnity,[31] although this would tend not to protect malicious acts.[32]

Modern emergency powers are mainly statutory. In a constitutional system which embodies parliamentary sovereignty as the governing relationship between the legislature and the courts, and which lacks an over-riding Bill of Rights, the courts cannot test the constitutionality of an admitted statute.[33] They may only interpret it to ascertain Parliament's intention as to the scope of the legal authority it confers on the body concerned. Emergency powers tend to confer on the executive discretionary powers to act, giving the decision-maker a choice between alternatives. Ostensibly the courts are not concerned with the merits of the choice but rather with its limits and with principles of good administration applicable to the making of the decision. Thus, in normal circumstances, they may insist that the discretion be not fettered by predetermined rigid rules of policy; that it be applied only for a proper purpose; that its exercise is not dependent on irrelevant considerations; that its exercise is not so unreasonable as would cause one to doubt that any such power was remitted to the decision-maker; that the decision-maker exercised it in good faith; and that those affected by it were given a right to be heard. The scope of permissible review is determined in part by the words of the statute, but these are interpreted against a background of presumptions of interpretation (*e.g.* that Parliament does not intend to contravene international obligations such as the European Convention on Human Rights),[34] constitutional principles and common law values—something like an "implied"

[29] *Ex p. Marais* [1902] A.C. 109; *Tilonko* v. *Att.-Gen. for Natal* [1907] A.C. 93; *R.* v. *Allen* [1921] 2 I.R. 241.

[30] M. Supperstone, *Brownlie's Law of Public Order and National Security* (2nd ed., 1981), p. 216.

[31] See, *e.g.* Indemnity Act 1920; Restoration of Order in Ireland (Indemnity) Act 1923.

[32] 8 *Halsbury's Laws of England* (4th ed.), para. 982.

[33] *B.R.B.* v. *Pickin* [1974] A.C. 765; *Manuel* v. *Att.-Gen.* [1983] Ch. 77.

[34] For the operation of this presumption see *Waddington* v. *Miah* [1974] 1 W.L.R. 683; *R.* v. *CIO Heathrow Airport, ex. p. Bibi* [1976] 1 W.L.R. 979; *R.* v. *Secretary of State for Home Department, ex. p. Phansopkar* [1976] Q.B. 606; *Kaur* v. *Lord Advocate* [1980] 3 C.M.L.R. 79.

Bill of Rights[35]—as well as the rarely expressed societal and political attitudes with which judges are imbued.[36] Commentators on administrative law also stress the importance of context, that the judicial approach to scrutiny of one area of governmental activity cannot be assumed to apply to another. Much may depend on judicial attitudes to the suitability for judicial control of the subject area concerned and to the respective worth of the particular interests advanced for protection by the protagonists before them and on the identity of the decision-maker.[37] It cannot be gainsaid that this is a policy or value-laden area of law in which it may be more difficult than in other areas to predict the outcome of cases.

There can be little doubt that one policy governing the framing of statutory emergency powers is to eliminate, or at least marginalise, judicial scrutiny of administrative action. This is reflected in the lack of rights of appeal to judicial bodies. It is exemplified in a willingness to alter the law—sometimes retrospectively—in response to unwelcome judicial decisions reducing executive freedom of action or to reduce the risk of judicial challenge. An example of the former is the Northern Ireland Act 1972 which was passed to negate the effect of the decision in *R.* v. *Londonderry JJ., ex p. Hume* [38] where D's conviction was quashed on the ground that the Northern Ireland legislature had exceeded its legislative powers embodied in the Government of Ireland Act 1920 by conferring powers on the armed forces. It could not, therefore, penalise disobedience to directions of officers in those forces. The Act retrospectively validated the enactment of such powers by that subordinate legislature.[39] The Emergency Powers (Defence) Act 1939 provides an example of reducing the risk of judicial challenge. Although the validity of internment regulations was upheld by the House of Lords in the First World War as within the general power to make regulations for the defence of the realm,[40] the 1939 Act provided

[35] D.L. Keir and F.H. Lawson, *Cases in Constitutional Law* (6th ed., 1979), pp. 15-22.

[36] J.A.G. Griffith, *The Politics of the Judiciary* (1977), esp. pp. 175-216.

[37] *Cf.* J.M. Evans, *Immigration Law* (2nd ed., 1983), pp. 414-415; E.C.S. Wade and G. Phillips, *Constitutional and Administrative Law* (9th ed., 1977, edited by A.W. Bradley) pp. 580-581.

[38] [1972] N.I.L.R. 91.

[39] For critical comment see P. O'Higgins (1972) 35 M.L.R. 295.

[40] *R.* v. *Halliday, ex p. Zadig* [1917] A.C. 260; *infra*, pp. 55-56.

specific powers for their enactment, just to make sure.[41]

In the eighteenth century, emergency powers were effectively conferred by Habeas Corpus Suspension Acts precluding recourse to that remedy in cases of treason.[42] In modern times, the executive has tended not to rely on direct exclusion of judicial review; most preclusive clauses are in any event readily circumventable after *Anisminic*[43] and would not protect jurisdictional errors.[44] A common clause in emergency powers authorising detention, however, is one stating that a person shall be deemed to be in lawful custody whilst detained under the legislation.[45] Such a clause has been held neither to oust habeas corpus nor to confer legality on detentions which did not otherwise comply with the terms of the legislation.[46] It merely provides authority for keeping detainees in places other than lawful prisons and settles possible doubts as to prison law and practice.[47]

The device used to limit the scope of judicial review has rather been indirect: to frame discretionary powers in subjective terms, rather than in the objective terms which more clearly impart a judicially reviewable standard,[48] and to be rather vague as to the criteria governing the exercise of the power, no doubt on the basis that detailed criteria might afford greater scope for judicial intervention. As Professor Evans has noted, "the effectiveness of judicial review is inversely proportionate to the extent of the discretion conferred by statute upon the repository of the

[41] s.1(2)(*a*). s.9 obviated challenge of the type upheld by the House of Lords in *Att.-Gen.* v. *De Keyser's Royal Hotel* [1920] A.C. 508 by providing that the statutory powers were additional to and not in derogation of the powers exercisable under the prerogative. See also Eaves, *op. cit.* n. 56, p. 18.

[42] R.J. Sharpe, *The Law of Habeas Corpus* (1976), pp. 91-93.

[43] *Anisminic* v. *Foreign Compensation Commission* [1969] 2 A.C. 147.

[44] See, *e.g.* P.P. Craig, *Administrative Law* (1983), pp. 518-526; Wade, *op. cit.* n. 24, pp. 598-609.

[45] See, *e.g.* Art. 12(2) of the Aliens Restriction (Consolidation) Order 1916 (S.R. & O. 1916 No. 122); PTA 1984, Sched. 3, para. 5(2).

[46] *R.* v. *Chiswick Police Station Superintendent, ex p. Sacksteder* [1916] 1 K.B. 578, at p. 586; *R.* v. *Governor of Brixton Prison, ex p. Sarno* [1916] 2 K.B. 742; *R.* v. *Secretary of State for Home Affairs, ex p. Greene* [1942] 1 K.B. 87, at p. 116-117; *Liversidge* v. *Anderson* [1942] A.C. 206, at p. 255 (Lord MacMillan) at p. 273 (Lord Wright).

[47] *Ex p. Greene* [1942] 1 K.B. 87, at p. 116-117; *Liversidge* v. *Anderson* [1942] A.C. 206, at p. 273 (Lord Wright).

[48] Sharpe, *op. cit.* n. 42, p. 97.

power."[49] It is thus more common to find powers conferred in such terms as "if X is satisfied that," "if/where it appears to X that," "where X is of the opinion that," or "where X suspects that" rather than "if X has reasonable grounds to suspect that" or "where A B and C are present, X may."

In the last 20 years, judges have not permitted the use of subjective formulae to negate judicial review, at least in some contexts, and have ventured into areas once thought to be remitted to the absolute discretion of the executive.[50] An important issue in terms of their potential review of the emergency powers covered in this book is how far this activist approach of recent years will be brought to bear in the context of such powers. Or, to put the matter another way, how far will the very different "hands-off" attitude of the leading wartime cases continue to limit their approach. The framers of the powers doubtless work on the basis that the latter attitude will exercise an over-riding influence. There is every reason to think them correct in that view.

The judicial attitude exhibited in the wartime cases was very much one of deference to the executive, permitting almost absolute freedom of decision-making, sacrificing the presumption that wide powers ought to be narrowly construed in favour of the traditional liberties of the subject, and proceeding on the basis that those liberties had to be sacrificed for a greater good, the survival of the nation in an acute crisis—*salus populi suprema lex.* This legitimation of executive freedom of decision has been criticised as an abdication of the judicial function.[51] One might equally well assert, however, that it may have provided yet another pillar in an edifice of national unity necessary to the successful prosecution of the war effort. This highly deferential approach was particularly apparent in cases concerning detention without trial.

In *R.* v. *Halliday, ex p. Zadig,*[52] a naturalised British subject, born in Germany of German parents, sought habeas corpus to challenge his internment under regulation 14B of the Defence of the Realm (Consolidation) Regulations 1914[53] as being outside the rule-making powers conferred by the Defence of the Realm

[49] Evans, *op. cit.* n. 37, p. 274.

[50] Wade, *op. cit.* n. 24, pp. 18-20, 395-396; J. M. Evans, De Smith *Judicial Review of Administrative Action* (4th ed., 1982), pp. 279, 296-298, 362-364.

[51] D.R. Lowry, "Terrorism and Human Rights: Counter-Insurgency and Necessity at Common Law" (1977) 53 *Notre Dame Law* 49, at pp. 53, 58.

[52] [1917] A.C. 260.

[53] S.R. & O. 1914 No. 1699.

(Consolidation) Act 1914 which made no specific mention of an internment power. That Act did, however, authorise the executive to issue regulations "for securing the public safety and the defence of the realm."[54] The majority of the House of Lords upheld the internment scheme as falling within that general power, thereby giving the statute a literal, virtually unlimited interpretation. In the grave peril in which the State found itself, the majority considered that Parliament could indeed have intended to confer near absolute powers on the executive, trusting that they would be exercised reasonably.[55] Although habeas corpus was still technically available as a remedy, as Lord Shaw pointed out, the interpretation adopted by the majority rendered it of little practical use.[56] The courts did, however, show more solicitude for the protection of property rights[57] ; for example, in one case a scheme for the expropriation of property was held not to be supportable under that same general power and was struck down.[58]

The 1939 legislation made express provision for the enactment of internment regulations[59] and of schemes for the regulation of property.[60] In considering the validity of regulations and of actions taken under them, the courts tended to take a literal approach to subjective powers. They were not prepared to review whether particular rules were necessary or expedient for the defence of the realm; these were matters for executive judgment. Provided that the regulation was within the four corners of the Act and the action within the scheme then, in the absence of bad faith, the decision was unreviewable.[61] In the context of internment the House of Lords went even further and decided that a power to detain without trial (reg. 18B), ostensibly framed in objective terms—"if the Secretary of State has reasonable cause to believe any person to be of hostile origin or associations . . . and that by reason thereof it is necessary to exercise control over him,

[54] s.1(1).

[55] [1917] A.C. 260, at pp. 268-269 (Lord Finlay L.C.), at pp. 270-271 (Lord Dunedin), at p. 271 (Lord Atkinson), and at p. 307 (Lord Wrenbury).

[56] [1917] A.C. 260, at p. 294 (dissent).

[57] Lowry, *loc. cit.* n. 51, at pp. 58-62; Griffith, *op. cit.* n. 36, p. 80.

[58] *Newcastle Breweries* v. *R.* [1920] 1 K.B. 854.

[59] Emergency Powers (Defence) Act 1939, s.1(1)(*a*).

[60] Emergency Powers (Defence) Act 1939, s.1(2)(*b*).

[61] See, *inter alia*, *R.* v. *Comptroller-General of Patents, ex p. Bayer Products Ltd.* [1941] 2 K.B. 306; *Progressive Supply Co.* v. *Dalton* [1943] Ch. 54; *Point of Ayr Collieries* v. *Lloyd George* [1943] 2 All E.R. 547; *Carltona Ltd.* v. *Commissioners of Works* [1943] 2 All E.R. 560; *Demetriades* v. *Glasgow Corporation* [1951] 1 All E.R. 457.

he may make an order against him directing that he be detained"[62] —imparted in the particular context under consideration, a purely subjective standard. It meant "if the Secretary of State honestly thinks he has reasonable cause to believe," so that unless the applicant could prove bad faith on the part of the Secretary of State, the internment order must stand. The House so held in *Liversidge* v. *Anderson* in which the internee sought further particulars of defence in an action for false imprisonment,[63] and in *Greene v. Home Secretary*, an application for habeas corpus.[64] Moreover, their Lordships held that mere production of the order without providing the reasons which supported the decision to make it, constituted a complete answer to any such action or application.[65]

Lord Atkin entered a solitary, if celebrated, dissent in *Liversidge.*[66] An objective standard was intended. This was the plain and natural meaning of the words used.[67] They were so used in other legislation.[68] Other provisions in the regulations were expressed subjectively, indicating that Regulation 18B imparted a different test.[69] An earlier form of the regulation had been framed subjectively indicating the importance of the change.[70] His interpretation was more in tune with accepted notions of the liberty of the subject.[71]

The majority preferred to see little significance in differences in wording between regulations, arguing that they were drafted at different times by different draftsmen and that too much stress ought not to be put on precise phraseology since regulations did not receive the same degree of consideration in their framing or scrutiny as did statutes.[72] Moreover, a difference in meaning was

[62] Defence (General) Regulations 1939 (S.I. 1939 No. 1681).

[63] [1942] A.C. 206, at pp. 219-220 (Viscount Maugham), at pp. 251-258 (Lord MacMillan), at pp. 261-273 (Lord Wright), at p. 278 (Lord Romer).

[64] [1942] A.C. 284, at p. 297 (Lord Macmillan), at pp. 300-305 (Lord Wright), at p. 309 (Lord Romer).

[65] [1942] A.C. 206, at p. 224 (Viscount Maugham), at p. 258 (Lord MacMillan); at pp. 277-278 (Lord Romer); [1942] A.C. 284, at p. 297 (Lord Macmillan), at pp. 305-306 (Lord Wright).

[66] [1942] A.C. 206, at pp. 225-247.

[67] [1942] A.C. 206, at pp. 227-228, 232.

[68] [1942] A.C. 206, at pp. 228-232.

[69] [1942] A.C. 206, at pp. 232-236.

[70] [1942] A.C. 206, at p. 237.

[71] [1942] A.C. 206, at pp. 244-245.

[72] [1942] A.C. 206, at p. 223 (Viscount Maugham), at p. 256 (Lord MacMillan), at p. 271 (Lord Wright), at p. 283 (Lord Romer).

given effect to by their Lordships' interpretation; "reasonable cause" admonished the Secretary of State to consider the matter personally and with great care whereas with "satisfied" he could merely rely on the report of a trusted subordinate.[73] Whether the construction adopted by the majority promoted or defeated the intention of the framers of Regulation 18B remains unclear.[74]

In any event, even Lord Atkin's approach would have afforded little practical comfort for the internee, as is indicated by his speech in *Greene*. There he upheld the decision of the Home Secretary who, unnecessarily in the view of the majority, had entered an affidavit stating that his belief that Greene was a person of hostile associations over whom it was necessary to exercise control was based on information from trustworthy and reliable sources. This was sufficient in law to justify the detention to Lord Atkin's satisfaction.[75] In *Liversidge*, moreover, the noble Lord said he would apply a different test to powers subjectively phrased: in such cases

> "It is plain that unlimited discretion is given to the Secretary of State, assuming as everyone does, that he acts in good faith."[76]

He also noted the near impossibility of establishing bad faith.[77]

Nor were the courts keen to apply stringent procedural standards. Decisions under wartime powers tended to be characterised as non-judicial or executive, as not attracting the operation of the rules of natural justice.[78] In *Ex p. Budd* (*No. I*), however, an internee's release was ordered on habeas corpus because failure to comply with the requirement in the regulation that he be given a document stating the ground of his detention, rendered that detention unlawful.[79] That decision did not preclude immediate re-detention with the proper ground stated.[80]

[73] [1942] A.C. 206, at p. 224 (Viscount Maugham), at p. 256 (Lord Macmillan), at p. 268 (Lord Wright).

[74] R.F.V. Heuston, "*Liversidge* v. *Anderson* in Retrospect" (1970) 86 L.Q.R. 33, at pp. 60-63; see, further, by the same author "*Liversidge* v. *Anderson: Two Footnotes*" (1971) 87 L.Q.R. 161, at p. 162.

[75] [1942] A.C. 206, at pp. 246-247; 284, at p. 296.

[76] [1942] A.C. 206, at p. 233.

[77] [1942] A.C. 206, at p. 226.

[78] *R.* v. *Halliday, ex p. Zadig* [1917] A.C. 260 (where the function was said to be "executive"); *Liversidge* v. *Anderson* [1942] A.C. 206; *Howell* v. *Addison* [1943] 1 All E.R. 29, at p. 32 (Goddard L.J.).

[79] Noted in *R.* v. *Home Secretary, ex p. Budd* [1942] 2 K.B. 14, at pp. 22-23.

[80] [1942] 2 K.B. 14, at p. 23 (Lord Greene M.R.).

Moreover, in *Greene* the House of Lords decided that an error in stating the grounds did not affect the validity of the order itself; it was a non-vitiating, directory rather than mandatory requirement.[81]

Several factors may be suggested as important in influencing this deferential approach. The periods were ones of grave national peril, of total war, and with the country fighting for survival, all had to make sacrifices for the common good. The need for mobilisation and direction of the nation's resources and to protect it against spies, saboteurs and subversives seemed obvious.[82] Construing legislative provisions so as to support those aims, even giving them a construction which would not normally apply, seemed appropriate.[83] The executive, by reason of its position as central director, rather than courts of law, seemed better placed to judge what was necessary in the public interest.[84] This was especially so in the internment context where the Secretary of State, "who, by reason of his position, is entitled to public confidence in his capacity and integrity, [and] who is answerable to Parliament for his conduct in office,"[85] had to appraise confidential information from intelligence sources and informants, disclosure of which to the internee or others might prejudice those sources.[86] Moreover the internee could make representations to an Advisory Committee chaired by a High Court judge, which suggested to the majority in *Liversidge* that judicial review was not envisaged by the regulation.[87] A further safeguard against abuse was provided by a requirement of monthly

[81] [1942] A.C. 284, at p. 298 (Lord MacMillan), at p. 300 (Lord Wright), at p. 309 (Lord Romer).

[82] See *R.* v. *Halliday, ex p. Zadig* [1917] A.C. 260, at pp. 270-271 (Lord Dunedin), at p. 271 (Lord Atkinson), at p. 307 (Lord Wrenbury).

[83] [1917] A.C. 260, at pp. 268-269 (Lord Finlay L.C.), at pp. 270-271 (Lord Dunedin), at p. 271 (Lord Atkinson); [1942] A.C. 206, at pp. 218-220 (Viscount Maugham), at p. 252 (Lord MacMillan), at p. 280 (Lord Romer).

[84] *R.* v. *Comptroller-General of Patents, ex p. Bayer Products* [1941] 2 K.B. 306, at pp. 311-312 (Scott L.J.); *Point of Ayr Collieries Ltd.* v. *Lloyd-George* [1943] 2 All E.R. 546 (Lord Greene M.R.).

[85] *Liversidge* v. *Anderson* [1942] A.C. 206, at p. 253 (Lord MacMillan); *cf.* at p. 222 (Viscount Maugham), at pp. 261, 269 (Lord Wright), at p. 282 (Lord Romer).

[86] *R.* v. *Halliday, ex p. Zadig* [1917] A.C. 260, at p. 269 (Lord Finlay L.C.); *Liversidge* v. *Anderson* [1942] A.C. 206, at pp. 220-222 (Viscount Maugham), at p. 253 (Lord MacMillan), at p. 267 (Lord Wright), at p. 280 (Lord Romer).

[87] [1942] A.C. 206, at p. 222 (Viscount Maugham), at p. 254 (Lord MacMillan), at p. 267 (Lord Wright).

reporting to Parliament.[88]

These cases were, of course, decided in the period which marked the nadir of judicial review.[89] The courts in recent years have not allowed the use of subjective formulae in statutory material to negate their power to review executive action. The wartime cases have been doubted and distinguished. In *Nakkuda Ali* v. *Jayaratne*, the Privy Council, obiter, criticised the construction of "reasonable cause" adopted by the majority in *Liversidge* because it reduced to nothing the restraint implied in those words by permitting the wielder of the power to determine conclusively whether the condition had been met.[90] In *Ridge* v. *Baldwin*, Lord Reid characterised *Liversidge* as a very peculiar decision.[91] Their Lordships in *Rossminster* thought it "expediently wrong" and that its ghost ought not to haunt us further.[92] Even Lord Atkin's statements on the meaning and effect of subjective formulae have been stated not to apply today.[93] In *Tameside* the House of Lords did not regard subjective language as excluding all review; Lord Wilberforce stated:

> "The section is framed in a subjective form—if the Secretary of State 'is satisfied.' This form of section is quite well known, and at first sight might seem to exclude judicial review. Sections in this form may, no doubt, exclude judicial review on what is or has become a matter of pure judgment. But I do not think that they go further than that. If a judgment requires, before it can be made, the existence of some facts, then, although the evaluation of those facts is for the Secretary of State alone, the court must enquire whether those facts exist, and have been taken into account, whether the judgment has been made on a proper self-direction as to those facts, whether the judgment has not been made on other facts which ought not to have been taken into account. If these requirements are not met, then the exercise of judgment, however bona fide it may be, becomes capable of challenge."[94]

[88] [1942] A.C. 206, at p. 255 (Lord MacMillan).

[89] H.W.R. Wade, *Administrative Law* (5th ed., 1982), p. 18.

[90] [1951] A.C. 66, at pp. 76-77 (Lord Radcliffe).

[91] [1964] A.C. 40 at p. 73.

[92] *Inland Revenue Commissioners* v. *Rossminster Ltd.* [1980] A.C. 952, at p. 1011 (Lord Diplock), at p. 1025 (Lord Scarman).

[93] *Secretary of State for Education and Science* v. *Metropolitan Borough of Tameside* [1976] 3 All E.R. 665, at p. 670 (C.A.—Lord Denning M.R.).

[94] [1976] 3 All E.R. 665, at p. 681 (H.L.). *Cf. Norwich C.C.* v. *Secretary of State for the Environment* [1982] 1 All E.R. 737.

It may now be true that the courts, if they so choose, can review the legality of any discretionary power.[95] The difficulty with these judicial utterances, however, is that they were made in non-emergency contexts: textile licensing (*Nakkuda Ali*); dismissal of a chief constable (*Ridge* v. *Baldwin*); entry and search powers of the Inland Revenue (*Rossminster*); the relationship between local authority freedom of choice and central government direction in education (*Tameside*). Only the latter involved a Minister. But similar statements were made in the Court of Appeal in *Secretary of State for Employment* v. *ASLEF* (*No. 2*),[96] in the context of the emergency procedure in the Industrial Relations Act 1971, section 141(*c*) of which permitted the Secretary of State to apply to the NIRC for a court-ordered ballot of workers

> "where it appears to the Secretary of State that . . . there are reasons for doubting whether the workers who are taking part or are expected to take part in the strike or other industrial action are or would be taking part in it in accordance with their wishes, and whether they have had an adequate opportunity of indicating their wishes."

Lord Denning M.R. denied that the Minister's decision was thus put beyond challenge.[97] He did note, however, that

> "the scope available to the challenger depends very much on the subject matter with which the Minister is dealing. In this case I would think that, if the Minister does not act in good faith, or if he acts on extraneous considerations which ought not to influence him or if he plainly misdirects himself in fact or in law, it may well be that a court would interfere."[98]

But scrutiny in this context was not to be too strict; thus

> "when he honestly takes a view of the facts or the law which could reasonably be entertained, then his decision is not to be set aside simply because thereafter someone thinks that his view was wrong. After all, this is an emergency procedure. It has to be set in motion quickly, when there is no time for minute analysis of facts or law. The whole process would be

[95] S.A. De Smith, *Constitutional and Administrative Law* (4th ed., 1981, edited by H. Street and R. Brazier), p. 584.

[96] [1972] 2 Q.B. 455.

[97] [1972] 2 Q.B. 455, at p. 487.

[98] *Ibid.* at p. 493.

> made of no effect if the Minister's decision was afterwards to be conned over word by word, letter by letter to see if he has in any way misdirected himself. That cannot be right."[99]

In the analogously sensitive context of deportation of aliens on grounds of public good, the Court of Appeal similarly asserted its power to intervene where the evidence was such as to suggest that the Home Secretary might have used the power for an ulterior purpose, to demand an answer from him and upset his order if none were given or it proved unsatisfactory.[1] There the Home Secretary had made a deportation order against Soblen, a United States' citizen convicted in the United States of spying for the Eastern bloc, which would effectively secure his return to the United States in circumstances in which he could not be extradited. The Court of Appeal considered that the evidence of improper purpose presented was insufficient even to call for an answer from the Home Secretary. In *ASLEF* (*No. 2*) the court was unwilling to draw adverse inferences, as the House of Lords' decision in *Padfield* [2] indicated it could, from the Secretary of State's refusal to disclose his reasons to the courts, although Lord Denning did say that he would apply *Padfield* particularly "in cases which affect life, liberty or property."[3] It may be suggested that the court, whatever its lip-service to a wider scope of review, is, by casting on the challenger an almost insurmountable burden, in effect reserving actual review for the type of clear case of gross abuse unlikely to arise, in short negating the usefulness of review by another method.

Clearly the emergency situations considered in this book do not attain the magnitude of the crises experienced in the two wars. This, and the judicial activism of the last two decades, may lead one to hope that the scope of review of modern emergency powers would not be so narrow as in wartime, that the lessons of the recent past will not wholly be forgotten.[4] That said, however, some of the other policy factors limiting review in the wartime cases—the status of decision-maker, the sensitive nature of the subject matter, a factual basis more properly within executive knowledge, the availability of other safeguards against abuse—are

99 *Ibid.*

1 *R.* v. *Brixton Prison Governor, ex p. Soblen* [1963] 2 Q.B. 243, at p. 302 (Lord Denning M.R.), at p. 308 (Donovan L.J.).

2 *Padfield* v. *Minister of Agriculture, Fisheries and Food* [1968] A.C. 997.

3 [1972] 2 Q.B. 455, at p. 493 (Lord Denning M.R.), at pp. 496-497 (Buckley L.J.), at p. 511 (Roskill L.J.).

4 *Cf.* Sharpe, *op. cit.* n. 42, p. 124.

also present in the context of powers dealing with terrorism and the maintenance of essential supplies and services. It is also arguable that the context is closer to war than to the issues raised by the cases asserting wider powers of review. Privy Council review of post-war colonial and Commonwealth emergency powers, and the few cases on legislative powers concerned with security and public order in Northern Ireland suggest that the wartime cases will still be influential; that while there may be suggestions that a more extensive power of review subsists even in emergency contexts, in practical terms, on substantive issues, discretionary powers, especially those clearly framed in subjective terms, are likely to be held to be effectively non-reviewable unless the challenger can surmount the near insurmountable hurdle of establishing bad faith or some other vitiating defect almost as difficult to prove as bad faith. That this is so draws some support from the almost complete lack of court challenge to most of the powers examined in this book.[5] Where, however, the preconditions to or limits on the exercise of powers are framed clearly objectively or deal with matters capable of independent objective verification (*e.g.* status or residence), the courts are likely to insist on their being met.[6] These submissions may be illustrated and supported by considering each stage in the deployment of emergency powers at which court intervention might be envisaged: the invocation of emergency powers; the making of delegated and sub-delegated legislation under such powers; the application of such powers, whether in primary or subordinate legislation, to individual cases.

Emergency powers may be invoked by procuring their enactment by Parliament, as with the NIEPAs and the PTAs. Clearly, the courts cannot challenge the necessity or expedience of their enactment. Another method is to use an executive proclamation to bring into force rule-making powers in an already existing statute. Judicial review of the validity of that proclamation is not precluded by Parliamentary sovereignty. Such a proclamation may be issued under the EPA 1920

[5] Note: Legal advice given to the NCCL was that it was impossible to challenge in court an exclusion order under the PTAs: see C. Scorer and P. Hewitt, *The Prevention of Terrorism Act: The case for repeal* (1981), p. 28; *cf.* p. 21 on proscription of organisations.

[6] *Cf. Eshugbayi Eleko* v. *Officer Administering the Government of Nigeria* [1931] A.C. 662, at p. 670; *R.* v. *Home Secretary, ex p. Budd* [1942] 2 K.B. 14, at pp. 21-22 (Lord Greene M.R.).

> "if at any time it appears to Her Majesty that there have occurred, or are about to occur, events of such a nature as to be calculated, by interfering with the supply and distribution of food, water, fuel or light, or with the means of locomotion, to deprive the community, or any substantial portion of the community, of the essentials of life."[7]

Powers in the Energy Act 1976 which enable the executive to regulate the use, supply or price of energy, may by order be declared exercisable to their full extent where

> "there exists, or is imminent, in the United Kingdom an actual or threatened emergency affecting fuel or electricity supplies which makes it necessary in Her Majesty's opinion that the government should temporarily have at its disposal exceptional powers for controlling the sources and availability of energy."[8]

On the face of it, under the first Act the existence of the emergency is made a matter of executive opinion whereas under the latter Act, although the necessity for powers is made a matter of opinion, the existence or imminence of the emergency is not clearly so. A trio of Privy Council decisions[9] on whether the courts can review a decision that an emergency exists, suggest that, in practical terms, courts will not intervene, whether the power be framed objectively or subjectively, either because the decision is non-justiciable, for example because it properly belongs in the political sphere, more properly a matter for executive judgment, or because if justiciable,

> "the onus of proof [of abuse of discretion] on anyone challenging a proclamation of emergency may well be heavy and difficult to discharge since the policies followed and the steps taken by the responsible Government may be founded on information and apprehensions which are not known to, and cannot always be made known to, those who seek to impugn what has been done."[10]

Moreover, bad faith cannot be imputed to the Crown.[11]

7 EPA 1920, s.1(1), as amended by the EPA 1964, s.1.

8 Energy Act 1976, s.3(1)(*b*).

9 *Bhagat Singh* v. *King-Emperor* (1931) L.R. 58 I.A. 169; *King-Emperor* v. *Benoari Lal Sarma* [1945] A.C. 14; *Ningkan* v. *Government of Malaysia* [1970] A.C. 379.

10 [1970] A.C. 379, at p. 390 (Lord MacDermott).

11 Evans, *op. cit.* n. 50, pp. 287, 336.

Several emergency powers are found in delegated rather than primary legislation. To be valid delegated legislation must comply with the limits set by the parent Act. It may be challenged as to its *vires.* Defects of procedure, however, will not always prove fatal. Courts may construe procedural requirements as mandatory or directory. They are more likely to take the latter path where to regard non-compliance as vitiating the regulation would have unfortunate consequences.[12] It has accordingly been suggested that requirements to lay emergency regulations before Parliament—and, perhaps indeed, to communicate the proclamation of emergency to it—are directory only.[13] While consultation requirements are usually mandatory,[14] they do not form typical features of emergency legislation.[15] As to substantive limits, the parent Act in emergency powers situations tends to confer rule-making power in wide terms, rendering challenge difficult because the limits of the power conferred are so vague that the requirement that the regulation fall within the four corners of the power or that it be referable to the purposes set out in the Act becomes meaningless.[16] For example, during the currency of a proclamation of emergency under the EPA 1920 Her Majesty in Council can by order make regulations

> "for securing the essentials of life to the community, and those regulations may confer or impose on a Secretary of State or other Government department, or any other persons in Her Majesty's service or acting on Her Majesty's behalf, such powers and duties as Her Majesty may deem necessary for the preservation of the peace, for securing and regulating the supply and distribution of food, water, fuel, light, and other necessities, for maintaining the means of transit or

[12] De Smith, *op. cit.* n. 95, pp. 349, 563-564.

[13] G.S. Morris, "The Emergency Powers Act 1920" [1979] P.L. 317, at pp. 331-332.

[14] De Smith, *op. cit.* n. 95, p. 349.

[15] But *cf.* Drought Act 1976, Sched. 1, *infra,* pp. 217-220 where prior notice of the application to the Secretary of State must be given and objections heard, if necessary, by way of a public local inquiry or by a person appointed by the Secretary of State. However, the inquiry or hearing may be dispensed with "where it appears to the Secretary of State that the order is required to be made urgently if it is to enable the authority effectively to meet the deficiency of supplies of water in their area" (para. 3), but he must not ignore objections already in and not withdrawn.

[16] *Cf.* Evans, *op. cit.* n. 50, p. 292.

locomotion, and for any other purposes essential to the public safety and the life of the community, and may make such provisions incidental to the powers aforesaid as may appear to Her Majesty to be required for making the exercise of those powers effective."[17]

That the regulations so made are to have effect as if enacted in the Act[18] does nothing to furnish the answer to the question: are they valid regulations; the Act would prevail in the event of conflict.[19] It is submitted that the courts are unlikely to undertake searching scrutiny of whether the powers would further the ends stated in the Act. The wartime stance on such issues was in substance adopted by the majority of the House of Lords in *McEldowney* v. *Forde*, [20] where the regulation at issue, declaring Republican Clubs to be unlawful associations membership of which constituted an offence, was made by the Northern Ireland Minister of Home Affairs in a relatively quiet period, well before the disorders necessitating the introduction of troops to Northern Ireland.[21] The parent statute, in objective terms, conferred on the Minister power to make regulations for the preservation of the peace and the maintenance of order in Northern Ireland.[22] The majority of the House of Lords held that the regulation could be related to the prescribed purpose, and that, in the absence of proof of bad faith, the Minister's decision as to its expediency was not challengeable. He was in the best position to know.[23] Similarly in *Ross-Clunis* v. *Papadopollous*, [24] the Privy Council upheld regulations during the Cyprus emergency in the 1950s, which permitted collective fines to be levied on the inhabitants of an area where terrorists were thought to be harboured, as clearly within a power "to make such regulations as appear to [the Governor] to be necessary or

[17] EPA 1920, s.2(1).

[18] EPA 1920, s.2(4).

[19] Morris, *loc. cit.* n. 13, at p. 323, n. 27, citing *Institute of Patent Agents* v. *Lockwood* [1894] A.C. 347 and *Minister of Health* v. *R., ex p. Yaffe* [1931] A.C. 494.

[20] [1971] A.C. 632.

[21] Reg. 24A of the Civil Authorities (Special Powers) Act Regulations (Northern Ireland) 1922 (S.R. & O. 1922 No. 35) as amended by Civil Authorities (Special Powers) Acts (Amending) (No. 1) Regulations (Northern Ireland) (S.R. & O. 1967 No. 42).

[22] Civil Authorities (Special Powers) Acts 1922-43, s.1(3).

[23] [1971] A.C. 632, at p. 645 (Lord Hodson), at p. 649 (Lord Guest), at p. 655 (Lord Pearson). Lords Pearce and Diplock dissented.

[24] [1958] 1 W.L.R. 546.

expedient for securing the public safety . . . or the maintenance of public order," although the Privy Council reserved power to nullify regulations if there were no grounds on which a reasonable authority could have been satisfied of the conditions precedent being fulfilled.[25] One suspects that it would only be in an overwhelmingly clear case, and one of a type unlikely to arise, that that power would be exercised.

Sometimes, however, very clear limits on rule-making power may be set out. Thus, the EPA 1920 does not authorise the making of regulations which impose any form of compulsory military service or industrial conscription, or which criminalise participation in a strike or the peaceful persuasion of others to participate in it.[26] While regulations may create other offences triable summarily, they are not to alter existing criminal procedure "or confer any right to punish by fine or imprisonment without trial."[27] It may confidently be submitted that the courts would insist on such limits being respected. In *Smith* v. *Wood*, where the proviso on the right to strike was re-iterated in the regulation in question, the fact that the interpretation adopted by the magistrates criminalised activity within the proviso, provided one reason for the Divisional Court to quash the conviction.[28]

The application of particular emergency provisions to particular cases may well prove more susceptible to judicial challenge than the two stages considered above, depending on context and on formulation. For example, to make an exclusion order excluding from the United Kingdom a person who could establish his British citizenship would clearly be outside the powers conferred by the PTA 1984.[29] A court could quash the order and if necessary direct the person's release if detained. The limitation on the power is judicially and objectively verifiable, rather than a matter of opinion or executive judgment. An order purporting to exclude from Great Britain a British citizen exempt from exclusion on grounds of residence would similarly be controllable.[30] By contrast, whether a person, not otherwise exempt on objective grounds of status, is a person who may

[25] [1958] 1 W.L.R. 546, at pp. 559, 560.
[26] EPA 1920, s.2(1).
[27] EPA 1920, s.2(3).
[28] (1927) 43 T.L.R. 178.
[29] PTA 1984, s.6(4) (*infra*, pp. 192-193).
[30] PTA 1984, s.4(4)(*a*) (*infra*, pp. 192-193).

legitimately be arrested and detained, or be interned without trial, or be excluded from a specified territory, or have his land or chattels requisitioned, raises more difficult issues.

Where an arrest power conferred on a constable is conditioned objectively in terms of reasonable cause or grounds for suspicion, as, for example, in section 12(1) of the PTA 1984 or in regulations under the EPA 1920,[31] the *Liversidge* v. *Anderson* construction will not apply. The House in that case[32] and the judge in a Northern Ireland decision, *Re McElduff*,[33] confined its operation to ministerial level, and even at that level the case has been so discredited that an objective construction of such powers even in time of war or civil commotion cannot be ruled out.[34] For that reason, perhaps, such powers given to ministers are now clearly framed in subjective terms. *Re McElduff* also demonstrates that even in an emergency context the courts will be slow to displace the common law requirement that proper and adequate reasons be provided for arrest. There a person was merely told that he was being arrested under the Special Powers Act and that the arrestor was not obliged to supply further information. The court held this insufficient and declared the arrest unlawful.[35] Moreover, the illegality of the arrest vitiated a detention order made against the arrestee by the Minister of Home Affairs; even though that power was framed subjectively it was so formulated that it could only be exercised against a person validly arrested.[36] As in *Ex p. Budd* (*No. 1*),[37] however, the defect could be countered by a valid re-arrest with sufficient reasons at the door of the court.[38] However, the illegality of any prior period of arrest and detention could not

[31] For an example see *infra*, p. 239.

[32] [1942] A.C. 206. Their Lordships laid stress on the status of the Secretary of State, responsible to Parliament; see especially at p. 222 (Viscount Maugham), at pp. 268-269 (Lord Wright).

[33] [1972] N.I.L.R. 1, at pp. 17-18 (McGonigal J.).

[34] Heuston, *loc. cit.* n. 74, at p. 68.

[35] [1972] N.I.L.R. 1, at pp. 14-15. McGonigal J. held that, since arrest under differing powers of the regulations had vastly differing consequences and gave rise to different rights for the arrestee, he had to be told under which power he had been arrested and why.

[36] [1972] N.I.L.R. 1, at pp. 12, 15-16, 26.

[37] *Supra*, p. 58.

[38] McElduff was so re-arrested. An earlier attempt to seek habeas corpus in the High Court in London so as to avoid this danger was unsuccessful: *Re Keenan* (1972) N.I.L.R. 118n. (Ackner J.); [1971] 3 W.L.R. 844 (C.A.).

taint an internment order made against that person; the power to make such an order, vested in a minister, framed in subjective terms, was not preconditioned on a power of arrest.[39]

The protection afforded by the *McElduff* reasoning is, however, limited. Where an objective arrest power demands reasonable suspicion of something inherently vague–for example, involvement in terrorism rather than a specific criminal offence–there may be little for the court to review, especially in terms of substance. In *Ex p. Lynch*, it was held that informing the person that he was being arrested as a suspected terrorist constituted sufficient information, and judicial scrutiny of the validity of the exercise of the power could be satisfied by the police stating that they were acting on non-disclosable information received.[40] Protection of those sources from identification would be ground for not probing further at that stage.[41]

Where the power of arrest is conditioned on mere suspicion, however, the courts have merely required the constable to have an actual, honest and bona fide belief.[42] They have proved unwilling to enquire into the reasonableness of the belief, arguably rendering illusory any benefits to be obtained from the review process. Where powers are vested in a Secretary of State in subjective form–for example to exclude or intern persons he is satisfied are involved in terrorism–the deferential approach of the wartime cases looms large. In *Kelly* v. *Faulkner*, [43] Gibson J. dealt with the appropriate scope of review of the power of the Northern Ireland Minister of Home Affairs to make an internment order

> "when it appeared to him that it was expedient that a person suspected of acting, or of having acted, or of being about to act in a manner prejudicial to the preservation of the peace and the maintenance of order in Northern Ireland,"

[39] *Kelly* v. *Faulkner* [1973] N.I.L.R. 31, at p. 39 (Gibson J.).

[40] [1980] N.I.L.R. 126 (Lord Lowry L.C.J.).

[41] *Marks* v. *Beyfus* (1890) 25 Q.B.D. 494, at p. 498; *R.* v. *Lewes JJ., ex p. Home Secretary* [1973] A.C. 388, at p. 407.

[42] *McKee* v. *Chief Constable for Northern Ireland* [1984] 1 W.L.R. 1358 (H.L.(N.I.)). In *Re Boyle, O'Hare and McAllister* (Jellicoe, para. 119), Donaldson L.J. noted that judicial review of the powers of examination at ports under the PTA 1984 and subordinate legislation (*infra*, pp. 170-173), exercisable without suspicion, merely meant examination of whether the officer bona fide thought that a person fell into a category of persons who should be questioned, although in an extreme case, the court might ask whether no reasonable person could have taken that view.

[43] [1973] N.I.L.R. 31.

should be restrained.[44] Kelly, a person not on the arresting officer's list, was nonetheless arrested when the Army platoon came for his brother, who was not in the house. The court accepted as bona fide the officer's statement that Kelly was arrested because the officer had recalled other information linking Kelly with the IRA.[45] Kelly challenged the internment order *inter alia* on the bases of "no evidence" and lack of bona fides in the Minister of Home Affairs. Gibson J. stated, after citing *Liversidge:*

> "it is not open to the court to inquire into the reasonableness of the belief or decision of a Minister of the Crown when making such an order. Whether it is expedient to make the order is a political decision into which the courts will not enquire and if a Minister says he suspects any person of any activity then failing evidence either of bad faith or that that conclusion could not reasonably be related to the circumstances of the case, the sufficiency of the statement must be taken as concluded. Here the plaintiff in his statement of claim denied the various elements requisite to the making of a valid order but no evidence has been led to support these averments. In the absence, therefore, of evidence specifically raising an issue of bad faith, or that the state of mind of the Minister which induced the order depended upon the application of incompetent standards or the admission of irrelevant consideration the averments on its face or otherwise requisite for its efficacy are to be taken as established without any further evidence."[46]

It has been suggested that this would enable review in cases of mistaken identity, or where the order was tainted with politico-religious discrimination, or where persons, clearly not a security threat, were nonetheless interned because they would be vociferous critics of internment.[47] Some support for such views might be drawn from the *Tameside* approach noted earlier.[48] A court might equally conceivably regard the factual basis as being

[44] Reg. 12(1) of the Civil Authorities (Special Powers) Act Regulations (Northern Ireland) 1922 (S.I. 1922 No. 191).

[45] [1973] N.I.L.R. 31, at p. 35.

[46] [1973] N.I.L.R. 31, at p. 41, citing *Point of Ayr Collieries Ltd.* v. *Lloyd-George* [1943] 2 All E.R. 546.

[47] M.P. O'Boyle, "Emergency Situations and the Protection of Human Rights: A Model Derogation Provision for a Northern Ireland Bill of Rights" (1977) 28 N.I.L.Q. 160, at p. 175, n. 78.

[48] *Supra*, pp. 60-61. Indeed, in *Att.-Gen. of St. Christopher* v. *Reynolds* [1980] A.C.

one essentially within the knowledge of the Secretary of State, as raising issues turning on confidential information from intelligence sources, and which depend on judgments unsuitable for the judiciary (for example, whether the security situation is such that X needs to be interned). The courts might assign the decision to the non-reviewable category of "pure judgment." In any event, the burden of proving any such allegations is likely to be set so high as to make any such challenge impractical.

Re McElduff suggests judicial keenness to ensure compliance with non-substantive limits. What role does natural justice or the duty to act fairly have to play? In a security context they will not apply to give a right to be heard before an order on which confinement depends is made; such prior notification, by alerting the suspect, would defeat the end in view.[49] They would probably apply after the event, but only in a limited form. In *Ex p. Mackay*, the court decided that an internee was entitled to be told the information on which the order was based, although the Secretary of State could withhold such of the information disclosure of which would in his opinion endanger the security forces or public safety. In some circumstances, but not the case at hand, legal representation might be required to assist him to present his case to the advisers.[50] In the analogous context of national security deportations, the Court of Appeal said it would interfere where the advisers refused to hear representations at all, but otherwise the balance between national security and the interest in a fair hearing was to be struck by a Secretary of State responsible to Parliament, and the court would not rule on how much information, if any, must be supplied to the deportee.[51]

A Bill of Rights might enhance judicial scrutiny of emergency powers.[52] The issue is examined in Chapter 6 (*infra*, pp. 274-286).

637, the J.C.P.C. interpreted "is satisfied" in detention regulations to mean "is satisfied on reasonable grounds," but did so chiefly in reliance on provisions in the Constitution protecting freedom of person and mandating the provision to the detainee in detail of the grounds for his detention, rather than on *Tameside* or other decisions. Insufficient reasons were provided in the particular case, raising an irresistible presumption that no reasonable grounds existed for the detention. The detention order was invalidated and an award of damages upheld (see esp. at pp. 655-662).

[49] Evans, *op. cit.* n. 50, p. 190.

[50] *Ex p. Mackay* (1972) 23 N.I.L.Q. 331.

[51] *R.* v. *Secretary of State for Home Affairs, ex p. Hosenball* [1977] 1 W.L.R. 766, at pp. 781, 783 (Lord Denning M.R.).

[52] Enhanced review because of a Bill of Rights may be seen in *Att.-Gen. of St. Christopher* v. *Reynolds* [1980] A.C. 637.

4. Committees, Inquiries and Reviews

Such investigative and reporting mechanisms are a common feature of public administration in the United Kingdom to inquire into matters of public concern; to review the operation of a particular legislative or administrative scheme, and to make appropriate recommendations; and as a means of "buying" time in an area of controversy.

Internal governmental reviews have produced a finely tuned Civil Contingencies machine. Otherwise the role of such mechanisms in the context of the maintenance of essential supplies and services has been concerned with the causes of particular industrial disputes which have threatened to cause, or have caused, the invocation of powers under the EPA 1920 and with how those disputes might be resolved, rather than with the operation of the legislation and what it might appropriately contain. For example, faced with the prospect of a transport stoppage in support of the miners in the summer of 1925, a confrontation for which it was not ready, the Baldwin Government gained time by providing a nine months' subsidy for the industry and setting up the Royal Commission on the Mines.[53] The miners' strike of January-February 1972, which led to a proclamation of emergency on February 9, was settled when the Government awarded a pay rise recommended by an official inquiry under Lord Wilberforce.[54]

As regards the Northern Ireland emergency, there have been two investigations into the causes of the disturbances in 1968-69 in the Province by Lord Cameron[55] and then by the Scarman Tribunal.[56] The Report of the Hunt Committee led to the restructuring of the Royal Ulster Constabulary (RUC), the disbanding of the partisan, paramilitary Ulster Special Constabulary (the "B" Specials recruited exclusively from Protestants) and their replacement by the Ulster Defence Regiment (UDR).[57] In the immediate aftermath of the introduction of internment in August 1971, two reports

[53] K. Jeffery and P. Hennessy, *States of Emergency: British Governments and Strikebreaking since 1919* (1983), pp. 91-94.

[54] *Keesing's Contemporary Archives* (1971-1972), p. 25185.

[55] *Disturbances in Northern Ireland; Report of the Commission Appointed by the Governor of Northern Ireland*, Cmd. 532 (N.I.) (1969).

[56] *Report of the Tribunal of Inquiry into Violence and Civil Disturbances in Northern Ireland in 1969*, Cmd. 566 (N.I.) (1972).

[57] *Report of the Advisory Committee on Police in Northern Ireland*, Cmd. 535 (N.I.) (1969).

considered the treatment and interrogation of internees and, in particular, the practice of "interrogation in depth" which involved the application in combination to 14 persons questioned at an unidentified interrogation centre of five aids to interrogation: hooding; wall-standing; subjection to "white noise"[58] ; deprivation of sleep, and of food and water. These aids were authorised by a high level directive and had been deployed in various internal security situations which accompanied British withdrawal from colonial empire.[59] The Compton Report was limited to allegations of *physical brutality.* [60] It concluded that ill-treatment had occurred but not brutality since Compton considered that the latter was

> "an inhuman or savage form of cruelty and that cruelty implies a disposition to inflict suffering, coupled with indifference to, or pleasure in, the victim's pain."[61]

The Parker Report considered the authorised procedures governing the interrogation of suspected terrorists. The majority report considered "interrogation in depth" acceptable but that an Act of Indemnity should be procured to protect its operators.[62] The Government accepted Lord Gardiner's minority report that the methods were morally objectionable, unlawful, ineffective and should be discontinued.[63] They were subsequently found to breach the prohibition on torture, inhuman or degrading treatment embodied in the European Convention on Human Rights. The Report of the Tribunal of Inquiry headed by Lord Widgery largely exonerated the Parachute Regiment in respect of the deaths of 13 civilians shot at an unlawful demonstration in Londonderry on "Bloody Sunday," January 30, 1972.[64] It also endorsed as

[58] This was a constant hissing noise like that of compressed air or a drill, designed to increase the victim's disorientation; see *Ireland* v. *United Kingdom*, European Commission of Human Rights (1973) 41 *Collection of Decisions* 55.

[59] *Report of the Committee of Privy Counsellors appointed to consider authorised procedures for the interrogation of persons suspected of terrorism*, Cmnd. 4901 (1972), pp. 2-3 (hereinafter cited as "Parker"); *Ireland* v. *United Kingdom* (1978) 2 E.H.R.R. 25, at p. 60 (para. 97).

[60] *Report of the enquiry into allegations against the security forces of physical brutality in Northern Ireland arising out of events on the 9th August 1971*, Cmnd. 4823 (1971) (hereinafter cited as "Compton").

[61] Compton, p. 23; for criticism see Brownlie (1972) 35 M.L.R. 501.

[62] Parker, majority report, para. 38 (p. 8).

[63] *Ibid.* at pp. 19-20; *Ireland* v. *United Kingdom*, European Commission of Human Rights (1973) 41 *Collection of Decisions*, at pp. 42, 50.

[64] H.C. 220 (1971-72).

satisfactory the standing instructions to troops on opening fire embodied in the "Yellow Card."[65] The Bennett Report[66] on interrogation by the RUC led to changes in the practice of, and the supervision of, interrogation of terrorist suspects by that force.

Such inquiries have been criticised on various levels: too narrow terms of reference; "conclusions which . . . with the possible exception of Cameron and Scarman were not always in accord with what might have been expected from an objective assessment of those findings"[67] (*e.g.* Compton's odd definition of brutality); a too heavy emphasis on the evidence of the security forces to which undue credence was paid; and the involvement of senior judges in an essentially political role which "blurred the distinction between executive and judicial functions and had an adverse effect on public confidence in the latter."[68]

There have been several reviews of the anti-terrorist legislation applicable exclusively in Ulster and throughout the United Kingdom. In 1972 a commission, chaired by Lord Diplock, was appointed to consider what legal procedures other than internment by the Executive could be used in the Province to bring terrorists to book.[69] Its recommendations formed the basis for NIEPA 1973, other parts of which resulted from an internal inquiry into the Special Powers Act regime (*infra*, pp. 98-99). In 1975 the Gardiner Committee was asked to

> "consider what provisions and powers, consistent to the maximum extent practicable in the circumstances with the preservation of civil liberties and human rights, are required to deal with terrorism and subversion in Northern Ireland, including provisions for the administration of justice, and to examine the working of the Northern Ireland (Emergency Provisions) Act 1973; and to make recommendations."[70]

[65] *Supra*, p. 36; *infra*, pp. 164-165.

[66] Cmnd. 7497 (1979).

[67] K. Boyle, T. Hadden and P. Hillyard, *Law and State: the case of Northern Ireland* (1975) p. 127.

[68] *Ibid.* p. 129; *cf.* J.A.G. Griffith, *The Politics of the Judiciary*, pp. 46-48.

[69] Cmnd. 5185 (1972).

[70] Cmnd. 5847 (1975).

Its report largely endorsed the Diplock approach.[71] Its recommendations, with some modifications, were given effect by NIEPA 1975. That Act, and NIEPA 1973, are now consolidated in NIEPA 1978, which is examined in Chapter Three. The late Sir George Baker, former President of the Family Division, reviewed the operation of NIEPA 1978. His terms of reference were

> "Accepting that temporary emergency powers are necessary to combat sustained terrorist violence, and taking into account Lord Jellicoe's review of the working of the Prevention of Terrorism (Temporary Provisions) Act 1976 as it affects Northern Ireland, to examine the operation of the Northern Ireland (Emergency Provisions) Act 1978 in order to determine whether its provisions strike the right balance between the need on the one hand to maintain as fully as possible the liberties of the individual and on the other to provide the security forces and the courts with adequate powers to enable them to protect the public from current and foreseeable incidence of terrorist crime; and to report."[72]

Some of his recommendations can be implemented administratively. Others require legislation. Apparently the Government plans to bring some legislation forward at an opportune moment and is in broad agreement with the tone of the Review and with most of its conclusions and recommendations.[73] In 1978 Lord Shackleton's *Review of the Operation of the Prevention of Terrorism (Temporary Provisions) Act 1974 and 1976* was published.[74] Most of the relatively minor changes it suggested were implemented by the Government. The Review of the PTA 1976, carried out by Lord Jellicoe, recommended more far-reaching changes.[75] Those that could be effected administratively were promptly accepted and implemented, some

[71] *Infra*, pp. 99-101, 132-146.

[72] Cmnd. 9222 (1984), para. 1.

[73] In the Common's debate on the Review, the Secretary of State for Northern Ireland, Mr. D. Hurd MP, stated that the Government had not made its decisions on several key issues, but would consult widely and take a note of points raised in the debate when formulating proposals which would be submitted when there is an opportunity to do so. No timescale was mentioned (H.C. Deb., Vol. 70, col. 580). For Baker's recommendations see *infra*, pp. 99-161.

[74] Cmnd. 7324 (1978).

[75] Cmnd. 8803 (1983).

through guidance in circulars. Others are enshrined in the PTA 1984.[76] The Police and Criminal Evidence Act 1984 and codes made thereunder house others.[77]

Some concern has been expressed that the more recent inquiries into emergency powers (Shackleton, Jellicoe, Baker) have been obliged by their terms of reference to accept as given a debatable proposition: that emergency legislation is necessary in the particular context.[78] The Diplock Report was criticised as too hurried and for taking evidence from too narrow sources.[79] The others have heard evidence from a wide range of sources indeed.[80] All the inquiries into the legislation represent a substantial contribution to the debate on emergency powers. They are essential reading.

5. Pressure Groups, the Media and Public Opinion

These are traditionally regarded as having an important though ill-defined role in the protection of civil liberties and in ensuring executive accountability in the United Kingdom.

In the context of anti-terrorist legislation, the NCCL, in particular, has done much to monitor the operation of the legislation, given evidence to the official reviews of its operation and provided briefings for interested MPs at the time of the renewal debates, thereby making for better informed scrutiny.[81] In the Province, groups such as the Association for Legal Justice, the Northern Ireland Civil Rights' Association, the Committee on the Administration of Justice (CAJ) and the Northern Ireland Association of Socialist Lawyers (NIASL), strive to improve the level of public debate on these important issues. Unofficial reports by various investigative bodies on the use of force have

[76] *Infra*, pp. 169-209.

[77] *Infra*, pp. 181-182; PCEA 1984, ss.56, 58, 60, 66, 67. See also Home Office Circular No. 26/1984, para. 95.

[78] Committee on the Administration of Justice. "Submission to the review by Sir George Baker of the Northern Ireland (Emergency Provision) Act 1978 (the EPA)," para. 1. A copy of this was kindly supplied to the author by Brice Dickson of the Faculty of Law, Queen's University, Belfast.

[79] Boyle, Hadden and Hillyard, *op. cit.* n. 67, p. 95; D.R. Lowry, "Internment: Detention without Trial in Northern Ireland" (1976) 5 *Human Rights* 261, at p. 296.

[80] See the "List of Witnesses" in the Appendices to the Reports.

[81] See, *e.g.* Scorer, *The Prevention of Terrorism Acts 1974 and 1976: A Report on the Operation of the Law* (NCCL, 1976), and Scorer and Hewitt, *op. cit.* n. 5.

contributed to that process.[82] Although Amnesty International has no prisoners of conscience in Ulster, reports by that body on interrogation abuses in 1971 and 1977 may be thought influential factors in the establishment of official inquiries into the area.[83] Revelations in the media can also be important. The whole area of media coverage of Northern Ireland affairs is, however, controversial and has attracted criticism from differing quarters.[84]

On a semi-official level, the work of the Standing Advisory Commission on Human Rights (SACHR) must be noted. This body, arguably a reflection of moderate opinion, was set up in 1973 to monitor discrimination. Its statutory remit in the Northern Ireland Constitution Act 1973[85] does not include investigation of emergency powers, and therefore it is not included in the section on official bodies. It has nevertheless taken that task upon itself and its monitoring of the area has been in practice endorsed by successive Secretaries of State. It is arguable that the remit should be so extended as to place such work on a more secure footing. Its annual reports contain useful information on the operation of and moderate attitudes to emergency powers. It has given evidence to official reviews and advice to the Secretary of State. Its influence is difficult to evaluate. Paul Maguire suggests that

> "from the Government's point of view, the Commission performs, at minimum, a useful public relations function and, at maximum, the function of a non-party political counterweight to sectarian forces . . . . No doubt the Commission's words are heard by Government but its status is advisory and it is noticeable that in many important areas the Government has not publicly sought the Commission's advice, for example, in relation to emergency powers generally."[86]

[82] See, *e.g.* S. Dash, *Justice Denied: A Challenge to Lord Widgery's Report on "Bloody Sunday"* (NCCL, 1972); T. Gifford, *Death on the Streets of Derry* (NCCL, 1978).

[83] Amnesty International, *Report of an Enquiry into Allegations of Ill-Treatment in Northern Ireland* (1972); *Report of an Amnesty International Mission to Northern Ireland (28 November–6 December 1977)*, AI Index: Eur 45/01/78 (1978).

[84] See, generally, L. Curtis, *Ireland: the Propaganda War. The British Media and "The Battle for Hearts and Minds"* (1984). There have occassionally been calls for the prosecution of editors over interviews with paramilitaries and filming of their activities; see, *e.g.* H.C. Deb., Vol. 987, col. 1009 (Att.-Gen. Havers).

[85] s.20(1)(*a*).

[86] P. Maguire, "The Standing Advisory Commission on Human Rights" (1981) 32 N.I.L.Q. 31, at p. 53.

On a more overtly political plane, although it has no powers in relation to security, the Northern Ireland Assembly[87] has discussed these matters. Ministers and the Northern Ireland Secretary have appeared before its security committee, notably in connection with the mass escape of Republican prisoners from the Maze Prison in September 1983.[88] This, and the evidence to reviews given by political parties in Northern Ireland and the representations of those parties to Ministers represent an important flow of public opinion helping to mould governmental response to the legislation and its operation. If the voice of Republican groups and of paramilitaries on both sides is muted in official channels, it is represented forcefully in demonstrations, meetings and in statements to the media, for example, on the "supergrass" issue.[89]

The police and the military might also be seen as pressure groups campaigning for retention of or changes in existing powers. They have direct channels of communication to the very heart of government. Doubtless their voice is highly influential.

In the context of maintenance of essential supplies and services, discussions between government and employers have been commonplace in planning for disputes in particular sectors and in the operation of emergency powers once taken. There has been a reluctance to involve trades unions in the process of contingency planning, given that their actions or potential actions have been its target. Their involvement has been more important in terms of discussions with a view to avoiding the need to resort to emergency powers in particular disputes.[90] TUC guidance on disputes in essential services and Codes of Conduct drawn up by the TUC affiliated unions in relevant industries may provide some moderating influence, precluding the necessity to invoke the EPA 1920, although breaches of such codes were said to be widespread in the 1978-79 "winter of discontent" disputes, "and there may be discrepancies in their interpretation and application at local level."[91] Emergency tasks discharged by strikers during the waterworkers' dispute in 1982/83 were important in limiting the

[87] See, generally, B. Hadfield, "The Northern Ireland Act 1982—Do it Yourself Devolution" (1982) 33 N.I.L.Q. 301.

[88] *The Times*, October 12, 1983, p. 2.

[89] See, *e.g.* BBC TV's "Panorama" programme, "Justice on Trial?" October 24, 1983.

[90] Jeffery and Hennessy, *op. cit.* n. 53, pp. 268-269.

[91] G.S. Morris, "The Regulation of Industrial Action in Essential Services" (1983) 12 I.L.J. 69, at pp. 80-81.

impact of the dispute,[92] while emergency work by striking miners on pumping and ventilation equipment is essential to the continued viability of some pits.[93]

6. Handling Individual Grievances: the Role of Complaints Agencies and Disciplinary Bodies

Individual grievances arise about emergency as about normal powers. Some may result in court action. Others may take the form of representations to Ministers directly or through MPs. Yet others may be brought into the disciplinary systems of the security forces.

The role of internal instructions, guidelines and hierarchical supervision within these forces has already been noted.[94] Both in England and Wales and in Northern Ireland,[95] complaints against the police by members of the public are investigated by the police themselves, subject to independent decision by the DPP in cases of criminal conduct, and to independent supervision of the outcome in Northern Ireland by the Police Complaints Board and in England and Wales by the Police Complaints Authority. In Northern Ireland the police also investigate complaints of criminal activity against the Army.[96] In both jurisdictions, police authorities exercise a general supervisory role. That in Northern Ireland has been criticised for not using its power to insist on tribunal investigation of a complaint affecting the public interest to look into deaths from the use of force by the police.[97] There are problems of public confidence in the system on both sides of the Irish Sea. That in England and Wales has recently been altered to

[92] D. Macintyre and P. Knightley, "Nightmare in the Pipeline" *The Sunday Times*, January 30, 1983, at p. 17.

[93] B. Silcock, "Hidden Cost of the Miners' Strike" *The Sunday Times*, June 17, 1984, at p. 4. Claims were made by the NCB that NUM refusal to provide rescue teams placed machinery in jeopardy as geological pressure caused roof supports to sag and coal faces to be closed; see *The Times*, June 5, 1984, at p. 2.

[94] *Supra*, pp. 35-37.

[95] On the system in Northern Ireland see Baker, paras. 324-337; C.A.J. Pamphlet No. 3, *Complaints Against the Police: A working party report* (1982). On the system operating until April 29, 1985 in England and Wales see P. Hewitt, *A Fair Cop: Reforming the Police Complaints Procedure* (1982). For the present system in England and Wales, see Police and Criminal Evidence Act 1984, Pt. IX and Sched. 4. For the rationale of the changes, see *Police Complaints and Discipline Procedures*, Cmnd. 9072 (1983).

[96] *Ireland* v. *United Kingdom* (1978) 2 E.H.R.R. 25, at p. 172 (para. 139).

[97] CAJ publication, *Civilian Deaths and the Police—the need for an Inquiry* (1983).

also provide for independent supervision of the investigatory process by the Police Complaints Authority but without providing a completely independent investigating system.[98] Published statistics do not indicate the volume of complaints relating to emergency powers, for example, by indicating those that come from terrorist suspects or from trade unionists arrested during industrial emergencies. Unpublished figures supplied by the RUC to the Bennett Committee and to Lord Jellicoe's Review indicate that between half and two-thirds of those making allegations against officers of that force of assaults during interrogation, were persons arrested under emergency legislation.[99]

The potential role of Parliamentary Commissioners for Administration (PCAs–ombudsmen), empowered to investigate and report to Parliament on injustice caused through maladministration in certain central government departments, requires brief consideration. The departments and authorities subject to investigation by the Northern Ireland PCA have no responsibilities with respect to security and related criminal investigation matters.[1] The United Kingdom PCA, by contrast, has within his remit the actions of the Ministry of Defence, the Home Office, the Northern Ireland Office, and the Northern Ireland Court Service.[2] However, he may not investigate matters which concern action taken by or with the authority of the Secretary of State for purposes of criminal investigation or protecting the security of the state[3]; the commencement or conduct of civil or criminal proceedings before any court of law in the United Kingdom[4]; or the exercise of the prerogative of mercy or of power to refer matters to the relevant Court of Appeal.[5] Nor do the Attorney-General or the DPPs fall within his remit.[6] Such restrictions leave little scope for a role in investigating areas affected by the anti-terrorist powers. As regards the maintenance of essential supplies and services, that the Cabinet Office (which houses the Civil Contingencies Unit) is

[98] Police and Criminal Evidence Act 1984, Pt. IX and Sched. 4.

[99] Bennett, App. 2, p. 143; Jellicoe, Table 14, p. 142.

[1] Parliamentary Commissioner Act (Northern Ireland) 1969, Sched. 1.

[2] Parliamentary Commissioner Act 1967, Sched. 2.

[3] *Ibid.* Sched. 3, para. 5.

[4] *Ibid.* Sched. 3, para. 6.

[5] *Ibid.* Sched. 3, para. 7.

[6] *Ibid.* not being within the list in Sched. 2.

outside his brief similarly limits his role.[7] Insofar as departments and authorities subject to the jurisdiction of these ombudsmen might be involved in the administration of the civil contingencies machine, it is possible that there could be entertained complaints of maladministration, which, in any event, focus more on the mode of decision-taking than on its substance.[8]

C. THE EUROPEAN COMMUNITY DIMENSION

Community law, subject to interpretation by the European Court of Justice, prevails over inconsistent national laws. Some of it is directly applicable in the sense that it may be invoked by individuals in United Kingdom courts without the necessity of further enactment by United Kingdom authorities. Parts of it have relevance to the areas covered by emergency powers.

Article 92(1) of the Treaty declares incompatible with the common market insofar as it affects trade between Member States, any aid, granted by a Member State or through State resources, in whatever form, which distorts or threatens to distort competition by favouring certain undertakings or the production of certain goods. However, aid to make good damage caused by natural disasters or exceptional occurrences (which could in certain circumstances cover the effects of terrorism in Northern Ireland[9] or, possibly, grave industrial disruption through industrial action in an essential service) is expressly declared compatible (Art.92(2)(*b*)).

Exclusion orders to combat terrorism can have an impact on those Community nationals and their families (*e.g.* Irish citizens) within the protection of Treaty provisions on the free movement of workers, the right of establishment and the right to provide and/or receive services. *Saunders* suggests that their protection does not extend to cover restrictions on the movement within the State of one's own nationals, at least where imposed as a form of penal measure.[10] But even if it did, exclusion orders against them or other Treaty protected persons could probably be justified in

7 *Ibid.* Sched. 2, note 6.

8 S.A. De Smith, *Constitutional and Administrative Law* (4th ed., 1981), p. 629; Justice, *Our Fettered Ombudsman* (1977), paras. 59-68.

9 Sweet & Maxwell, *Encyclopedia of European Community Law* (1983), Vol. B II, para. B 10-212, p. B 10082/1.

10 *R.* v. *Saunders* [1979] 2 C.M.L.R. 216, at p. 227. The principle was extended to detention of an Irish citizen pending his return to the Republic of Ireland under the Backing of Warrants Act 1965: *R.* v. *Governor of Pentonville Prison, ex p. Healy,* (1984) 128 S.J. 498.

terms of exceptions relating to public policy or public security, in the same way as was the refusal of entry to a Dutch scientologist in *Van Duyn.* [11] Directive 64/221/EEC,[12] provides that measures taken on these grounds must be based exclusively on the personal conduct of the individual (Art.3(1)) and that previous criminal convictions do not in themselves constitute grounds for taking such measures (Art.3(2)). The conduct must constitute a genuine or sufficiently serious threat[13] to the fundamental interest of the society.[14] Action merely *pour encourager les autres* is not included.[15] Nor is mere failure to comply with formalities in respect of entry, movement and residence of non-patrials.[16] Article 6 of the Directive requires that the person be informed of the ground on which the decision has been taken, unless that would be contrary to the interest of the security of the State concerned. Whether review of exclusion orders by an advisory body (*infra,* pp. 193-195) complies with Article 9(1) of the Directive is debatable.[17]

Powers taken under the EPA 1920 might conceivably raise issues under provisions concerned with the free movement of goods (Arts. 30-34) were they to prohibit the export of a scarce commodity needed during an emergency. Article 36 affords possible justification in terms of public policy or public security so long as the restrictions or prohibitions were not a means of arbitrary discrimination or a disguised restriction on trade between Member States.

Community obligations to take emergency measures in connection with the reduction or threatened reduction of fuel supplies, can be given effect to under the Energy Act 1976, s. 3, which enables the issue of an Order in Council calling into play powers to regulate the production, supply, acquisition and use of energy, including powers to fix its price (*infra,* pp. 220-223).[18]

[11] *Van Duyn* v. *Home Office* [1974] 1 W.L.R. 1107.

[12] J.O.1964/850.

[13] *Rutili* v. *Minister of the Interior* [1975] E.C.R. 129.

[14] *R.* v. *Bouchereau* [1978] Q.B. 732.

[15] *Bonsignore* v. *Director of City of Cologne* [1975] 1 C.M.L.R. 472.

[16] *Royer* [1976] E.C.R. 497.

[17] Contrast T.C. Hartley, *EEC Immigration Law* (1978), p. 239 with L. Grant and I. Martin, *Immigration Law and Practice* (1982), pp. 252-257.

[18] Crisis management obligations arise under Dir. 73/238/EEC, O.J. 1973, L.228/1. Obligations to maintain fuel stocks at power stations (Dir. 75/339/EEC, O.J. 1975, L.153/35) and on the fuelling of power stations (Dirs. 404 and 405/75/EEC, O.J. 1975, L.176/24, 26) are given effect to by permanent provisions in the Energy Act 1976, in particular ss.7 and 14.

D. THE INTERNATIONAL DIMENSION

1. Powers to Combat Terrorism

(1) *The European Convention on Human Rights 1950*

This provides a yardstick of liberal-democratic values with which the United Kingdom must comply. It embodies predominantly civil, political and legal rights and demands that they be secured to all within the State's jurisdiction on a non-discriminatory basis. It has a possible role on three levels. It may, first of all, exercise a formative influence on governmental decision-making, the precise extent of which must remain speculative, although, for example, the Diplock Commission chose Article 6 as its minimum embodiment of a fair trial, and suggested the Article 3 standard (no torture, inhuman or degrading treatment) as the appropriate regulatory standard to govern the admission in court of inculpatory statements of the accused.[19] Secondly, it provides a yardstick whereby courts can interpret ambiguous statutory material; it is now well established that they ought to give statutory provisions the meaning most consonant with Convention obligations.[20] That emergency provisions tend to be drafted with a degree of clarity, albeit violative of the Convention, renders it of little use; the statute must then prevail.[21] The Convention's third and most important role is as a regional system of human rights' protection.

Its enforcement machinery (Commission, Court and Committee of Ministers of the Council of Europe), backed up by sanctions of publicity and possible expulsion from the Council of Europe, can be set in motion by other Member States or by individuals.[22] The process is convoluted and lengthy.[23]

Many of the Convention's substantive provisions permit qualification of the protected rights and freedoms to accommodate competing societal values. So, for example, the right to privacy is not absolute but may legitimately be restricted by law where necessary in a democratic society in the interests of

[19] Diplock, paras. 12-16, 90.

[20] *Supra*, pp. 52-53; see, *e.g. Waddington* v. *Miah* [1974] 1 W.L.R. 683.

[21] *R.* v. *Secretary of State for Home Affairs, ex p. Bhajan Singh* [1976] Q.B. 198.

[22] Arts.24, 25.

[23] See, further, R. Beddard, *Human Rights and Europe* (2nd ed., 1980); F.G. Jacobs, *The European Convention on Human Rights* (1975).

national security, public safety or the economic well-being of the country, for the protection of health and morals, or for the protection of the rights and freedoms of others (Art.8). Similarly Article 5, protecting liberty and security of person, sets out permissible "heads" of deprivation of liberty, for example after conviction by a competent court (Art.5(1)(*a*)). Capital punishment does not violate the right to life (Art.2). Guarantees of freedom of expression, of assembly and association, and of non-discrimination do not prevent the State from restricting the political activities of aliens (Art.16). Most importantly, for purposes of this study, a State may derogate from most of its Convention obligations, but only to the extent strictly warranted by the exigencies of the situation, in time of war or other public emergency threatening the life of the nation (Art.15(1)). No derogation can be made in respect of the right to life (apart from deaths resulting from lawful acts of war), of freedom from torture or inhuman or degrading treatment or punishment, of freedom from slavery or forced or compulsory labour, or of freedom from retroactive criminal law (Art.15(2)). Any State availing itself of the right to derogate must keep the Secretary-General of the Council of Europe fully informed of the measures it has taken, and the reasons for them. It must also inform him when those measures have ceased to operate and the provisions of the Convention are again being fully executed (Art.15(3)).

In applying restrictions the State must act in good faith, deploying them only for the purposes for which they have been prescribed (Art.18). Nor may anything in the Convention "be interpreted as implying for any State, group or person any right to engage in any activity or perform any act aimed at the destruction of any of the rights and freedoms set forth herein or at their limitation to a greater extent than is provided for in the Convention" (Art.17).

Emergency situations have been examined under the Convention in several cases[24] and another application challenging its invocation has been declared admissible.[25] The approach taken

[24] *First Cyprus Case: Greece* v. *U.K.* [1958-59] 2 Y.B.E.C.H.R. 174; *Lawless* v. *Ireland* (1961) 1 E.H.R.R. 15; *First Greek Case* [1969] 12 Y.B.E.C.H.R., Vol. *bis; Ireland* v. *United Kingdom* (1978) 2 E.H.R.R. 25. See, generally on derogation, R. Higgins, "Derogation Under Human Rights Treaties" (1976-77) 48 B.Y.B.I.L. 281.

[25] *Denmark, France, the Netherlands, Norway and Sweden* v. *Turkey,* (1983) 6 E.H.R.R. 241.

has been consistent: Article 15, if invoked, is to be considered where a violation of the substantive provisions of the Convention as normally applicable would otherwise arise.

Article 15(1) permits derogation in time of war or other public emergency threatening the life of the nation. "Time of war" awaits interpretation. "Other public emergency threatening the life of the nation" was defined by the Court in *Lawless*, a case challenging detention without trial in the Republic of Ireland, as

> "an exceptional situation of crisis or emergency which affects the whole population and constitutes a threat to the organised life of the community of which the State is composed."[26]

This definition was accepted by the Commission in the *First Greek Case*, [27] which arose out of the Colonels' *coup* in Greece in 1967, and was endorsed by both Commission and Court in *Ireland* v. *United Kingdom*, [28] which was concerned with emergency legislation and the treatment of suspects in Northern Ireland in the period 1971-78. In the former case the Commission stressed the need for the imminence or actuality of such a situation and that its exceptional nature must be such "that the normal measures or restrictions permitted by the Convention for the maintenance of public safety, public health and order are plainly inadequate."[29]

The Convention organs have the right and duty to decide whether the requisite conditions have been met. The government concerned is not the final arbiter. Nor are they limited to ascertaining whether it acted in good faith. The burden of proof rests on the government seeking to rely on Article 15.[30] But the Convention agencies have the benefit of hindsight and the detached atmosphere of the courtroom whereas the government has to act in the heat of the moment. The national authorities are in direct and continuing contact with the pressing needs of the moment. They are therefore viewed as being in principle in a better position than the international judge to assess the existence of an emergency.[31] Accordingly, and perhaps realistically since they are interpreting a key State sovereignty provision and their position depends on State support, the Convention agencies

[26] [1961] 1 E.H.R.R. 15, at para. 28.

[27] [1969] 12 Y.B.E.C.H.R., Vol. *bis.*

[28] [1978] 2 E.H.R.R. 25, at para. 205.

[29] [1969] 12 Y.B.E.C.H.R., Vol. *bis*, at p. 72.

[30] [1958-59] 2 Y.B.E.C.H.R. 174, at p. 176; (1961) 1 E.H.R.R. 15, at p. 30; [1969] 12 Y.B.E.C.H.R., Vol. *bis*, at pp. 71-76.

[31] (1978) 2 E.H.R.R. 25, at para. 207.

accord the government a wide "margin of appreciation" in the application of Article 15. The agencies examine whether the government acted manifestly unreasonably or arbitrarily, whether it had sufficient reason to believe that there existed a public emergency, rather than whether the agency would have acted differently had it been faced with the decision. As Sir Humphrey Waldock, then President of the Commission, put it in *Lawless:*

> "The concept of the margin of appreciation is that a Government's discharge of [its] responsibilities [for maintaining law and order during emergency] is essentially a delicate problem of appreciating complex factors and of balancing conflicting considerations of the public interest; and that, once the Commission or the Court is satisfied that the Government's appreciation is at least on the margin of the powers conferred by Article 15, then the interest which the public itself has in effective Government and in the maintenance of order justifies and requires a decision in favour of the legality of the Government's appreciation."[32]

Insofar as it involves according the State the benefit of the doubt, too wide a margin could operate to the detriment of effective protection of human rights by the Convention agencies.[33]

In *Lawless*, the Court held that the Irish Government had reasonably deduced the existence of an emergency warranting derogation from a trilogy of inter-related circumstances: firstly, the existence in the Republic of the unconstitutional and secret IRA, a body using violence to attain its purposes; secondly, the armed cross-Border campaign by that body to drive the British out of Ulster, thereby jeopardising relations between the two governments; and a steady increase in terrorist activities during the period Autumn 1956-July 1957. In particular, as regards the latter point, a murderous IRA ambush across the Border in Ulster, in the traditionally tense period of 3-4 July leading up to the anniversary of the Battle of the Boyne, was perceived as showing the imminence of the danger to the State.[34] There was, however, little violence in the Republic itself, and the decision has been

[32] *Lawless* v. *Ireland*, Verbatim Report of the Hearings Held by the Court, April, 7, 8, 10, 11, 1961, Doc. A61.501, p. 68.

[33] See, *e.g.* [1969] 12 Y.B.E.C.H.R., Vol. *bis*, at p. 116 (dissenting opinion of M. Busuttil). For further comment see K.J. Partsch, "Experience Regarding the War and Emergency Clauses of the European Convention on Human Rights" (1971) 1 *Israel Y.B. on Human Rights* 327.

[34] (1961) 1 E.H.R.R. 15, at paras. 28, 29.

criticised as according too much deference to State needs as opposed to those of the individual.[35] Possible friction between two State parties seems an important factor in the decision.

In the *First Greek Case*, the Greek Government identified three threats justifying the Colonels' *coup* and its derogation under Article 15. First, a Communist threat to overthrow the legitimate government by force, indicated in several policy documents, the discovery of caches of arms and munitions, civil disturbances in major centres of population and Communist infiltration of Greece's conscript Armed Forces.[36] Secondly, a crisis of constitutional government, since it was alleged that the Left were proposing to abolish the Monarchy and the Constitution.[37] Finally, a crisis in public order bordering on anarchy, manifested in numerous politically-motivated strikes and demonstrations.[38] The majority of the Commission, clearly appreciating that these factors were inter-related and interacting, held that Greece had failed to establish the existence of the requisite public emergency.[39] The situation was instead characterised as a "period of instability and tension," in which the forces of the Left had gained ground, accompanied by some public disorder.[40] Arms caches were small[41] and such para-military activity as existed was aimed, not against the lawful government, but rather to combat the threat from the Right which came to fruition with the *coup* itself.[42] Such strikes and demonstrations were common throughout Europe, and had been dealt with by the police, without military aid, and by using methods (*e.g.* banning marches) which might be thought legitimate under restrictions normally allowed under the Convention.[43] Throughout the authorities had seemed well able to cope with the situation, while "the speed with which a large number of Communists and their allies were 'neutralised' on 21 April 1967 the date [of the *coup*] suggest[ed] that, for all their supposed plans, they were incapable of any organised action in a crisis."[44]

[35] P. O'Higgins, "The Lawless Case" [1962] C.L.J. 234.

[36] [1969] 12 Y.B.E.C.H.R., Vol. *bis*, at pp. 45-48, 73-74.

[37] *Ibid.* at pp. 58-65, 73-74.

[38] *Ibid.* at pp. 65-71, 74-75.

[39] *Ibid.* at pp. 73, 76.

[40] *Ibid.* at pp. 73.

[41] *Ibid.* at pp. 73-74.

[42] *Ibid.* at p. 74.

[43] *Ibid.* at pp. 74-75.

[44] *Ibid.* at p. 76.

In *Ireland* v. *United Kingdom* the applicant government accepted that the requisite public emergency existed in Northern Ireland. Both Court[45] and Commission thought its existence in the Province abundantly clear. The latter noted that

> "[t]he degree of violence, with bombing, shooting and rioting was on a scale far beyond what could be called minor civil disorder. It is clear that the violence used was in many instances planned in advance, by factions of the community organised and acting on para-military lines. To a great extent the violence was directed against the security forces which were severely hampered in their function to keep or restore the public peace."[46]

Although the level of violence in Ulster has waned (*infra*, pp. 95-96) it remains far in excess of that accepted as warranting derogation in *Lawless* and on a different scale and provenance to that considered in the *First Greek Case*. Probably the requisite public emergency still exists in Ulster, although for the moment the Government sees no need to rely on Article 15 to support its security measures in the Province.

What situations and measures has the United Kingdom sought to protect pursuant to Article 15? The answer is found in its notices under Article 15(3), ultimately withdrawn on August 22, 1984, which referred only to Northern Ireland, to the Special Powers Acts and Regulations, and to the measures which replaced that legislation: the Detention of Terrorists Order 1972 and NIEPA, 1973, 1975 and 1978.[47] No mention was made of any emergency in Great Britain or, even in Northern Ireland, of the PTAs 1974, 1976 and 1984. As the Commission noted in *McVeigh* v. *United Kingdom*

> "the Government have not sought to invoke Article 15 in respect of the situation in Great Britain. In respect of the present measures they have based their case solely on the contention that the measures taken did not breach the applicants' rights under the substantive provisions of the Convention."[48]

[45] (1978) 2 E.H.R.R. 25, at para. 205.

[46] *Ireland* v. *U.K.*, *Report of the Commission*, January 25, 1976, at p. 95.

[47] For text of these derogations see: [1971] 14 Y.B.E.C.H.R. 32; [1973] 16 Y.B.E.C.H.R. 24, at p. 26; [1973] 16 Y.B.E.C.H.R. 26, at p. 28; [1975] 18 Y.B.E.C.H.R. 18; [1978] 21 Y.B.E.C.H.R. 22. For the statement on withdrawal, see (1984) 128 S.J. 600.

[48] (1981) 5 E.H.R.R. 71, para. 155.

Accordingly, apart from issues, arising before withdrawal of the derogation notice, concerning the operation and terms of emergency legislation to combat terrorism applicable only in Northern Ireland, the examination of Convention issues raised by the emergency powers in this book proceeds, like the Commission in *McVeigh*, on the basis that Article 15(1) is irrelevant.

It should be noted, however, that, should the Government choose to invoke Article 15(1) in particular proceedings, in a context not covered by a notice of derogation under Article 15(3), for example, with respect to the operation of the PTAs in Northern Ireland or in Great Britain, it by no means follows that its failure to comply with Article 15(3) would preclude it from doing so, or the Convention agencies from examining Article 15 questions. In *McVeigh* the Commission only considered itself not called on to deal with the Article 15 issue "in these circumstances," *i.e.* where the Government made no attempt to rely on it. Article 15(3) is a mechanism designed to warn other State parties that the Convention can no longer be fully adhered to in the derogating State, and to enable one or more of them to decide whether to take proceedings under Article 24 to protect human rights.[49] It ought not to be open to a State to rely first on Article 15 only when a case alleging breach has been brought before the Convention agencies. In the present state of the authorities, however, one can only say that to do so would cast doubt on the government's good faith and cause those agencies to look closely and sceptically at the claim.[50] No case suggests that breach of paragraph three precludes reliance on Article 15(1). In any event, even where no reliance is sought to be placed on Article 15, *McVeigh* makes it clear that the Commission will interpret the substantive provisions of the Convention mindful of the need for democratic governments to combat terrorism.[51] In short, it may be inclined to take a State-oriented rather than individual-oriented approach to interpretation.

[49] *First Greek Case* [1969] 12 Y.B.E.C.H.R. Vol. *bis*, at p. 40.

[50] Higgins, *loc. cit.* n. 24, at pp. 290-293. In its Report in *Cyprus* v. *Turkey* (6780/74, 6950/75), adopted July 10, 1976, the Commission noted that reliance on Art.15(3) required some formal public act of derogation, such as a declaration of martial law or a state of emergency. See (1976) 4 E.H.R.R. 482, at paras. 526-530. It is suggested here that the passage of the NIEPAs and the PTAs as emergency legislation might constitute that formal act, although the position *re* Great Britain is more questionable as the Government has never described it as in a state of emergency.

[51] (1981) 5 E.H.R.R. 71, at para. 157.

A decision that a public emergency exists does not exhaust Article 15: there still remains the issue, whether the measures taken exceed what was required by the exigencies of that situation. That issue will be explored in the particular context of internment without trial in Chapter Three (*infra*, pp. 152-161). The same broad approach to the issues—ultimately a matter of appreciation and judgment in the circumstances of each case—would be applicable elsewhere.

(2) *The United Nations' Covenant on Civil and Political Rights 1966*[52]

The United Kingdom is a party to this Covenant which protects much the same rights and freedoms as the European Convention, but not the right to property, and similarly permits restriction of and derogation from many of its provisions. Until August 22, 1984 the United Kingdom derogated from certain of its obligations under it in respect of legislation, covering *inter alia* powers of arrest, detention and exclusion, passed to deal with terrorism related to Northern Ireland affairs. The obligations in question concern liberty and security of person (Art.9); aspects of the penal system (Art.10(2),(3)); freedom of movement and choice of residence (Art.12(1)); the right to fair trial (Art.14); protection of privacy, family, home and correspondence (Art.17); freedom of expression (Art.19(2)); the right of peaceful assembly (Art.21); and freedom of association (Art.22). Much the same issues are likely to arise under it in respect of emergency powers to combat terrorism as would arise under the European Convention, although the derogation was wider in that it covered the United Kingdom as a whole and the PTAs.[53] As under the Convention, powers taken under the EPA 1920 would fall to be judged according to normal standards (*infra*, pp. 92-93). Issues of compliance with the Covenant are not separately considered in this book which takes the Convention as a more practically relevant yardstick.

[52] For text, see I. Brownlie, *Basic Documents on Human Rights*(2nd. ed., 1981), pp. 128-150.

[53] For the text of the U.K.'s Reservation on ratification of the Covenant see SACHR, *The Protection of Human Rights by Law in Northern Ireland*, Cmnd. 7009 (1977), Annex C, p. 137. For the statement on withdrawal, see (1984) 128 S.J. 600.

The Covenant's enforcement machinery is much weaker than that under the Convention.[54] The United Kingdom has not recognised the right of individual petition. A measure of supervision is exercised through the Human Rights Committee's scrutiny of periodic reports which States are obliged to submit. Its questioning of the United Kingdom's reports in respect of Northern Ireland appears perfunctory.[55] The United Kingdom has also recognised the Committee's competence to receive petitions against it from other States on condition that the petitioner has itself recognised that competence.[56] No such petitions have been brought against it. In any event the Committee's role is primarily conciliatory in this sphere; it lacks jurisdiction to issue a binding public judgment.

2. Maintenance of Essential Supplies and Services: the Relevance of International Labour Law[57]

A number of international instruments–International Labour Organisation Conventions (ILO), the European Convention on Human Rights (ECHR), the European Social Charter (ESC), and the United Nations' Covenants on Civil and Political Rights (UNCTPR) and on Economic Social and Cultural Rights (UNCESC)–contain provisions relevant to this sphere of emergency action. They arguably recognise, implicitly if not always explicitly, the right to strike, and clearly prohibit forced or compulsory labour. Explicitly or through interpretation, however, they accommodate the need for some modification in times of emergency. The national decision to take emergency action could be accompanied by a measure of international supervision by the relevant international institutions. This might

[54] For analysis, see M. Nowak, "The Effectiveness of the International Covenant on Civil and Political Rights–Stocktaking After the First Eleven Sessions of the UN Human Rights Committee" (1980) 1 Human Rights L.J. 136.

[55] D. O'Donnell, "Observations and Conclusions" in ICJ Study, *States of Emergency: Their Impact on Human Rights* (1983), p. 455.

[56] Art.41.

[57] Essentially, much of this section of this chapter is a compression of a more detailed examination of the area by Professor N. Valticos, "International Labour Law" (1979) in Professor D.R. Blanplain (Ed.), *International Encyclopaedia for Labour Law and Industrial Relations*, esp. pp. 85-86, 233. Compression inevitably results in imprecision. For texts, see Brownlie, *op. cit.* n. 52.

be achieved through reporting mechanisms (ILO, ESC, UN Covenants) or direct complaints by other States (ILO, ECHR, UNCCPR), associations of employers and employees (ILO) or other groups or individuals (ECHR). The State's right to limit or in some cases prohibit the right to strike of particular groups in the public service (police, armed forces, civil servants) is recognised, although the Freedom of Association Committee of the ILO has stressed that there should be adequate provision, through binding conciliation or arbitration proceedings, to ensure protection for the rights of workers thus barred from using the strike weapon to protect their occupational interests.[58] Service exacted to cope with emergency or calamity affecting the life or well-being of the community tends to be excluded from the notion of forced labour.[59]

In the United Kingdom, in effect, only the police and the armed forces cannot strike (*infra*, pp. 214-215). The EPA 1920, of course, does not authorise the making of regulations to effect military or industrial conscription or to criminalise participation in or peaceful encouragement to participate in a strike. It has not been thought necessary to enter notices of derogation under the ECHR. The issue has not yet arisen since obligations under the UNCCPR became effective, although there is no reason to expect a different approach. Such interferences with the protected rights and freedoms as may arise would arguably be protected by the modifying clauses attached to them. This is especially so in terms of likely interferences, through requisition powers, with the right of every natural and legal person to the peaceful enjoyment of his possessions (ECHR, Protocol 1, Art.1). That Article permits deprivation of possessions, subject to compensation, in the public interest and is not to impair the State's right "to enforce such laws as *it deems necessary* to control the use of property in accordance with the general interest" (emphasis added). Rights of property are not protected by the UN Covenants.

Were it invoked the jurisprudence on Article 15 ECHR (*supra*, pp. 83-90) would be equally applicable to emergencies in this context. The definition of "public emergency threatening the life of the nation" is arguably narrower than that required by the EPA 1920. Morris notes:

[58] *Ibid.* p. 86.

[59] ECHR, Art.4(3)(*c*); UNCCPR, Art. 8(3)(*c*)(iii); ILO Convention Concerning Forced or Compulsory Labour, 1930, Art.2(2)(*d*).

"It is . . . possible that even where the circumstances clearly justified a proclamation under the Act, the Commission and the Court might hold that the United Kingdom could not avail itself of Article 15."[60]

[60] G.S. Morris, "The Emergency Powers Act 1920" [1979] P.L. 317, at p. 321.

Chapter 3

EMERGENCY POWERS TO COMBAT TERRORISM IN NORTHERN IRELAND

1. Background and Overview

In 1969 in accordance with accepted constitutional proprieties whereby the Northern Ireland Government asked the Westminster Government for such help, troops were deployed in Ulster as a peace-keeping force to aid the civil power to maintain order in the face of sectarian rioting.[1] Since then violence has escalated as an initial campaign for civil rights for Catholics in the Province was overtaken by the more traditional use of violence to attain a united Ireland.[2] Statistics on the security situation in the Province paint a partial, if depressing, picture of the conflict. To December 31, 1984, 2,410 people have been killed: 200 policemen; 526 soldiers and members of the Ulster Defence Regiment (UDR); and 1,684 civilians (including suspected terrorists). There have been 29,949 terrorist shootings; 11,493 bomb, including defused bomb, incidents; and, since 1973, 5,618 malicious fires. Over 9,700 firearms, 1 million rounds of ammunition and some 170,000 lbs of explosives were discovered. Violence peaked in 1972, in the aftermath of the introduction of internment and of Direct Rule, and has quite markedly declined since 1976. Nonetheless in the "quiet" year 1984: 64 people died (28 from the security forces); there were 230 terrorist shootings, 248 bombing incidents and 840 malicious fires; 197 weapons, 27,211 rounds of ammunition and

[1] K. Boyle, T. Hadden and P. Hillyard, *Ten Years On In Northern Ireland: The legal control of political violence* (1980), p. 25; C. Palley, "The Evolution, Disintegration and Possible Reconstruction of the Northern Ireland Constitution" (1972) 1 Anglo-Am. L.R. 368, at pp. 411-414. For some differing views on the legal basis for the use of troops, see S. Greer, "Military Intervention in Civil Disturbances: The Legal Basis Reconsidered" [1983] P.L. 573; R. Evelegh, *Peace-Keeping in a Democratic Society: The Lessons of Northern Ireland* (1978), pp. 6-59; M. Supperstone, *Brownlie's Law of Public Order and National Security* (2nd ed., 1981), pp. 210-213.

[2] K. Boyle, T. Hadden and P. Hillyard, *Law and State: The Case of Northern Ireland* (1975), Chap. 3; K. Kelley, *The Longest War: Northern Ireland and the IRA* (1982), Chaps. 3-8.

8,534 lbs of explosives were found. In the period 1971-December 31, 1984 there were some 325,000 house searches, over half of which occurred in the years 1972-1974.[3] It should be recalled that the population of Northern Ireland is only some 1.5 million in some 450,000 dwellings.

Such statistics cannot convey the horror of particular incidents. They give only a crude picture of the nature of terrorist violence in the Province which is a complex of insurgent guerrilla warfare, sectarian killings and attacks, inter and intra-factional conflicts within both communities, knee-cappings, punishment shootings and other modes of enforcing discipline, and activity of more traditional criminal provenance (*e.g.* protection rackets). The roots of the problem cannot be explored here.[4] However, without in any way condoning their methods, denying the appropriateness of other epithets such as "evil" or "criminal" or that some may be psychopaths, and without suggesting that those convicted of terrorist crimes ought to receive better treatment than other convicted prisoners, it is nevertheless important to grasp that much of the violence perpetrated by Republican and Loyalist paramilitaries is politically motivated and centres ultimately on the issue of the status of Ulster as part of the United Kingdom. Each group is rooted in its respective community and shares its traditional fears, concerns and political aspirations. They have a permanence transcending the membership at any given time, and there seems to be little shortage of new recruits or leaders.[5] As Boyle, Hadden and Hillyard have noted, to recognise this political dimension and

> "[c]ultural permanence has important implications for security policy. It means that elimination of IRA (and INLA) activity and Loyalist reaction to it is not just a matter of

[3] *Review of the Operation of the Northern Ireland (Emergency Provisions) Act 1978 by Rt. Hon. Sir George Baker OBE*, Cmnd. 9222 (1984), Apps. D1 and D2, P (covering 1971-1983) (hereinafter cited as "Baker"); earlier figures came from *RUC Chief Constable's Report 1982, Presented to the Police Authority for Northern Ireland* (1983), App. 4. Updated statistics come from H.C. Deb., Vol. 72 cols. *650-652* (written answer).

[4] See, *inter alia* C.C. O'Brien, *States of Ireland* (1972); L. De Paor, *Divided Ulster* (1971); Kelley, *op. cit.* n. 2; Palley, *loc. cit.* n. 1, at pp. 368-83, and sources cited therein. W.D. Flackes, *Northern Ireland: A Political Directory 1968-83* (1983) is an invaluable companion. For an interesting perspective, based on interviews with key participants amongst politicians and paramilitaries in Great Britain, Ulster and the Republic see P. O'Malley, *The Uncivil Wars: Ireland Today* (1983).

[5] Boyle, Hadden and Hillyard, *op. cit.* n. 1, p. 23.

> arresting and putting behind bars the existing members of the various groups. Terrorist activity can be contained by that means. But it cannot be eliminated as long as the conditions for continued recruitment or regeneration remain."[6]

Only a political settlement acceptable to the vast majority of both communities in Northern Ireland can hope to bring lasting peace and stability. Security laws and policies can only assist in holding the ring, in containing violence at the minimum level possible. It is important to ensure that, so far as is possible, the existence and application of such laws and policies does not, by exacerbating tension between the security forces and the community and increasing suspicion of government and authority, retard the attainment of a political solution. This has sometimes been recognised by Government but has been an uncertain feature of its security policy.[7]

Widely drawn emergency powers to combat security problems centering on the issue of British rule in Ireland have a long tradition. Various statutes in the nineteenth century included special powers of arrest, detention and search, made provision for trial by special juries and increased use of summary trial, and provided for non-jury trial of serious offences, although this last was never operated.[8] Wartime emergency powers enabled internment of those rebels of 1916 not executed.[9] The Restoration of Order in Ireland Act 1920 enabled the executive to make regulations under wartime powers (deemed to continue in force for the purpose) for securing the restoration and maintenance of order in Ireland. The Act made provision for civilian trial by military courts. Regulations could be issued "where it appears to His Majesty in Council that owing to the existence of a state of disorder in Ireland the ordinary law is inadequate for the prevention and punishment of crime and the maintenance of order," and could apply throughout or only to a part of Ireland.[10]

6 *Ibid.*

7 R.J. Spjut, "Prevention of Terrorism and Liberal Democracy," a paper delivered at the Institute of Advanced Legal Studies Workshop on Constitutional Law, July 3-6, 1979. It was, however, recognised in respect of internment (*infra*, pp. 152-161).

8 Boyle, Hadden and Hillyard, *op. cit.* n. 2, Chap. 9; S.H. Bailey, D.J. Harris and B.L. Jones, *Civil Liberties: Cases and Materials* (1980), p. 186.

9 J. McGuffin, *Internment* (1973), Chap. 3; D.R. Lowry, "Internment in Northern Ireland" (1976) 8 U.Toledo L.Rev. 169, at pp. 171-172.

10 Palley, *loc. cit.* n. 1, p. 400. For the text of regulations under the Act see S.R. & O. 1920 No. 1530.

These regulations were adopted as part of the initial regime created by the Civil Authorities (Special Powers) Act 1922 (hereinafter "Special Powers Act"), passed by the Northern Ireland legislature to combat Republican violence when the Imperial Government decided that it was no longer willing to permit the Restoration of Order in Ireland Act 1920 to be used in any part of the island.[11] This regime of Special Powers Act and regulations made under it as amended provided *inter alia* wide powers of arrest for purposes of interrogation, of detention and internment without trial, of effective exclusion from all but a small area of the Province, of stop and search of vehicles and persons, and of stop and question. Most such powers were conferred on the armed forces as well as the police. Mere failure to inform was an offence against the regulations. There were powers to order assemblies to disperse.[12] Section 2(4) of the Act was a clear violation of the principle *nulla poena sine lege*, a non-derogable principle in the European Convention on Human Rights[13]; it provided:

> "[i]f any person does any act of such a nature as to be calculated to be prejudicial to the preservation of the peace or maintenance of order in Northern Ireland and not specifically provided for in the regulations, he shall be deemed to be guilty of an offence against the regulations."

The executive had power to ban organisations.[14] In short, as Professor Palley has concluded,

> "the result of the Act, when taken in conjunction with the existence of the Special Constabulary . . . was that apart from the establishment of military courts, the Government enjoyed powers similar to those current in time of martial law."[15]

The powers conferred were directed almost exclusively against

[11] Palley, *loc. cit.* n. 1, pp. 400-401, 436-438.

[12] *Ibid.* p. 437; H. Calvert, *Constitutional Law in Northern Ireland: A Study in Regional Government* (1968), Chap. 20; Boyle, Hadden and Hillyard, *op. cit.* n. 2, pp. 7-9, 37-39; *Report of a Commission of Inquiry into the Special Powers Acts* (NCCL, 1936; republished 1972); J. Edwards, "Special Powers in Northern Ireland" [1956] Crim.L.R. 7.

[13] Arts. 7 and 15(2).

[14] Reg. 24 (see sources cited *supra*, n. 12); *McEldowney* v. *Forde* [1971] A.C. 632.

[15] Palley, *loc. cit.* n. 1, at p. 400.

Catholics.[16] They provided a large element of the legal basis for security operations in the Province from 1969 to 1973. It is, however, noteworthy that similar legislation providing for internment without trial and for trial by special non-jury courts, until recently composed of military personnel, was also enacted in the Republic of Ireland to deal with militant Republicanism.[17]

The legal response since 1971 to security problems in Northern Ireland may be analysed as a mixture of two processes for removing terrorists from circulation in the community: executive or non-court-oriented options (internment, detention without trial and exclusion orders); and judicial or court-oriented options, the criminal prosecution approach using, since 1973, non-jury, so-called Diplock courts. The current emergency powers are contained in the Northern Ireland (Emergency Provisions) Act 1978 (hereinafter "NIEPA 1978"), which consolidated 1973 and 1975 legislation of the same name, and in the Prevention of Terrorism (Temporary Provisions) Act 1984 (hereinafter "PTA 1984"), which replaced with modifications Temporary Provisions Acts of 1974 and 1976. Together these statutes (but principally NIEPA 1978) have effected several significant changes: extended the criminal law, including giving the executive a power to proscribe organisations; increased the powers of the security forces (RUC, UDR and Army) to stop, question and search and otherwise interfere with property; provided the security forces, but particularly the RUC, with extended powers of arrest and detention for questioning; altered the pre-trial criminal process in respect of bail and preliminary hearings; established non-jury trial before a single judge subject to modified rules of evidence as the norm for those offences commonly committed by terrorists (scheduled offences); and created the executive processes of detention without trial and exclusion orders which have supplemented recourse to the ordinary and/or modified criminal processes. Baker proposed the enactment of a new statute to house for Northern Ireland, with some modifications, many of the anti-terrorist powers now split between NIEPA 1978 and the PTA

[16] Boyle, Hadden and Hillyard, *op. cit.* n. 2, p. 38.

[17] J.M. Kelly, *Fundamental Rights in the Irish Law and Constitution* (2nd ed., 1967), pp. 77-88; M. Robinson, "The Protection of Human Rights in the Republic of Ireland" in C. Campbell (Ed.), *Do We Need a Bill of Rights?* (1980), pp. 55-69.

1984 to reduce confusing duplication and overlap. He thought that this statute should have a new name, but conceded that his own preference, the Protection of the Peoples Act, had won little support, while the Prevention of Terrorism (Northern Ireland) Act was unimaginative and little improvement on NIEPA 1978.[18]

Since December 1975, when detention without trial was finally phased out, the emphasis has been firmly on policies of *criminalisation* (the use of the court-oriented option, of the criminal prosecution approach) and of *Ulsterisation* (placing primary reliance on the locally recruited forces, the RUC and UDR, with the Army, in much reduced numbers, in a supportive role).[19] Given the problematic nature in the Ulster context of the executive processes, that emphasis is likely to continue. Indeed Baker recommended that powers of detention without trial at present in abeyance, be repealed, so that legislation would be required to effect their reintroduction.[20]

The perceived need for many of the powers is founded on the unreliability of jury trial for certain types of offence in the Province and on the problems posed there to the gathering of evidence through normal policing methods during the current emergency.[21] The latter were well summarised in the Bennett Report and re-emphasised by Baker.[22] Meticulous and expert examination of the scene of the crime is often difficult because the crime may have occurred in an area "hostile" to the presence of the security forces, evidence may have been destroyed or booby-trapped, and, at certain times, there may be too many incidents to make it possible for the available experts to give the kind of full coverage they would wish. While the police obtain a flow of information (much of it anonymous) through the confidential telephone system, its reliability cannot easily be checked without interviewing the suspect it points to. Collecting evidence from witnesses is difficult. Methodical routine enquiries

[18] Baker, paras. 26, 27, 267, 300. His specific proposed modifications are noted at appropriate points in this chapter.

[19] *Ibid.* paras. 33, 34.

[20] *Ibid.* para. 236.

[21] *Report of the Commission to consider legal procedures to deal with terrorist activities in Northern Ireland*, Cmnd. 5185 (1972) (hereinafter cited as "Diplock"); *Report of the Committee of Inquiry into Police Interrogation Practices in Northern Ireland*, Cmnd. 7497 (1979) (hereinafter cited as "Bennett").

[22] Bennett, paras. 21-31; Baker, paras. 254-257.

in the vicinity of a crime are not always possible, since the environment may be hostile, or, where possible, might tend to prove unfruitful. Witnesses may be understandably reluctant to come forward, whether through hostility to authority or fear of intimidation and reprisals, and neither key witnesses nor informants would be likely to want to appear in open court. The questioning of suspects, accordingly, has had to be heavily relied on. Whereas in Great Britain this might readily be effected away from the police station, or the individual might readily agree to go there to help with inquiries, this

> "was not so in some districts in Northern Ireland, where an arrest may be the only means of making contact with a suspect. In hostile areas, arrests may have to be made at a time of day or night when the street will not be roused. The police may need Army support, and the suspect may need to be moved from his neighbourhood speedily for the safety of the officers to a place of security from which he cannot escape or be rescued."[23]

Such difficulties have produced a legislative scheme: (a) making provision to enable the police to interview suspects for longer than normal at the police station (*infra*, pp. 117-132); (b) effecting alterations to rules of evidence to enable the more ready admission at the criminal trial of inculpatory statements which were the fruits of such extended interrogation (*infra*, pp. 121, 137-142); (c) modifying the onus of proof as to the "knowledge" element in cases concerned with possession of firearms and/or explosives discovered in the course of a search pursuant to existing or emergency powers (*infra*, pp. 138-139). More recently the police have successfully relied on the evidence of so-called "converted terrorists" or "super-grasses" (*infra*, pp. 144-146).

2. *Some Vital Concepts*

Before examining each of the matters effected by the emergency legislation which were identified above, it is necessary to examine some key concepts central to one's understanding of it: "terrorism," "terrorist" and "scheduled offence."

[23] Bennett, para. 28.

(1) *Terrorism and terrorist*

"Terrorism" is defined in section 31(1) of NIEPA 1978 and section 14(1) of the PTA 1984 as

> "the use of violence for political ends and includes any use of violence for the purpose of putting the public or any section of the public in fear."

The term "terrorist," relevant only to NIEPA 1978, is defined therein as

> "a person who is or has been concerned in the commission or attempted commission of any act of terrorism or in directing, organising or training persons for the purpose of terrorism" (s.31(1)).

Such definitions are wide indeed and could cover violence at a political demonstration or, depending on the aims of the dispute, on a trade union picket line.[24] But it is arguable that they are not apt to cover ordinary criminals using violence to carry out robberies for personal gain.[25] Insofar as the definitions do not distinguish between state and non-state actors, enabling propagandists to characterise security forces' actions as "terrorism", their width is indeed unfortunate.[26] The definitions are, however, much narrower than the definition of terrorism in South African security legislation "which prima facie includes, *inter alia*, any act likely to embarrass the administration of the affairs of the state."[27] In Northern Ireland neither terrorism nor being a terrorist constitutes as such a criminal offence.[28]

Baker recommended making it crystal clear that a member of a proscribed organisation is a terrorist.[29] He was concerned that the reference in the definition to political ends was at odds with "criminalisation," enabling terrorists to point to the definition "as

[24] Street [1975] Crim.L.R. 192, p. 197.

[25] K. Boyle, annotations to s.31 of NIEPA 1978 in *Current Law Statutes Annotated*.

[26] C. Warbrick, "The European Convention on Human Rights and the Prevention of Terrorism" (1983) 32 I.C.L.Q. 82.

[27] J. Dugard, *Human Rights and the South African Legal Order* (1978), pp. 262-263.

[28] In 1975, it was recommended that a new indictable offence of being concerned in terrorism be enacted, but this proved unacceptable to the government. See *Report of a Committee to consider, in the context of civil liberties and human rights, measures to deal with terrorism in Northern Ireland*, Cmnd. 5847 (1975), paras. 70-71 (hereinafter cited as "Gardiner").

[29] Baker, para. 440. The majority of the Northern Ireland Court of Appeal in

proof of the recognition of their political motivation."[30] He recommended that further thought be given to finding a new definition to eliminate this.[31] That advanced by Professor Wilkinson found some favour with him:

> "The systematic use of violence to create a climate of fear, to publicise a cause or to coerce a target into conceding the terrorists' aims."[32]

This, however, seems neither narrower nor clearer than the present formulation. It may be preferable to retain the present concepts, which at least have the benefit of familiarity, with possible extensions to bring violence for sectarian ends within the notion "terrorism" and to embrace those who recruit others for terrorism within the concept "terrorist."[33]

(2) *"Scheduled Offence"*

This concept is central to NIEPA 1978. The offences are listed in Schedule 4 subject to the modifications set out in the notes therein. The purpose of the concept was to focus the new system on those offences commonly committed by terrorists, to limit its operation to offences connected with the emergency; "that is to say," in the words of the Diplock Commission, where "the prevalence of violence in pursuit of political aims results in the intimidation of witnesses and so prevents the prosecution from calling them to give evidence in a court of law where there is any risk that their identity may become known" or where there was a risk of intimidation of jurors of similar provenance or there was a risk of a perverse verdict by partisan jurors.[34] The list of offences consists in the main of already existing crimes: murder, manslaughter and other serious offences against the person; the majority of firearms and explosives offences; arson and other

McKee v. *Chief Constable* (1983) 11 N.I.J.B; [1984] 2 C.L. 237 took the view that suspicion of membership of a PO was not enough to ground arrest under NIEPA 1978, s.11 because of itself it did not suffice to bring the suspect within the s.31 definition. The House of Lords, allowing the Chief Constable's appeal, declined to express any view on that issue: [1984] 1 W.L.R. 1358, 1362.

30 Baker, paras. 438-439.

31 *Ibid.* para. 441.

32 *Ibid.* para. 440.

33 *Ibid.* para. 441. *Cf.* Gardiner, paras. 70 and 71.

34 Diplock, para. 114; *cf.* Gardiner, para. 62, Boyle, Hadden and Hillyard, *op. cit.* n. 1, pp. 57-58.

serious criminal damage; robbery and aggravated burglary; intimidation; offences related to the manufacture, possession and use of petrol bombs; bomb hoaxes; extra-territorial offences under section 1 of the Criminal Jurisdiction Act 1975[35]; new criminal offences under the PTA 1984 (*infra*, pp. 188-191) applicable to Northern Ireland; and a number of offences created by NIEPA 1978 itself (*infra*, pp. 107-109). Aiding, abetting, counselling or procuring, attempting or conspiring to commit a scheduled offence; doing any act with intent to impede the arrest or prosecution of a person who has committed one (s.4 Criminal Law Act (Northern Ireland) 1967)[36]; and failing to give information to the police which is likely to secure, or to be of material assistance in securing, the apprehension, prosecution or conviction of such a person (Criminal Law Act (N.I.) 1967, s.5(1)), are all to be treated as scheduled offences for the purposes of NIEPA 1978.[37] That an offence is scheduled involves no change in its substantive elements or in the availability of defences to it.[38]

No express distinction is made between those crimes executed for a political motive and those executed for some private advantage; the Diplock Commission considered that

[35] This Act provides courts in Northern Ireland with extra-territorial jurisdiction to try certain offences committed in the Republic of Ireland. Reciprocal legislation exists there (Criminal Law Jurisdiction Act 1976, No. 14). For the background to the legislation see *Report of the Law Enforcement Commission to the Secretary of State for Northern Ireland and the Minister for Justice of Ireland*, Cmnd. 5627 (1974).

[36] This provides that "where a person has committed an arrestable offence any other person who, knowing or believing him to be guilty of the offence, or some other arrestable offence, does without lawful authority or excuse any act with intent to impede his apprehension or prosecution, shall be guilty of an offence."

[37] This provides that

> " . . . where a person has committed an arrestable offence, it shall be the duty of every other person, who knows or believes–
> (*a*) that the offence or some other arrestable offence has been committed; and
> (*b*) that he has information which is likely to secure, or to be of material assistance in securing, the apprehension, prosecution or conviction of any person for that offence;
>
> to give that information, within a reasonable time, to a constable and if, without reasonable excuse, he fails to do so he shall be guilty of an offence and shall be liable on conviction on indictment to imprisonment according to the gravity of the offence about which he does not give that information. . . ."

[38] Boyle, *op. cit.* n. 25, note to Sched. 4.

> "[a]lthough what distinguishes terrorist activities from other crimes involving acts or threats of violence is the motive that lies behind them, motive does not provide a practical criterion for defining the kinds of crime with which we need to deal. The object of the terrorist organisations which concern us is to bring about political change in Northern Ireland by violent means: but terrorist organisations inevitably attract into their ranks ordinary criminals whose motivation for particular acts may be private gain or personal revenge. If those who commit such acts for non-political motives are associated with a known terrorist organisation, the effect on public safety and on public fear is no different because the motive with which they are committed is more base. We do not exclude these from the category of terrorist acts with which we are bound to deal."[39]

Two devices are, however, employed to limit the modified bail, preliminary hearing and trial processes to offences connected with the emergency:

(i) the Attorney General's power to certify that certain offences are not to be treated as scheduled in particular cases (see Sched. 4, Pt. 1, notes 1 and 2), *e.g.* murder and manslaughter are scheduled offences but if the evidence revealed a killing in the course of a domestic quarrel, with no paramilitary overtones, it would be certified out and prosecuted in the normal manner[40];

(ii) certain offences are only to be treated as scheduled offences in certain circumstances (Sched. 4, Pt. 1, notes 3 and 4), *e.g.* robbery and aggravated burglary are only scheduled offences where "it is charged that an explosive, firearm, imitation firearm or weapon of offence was used to commit the offence."

Certification by the DPP for Northern Ireland of suitability for summary trial is effectively certifying out; the post-Diplock modifications to evidentiary rules are now only applicable to trials on indictment (ss.8(3), 9(5)).[41] The Attorney General is responsible to Parliament for his decisions, but there is no appeal to a court from certification decisions. The Act sets out no guidelines to govern their making. In the debates on NIEPA 1975, Attorney General Silkin indicated that his aim in making such decisions, which he regarded as a personal responsibility, was "to try to ensure that justice will follow. . . . When I speak about

[39] Diplock, para. 5.

[40] Boyle, *op. cit.* n. 25, note to Sched. 4.

[41] Gardiner, para. 57.

justice I mean "justice to the public as much as the defendant."[42] There seems to have been no further elaboration of the criteria which influence the decisions.

A similar device to certifying out is employed in the Republic of Ireland in the operation of its non-jury Special Criminal Court under the Offences Against the State Act 1939.[43] Such courts can be activated by the executive, through a proclamation annullable by Dail Eireann (their Commons) which can be issued

> "if and whenever and so often as the Government is satisfied that the ordinary courts are inadequate to secure the effective administration of justice and the preservation of public peace and order" (s.35(1)).

Such courts have operated during the periods 1939-46, 1961-62 and 1972-date. Offences specified as scheduled will be tried there unless the Attorney General otherwise directs, but he also has power to direct that non-scheduled offences be referred to that court by certifying that "the Ordinary Courts are, in his opinion, inadequate to secure the effective administration of justice and the preservation of public peace and order in relation to the trial of . . . a person on such charge" (ss.45-47).

The present system in Northern Ireland, like that in the Republic,[44] enables serious crimes, unconnected with the emergency, to be tried without a jury. Thus an armed robbery, wholly unconnected with the paramilitaries, must be tried before a Diplock Court.[45] Apparently some 41 per cent. of cases appearing before those courts in the first three months of 1981 were non-terrorist, that is, not being "motivated by loyalist or republican paramilitar(ism) or by sectarianism or having been committed by the security forces in dealing with terrorism."[46] Most were armed robberies carried out for ordinary motives.[47] The wide reach of the scheduled offence notion also produces problems with the bail process, bringing ordinary crimes, for a time at least, within a much modified process popularly thought to be reserved for terrorist crime (*infra.* pp. 132-134).

[42] H.C. Debs., Vol. 894, cols. 974-975.

[43] M. Robinson, *The Special Criminal Court* (1974), *passim.*

[44] *Ibid.* pp. 35-36.

[45] NIEPA 1978, s.30, Sched. 4, n. 4.

[46] D. Walsh, "The Diplock Process in Northern Ireland Today" in *Emergency Laws in Northern Ireland* (CAJ Pamphlet No. 2, 1982), p. 8.

[47] D. Walsh, *The Use and Abuse of Emergency Legislation in Northern Ireland* (1983), p. 60.

The Baker recommendation that the number of scheduled offences capable of being certified out be increased (*infra*, pp. 150-151) should, if implemented, reduce the number of trials on indictment without a jury. It would not dispose of the associated bail problem.

3. *New Criminal Offences in NIEPA 1978*

Prosecutions for these offences may only be instituted by or with the consent of the DPP for Northern Ireland (s.29).

(1) *Scheduled offences*

Where tried on indictment, these are punishable with up to ten years in prison, a fine or both. If convicted summarily, the accused is liable to imprisonment not exceeding six months, a fine not in excess of the prescribed maximum, or both.[48]

Section 21 deals with proscribed organisations. They are listed in Schedule 2 and transcend the sectarian divide. The Secretary of State can add to the list any organisation appearing to him to be concerned in terrorism or in its promotion or encouragement (s.21(4)). He may deproscribe an organisation, and can re-proscribe it at a later date (s.21(4), (5)). All such powers are exercised by order requiring the affirmative approval of both Houses of Parliament (*supra*, pp. 43-44). Those organisations presently proscribed are: the Irish Republican Army (IRA); the Irish National Liberation Army (INLA); Cuman na mBan; Fianna na hEireann; the Red Hand Commando; Saor Eire; the Ulster Freedom Fighters (UFF); and the Ulster Volunteer Force (UVF). It is an offence to belong or profess to belong to such an organisation (s.21(1)(*a*)); or to solicit or invite financial or other support for it; or to knowingly make or receive any monetary or other contribution to its resources (s.21(1)(*b*)). To solicit or invite anyone to join or to carry out on its behalf orders or directions given, or requests made, by a member, is likewise an offence (s.21(1)(*c*)).[49] The accused's possession of a document addressed to

[48] NIEPA 1978, ss.21(1), 22(4), 23(1). Baker recommended seven years as the maximum sentence under s.21. The level of fine on summary conviction was altered by the Fines and Penalties (NI) Order 1984 (S.I. 1984 No. 703) as amended by the Criminal Penalties (Increase) Order (NI) 1984 (S.R. No. 253). The prescribed maximum is now £2,000.

[49] Baker proposed that the offence in PTA 1984, s.1(1)(*c*) (*infra*, pp. 183-184), at

him as a member, or relating or purporting to relate to the organisation's affairs, or emanating or purporting to emanate from it or one of its officers, is evidence of his membership at the time he possessed the document (s.21(6)).[50] In this respect the Act goes further than the proscription provisions applicable in Great Britain (*infra*, pp. 183-184). The legislation, however, eschews more far-reaching provisions, of the type contained in the Irish Republic's Offences Against the State (Amendment) Act 1972, which permit the court to accept as prima facie evidence of the accused's membership, a statement by a senior police officer that to the best of his belief the accused is a member of the organisation in question.[51] The Diplock and Gardiner committees rejected such a provision because the only way of effectively testing the statement would be to cross-examine the officer concerned on the sources grounding his belief, and this could only safely be done, without prejudice to those sources and a continuing flow of information, in the absence of the accused and his lawyers, a device those committees considered unacceptable in a regular court of law.[52] The possibility of offending against the principle *nulla crimen sine lege*, embodied as non-derogable in Article 7 of the European Convention on Human Rights,[53] is avoided by providing that a person shall not be guilty of a "belonging" offence if he has not taken part in the organisation's activities while proscribed (s.21(7)). Proscription is clearly an interference with freedom of association: its wider implications in that respect are examined in Chapter Four in the context of similar provisions in the PTA 1984 (*infra*, pp. 183-188).

Section 22 makes it an offence to collect, record (including to photograph), publish, communicate or attempt to elicit any information, of a nature likely to be useful to terrorists,

present applicable only in Great Britain, be extended to Northern Ireland in the proposed new legislation (para. 408). He recommended that the meaning be clarified of the terms "financial or other support" and "any contribution in money or otherwise."

50 Baker recommended substituting "may" for "shall" in s.21(6).

51 s.3(2). See M. Robinson, *loc. cit.* n. 17, at p. 59.

52 Diplock, para. 22; Gardiner, para. 68.

53 Art. 7(1) provides: "No one shall be held guilty of a criminal offence on account of any act or omission which did not constitute a criminal offence under national or international law at the time when it was committed. Nor shall a heavier penalty be imposed than the one that was applicable at the time the criminal offence was committed." Art. 15(2) renders it non-derogable.

concerning police officers, members of Her Majesty's forces, judges, court officers or full time employees in the prison service in Northern Ireland, many of whom have been murdered during the current emergency (s.22(1)(*a*), (2)). It also penalises the collection or recording of information of a nature likely to be useful to terrorists in the planning or execution of any act of violence (s.22(1)(*b*)). Possession of any record or document containing any of the information covered by the section is likewise an offence (s.22(1)(*c*)). The burden of proving a defence of lawful authority or reasonable excuse lies on the accused (s.22(1)). Forfeiture of any such records or documents can be ordered by the court on conviction (s.22(5)). These "spying" offences do not detract from those available under the Official Secrets Acts 1911 and 1920 (s.22(6)). A typical situation covered by the section is the "logging" of security forces' movements or of police or army vehicle registration numbers. The communication offence would also embrace a person acting as a lookout for those perpetrating an ambush of a police or army patrol. Both sections 21 and 22 contain the potential for oppressive application, and *pace* Baker could be so deployed against journalists or the media.[54] Some safeguard against this lies in an alert judiciary and benevolent prosecutorial discretion.[55] Baker considered that section 22 was too limited in the persons about whom it was an offence to collect, etc., information, and that it should be extended to cover persons at special risk, that is, at least, MPs, former MPs, former members of the security forces, senior civil servants and former holders of judicial office.[56]

Section 23 supplements the effect of the Unlawful Drilling Act 1819 (s.23(4)), and criminalises the giving or receipt of training or instruction in the making or use of firearms, explosives or explosive substances (s.23(1)). It is a defence to prove that the training or instruction was given or received for industrial, agricultural or sporting purposes only, or with lawful authority, or for other good reason (s.23(2)).[57]

[54] Baker disagreed that they had a potential for media censorship, but gave no reasons for his view (para. 431).

[55] See, generally, K. Boyle, *op. cit.* n. 25, annotation to s.22.

[56] Baker, para, 431.

[57] Boyle, *op. cit.* n. 25, annotation to s.23, noted that "the pattern of conviction in Northern Ireland remains one of catching the volunteers and not the leaders or instigators."

(2) *Summary offences connected with public order*

These are punishable with maximum imprisonment of six months, a fine up to level 5 on the standard scale, or both.[58] Under section 24 any member of the security forces can order the dispersal of any assembly of three or more persons where any commissioned officer of Her Majesty's forces or any officer of the RUC not below the rank of chief inspector is of opinion that it might make undue demands on the police or Her Majesty's forces, or that it might lead to public disorder or a breach of the peace (s.24(1)). Persons who knowingly join or remain in the assembly after the order to disperse, or who otherwise fail to comply with it, commit an offence (s.24(2)). Although there had been no recent prosecutions under this section, Baker thought it valuable as much more convenient than proceedings on indictment for riot, unlawful assembly or affray, and that the power obviously should be retained.[59] It is an offence for a person in any public place to dress or behave in such a manner as to give reasonable grounds to suppose that he is a member of a proscribed organisation (s.25). Section 26 prohibits the wearing of hood, mask, or other article for concealing identity or features, in a public place or in the curtilage of any dwelling-house other than that in which the wearer resides. Sections 25 and 26 are designed to deter the public display of paramilitary activity, for example, at funerals, or for the purpose of terrorism and intimidation of innocent citizens.[60] Baker rejected views that section 25 should apply to any place or that section 25 or 26 conduct should be evidence of membership of a proscribed organisation.[61] Section 27 empowers the Secretary of State to make additional regulations to promote the preservation of the peace and the maintenance of order. The regulations set out in Schedule 3 cover such matters as the regulation of road and rail traffic,[62] and of the routes of funerals (including power to stop entry to any particular place and to insist that participants travel in vehicles),[63] and powers to require

[58] NIEPA 1978, ss.24(2), 25, 26, 27(2). The level of fine was altered by the Fines and Penalties Order as amended, *op. cit*, n. 48. Level 5 is currently £2,000.

[59] Baker, para. 434.

[60] Gardiner, para. 72; Boyle, *op. cit.* n. 25, annotations to ss.25, 26.

[61] Baker, para. 433. The offences should, however, become hybrid, *i.e.* capable of trial on indictment where appropriate because of other charges to be tried on indictment (*ibid.*).

[62] NIEPA 1978, Sched. 3, paras. 2 (road), 3 (rail).

[63] *Ibid.* para. 4.

the closing of licensed premises or clubs.[64] A regulation made under NIEPA 1973 requires motor vehicles not to be left unattended unless any keys (including the ignition key) are taken away and the vehicle is locked and immobilised. Certain exceptions are made, *inter alia*, for security forces' and emergency services' vehicles, and for buses.[65] Breach of the regulations, or of instruments or directions under them, is an offence.[66]

(3) *Summary offences of non-co-operation with the exercise by the security forces of specific statutory powers*

These attract the same penalties as the summary offences above. Failing to stop when required to do so by the security forces under sections 18 and 20 constitutes an offence, as does refusal to answer questions lawfully put under section 18 (*infra*, pp. 112-113) or failure to answer the same to the best of one's knowledge and ability.[67] Interference without lawful authority or reasonable excuse with works erected or anything used in or in connection with the security forces' general powers of interference with property or highways conferred by section 19, is likewise criminal.[68] The reasonableness of such offences depends on whether the powers they support have that same quality.

4. Criminal Offences in the PTA 1984

A number of such offences apply to Northern Ireland. Some are scheduled offences, proceedings in respect of which require the consent of the Attorney General for Northern Ireland (Sched. 3, para. 3). They cover: contributions towards acts of terrorism (s.10); failure to disclose information about acts of terrorism (s.11); and offences ancillary to the exclusion process (s.9). There is also a summary offence of knowing contravention of or non-compliance with orders establishing the immigration-type security control permitted under this legislation (Sched. 3, para. 9). The scope of these offences is examined more fully in Chapter 4 (*infra*, pp. 188-191). Baker proposed that the offences under

[64] *Ibid.* para. 5.

[65] The Northern Ireland (Emergency Provisions) Regulations 1975 (S.I. 1975 No. 2213); Baker, para. 435.

[66] NIEPA, s.27(2).

[67] *Ibid.* ss.18(2), 20(7).

[68] *Ibid.* s.19(4).

sections 10 and 11 be included in replacement legislation for Northern Ireland, and the PTA 1984 amended accordingly.[69]

5. Powers to Stop, Question and Search, and to Interfere with Property

NIEPA 1978 confers sundry such powers on constables and members of Her Majesty's forces on duty. The latter, if not in uniform, are obliged to produce on request documentary evidence of their status (s.20(8)). A number of less sweeping powers are granted by the PTA 1984; they are examined in Chapter 4 (*infra*, pp. 172-173).

Any member of the security forces may stop any person, vehicle or non-airborne aircraft and may question any person to ascertain any one or more of the following matters: his identity and movements; or what he knows concerning any recent explosion or other incident endangering life, or about any person injured or killed therein (ss.18(1), 20(6)). "Recent" is not defined. Its meaning should be clarified.[70] Any constable, or soldier on duty, can stop and search persons, vehicles, vessels or non-airborne aircraft for munitions or radio-transmitters (ss.15, 20(1), (6)). These powers of search are not confined to persons or objects in a public place. However, where the search is not in a public place there must be suspicion that the subject of the search has a transmitter or unlawfully held munitions with him. No suspicion is required to search in a public place: the power can be exercised to see whether the person has such objects with him. Baker considered these powers necessary.[71] "Munitions" means explosives, explosive substances, firearms, ammunition, and anything capable of being used in their manufacture. "Transmitter" is defined as any apparatus for wireless-telegraphy, or any part thereof, designed or adapted for emission as opposed to reception (s.15(5)).[72] Munitions found may be seized and retained or destroyed, and transmitters seized and retained, unless their use appears to be for a lawful purpose (s.15(4)). Vehicles or vessels which cannot

[69] Baker, paras. 238-240. In the new enactment, s.5(1) of the Criminal Law Act (N.I.) 1967 should be amalgamated with s.11 insofar as s.5(1) concerns scheduled arrestable offences.

[70] Baker, paras. 382-384.

[71] *Ibid.* para. 359.

[72] Baker recommended that an immediate technical study be made to see whether the definitions needed amendment, *e.g.* to make misuse of CB Radio to alert others of the security forces' movements or roadchecks "a punishable or even scheduled offence insofar as it is not already an offence under the Wireless Telegraphy Acts" (para. 369).

conveniently be searched *in situ* may be taken to some more convenient spot (s.20(4)). There is power to search containers (s.20(1)). Power to search vessels, vehicles, aircraft or containers includes power to examine them (s.20(5)). An explosives inspector has similar powers with respect to explosives and explosive substances (s.16(2), (3)), but his power to stop and search persons is confined to a public place (s.16(2)). Members of the Civilian Search Unit (CSU), whose main function is to search those wishing to enter the secure zone in the main shopping area in Belfast City Centre, are explosives inspectors. Where the CSU find offending objects, arrests are executed by the Army or the RUC.[73]

NIEPA 1978 confers specific powers of entry to premises or other places for search and seizure purposes, including powers to search vehicles, vessels and aircraft (s.20(1)). Explosives inspectors may enter any premises or places other than a dwelling-house, without prior suspicion or a search warrant, to ascertain if explosives or explosive substances are unlawfully held there (s.16(1)). Their entry to a dwelling-house is regulated by ordinary powers requiring reasonable suspicion and a warrant.[74] Powers conferred on the security forces are exercisable without a search warrant. Section 15(1) permits any member of Her Majesty's forces on duty or any constable to enter and search any premises or place other than a dwelling-house to ascertain whether munitions are unlawfully held there or if there is a transmitter there. Offending items may be seized and retained, and munitions may be destroyed (s.15(4)). Section 17 sanctions their entry and search for any person thought to be unlawfully detained and in danger of his life, but entry and search of a dwelling-house for that purpose demands authorisation by, in the case of the Army, a commissioned officer, and, as regards the police, an officer not below the rank of chief inspector, thus affording some protection against arbitrary invasion of the citizen's home (s.17(2)). Such authorisation is also required in respect of dwelling-houses by section 15(2) which furthermore demands suspicion that a transmitter or unlawfully held munitions are to be found there. Baker recommended that section 15(2) require reasonable suspicion on the part of the authorising officer but that personal suspicion on the part of the person duly authorised to enter should not be required.[75] Powers of entry and search also

[73] Baker, paras. 374-376.

[74] Explosives Act 1875, s.73.

[75] Baker, paras. 361-363. He further suggested that it be made clear that the

accompany the powers of arrest conferred by NIEPA 1978 (*infra*, pp. 117-119). To effect the arrest of a suspected terrorist or of a person suspected of an offence under NIEPA 1978 (*supra*, pp. 107-111) or of a scheduled offence (*supra*, pp. 103-107), a constable may enter and search any premises or place where that person is or the constable suspects him of being (ss.11(2), 13(2)). A soldier on duty has a narrower power: with a view to exercising his power of arrest under section 14(1) (*infra*, pp. 117-118), he may only enter and search premises or places where that person is, or in the case of a suspected terrorist or a person suspected of having committed an offence involving the use or possession of a firearm, explosive or explosive substance, where he is suspected of being (s.14(3)). A constable, but not a soldier, has a general power to seize anything he suspects is being, has been or is intended to be used in the commission of an offence under NIEPA 1978 or of a scheduled offence (s.13(3)). This is a very wide power indeed, far exceeding those powers which are available at common law[76] or those in the Police and Criminal Evidence Act 1984,[77] none of which sanction seizure of articles merely on the basis that they might be used in future offences.[78] In line with his proposals on arrest powers (*infra*, pp. 127-131), Baker recommended that "reasonable suspicion" be required to exercise these powers of entry search and seizure ancillary to arrest.[79]

Section 19 gives general powers of entry to and interference with rights of property and with highways. A policeman or soldier can enter any premises or place when he considers it necessary to do so in the course of operations for the preservation of the peace and the maintenance of order (s.19(1)(*a*)). They may do likewise when so authorised by or on behalf of the Secretary of State (s.19(1)(*b*)). Constables, soldiers and persons authorised by or on behalf of the Secretary of State, may, on particular

authorities can detain all or any of the occupants in one place during the search in order to prevent their interfering with it, but not for more than four hours (para. 367).

[76] See L.H. Leigh, *Police Powers in England and Wales* (1975), pp. 50-53, Chap. IX; Royal Commission on Criminal Procedure, *The Investigation and Prosecution of Criminal Offences in England and Wales: The Law and Procedure*, Cmnd. 8092-I (1981), paras. 27-29, 34-35 (hereinafter cited as "RCCP: Law and Procedure").

[77] Police and Criminal Evidence Act 1984 (hereinafter PCEA 1984), ss.8-23.

[78] However, similar powers to those in NIEPA 1978 were a feature of pre-Second World War codes of emergency regulations issued pursuant to a proclamation of emergency under the Emergency Powers Act 1920. See *infra*, pp. 238-239.

[79] Baker, paras. 284, 303, 346.

authorisation given by him or on his behalf (which affords some protection for the citizen), take possession of any land or other property; take steps to place buildings or other structures in a state of defence; destroy any property or cause it to be moved or destroyed; or do anything else interfering with private rights of property or any public right, including executing any works on land possession of which has been taken pursuant to these powers (s.19(2)). Such wide powers, possibly otherwise available under the prerogative, have enabled the construction of fortified army posts on roads, pavements and in private (usually derelict) houses,[80] and permit the Army to blow up vehicles suspected of being booby-trapped.[81] Any such person may also wholly or partly close, divert or otherwise interfere with a highway or its use, or prohibit or restrict exercise of any right of way or use of any waterway, but only so far as he considers it to be immediately necessary for the preservation of the peace and the maintenance of order (s.19(3)), a limitation claimed not to be observed in practice.[82] Such a power is of vital importance in denying access to areas, for example, when dealing with car bombs.[83]

Section 28 provides for compensation to be payable by the Secretary of State where, pursuant to the Act, real or personal property has been occupied, taken, destroyed or damaged, or private rights of property have been otherwise interfered with. No such right to compensation accrues to an offender in respect of the taking, occupation, destruction or damaging of property or in respect of any other act done in connection with the offence.[84] The scope of this limitation is uncertain. The SACHR thought that it might exclude *any* offender. Baker considered that it probably only excluded compensation where the search in question revealed evidence of an offence connected with the search, and recommended that in any event the exclusion should be limited to that.[85]

It is difficult to disagree with the SACHR that

[80] Boyle, *op. cit.* n. 25, annotation to s.19. See also *supra*, pp. 8-9; Baker, para. 397.

[81] Baker, para. 397.

[82] Committee on the Administration of Justice, *Submission to the review by Sir George Baker of the Northern Ireland (Emergency Provisions) Act 1978 (the EPA)*, para. 39 (hereinafter cited as "CAJ, Baker Submission").

[83] Boyle, *op. cit.* n. 25, annotation to s.19(3).

[84] Baker, paras. 370-373, App. Q.

[85] Baker, para. 371.

> "while violent attacks on people and property continue in Northern Ireland most responsible people would accept that the police and Army should have available to them extraordinary powers to stop, search [and] question."[86]

Such powers, however, emphasise the degree to which life is not normal in the Province. Over-zealous use of such powers, in particular of those of stop and question, or of search (especially of small terraced houses), may prove alienating and counter-productive. There is, therefore, merit in suggestions that entry and search of dwelling-houses should normally require a judicial warrant issued on reasonable suspicion that munitions or transmitters are held there[87]; that such searches at night always require a warrant[88]; and that steps be taken to ensure that powers are used for preventive not punitive or harassment purposes (*e.g.* through enhanced training and by making greater use of the element of control inherent in supervision by senior officers). Equally valuable are proposals that the power to stop and question (s.18) be confined to questions relating to identity and movements and be limited in time to 15 or 20 minutes,[89] that so far as possible the powers examined in this section of this chapter should require reasonable suspicion; and that the Army should adopt a lower profile and act only as delegates of or in concert with the force permanently on the spot, the RUC.[90]

Baker supported this last suggestion but was unable to accept as appropriate a requirement for a judicial warrant before search. He rejected time restrictions on section 18 in favour of flexibility to suit the particular case with the Army authorities ensuring through specific orders that no person stopped is delayed for longer than necessary.[91] It may not be feasible to condition every power on reasonable suspicion. As Secretary of State Whitelaw

[86] SACHR, *Annual Report for 1977-78*, H.C. 176 (1978-79), para. 35.

[87] SACHR, *Annual Report for 1982-83* H.C. 262 (1983-84) at p. 18 (para. 22 of their submission to Baker).

[88] Boyle, Hadden and Hillyard, *op. cit.* n. 1, pp. 27, 33-34.

[89] SACHR, *op. cit.* n. 87, para. 20. *Cf.* The Alliance Party of Northern Ireland, *Submission to Review of the Northern Ireland (Emergency Provisions) Act 1978 to Sir George Baker*, para. 30 (hereinafter cited as "Alliance Party Baker Submission.") I am indebted to Alliance Party Assemblyman, Paul Maguire, for providing me with this submission.

[90] CAJ Baker Submission, paras. 39-40; Boyle, Hadden and Hillyard, *op. cit.* n. 1, p. 34, make a related point.

[91] Baker, paras. 363, 394.

noted in 1973, to deter the movement of terrorists and their equipment may require powers to be exercised randomly, requiring no suspicion at all; to take his example, where

> "the security forces have reason to suspect that arms are being moved by a particular route, [it] is only reasonable that they should search all the traffic on that route; but they cannot say that they suspect each vehicle of carrying the arms."[92]

6. *Arrest, Detention and Interrogation*

A number of overlapping powers of arrest without warrant exist in Northern Ireland for deployment against terrorist suspects. There are the "normal" powers to arrest for arrestable offences conferred by section 2 of the Criminal Law Act (Northern Ireland) 1967,[93] and specific powers of summary arrest in particular non-emergency statutes. Section 13(1) of NIEPA 1978 is an addition to this general pattern of powers which require the appearance of the detainee before a magistrate as soon as is practicable and in any event not more than 48 hours after his arrest.[94] It empowers a constable to arrest without warrant someone he suspects of committing, having committed or being about to commit a scheduled offence or an offence under the Act which is not a scheduled offence. Under the "normal" powers, of course, suspicion must, generally speaking, be reasonable.

The emergency legislation supplements normal powers with arrest powers which do not require an early court appearance. Any member of Her Majesty's forces on duty may arrest without warrant a person whom he suspects of committing, having committed or being about to commit any offence (NIEPA, s.14(1)). The arrestor is deemed to comply with any rule of law (*e.g.* that in *Christie* v. *Leachinsky*) requiring him to give the ground of arrest by stating that he is effecting the same as a member of Her Majesty's forces (s.14(2)). If not in uniform he must produce, if requested, documentary evidence of his status (s.20(8)). A person may be detained in right of the arrest for not more than four hours (s.14(1)). The rationale of the power and its accompanying modification of common law safeguards of the liberty of the

[92] H.C. Deb., Vol. 855, col. 276.

[93] s.2 is in much the same terms as s.2 of the Criminal Law Act 1967. It may be that the powers in ss.24, 25 of the PCEA 1984 will be extended to the Province.

[94] Baker, para. 301; Art. 131, Magistrates' Court Order (NI) 1981 (S.I. 1981 No. 1675).

subject reflects the concern of the Diplock Commission about the practicalities of arrests by soldiers in "extremist strongholds" (no-go areas for the police) where they may come under attack from snipers or be hindered by sympathisers in the local populace.[95] It recommended a power of arrest and short period of detention for purposes of establishing identity which would embrace those merely suspected of having information about offences committed or about to be committed by someone else.[96] This wider power was not enacted. Those arrested are either released after a period of questioning up to the permitted limit or, before it expires, handed on to the RUC for rearrest and further questioning where this seems appropriate. In the year to May 31, 1981, 1,503 people were arrested by the Army, of whom 418 were transferred to RUC custody.[97] The SACHR estimate that between one quarter and one half of suspects are handed over to the RUC. At the handover stage, unless the arrest was pre-planned with the RUC, the soldier will explain the circumstances of the arrest (*e.g.* "he would not answer questions" or "he threw a petrol bomb").[98]

In practice, even where a person is caught in the act of committing a specific offence, the RUC choose to deploy a power of arrest carrying with it an extended period of non-judicially authorised detention.[99] Section 11 of NIEPA 1978 confers one such power to arrest "any person whom [the constable] suspects of being a terrorist" (s.11(1)) and grants power to detain him for up to 72 hours (s.11(2)). An RUC officer not below the rank of chief inspector may order him to be photographed and finger-printed, and a constable may use such reasonable force as is necessary for that purpose (s.11(4)). Section 12(1) of the PTA 1984 permits a constable to arrest without warrant anyone he has reasonable grounds to suspect to be subject to an exclusion order excluding him from Northern Ireland, guilty of an offence under section 9 or 10 of the Act, or a person who is or has been concerned in the commission preparation or instigation of acts of terrorism connected with the affairs of Northern Ireland or of acts of terrorism of any description apart from acts solely connected with the affairs of the United Kingdom or any part thereof other than Northern Ireland. Anyone so arrested may be detained for up to 48 hours, a period extendible by a Secretary of State for a period or

95 Diplock, para. 44.
96 *Ibid.* para. 49.
97 Walsh, *op. cit.* n. 47, p. 38.
98 Baker, paras. 351, 352.
99 Bennett, para. 70; Baker, para. 302.

periods specified by him up to a maximum of a further five days (s.12(4), (5)). Similar powers conferred on examining officers at ports and airports as part of the travel control established by the Act and subordinate legislation are examined in detail in Chapter 4 (*infra*, pp. 170-176). They have scarcely been used in the Province.[1] Steady use has been made of section 12 powers, particularly since 1976. Up to December 31, 1984, 4,361 people had been detained under the section; 3,087 extensions of detention were granted; 1,652 charges arose, 266 without extension, 1,386 after extension. The success rate in terms of charges to extensions granted was 46 per cent. Many charges were serious.[2] No comparable figures exist on arrests under section 11 of NIEPA 1978. Statistics on persons arrested under both Acts and detained for more than four hours between September 1, 1977 and August 31, 1978 were published in the Bennett Report on Police Interrogation, and suggest that the arrest rate was 19 times greater under the NIEPAs. About 35 per cent. of those so detained in that period were charged.[3] In 1983, section 12 arrests formed just under half of arrests under both sections.[4] Which power is used reflects the time for which the police consider they will need to interview the suspect.[5] That section 12 requires a higher level of suspicion is not a factor in the choice,[6] and police are "now trained to treat arrest for terrorist offences as requiring similar suspicion as for all other offences."[7] Although it may legally be possible to do so, it is not RUC practice to arrest first under one power and then immediately re-arrest under the other at the end of the permissible period of detention, to make for up to 10 days' detention in all.[8] Whichever power is used, however, the greater proportion (76 per cent.) of those arrested are released without charge or subjection to an exclusion order.[9] The police must comply with *Christie* v.

1 *Review Of The Operation Of The Prevention Of Terrorism (Temporary Provisions) Act 1976 by The Rt. Hon. Earl Jellicoe, DSO, MC,* Cmnd. 8803 (1983), para. 51 (hereinafter cited as "Jellicoe").

2 *Ibid.* paras. 52, 53; Tables 10 and 13, Annex D. Updated statistics are taken from the Northern Ireland Information Service, *Statistics on the PTAs–Fourth Quarter 1984* (January 24, 1985).

3 Bennett, App. 1, p. 141.

4 Baker, paras. 281-282, App. M.

5 Jellicoe, para. 52; Baker, paras. 281-283.

6 Baker, para. 283.

7 *Ibid.*

8 *Ibid.* paras. 293-294. Baker proposed that such re-arrest in the absence of fresh evidence be precluded when framing the new Act.

9 *Ibid.* para. 276.

Leachinsky.[10] Informing the suspect that he is being arrested on suspicion of involvement in terrorism apparently suffices.[11] Boyle, Hadden and Hillyard found that arrests in Republican areas tended to be effected by the Army alone, or by the RUC with Army support, and were more likely to be effected in the early morning to avoid confrontation with the local populace.[12] Recent research suggests an increasing rate of arrests by the RUC alone in Republican areas with a heavy emphasis on early morning arrests in both Loyalist and Republican areas.[13]

Actual or perceived maltreatment of suspects has been a significant factor in community discontent. That there have been grave abuses in the sphere of interrogation in Ulster in the past is testified to by the Compton Report (1972), the Report of the Bennett Committee on RUC Interrogation (1979) and two Amnesty International Reports (1971 and 1978).[14] Interrogation practices of the Army in 1971 ("interrogation in depth") and the RUC at Palace Barracks in 1971-72 were challenged in *Ireland* v. *United Kingdom* as violations of the European Convention's non-derogable prohibition on torture, inhuman and degrading treatment (Art. 3). The European Commission of Human Rights characterised the Army practice as torture and that of the RUC as inhuman treatment.[15] The Court unanimously endorsed the latter opinion.[16] Inhuman treatment, it said, is the infliction of "intense suffering."[17] Torture, in its view, is "deliberate inhuman treatment causing very serious and cruel suffering," whether mental or physical.[18] Notwithstanding that interrogation in depth "caused, if not actual bodily injury, at least intense physical and mental suffering to the (fourteen) persons subjected thereto and also led to acute psychiatric disturbances during interrogation . . . (it) did not occasion suffering of the particular intensity and cruelty

[10] [1947] A.C. 573.

[11] *Ex p. Lynch* [1980] N.I.L.R. 126, at p. 131.

[12] K. Boyle, T. Hadden and P. Hillyard, *Ten years on in Northern Ireland: The legal control of political violence* (1980), p. 29.

[13] Walsh, *op. cit.* n. 47,pp. 34-37.

[14] For detailed references, see *supra*, pp. 72-74.

[15] M.P. O'Boyle, "Torture and Emergency Powers under the European Convention of Human Rights: Ireland v. The UK" (1977) 71 A.J.I.L. 674; *The Republic of Ireland* v. *The United Kingdom* (1978) 2 E.H.R.R. 25, at pp. 79, 81. (paras. 165, 173).

[16] (1978) 2 E.H.R.R. 25, at pp. 81-82, 107.

[17] (1978) 2 E.H.R.R. 25, at p. 80 (para. 167).

[18] (1978) 2 E.H.R.R. 25, at p. 80 (para. 167).

implied by the word torture" to which a special stigma attached. It did, however, constitute inhuman treatment. The techniques were also degrading treatment "since they were such as to arouse in their victims feelings of fear, anguish and inferiority capable of humiliating them and debasing them and possibly breaking their physical or moral resistance."[19]

Apart from declaring inadmissible at trial statements of the accused which may have been procured as a result of torture or inhuman or degrading treatment (s.8, *infra*, pp. 139-143), NIEPA 1978 is silent on the regulation of the interrogation process. So have been successive PTAs. But neither legislation attempts to exempt the process from the law of torts or the criminal law. Nor do they sanction "hardline' methods. Professor Boyle has suggested that there is some doubt about the applicability of the Judges' Rules, formulated for a context of arrest on reasonable suspicion of a specific offence, to arrests based on mere suspicion of terrorism where "the police may be aware of no such offence and be concerned only to gather intelligence through the interviews."[20] They are, however, reflected to a degree in the RUC Code, the standing body of instructions from the Chief Constable and senior officers with which every member of the RUC is required to comply, which is enforceable as a matter of internal discipline.[21] On the recommendations of the Bennett Committee a number of changes were made, not always precisely in line with the Committee's proposals, in terms of: the supervision by the uniformed branch, in part through closed-circuit television, of interviews conducted by the plain clothes branch; the better training of interrogators; increased involvement of senior officers in the process; the conduct of the interviews, for example, in terms of timing and breaks; notification to suspects of their rights; medical examination; access to legal advice and notification of arrest to third parties, for example, relatives. Most are embodied in the RUC Code.[22] Inevitably, the rules are hedged about with restrictions conferring discretion on officers. For instance, interviews are not to take place between midnight and 8 a.m. except where required by urgent operational reasons.[23] Similarly,

[19] (1978) 2 E.H.R.R. 25, at p. 80 (para. 167) For a critique see Bonner (1978) 27 I.C.L.Q. 897, at pp. 898-902.

[20] *Op. cit.* n. 25, note to s.8.

[21] Boyle, Hadden and Hillyard, *op. cit.* n. 12, p. 49. On the nature and role of the RUC Code, see Bennett, Chap. 6, and para. 85.

[22] Jellicoe, para. 87.

[23] *Ibid.*

although there is an unconditional right of access to a lawyer after 48 hours, if an RUC officer of the rank of Assistant Chief Constable or above considers that a private interview might unreasonably hinder the investigation or the administration of justice, he can direct that it take place within the sight and/or hearing of a uniformed officer, not below the rank of inspector or connected with the case.[24] Subject to worries about verbal abuse of suspects and the issue of discretionary access to a solicitor within the 48 hour period, Lord Jellicoe was convinced

> "that on the whole these recommendations have been implemented fully and fairly, and that the present system for supervising the detention of terrorist suspects in Northern Ireland is thorough and effective and reflects well on the professionalism of the RUC."[25]

His view was endorsed by Baker.[26] There has clearly been a decline in the incidence of physical abuse of suspects.[27] But it has been questioned whether it is appropriate to leave matters so heavily dependent on attitudes within and supervision by the higher echelons of the police themselves.[28]

The provisions authorising arrest and extended detention for questioning constitute far-reaching departures from Article 5 of the European Convention on Human Rights which provides an exhaustive list of the permissible grounds of deprivation of liberty and sets out guarantees applicable to persons deprived of their liberty. The provisions violate Article 5(1)(*c*) read with Article 5(3) in several respects. The former permits

> "the lawful arrest or detention of a person effected for the purpose of bringing him before the competent legal authority on reasonable suspicion of having committed an offence or when it is reasonably considered necessary to prevent his committing an offence or fleeing after having done so."

The latter requires that persons so detained "be brought promptly before a judge or other officer authorised by law to exercise judicial power and shall be entitled to trial within a reasonable time or to release pending trial. Release may be conditioned by

[24] Jellicoe, para. 93.

[25] Para. 84.

[26] Baker, paras. 308-313.

[27] Jellicoe, para. 86 and Annex D (Table 14).

[28] D.P.J. Walsh, "Arrest and Interrogation: Northern Ireland 1981" (1982) 9 B.J.L.S. 37.

guarantees to appear for trial." Some of the arrest powers do not require reasonable suspicion. Nor need there be suspicion of a specific offence. Although many of those arrested are brought into the criminal process, insofar as the powers are exercisable and exercised solely for purposes of intelligence-gathering, with no intention that the person interviewed be charged, they do not comply with the dictates of those Convention paragraphs which require in all cases the existence of a sufficiently firm intention to bring the person into the criminal process of charge and trial on the basis of the requisite reasonable suspicion or belief. In *Ireland* v. *United Kingdom* the Court impugned the similar provisions of Regulation 10, made under the Special Powers Act, on that ground.[29] The time-lag before the arrestee is brought before a resident magistrate may not be sufficiently prompt to satisfy paragraph three; a maximum of 48 hours seems standard in Convention countries although three and five days have been permitted in exceptional cases.[30] Article 5(2), analogous to *Christie* v. *Leachinsky* principles, provides

> "Everyone who is arrested shall be informed promptly, in a language which he understands, of the reasons for his arrest and of any charge against him."

This provision requires adequate information about the legal basis for the arrest and the relevant facts grounding its lawfulness to enable the victim to judge its legality and take steps to challenge it, should he so wish.[31] Section 14(2) of NIEPA 1978 would clearly violate this. So might the paucity of information provided in the exercise of the other powers although this is less clear.[32] The limited nature of judicial review probably violates Article 5(4) by not tackling the substance of the decision to detain.[33] The departures from Article 5 can only be justified during an Article 15 emergency. The United Kingdom's position on the PTA, insofar as its provisions do not comply with Article 5, may prove

[29] (1978) 2 E.H.R.R. 25, at pp. 87-88 (para. 196).

[30] See F.G. Jacobs, *The European Convention on Human Rights* (1975) p. 63.

[31] *McVeigh, O'Neill and Evans* v. *United Kingdom* (1981) 5 E.H.R.R. 71 (para. 208).

[32] In *McVeigh*, in the context of detention for examination under the "port powers" provided under the PTA, the Commission held that it was enough that the applicants had been told in general terms of the legal basis for their detention ("pending examination") and that it was not necessary that they be told the reasons why the examining officer was suspicious of them (*ibid.* para. 209). It should be noted, however, that the relevant power did not even require "suspicion."

[33] *Ireland* v. *United Kingdom* (1978) 2 E:H.R.R. 25, at p. 90 (para. 200).

problematic; that legislation was not embraced by its notice of derogation, the withdrawwal of which in respect of NIEPA 1978 seems premature (*supra*, pp. 88-90).

Justification for these powers is put in terms of the difficulties of policing in the Province making it imperative that suspects be interviewed at the police station and placing a premium on the evidence obtained from such interviews,[34] and of the need to gather reliable intelligence about terrorists, their plans and the communities in which they operate so as to make the terrorists more readily identifiable. Intimate knowledge of the terrorists' *milieu*, even of ways of pronouncing particular words or names, is said to be essential to enable the interviewer to gain vital leads through highlighting gaps and inconsistencies in a suspect's story. Such careful interrogation, where the interviewer may initially have little to go on, requires time.[35] Lord Jellicoe thought extended detention valuable in that it gave the police adequate time to complete forensic inquiries, check out identities and statements against existing intelligence and follow up new lines of inquiry.[36] He reported that it had proved useful in the Province in building up an interrogation so as the better to confront, with successful results, an unco-operative suspect with information against him obtained from a "converted terrorist."[37] This was especially important as the terrorist groups were more than ever conscious of the need to ensure "that their activists are well trained in the techniques of remaining silent under prolonged police questioning."[38] He opined that the police would be "seriously handicapped" if such powers were abolished,[39] a view shared by Baker.[40] Robin Evelegh, indeed, has argued for more extensive powers: that citizens should be obliged to attend periodic census-type security surveillance interviews the better to enable the security forces to build up an intelligence profile of the population in terms of the fingerprints, photographs and

[34] Bennett, paras. 28, 29.

[35] R. Evelegh, *Peace-keeping in a Democratic Society: The Lessons of Northern Ireland* (1978), pp. 60-75, 143-147, 150; Jellicoe, paras. 56-60; *Review of the Operation of The Prevention of Terrorism (Temporary Provisions) Acts 1974 and 1976 By The Rt. Hon. Lord Shackleton, KG. OBE*, Cmnd. 7324 (1978), paras. 69-77 (hereinafter cited as "Shackleton"); Baker, paras. 270, 272, 282.

[36] Jellicoe, paras. 59-60; Baker, para. 270.

[37] Jellicoe, para. 63.

[38] Jellicoe, para. 67. *Cf.* Shackleton, para. 72; Baker, paras. 272, 282.

[39] Jellicoe, para. 65.

[40] Baker, para. 257.

signatures (which might be included on identity cards which it would be compulsory to carry) as well as the political views and attitudes to authority of everyone in a particular "rebel-affected" area. Such information would be stored on computer.[41] Evelegh also stresses the necessity of extended detention for questioning, cash payments and immunity from prosecution as means of encouraging defectors or informers within terrorist groups, which he perceives as vital to destroying those groups.[42] He notes the success of the paid informer policy in the colonial Malayan emergency.[43]

It is evident that some such surveillance has already been achieved through practices of dubious legality in terms of existing powers.[44] A continuing cause for concern in the Province has been their use by the Army and the RUC, on the basis of no more suspicion than a person's residence in a particular area, not in order to prosecute the individual concerned but for "the ulterior motives of screening, building-up dossiers of information on people in an area, harassment and inducing suspects to pass on information."[45] This was particularly prevalent during the currency of internment and detention without trial as the Army put into practice in Ulster counter-insurgency tactics developed during colonial emergencies and refined and brought to the fore by such military theoreticians as the then Brigadier Kitson.[46] That general "trawling" operations persist is indicated by the low charge rate referred to above (pp. 119-120), but the thrust of policing, with a lower Army profile, is much more towards prosecution. There is said to have been an increase in Army "undercover intelligence and surveillance operations" employing "new technological devices, such as concealed cameras, telephone-tapping and a computerised data bank on the bulk of

[41] *Op. cit.* n. 35, pp. 119-132. *Cf.* Frank Kitson, *Low Intensity Operations: Subversion, Insurgency and Peacekeeping* (1971), pp. 107-112. For a critique see D.R Lowry, "Terrorism and Human Rights: Counter-Insurgency and Necessity at Common Law" (1977) 53 *Notre Dame Law* 49.

[42] *Op. cit.* n. 35, pp. 67-75, 133-151; *cf.* Kitson, *op. cit.* n. 41 at p. 100.

[43] *Op. cit.* n. 35, pp. 68-69, 140.

[44] *Ibid.* p. 119-20; Boyle, Hadden and Hillyard, *op. cit.* n. 12, pp. 25-31; Walsh, *op. cit.* n. 47, pp. 33-34, 38-40.

[45] D. Walsh, "Arrest and Interrogation" in C.A.J. Pamphlet No. 1, *The Administration of Justice in Northern Ireland: The proceedings of a conference held in Belfast on June 13, 1981,* pp. 7-8.

[46] Boyle, Hadden and Hillyard, *op. cit.* n. 12, pp. 25-29; Frank Kitson, *op. cit.* n. 41; D.R. Lowry, *loc. cit.* n. 41.

the population."[47] Such tactics may, of course, materially assist the security forces to bring terrorists to justice. Boyle, Hadden and Hillyard have warned, however, that

> "it is much more doubtful whether the adverse effects of the screening policy [in the early 1970s], when combined with the obvious risk that large numbers of innocent persons would be ill-treated or abused in the course of the arrest and questioning process, was not counter-productive in the sense that it increased the alienation of the civilian population in troubled areas from the security forces, and thus helped to ensure a continuing flow of recruits to terrorist organisations to replace those who were successfully identified and locked up"[48]

and have suggested that

> "there is a strong case . . . for some more effective control over the use of the power to arrest for questioning if public confidence in the legitimacy of police powers and practice is to be restored in some Catholic areas."[49]

How might the powers of arrest and detention be reformed? Ordinary powers must remain. The crucial issues are how far special powers should supplement them, and how they ought to be framed. It is submitted that all the powers should require reasonable suspicion, a view accepted by Baker.[50] This criterion, determined with regard to something like the average citizen's reaction, would afford greater scope for judicial intervention to check abuse.[51] Judicial willingness (or lack thereof) to use it to full effect is another matter. To require such suspicion would not unduly hinder the security forces; it is not the same thing as a solid prosecution case based on admissible evidence and would still permit positive action on information received. Courts are not quick to order disclosure of informants' identities. Significant use is already made of section 12 of the PTA 1984 which requires reasonable suspicion. Apparently police training proceeds as if such suspicion were required to arrest for terrorist offences.[52]

[47] Boyle, Hadden and Hillyard, *op. cit.* n. 12, p. 27.

[48] Boyle, Hadden and Hillyard, *Law and State: The Case of Northern Ireland* (1975), p. 53.

[49] *Op. cit.* n. 12, p. 31.

[50] Baker, paras. 280-284, 303, 304, 306-307.

[51] *Ibid.* para. 280.

[52] Baker, paras. 381-384; *supra*, pp. 118-120.

Requiring such suspicion would be an additional indication of a move towards normalisation.[53] Section 13 of NIEPA 1978 (the constable's general power of arrest), thus amended, could usefully remain covering non-scheduled offences under the Act and such scheduled offences as are not arrestable under the Criminal Law Act (Northern Ireland) 1967.[54] Section 14, or something close to it, seems inevitable so long as troops are actively deployed in the Province, although careful consideration ought to be given to their acting under RUC direction during policing operations; troops are in Ulster for relatively short periods, the police provide the element of continuity and expertise.[55] Baker proposed a power to arrest someone

> "whom [the soldier] reasonably suspects of being a terrorist or a member of a proscribed organisation or of committing, having committed or being about to commit any act of terrorism, or violence or of rioting or of an offence involving the use of an explosive substance or firearms, or of making or possessing a petrol bomb."[56]

It could not be limited to scheduled offences; such a concept was too complex for ordinary soldiers.[57] He suggested that a requirement of more informative "plain language" reasons for the arrest be considered (*e.g.* "you were throwing a petrol bomb"),[58] a welcome move given the SACHR's doubts about the force of the Diplock arguments on the giving of reasons, particularly in the current climate.[59] Baker thought that the power should further emphasise that the person be handed over to the RUC as soon as possible, and at the latest after four hours, or else released.[60] Such a reformulation might open up this arrest power to more far-reaching judicial scrutiny,[61] if it were challenged by aggrieved

[53] SACHR, *Annual Report for 1979-80*, H.C. 143 (1980-81), paras. 6-7.

[54] Baker, paras. 302-304.

[55] CAJ, Baker Submission, para. 31.

[56] Baker, para. 348.

[57] *Ibid.*; such a proposal was made by the Alliance Party (Baker Submission, para. 28).

[58] Baker, paras. 350-351.

[59] SACHR, *Annual Report for 1979-80*, H.C. 143 (1980-81), para. 7.

[60] Baker, paras. 353-354.

[61] Baker, para. 280. The reformulation provides an objective rather than subjective standard (*supra*, pp. 54-63, 68-71).

individuals. That it does not require reasonable suspicion of a specific criminal offence, but of something vaguer, may inhibit any such challenge.

There can be little doubt that in the straitened circumstances of policing in the Province, there is need for some power of arrest and extended detention enabling the police to question suspects at the police station. Little admissible evidence, other than that procured through interrogation, is likely to be forthcoming given the problems posed in Northern Ireland to gathering evidence through normal policing methods (*supra*, pp. 100-101). Baker proposed the enactment of a single special police power of arrest and extended detention combining features of section 11 of NIEPA 1978 and section 12 of the PTA 1984, which ought at least to avoid the confusion generated by a multiplicity of similar powers.[62] Several issues require further exploration in the light of his proposal.

The first issue is what should be the scope of the arrest power, of what should a person be reasonably suspected to justify his arrest? Some suggest that it should be of a specific scheduled offence.[63] This would certainly harmonise with the policy of criminalisation and that underlying normal powers' interference with personal liberty. "It would strengthen safeguards against the abuse of powers and bring the law more into harmony with the spirit if not the letter of Article 5 of the European Convention on Human Rights."[64]

Baker rejected this option apparently because (a) section 12 of the PTA is vital for the RUC and the power was about to be re-approved by Parliament in the Prevention of Terrorism Bill, and (b) it does not go far enough, but articulated no further reasons.[65] Presumably he desires the police to be able to operate on less specific information received than would constitute reasonable suspicion of a specific offence (itself much lower than a prima facie case based on admissible evidence)[66] on the basis "better safe than sorry"; given the possible consequences of terrorist action, the police must be able to arrest suspects on a

[62] Para. 304.

[63] Para. 302 (Dr. T. Hadden and the SACHR).

[64] SACHR, *Annual Report for 1982-83*, H.C. 262 (1983-84), p. 9. Although advanced in the context of a submission to the Home Secretary on PTA, s.12 the point is equally applicable here.

[65] Baker, paras. 299, 302.

[66] *Ibid.* para. 280.

relatively low level of information if only to check its reliability. He recommended that a new power of arrest without warrant should cover

> "a person whom the constable has reasonable grounds for suspecting to be:
> (i) a person who is or has been concerned in the commission, preparation or instigation of acts of terrorism or of directing, organising or training persons for the purpose of such acts;
> (ii) a person who is or professes to be a member of a proscribed organisation;
> (iii) a person who is guilty of any other offence under the present section [21 of NIEPA 1978];
> (iv) a person guilty of an offence under section 9 or 10 (and possibly 11) of the PTA."[67]

He left for consideration whether it should cover the arrest of someone subject to an exclusion order.[68]

To obviate the alienating over-use of such powers he suggested "that the RUC be told to arrest only after they have checked and double-checked [presumably in the context of existing intelligence] the reasonable suspicion that the person is or has been concerned in acts of terrorism, and that all ranks are made aware that alienation arises particularly from arresting then having to release."[69] The reformulated power represents such little change in the legal position that one cannot expect much change in practice, and further consideration ought to be given to requiring reasonable suspicion of a specific scheduled offence or at the very least that the reasonable suspicion required be such as to link the suspect with specific terrorist incidents.[70] Neither is likely to unduly hinder the police but might serve to reduce over-zealous use of the power.

The second issue concerns the length of detention after arrest. All the official reports endorse the view that adequate time is needed to interview the suspect, to enable forensic enquiries to be carried out, alibis to be verified, and information checked against existing intelligence (*supra*, pp. 124-125). Extended detention may,

[67] *Ibid.* para. 305.
[68] *Ibid.*
[69] *Ibid.* para. 292.
[70] D. Bonner, "Combating Terrorism: the Jellicoe Approach" [1983] P.L. 224, at. p. 227.

however, have adverse effects on the individual and his family (*e.g.* with respect to employment), and may enhance the risk of false confessions.[71] Lord Jellicoe noted that most initial admissions come within the first 48 hours but occasionally more time was needed, *e.g.* to confront the suspect with a "supergrass."[72] Gardiner thought a maximum 72 hours was about right.[73] The SACHR, in view of the Police and Criminal Evidence Act, question whether more than four days can be justified.[74] Flexibility within a maximum period is needed, and adequate safeguards should be provided, in addition to important internal scrutiny by the police themselves (as under the Police and Criminal Evidence Act),[75] to ensure that persons are not detained for longer than necessary. The Baker proposal—48 hours in right of the arrest extendible up to a further five days by the Secretary of State for Northern Ireland or a junior minister in the Northern Ireland Office[76] —gives the requisite flexibility, but articulates no criteria to govern extensions of detention. The SACHR consider it "reasonable to suggest that such authorisation should only be given where there are reasonable grounds for believing that the suspect may be guilty of a specific and serious terrorist-type offence."[77] An alternative would be a presumption (becoming heavier as time goes on) that further extensions would only be granted if the information being obtained linked the suspect with a specific criminal offence. The legislation, moreover, should only authorise extensions for no more than 24 hours at a time up to the maximum five days.

The Baker proposal is also deficient with regard to the third issue: the provision of adequate, independent safeguards against abuse. It would be preferable to place authorisation of extensions in the hands of a High Court judge, with some opportunity for representation of the individual's interest through an *in camera* inquisitorial rather than adversarial process to protect witnesses and intelligence operatives from prejudicial revelation.[78] It may

[71] Baker, para. 276.

[72] Jellicoe, paras, 59, 63. *Cf.* Boyle, Hadden and Hillyard, *op. cit.* n. 12, pp. 45-46, raising doubts about the need to hold suspects as long as three days, given that most defendants made their first statement after less than six hours' interrogation.

[73] Gardiner, para. 91.

[74] SACHR, *Annual Report for 1982-83*, H.C. 262 (1983-84), pp. 9-10, 17.

[75] ss.33-40 of the PCEA 1984.

[76] Baker, paras. 273, 279, 305.

[77] *Annual Report for 1982-83*, H.C. 262 (1983-84), p. 10.

[78] SACHR, *ibid.* Bonner, *loc. cit.* n. 70, at pp. 228-229.

be conceded that the ministerial check under section 12 of the PTA is no rubber-stamp and that police officers are unlikely to try to deliberately mislead their superiors or the Secretary of State.[79] The latter's independence and availability to give personal consideration to each individual case might, however, be questioned. The proposed judicial scrutiny could provide better decision-making in terms of independent scrutiny of the evidence, possibly enhanced availability of a senior decision-maker (habeas corpus applications can be made to a judge at home), arguably greater protection for the suspect, and a closer approximation to the regime of magisterial scrutiny embodied in the Police and Criminal Evidence Act 1984. It is difficult to accept that "the decision whether to extend detention depends upon criteria which are not susceptible of judicial assessment."[80] Much the same types of question are likely to arise as under that regime of magisterial scrutiny. In principle emergency powers should only be invoked in individual cases where necessary. The directions to that effect in circulars from central government to the police, as recommended by Lord Jellicoe, are welcome.[81] That ordinary powers would have sufficed ought also to be a factor that the judge authorising extension should take into account and to provide grounds for an action in false imprisonment as further means of inducing police compliance.

It is imperative given the heavy reliance on the accused's statements as evidence against him, the history of abuse in this sphere in Northern Ireland and the drastic effects this has had on community confidence in the security forces, that the interrogation process be, and be clearly seen to be, well regulated. The Bennett recommendations and their implementation (*supra*, pp. 121-122) are a step in the right direction. Baker's proposed clarificatory and codificatory redraft of section 8 of NIEPA 1978 (*infra*, pp. 146-147) is an improvement. Consideration ought to be given to drafting a detailed code on interrogation and treatment of suspects[82] and to determining exactly which sanctions–tortious

[79] Baker, para. 271.

[80] Jellicoe, para. 70.

[81] *Ibid.* para. 68. Those recommendations were accepted by the Government (Mr. W. Whitelaw, MP, Home Secretary, H.C. Deb., Vol. 38, col. 569). Mr. D. Waddington, MP, Minister of State at the Home Office informed the House of Commons' Standing Committee on the Prevention of Terrorism Bill 1983 that the requisite circulars had been issued (*Official Report*, Standing Committee D (1983-84), col. 242).

[82] A model, backed up by an absolute exclusionary rule, has been drafted by Boyle, Hadden and Hillyard, *op. cit*, n. 12, App. pp. 110-113.

(statutory torts with set minimum levels of damages), criminal, internal disciplinary, or absolute or flexible exclusionary evidence rule—should apply to each specific provision (*infra*, pp. 146-148).

7. *Bail and Committal Proceedings*

Unless his offence is tried summarily or certified as suitable for it, any person 14 or over, other than a member of the regular Armed Forces, who is charged with a scheduled offence can only be admitted to bail by a judge of the Supreme Court or by the trial judge on adjourning the trial. The process is centralised in Belfast. Legal aid is available for the application (s.3). The Diplock Commission had considered that bail was too readily granted by magistrates.[83] There appears to be a presumption that bail is not to be granted unless certain conditions, more restrictive than those in the Bail Act 1976 (not applicable to the Province), are satisfied. Section 2(2) of NIEPA 1978 provides that

> "A judge shall not admit . . . to bail unless he is satisfied that the applicant—
> (*a*) will comply with the conditions on which he is admitted to bail; and
> (*b*) will not interfere with any witness; and
> (*c*) will not commit any offence while he is on bail."

Some 40 per cent. of adult and 65 per cent. of juvenile bail applications in scheduled cases are granted.[84] Some make no application on advice that it would be pointless in their case.[85] A judge granting bail may, without prejudice to the imposition of conditions under other powers, impose such conditions on a person's bail as seem likely to ensure his appearance when required or otherwise necessary in the interests of justice or to prevent crime. A common condition is regular reporting to a police station.[86] Baker opined that the judiciary have interpreted section 2 "liberally and sensibly."[87]

[83] Diplock, paras. 51-57.

[84] Baker, paras. 72-76, App. G(1)-(4). Figures in Boyle, Hadden and Hillyard, *op. cit.* n. 12, p. 66 reveal a 37 per cent. success rate (August 1973 to December 1979). Walsh's research (*The Use and Abuse of Emergency Legislation in Northern Ireland* (1983), pp. 82-85) showed a 36 per cent. success rate.

[85] Boyle, Hadden and Hillyard, *op. cit.*, n. 12, p. 66.

[86] Boyle, annotations to NIEPA 1978 in *Current Law Statutes Annotated*, note to s.2(2), (3).

[87] Baker, para. 75.

Serving members of the regular Armed forces are not subject to this regime (s.2(5)), the nature of those forces being such as to enable the accused's secure custody pending trial.[88] That the exemption does not extend to other members of the security forces, so that they are subject to a system perceived as designed for terrorists, has proved a bone of contention. Baker endorsed such an extension to the RUC and its Reserve.[89] The wide scope of the scheduled offence concept also gives rise to problems. Until an offence (*e.g.* an assault causing grievous bodily harm in a pub brawl) is descheduled, it must proceed in the system for scheduled offences, giving rise to resentment that ordinary crimes are, for a short period at least, being dealt with in a terrorist process. An increase in the power to certify out will not solve this. Centralisation in Belfast with concomitant delays, and delays in release pending the processing of successful applicants were mentioned to the author by practising lawyers as other irritants. A welcome reform would be to extend the Bail Act 1976 to the Province and return the power to grant bail in all cases to magistrates, who are legally qualified in Northern Ireland, and already deal with scheduled offences through the committal process.[90] Baker rejected a change in decision-maker,[91] but was much in favour of a change in criteria. He proposed for discussion a formulation on these lines:

> "There shall be a presumption in favour of bail. A judge may admit any such person to bail but need not do so if he is satisfied that the applicant:
>
> (*a*) may fail to surrender to custody; or
> (*b*) may not comply with all or any conditions on which he is admitted to bail; or
> (*c*) may commit an offence when on bail; or
> (*d*) may interfere with any witness or anyone related to or associated with a witness; or
> (*e*) may obstruct or attempt to obstruct the course of justice.
>
> In exercising his discretion the judge shall have regard to all the circumstances of the case including:

[88] Gardiner, para. 37.

[89] Baker, para. 67.

[90] Boyle, Hadden and Hillyard, *op. cit.*, n. 12, at p. 67. The Alliance Party Baker Submission recommends such a change in criteria but not decision-maker (para. 13). The SACHR called for amendment of the conditions to increase the numbers admitted to bail (H.C. 262 (1983-84), p. 19, para. 33).

[91] Baker, para. 73.

(1) the nature and seriousness of the offence charged;
(2) the character, antecedents, associations and community ties of the defendant;
(3) the nature of the evidence;
(4) the time spent or likely to be spent in custody if bail is refused."[92]

Greater decentralisation of court business and a radical reformulation of the notion of scheduled offence could do much to ease the position. There seems no reason to suppose that the bail process as such is incompatible with the European Convention on Human Rights.

Committal proceedings for scheduled offences take place before a Resident Magistrate. Where the prosecution requests him to proceed by way of preliminary enquiry (written evidence only) rather than preliminary investigation (the equivalent of full oral committal proceedings in England and Wales) he must grant that request, even if the accused objects, unless he considers that the interests of justice require the latter proceedings (s.1(1)). Most cases proceed on the former basis, limiting but not wholly precluding the possibility of cross-examination of prosecution witnesses, given that another statute permits the defence to require a prosecution witness to give oral evidence.[93] Some concern has been expressed about this limitation on preliminary investigation. Since the trial judge, who sits alone, reads the committal papers it may involve otherwise inadmissible evidence being brought to the notice of the arbiter of fact.[94] Recently, the Lord Chief Justice has instituted a pre-trial review where another judge reads the committal papers, to obviate this danger.[95] Preliminary investigation tends to be permitted where identification evidence is in issue.[96] Fearful of pressure to withdraw evidence being exerted on "supergrasses" by relatives in the public gallery at committal proceedings, the Crown has in some cases bypassed the proceedings using the voluntary bill of indictment procedure, a practice which has been roundly criticised for depriving the defence of an early opportunity to test the credibility of the

[92] *Ibid.* para. 81. He thought the ultimate aim should be to have the same provisions as in the Bail Act 1976 but doubted its acceptability in Northern Ireland *at present* (para. 80).

[93] Boyle, *op. cit.* n. 86, note to s.1(1).

[94] *Ibid. Cf.* Walsh, *op. cit.* n. 84, pp. 86-87.

[95] Baker, para. 54.

[96] Walsh, *op. cit.* n. 84, p. 85.

witness and to seek, by having the case rejected at the preliminary stage, an earlier release.[97] Baker thought that the practice should be discouraged and employed in a scheduled case solely by the Attorney General.[98]

Concern has also been expressed about the length of time spent on remand in custody pending trial. Some see it as a form of executive detention without trial,[99] a view rejected by the SACHR which felt delays reflected genuine logistical, court and manpower difficulties.[1] In October 1977, the average period on remand was 45 weeks, two-thirds of which elapsed before committal.[2] By October 1983, it was 25.3 weeks, but the numbers in custody for over 46 weeks rose sharply in some months in that year.[3] Such delays are unlikely to violate the right to trial within a reasonable time enshrined in Article 5(3) of the European Convention on Human Rights.[4] To ease the position, Baker proposed a power to hold trials outside Belfast, and that any person held in custody for twelve months or more without committal must be granted bail without surety.[5]

8. *Mode and Conduct of Trial on Indictment of Scheduled Offences*

(1) *The present system*

These trials are centralised at Belfast Crown Court before a single judge sitting without a jury but clothed with its powers and duties (ss.6, 7). A reasoned judgment must be given for conviction (s.7(5)). A person convicted may appeal without leave to the Court of Appeal on any ground against conviction or sentence (except a sentence fixed by law) (s.7(6)). The grounds of appeal

[97] The procedure is provided for in s.2 of the Grand Jury (Abolition) Act (Northern Ireland) 1969 and Sched. 5 to the Judicature (Northern Ireland) Act 1978: see J.D. Jackson, *Northern Ireland Supplement to Cross on Evidence* (*Fifth Edition*) (1983), p. 53. For criticism see Alliance Party Baker Submission, para. 24(d); Walsh, *op. cit.* n. 84, pp. 88-90; SACHR, H.C. 262 (1983-84), pp. 19-21, 32-35.

[98] Baker, para. 59.

[99] Walsh, *op. cit.* n. 84, p. 85.

[1] *Annual Report for 1979-80, H.C. 143 (1980-81), para. 11.*

[2] *Ibid.*

[3] Baker, para. 176.

[4] See, generally, Jacobs, *op. cit.* n. 30, at pp. 68-71. Delays in Continental criminal procedure can be very lengthy.

[5] Baker, paras. 181, 185.

remain unchanged by NIEPA 1978.[6]

The Diplock Commission considered jury trial unsuitable for such offences during the emergency because of fear of intimidation of jurors and the danger of partisan verdicts.[7] Evidence of intimidation cited related largely to that of witnesses,[8] but fear of it extended to jurors: "a frightened juror is a bad juror even though his own safety and that of his family may not be at risk."[9] Its effects could not adequately be met by using the prosecution's right to challenge so as to exclude jurors from areas where intimidation was likely; such challenge merely enhanced the already strong Protestant representation on juries, and Loyalist violence, with threat of accompanying intimidation, was increasing.[10] While the judge could avert the danger of a perverse conviction by removing the case from the jury, there was no similar safeguard against perverse acquittal.[11] In the debates on NIEPA 1973, the Attorney General referred to a number of such acquittals of members of Loyalist organisations.[12] The Commission concluded:

> "The jury system as a means for trying terrorist crime is under strain. It may not yet have broken down, but we think that the time is already ripe to forestall its doing so."[13]

Baker accepted that jurors would be in greater danger now than ever before.[14]

Trial by a single judge has been thought by all three official reviews of the Northern Ireland powers to be preferable to collegiate trial. Diplock and Gardiner noted that non-jury civil actions are so tried; oral adversarial procedure was thought ill adapted to collegiate trial of fact; in criminal proceedings instant decisions had to be made on admissibility of evidence and other

6 They are to be found in the Criminal Appeal (Northern Ireland) Act 1980, ss.2(1), 3, 6.

7 Diplock, paras. 36-37.

8 Diplock, para. 17, and see Baker, para. 99. For criticism see W.L. Twining, "Emergency Powers and Criminal Process: The Diplock Report" [1973] Crim.L.R. 406. Arguably, insufficient evidence was cited in Diplock.

9 Diplock, para. 36.

10 *Ibid.*

11 Diplock, para. 37.

12 *Official Report*, Standing Committee B, Vol. 2 (1972-73), cols. 70-71 (Att. Gen. Rawlinson).

13 Diplock, para. 37.

14 Baker, para. 107.

matters of procedure, and, if these had to be made after consultation with colleagues, "it would gravely inconvenience the progress of the trial and diminish the value of oral examination and cross-examination as a means of eliciting the truth."[15] Baker doubted the force of these arguments other than that on delays.[16] All three agreed, however, that collegiate trial would be problematic given limited judicial manpower and the small senior bar in Northern Ireland.[17]

In a context in which intimidation of winesses is a reality and normal policing difficult, the prosecution must inevitably rely heavily on testimony from security forces' members, who can be adequately protected, on physical evidence and on the admissible statements of the accused.[18] Several devices in varying combination might be contemplated to enable increased use of civilian testimony at trial: *in camera* trials, with press, public, the accused and/or his lawyer excluded, during the witness' testimony; an anonymous witness screened from view, his voice distorted by a scrambler mechanism; the increased use of written statements by unidentified witnesses who will not appear in court; a relaxation of the hearsay rule. Some of these processes are employed in "security" trials in Malaysia.[19] Their use in Northern Ireland has been thought inappropriate; Diplock and Gardiner accepted the right to cross-examination, enshrined in Article 6 of the European Convention on Human Rights, as a minimum requirement of a fair judicial process.[20] Neither, therefore considered the modifications that Article 15 of the Convention might permit to that right (*infra*, pp. 156-158). On this view, at the very least the defendant's lawyer would have to be present. Anonymity and other protective mechanisms would reduce his opportunity of testing credibility. Proper evaluation of the probative value of written statements demanded knowledge of matters which would identify their makers. In any event, witnesses would still have an understandable fear of coming to court, might doubt the adequacy of protection offered, and would not believe that the defendant's lawyer would not pass on to him,

15 Diplock, para. 39; Gardiner, para. 31.

16 Baker, para. 114.

17 Diplock, para. 39; Gardiner, para. 31; Baker, paras. 114-118. The number of Q.C.s is to be increased: *The Sunday Times*, December 2, 1984, p. 3.

18 Diplock, para. 17.

19 "The Grim Final Judgment . . . " (1983) 2 *Amnesty* (The Journal of the British Section of Amnesty International) 31, at pp. 31-32.

20 Diplock, paras. 12-16.

as might be his duty, details of the evidence given which might of itself be enough to make the witness known to the defendant with all the dangers that might entail to the witness.[21] The use of such devices in Commissioners' hearings under the system of detention without trial (*infra*, pp. 152-155), may have helped bring the processes of law into disrepute.[22]

The Diplock Commission did recommend a number of changes in the conduct of the trial to reduce the risk of acquittal of significant numbers of persons guilty of terrorist crimes.[23] Two remain in NIEPA 1978.[24] The first affects the onus of proof in relation to certain offences of possession of firearms, imitation firearms, ammunition, explosives and petrol bombs. These were often found in circumstances involving groups of people on premises or in vehicles, where it was not possible to prove beyond reasonable doubt which person had the knowledge of the article required to ground possession.[25] Section 9(1) now provides:

> "Where a person is charged with possessing [one or more of the above articles] in such circumstances as to constitute an offence to which this section applies and it is proved that at the time of the alleged offence–
> (*a*) he and that article were both present in any premises; or
> (*b*) the article was in premises of which he was the occupier or which he habitually used otherwise than as a member of the public,
> the court may accept the fact proved as sufficient evidence of his possessing (and, if relevant, knowingly possessing) that article at that time unless it is further proved that he did not at that time know of its presence in the premises in question, or, if he did know, that he had no control over it."

[21] Diplock, para. 20.

[22] Gardiner, para. 153.

[23] Diplock, paras. 58-100.

[24] The third, permitting the admission of certain written statements of certain witnesses unable to come to court to give evidence (paras. 93-100), was enshrined in s.5 of NIEPA 1973. It was repealed, on the recommendation of the Gardiner Committee, because the accused had no opportunity to test it through cross-examination and "the accuracy and quality of the statement might, depending on the circumstances in which it was taken and the character and intelligence of those concerned in making it, be open to grave doubt." (para. 43). "It contribut[ed] nothing sufficient to override [those] objections to its use." (para. 44).

[25] Diplock, paras. 61-72; Gardiner, para. 53; Baker, para. 202.

This applies as much to vessels, aircraft and vehicles as to premises (s.9(2)). The defendant, however, does not have the onus of proof of innocence. The burden of establishing guilt remains with the prosecution, and the judge must satisfy himself that the accused's guilt has been established beyond reasonable doubt. The judge *may* apply the section to decide whether it has.[26] Section 9 "is really a procedural device for ascertaining the truth by forcing, in some but not by any means all cases, the accused to say on oath [and subject to cross-examination] that he had no knowledge."[27] Some cases resulted in acquittals without the defendant having to enter the witness-box.[28] In the seven months after its introduction in NIEPA 1973, the defence of "no knowledge" or "knowledge but no control" was more readily accepted in relation to houses than vehicles. In a number of joint possession cases, one defendant would accept responsibility in order that the others might go free.[29]

The second change applies to all scheduled offences, and is concerned with making more readily admissible at trial inculpatory statements made by the accused during the extended interrogation envisaged by the legislation. In a number of cases, the Northern Ireland courts had excluded statements obtained during such interrogation on the broad basis that they had been obtained through oppression since they had been gathered as a result of an interrogation set up, officially organised and designed to get information from those who would otherwise have been less willing to give it.[30] As the Diplock Commission saw it, the fruits of effective but not cruel and degrading questioning, so vital to the drive to protect lives and property, thus barred from the criminal trial, were left to be used in the less satisfactory process of detention without trial.[31] There was, therefore, a need to suspend for scheduled offences the existing "technical" rules, practices and judicial discretions as to the admissibility of confessions so as to render admissible the products of legitimate extended

[26] Gardiner, para. 52; Boyle, *op. cit.* n. 86, note to s.9; Jackson, *op. cit.* n. 97, at pp. 25-26.

[27] Baker, para. 207.

[28] Baker, para. 213.

[29] K. Boyle, T. Hadden and P. Hillyard, *Law and State: The Case of Northern Ireland*, p. 100.

[30] Diplock, para. 83. The leading case was *R.* v. *Flynn and Leonard* [1972] N.I.J.B. (May). D.S. Greer, "Admissibility of Confessions and the Common Law in Times of Emergency" (1973) 24 N.I.L.Q. 199.

[31] Diplock, paras. 84-85.

interrogation but to keep out, so as to leave unsullied the reputation of the courts, statements obtained by means that flouted accepted standards such as Article 3 of the European Convention on Human Rights.[32] Section 8 of NIEPA 1978 is the salient provision. It permits the prosecution to give in evidence a statement made by the accused insofar as it is relevant to any matter at issue in the proceedings (s.8(1)). The trial judge must, however, exclude it where

> "prima facie evidence is adduced that the accused was subjected to torture or to inhuman or degrading treatment in order to induce him to make the statement . . . unless the prosecution satisfies [him] that the statement was not so obtained." (s.8(2)(*a*))

Similarly where such a statement has already been received in evidence, he must either proceed with the trial disregarding the statement (so far as is humanly possible!) or direct that it be restarted before another judge before whom the statement shall be inadmissible (s.8(2)(*b*)). Despite Diplock's recommendation that judicial discretions be suspended, it has been held, contrasting the permissive "may be given in evidence" in section 8(1) with the obligatory "shall be excluded" in section 8(2),[33] that there remains a general judicial discretion to exclude statements which would not fall foul of section 8.[34] This view was endorsed by the Gardiner Committee which recommended its clear statutory recognition.[35] This, unfortunately, was not forthcoming. Baker has repeated the call.[36]

Section 8, like Article 3, regulates admissibility by reference to improper conduct rather than reliability.[37] In interpreting "torture, inhuman or degrading treatment" the judiciary have been guided by definitions of those terms advanced by the Convention organs in interpreting Article 3. As a result it may not be crystal clear that all forms of physical maltreatment are outlawed. In *R.* v. *McCormick and Others*, the trial judge (McGonigal L.J.) concluded that the test

[32] Diplock, paras. 87-92.

[33] Baker, para. 194.

[34] Jackson, *op. cit.* n. 97, pp. 151-155; D.S. Greer, "The Admissibility of Confessions Under The Northern Ireland (Emergency Provisions) Act" (1980) 31 N.I.L.Q. 205, at pp. 217-228; Baker, paras. 194-200.

[35] Gardiner, para. 50.

[36] Baker, para. 196.

[37] Greer, *loc. cit.* n. 34 at p. 211.

"leaves it open to an interviewer to use a moderate degree of physical maltreatment for the purpose of inducing a person to make a statement."[38]

Doubt has been cast on this view by the Northern Ireland Court of Appeal.[39] In any event, the general judicial discretion could be prayed in aid to exclude such evidence.[40] Professor Greer and Baker are of the view that the judiciary have clearly set their faces against the use of violence to extract a statement.[41] It is less clear how far threats of violence to the accused or his loved ones is covered. The definition of degrading, "driving the individual to act against his will and conscience," leaves "the precise extent to which section 8 permits psychological pressure to be applied to a suspect . . . as yet uncertain and unclear."[42] The prohibited treatment must have been employed to induce the accused to make the statement and in fact cause him to make it.[43] Section 8 does not operate to exclude other evidence obtained as a result of an inadmissible statement.[44]

The scope of the available judicial discretion has been left undefined, but cannot be so wide as to permit a *de facto* return to the pre-NIEPA 1973 position.[45] It could provide a vehicle for exclusion of statements obtained in breach of the Judges Rules or pertinent RUC Force Orders. Probably a breach in conjunction with some other maltreatment would be required.[46]

The defence must adduce prima facie evidence of treatment prohibited by section 8, or which calls in issue the judicial discretion to exclude, used to induce the accused to make a statement. In practice this means that the defendant says he was subjected to such treatment.[47] It then is up to the prosecution to establish beyond reasonable doubt: that he made the statement and that it was not obtained through torture, inhuman or degrading

[38] [1977] N.I. 105, at p. 111.

[39] *R.* v. *O'Halloran* [1979] 2 N.I.J.B. (C.A.).

[40] *Per* McGonigal L.J., [1977] N.I. 105, at p. 114.

[41] Greer, *loc. cit.* n. 34, at p. 213; Baker, para. 193.

[42] Greer, at p. 215.

[43] Greer, at pp. 215-217.

[44] Greer, at p. 217.

[45] *Per* McGonigal L.J. [1977] N.I. 105, at p. 114.

[46] Greer, *loc. cit.* n. 34, at p. 225. A mere breach of the "Bennett" rules does not amount to torture, inhuman or degrading treatment; *R.* v. *Culbert* [1982] N.I.L.R. 90.

[47] Baker, para. 191.

treatment or through other means sufficient to justify exercise of the exclusionary discretion. If the statement is admitted, the trial judge will have to decide what weight (if any) to give it.[48]

In appearance, apart from the absence of the jury, Diplock trials do not differ radically from their mainland counterparts. The court conditions themselves, however, are not of the best, particularly as regards space and acoustics.[49] The majority of defendants plead guilty (79 per cent. in 1979).[50] On average the trials themselves are speedy. The process has worked without sectarian discrimination.[51] The conviction rate in contested cases is high (60 to 70 per cent. since 1976).[52] The trials are heavily reliant on the accused's statement as the only or main evidence against him. Boyle, Hadden and Hillyard's survey of Diplock trials January-April 1979 revealed that 56 per cent. of cases relied solely on his statement while in 30 per cent. of cases it was supplemented by other evidence which, while pointing to his guilt, would often not have been enough to justify a conviction on its own.[53] That pattern applied also to the first three months of 1981.[54] By contrast Baldwin and McConville in a study carried out in London and Birmingham, discovered that in only about one-fifth of the cases would the prosecution case have been fatally weakened if the accused's statement had not been taken into account.[55] Although challenge to the admissibility of a statement is common in contested Diplock trials, few statements are excluded.[56] Of those that were excluded, about 40 to 45 per cent.

[48] Greer, *loc. cit.* n. 34, at pp. 231-233, 237.

[49] A personal observation from a visit in April 1983. For a description of a trial see T. Hadden and S. Wright, "A terrorist trial in Crumlin Road" *New Society*, June 28, 1979.

[50] K. Boyle, T. Hadden and P. Hillyard, *Ten Years On In Northern Ireland: The legal control of political violence* (1980), pp. 60, 70.

[51] *Ibid.* p. 86, but *cf.* Walsh, *op. cit.* n. 84, pp. 102-104 who noted some indication that Catholics were treated more harshly as regards charge and sentence. His sample was such, however, that definite conclusions could not be made.

[52] Boyle, Hadden and Hillyard, *op. cit.* n. 50 p. 61; Walsh, *op. cit.* n. 84, p. 94.

[53] Boyle, Hadden and Hillyard, *op. cit.* n. 50 p. 44. *Cf.* Bennett, para. 30: "We were informed by the [DPP] that in 75-80% of these cases [January 1–June 30, 1978] the prosecution case depended wholly or mainly on the confession of the accused."

[54] D. Walsh, "The Diplock Process in Northern Ireland Today" in (C.A.J. pamphlet No. 2), *Emergency Laws in Northern Ireland: The proceedings of a conference held in Belfast on 24 April 1982* 6, at p. 9.

[55] J. Baldwin and M. McConville, *Confessions in Crown Court Trials* (RCCP, Research Study No. 5, 1980), pp. 30-32, 35.

[56] Greer, *loc. cit.* n. 34, at pp. 232-233; Baker, para. 198.

were rejected by means of the judicial discretion.[57] A declining acquittal rate in contested cases, much lower than in jury trials in Northern Ireland or Great Britain, led to the suggestion "that judges may have become case-hardened and are thus no longer in a position to give to the defendant the full benefit of his right to acquittal in any case where the prosecution has not proved its case beyond a reasonable doubt,"[58] a conclusion which, allied to the heavy dependence on confession evidence in a context of proven maltreatment of suspects in the past, "can only increase the general concern that the risk of innocent persons being convicted in Diplock courts is substantially greater than in jury trials."[59] On the other hand, that declining rate might have been attributable to better preparation of cases by the prosecution.[60] Baker, noting an increased acquittal rate, was sceptical about the existence of case-hardening in the Northern Ireland judiciary and stressed their independence, stating that they were very careful never to assist the Crown or to take over the prosecution.[61] Moreover, it should be noted that, in trials in England dependent on confessions, Baldwin and McConville's research reveals a not dissimilar acquittal rate.[62]

Writing in 1980, Boyle, Hadden and Hillyard noted that use of witnesses from outside of the interrogation process was limited:

> "There are rarely any witnesses whose evidence relates directly to the guilt or innocence of the defendant. Most are called only to establish that the particular shooting or bombing or other incident actually took place. Such witnesses, whether civilian or members of the security forces, are merely taken through their depositions in a routine manner."[63]

Latterly, however, increased reliance has been placed on the evidence of "converted terrorists" or "supergrasses" to point directly to the guilt of the accused in multi-defendant trials.[64]

57 Baker, para. 198.

58 Boyle, Hadden and Hillyard, *op. cit.* n. 50, p. 80.

59 *Ibid.* p. 62.

60 *Ibid.* p. 61.

61 Baker, paras. 123-125.

62 *Op. cit.* n. 55, p. 19.

63 Boyle, Hadden and Hillyard, *op. cit.* n. 50, p. 59.

64 See Tony Gifford Q.C., *Supergrasses: The use of accomplice evidence in Northern Ireland* (1984); Paddy McGrory, "Time to Reappraise the Supergrass System" (December 1983-January 1984) 200 *Fortnight* 12-14.

These alleged accomplices to crime have turned Queen's Evidence (testified against their colleagues) in return for immunity from prosecution, or the prospect of favourable treatment in terms of earlier release under the prerogative, money, and the offer of a new life and job elsewhere. The use of their sometimes uncorroborated evidence resulted in the conviction of terrorist offences of a significant number of persons on both sides of the sectarian divide, although some convictions have since been quashed, and recent prosecutions on such evidence, less successful.[65] The process has been regarded by the RUC as a major breakthrough in the battle against terrorism, the use of "insider" evidence making possible the implication in crime of those in the higher echelons of the secretive, paramilitary groups, the terrorist "Godfathers," and throwing those groups into some disarray by breaking down the trust between members.[66] The Attorney General has noted that

> "where the evidence of an accomplice appears to be credible and cogent and relates to serious terrorist crime, there is an overriding public interest in having terrorist charges brought before the court. This is especially so where the evidence . . . relates to murder, robbery, explosions and other similar atrocious crimes."[67]

There are, however, moral and social problems in deals with self-confessed heinous criminals. The evidence is suspect because of the character of the witness and the advantage he gains from giving it. There must be a strong temptation to add names to his list at police behest. The use of accomplice evidence is no new phenomenon to the law.[68] Its use as a major plank in security policy probably is.[69] The law has traditionally attempted to deal with the problems of accomplice evidence by requiring the trial judge to warn the arbiter of fact—normally a sceptical jury but in Northern Ireland, himself—of the dangers of convicting on such

[65] McGrory, *loc. cit.* n. 64, at p. 14; Workers' Research Unit, *Supergrasses* Belfast Bulletin No. 11 (Summer 1984), pp. 20-21.

[66] *RUC, Chief Constable's Report 1982 Presented to the Police Authority for Northern Ireland* (1983) pp. xi-xii.

[67] H.C. Deb, Vol. 47, cols. *3-5* (written answer—Sir Michael Havers).

[68] Gifford, *op. cit.* n. 64 pp. 4-5.

[69] McGrory, *loc. cit.* n. 64, at p. 12.

testimony where uncorroborated.[70] On an administrative level, following judicial disapproval of complete supergrass immunity in the Court of Appeal, the granting of unconditional immunity was dropped in England and Wales. Instructions from the DPP now preclude cases being brought there on the uncorroborated testimony of supergrasses. Not so in the Province, although "the police and the DPP have now established a rule of thumb . . . that immunity will not be given to those murderers who actually carry out killings, as opposed to accomplices."[71] These officials exercise a sifting and checking role to establish the veracity of the evidence proffered. The decision to grant immunity is taken personally by the DPP (NI) and immunity relates only to those offences disclosed by the individual and of which he has given a truthful account. The DPP (NI) is aware of all the financial arrangements made for the person and his family, and these are now disclosed to the court and the defence. Some of the general criteria applied by the DPP (NI) in considering immunity are: whether it is better in the interests of justice to have the person as Crown witness rather than defendant; whether, in the interests of public safety and security, the obtaining of information about the extent and nature of criminal activities is such as to outweigh the benefits of conviction of the person; whether it is likely that the information could be obtained without a grant of immunity. The Attorney General, who exercises general supervision and direction of the process, is fully satisfied with the way in which decisions are made.[72] The use of such evidence, however, has further highlighted problems of public confidence in the Diplock system.[73]

[70] T. Hadden, "The High Price of the Supergrass Strategy" (May 1983) 194 *Fortnight* 9. On accomplices and corroboration, see *Cross on Evidence* (5th ed., 1979), pp. 196-203; Gifford, *op. cit.* n. 64, pp. 4-5.

[71] Beresford, "How the informer casts a shadow over justice in Ulster" *The Guardian*, July 29, 1983. Judicial disapproval was expressed in the so-called "Bertie Smalls" case: *R.* v. *Bryan James Turner* (1975) 61 Cr.App.R. 67 (C.A.); Gifford, *op. cit.* n. 64, pp. 6-8.

[72] All information on the role of these officials comes from H.C. Deb., Vol. 47, cols. *3-5* (written answer: Att. Gen. Sir Michael Havers). *Cf.* E. Graham, "A vital weapon in the anti-terrorist arsenal" (October 1983) 198 *Fortnight* 10.

[73] M. Holland, "Using tainted evidence" *New Statesman*, September 23, 1983, at pp. 8-9; Hadden, *loc. cit.* n. 70; S. Greer, "The Seeds of Another Bitter Harvest" (October 1983) 198 *Fortnight* 11; Workers' Research Unit, *loc. cit.* n. 65, *passim.*

(2) *Evidence, the court and the mode of trial: some proposals for reform*

Baker recognised "an underlying and widespread unease" about trial by judge alone.[74] In part, it reflects concern about "case-hardening," the controversial nature of the evidence used, and the fear that there is a greater risk of an innocent person being convicted than with jury trial, since his fate depends so much on the judgment, perceptions and attitude of one man.

Section 8 and the supplemental judicial discretion provide a too uncertain guide for action in the regulation of the interrogation process, which uncertainty would not be altogether reduced by Baker's largely declaratory redraft. This would make it clear: (a) that torture, inhuman or degrading treatment includes and always has included the use or threat of physical violence; (b) "that the court has a discretion to exclude or disregard any statement made by the accused or any other evidence, if it considers that to receive it would be unfair to the accused or the interests of justice so require"; and (c) that the court, having excluded or disregarded any statement under (a) or (b) may continue the trial or direct its restart before a different court before which that statement would be inadmissible.[75] The scope of the discretion is, however, left uncertain. Nor is it crystal clear whether threats of violence or prejudice to third parties connected with the accused are covered. Such uncertainty may, as Bennett noted,[76] tempt the interrogator to see what he can get away with. Section 8 and the accompanying discretion should be replaced by a detailed statutory code regulating the interrogation and treatment of suspects.[77] The prime role in enforcing this would, given its immediacy, lie with police supervision and internal discipline. Declaring breach of its provisions to be a statutory tort and providing set minimum levels of damages could also help. The code should, *inter alia*, outlaw the use or threat of violence to the suspect and/or his loved ones; provide detailed rules on the permissible times and duration of interrogation sessions and refreshment breaks; and make provision for access to the suspect by his doctor and relatives and

[74] Baker, para. 110.

[75] Baker, para. 200, App. J.

[76] Bennett, para. 84.

[77] *Cf.* Boyle, Hadden and Hillyard, *op. cit.* n. 50, pp. 50-52, 110-113. The Codes made under the PCEA 1984 would afford another model.

for his access to legal advice. Video and tape-recording of interviews should be introduced.[78] A requirement that a statement should only be admissible if the code were completely complied with and there was corroboratory evidence,[79] goes too far. An absolute exclusion rule should back up provisions on the use or threat of violence and on access, although there would have to be exceptions permitting denial of access in appropriate circumstances (*e.g.* because it might alert accomplices). There is room for a more flexible approach to other provisions (*e.g.* exceeding the permitted interrogation period) where it might be more appropriate to look to such factors as the seriousness of the breach, whether it was deliberate or accidental, whether there were extenuating circumstances, what effect it had on the suspect or on the reliability of his statement. Such flexible exclusion rules, with perhaps a presumption in favour of exclusion rather than inclusion, have been suggested for or feature in evidentiary laws elsewhere.[80] It seems unrealistic to insist on corroboration in every case, given the circumstances of policing in the Province. A flexible rule, to enable the court to look sceptically after due warning at the statement or to exclude it where not supported by other evidence where that evidence might have been obtainable had the police sought it, might encourage the search for corroboratory evidence. There is merit in the SACHR's suggestion that issues on the admissibility of statements be taken at an earlier separate *voire dire* before a judge other than the one who will try the case proper:

[78] Both Baker (paras. 308-319) and Jellicoe (para. 107) supported tape recording.

[79] Boyle, Hadden and Hillyard, *op. cit.* n. 50, pp. 50-52, 110-113.

[80] For example, Australian Law Reform Commission, *Criminal Investigation: Report No. 2. An Interim Report*, Australian Govt. Publishing Service, Canberra (1975), para. 298. Scots law is similar with respect to unlawfully obtained evidence (see L.H. Leigh, *Police Powers in England and Wales* (1975), pp. 159-160). The Canadian Charter of Rights and Freedoms, Pt. I of the Constitution Act 1982, set out as Sched. B to the Canada Act 1982 passed by the U.K. Parliament, enables a court to exclude evidence obtained in breach of the Charter "if it is established that, having regard to all the circumstances, the admission of it in the proceedings would bring the administration of justice into disrepute." The SACHR recommended publication of a statutory police code of conduct concerning the treatment of persons in custody under emergency legislation, breach of which would not result in the automatic exclusion of a confession from evidence. Only if the confession were obtained through torture, inhuman or degrading treatment or in consequence of other police misconduct tending to cast doubts on its reliability, should it be excluded (H.C. 262 (1983-84), p. 18).

> "it would allow an early decision as to whether interrogation practices had been legitimate. This would not only expose those who broke the rules, it would also expose false rumours, allegations and slurs. . . . [It] should also be possible to ensure that complaints about treatment in custody must either be raised at an early stage or not at all. If there were no complaints, a subsequent trial could proceed quickly. Certification as to the truth or falsity of the complaint of ill-treatment would be regarded as final. This might result in a re-allocation of judicial resources but not necessarily in an increased workload."[81]

It seems inappropriate to ban "supergrass" evidence altogether. Yet this would probably be the result in a significant number of cases of requiring corroboration of the same for conviction,[82] which requirement might otherwise be thought desirable since the accused has already lost the safeguard of a sceptical jury.[83] Baker stressed the importance as safeguards of an independent Northern Ireland judiciary, which has not accepted such evidence automatically or uncritically, and of the need to give reasons for conviction which can be (and have successfully been) attacked in the appellate court.[84] There should also be continuance of a careful prosecution policy, with no immunity for the most serious offences, and of the fullest possible disclosure, consonant with the accomplice's future security, to the judge and the defence of *all* the arrangements made with the accomplice, in order to promote

[81] *Annual Report for 1978-1979*, H.C. 433 (1979-80), para. 17.

[82] Graham, *loc. cit.* n. 72. McGrory, (*loc. cit.* n. 64, at p. 14) produced a table on supergrasses in Northern Ireland, 1980-Nov. 1983. Five trials had then been completed: 66 persons were convicted; 26 without corroboration.

[83] Gifford, *op. cit.* n. 64, pp. 35-36; McGrory, *loc. cit.* n. 64 at p. 14.

[84] Baker, paras. 169-170 noting Lord Lowry, C.J.'s judgment at trial in *R.* v. *Gibney* [1983] 13 N.I.J.B. (delivered October 26, 1983) in which he rejected Kevin McGrady's evidence against a number of defendants. See also A. Pollak, "The Strange Tale of the Collapsing Supergrass and his RUC Accomplices" (December 1983-January 1984) 200 *Fortnight* 10-11 noting the trial in which Gibson J. rejected the evidence of Jackie Grimley. The appeal of Charles McCormick was successful (noted in (February 1984) 201 *Fortnight* 17; [1984] 1 N.I.J.B.; [1984] 4 C.L. 217). In December 1984, Lord Lowry L.C.J. rejected Raymond Gilmour's evidence as "entirely unworthy of belief" and acquitted the 35 defendants while, in the same month, the Northern Ireland Court of Appeal quashed the 14 convictions obtained on the evidence of Joseph Bennett in April 1983 as unsafe and unsatisfactory, but re-affirmed the legality of using supergrass evidence. Is this "goodbye to the Supergrasses?" (see S. Greer and T. Jennings, January 1985, 212 *Fortnight*, 4).

effective testing of his credibility. Efforts should also be made to set a maximum number of defendants for each trial (Baker proposed 20) and to reduce delays in starting and in the length of supergrass trials.[85] It remains to be seen, however, how much longer use of supergrasses will remain as a significant part of security strategy.

Public concern might also be alleviated by making changes in the structure of the trial court itself. A return to jury trial was rightly rejected by Baker as unrealistic in view of intimidation and/or the fear of it.[86] Nor can one be sanguine about the prospects of non-partisan juries in a divided society. A single judge sitting with two lay assessors or resident magistrates, raised problems of selection and (especially with the former) problems of intimidation and protection. Baker was unconvinced that they would provide a better mode of trial.[87] The option of a multi-judge court—two or three judges, the former alternative requiring unanimity for conviction[88] —is more attractive. A three judge court was the model envisaged by the Prevention of Crime (Ireland) Act 1882, was deployed in colonial India, and is used to try terrorist cases in the Republic of Ireland.[89] Although trials by such a court might be longer, the prime argument in favour of a multi-judge court is that it would promote better decision-making in that one judge would have to justify his reactions and decisions in discussions with expert colleagues who had also seen the witnesses. This appears preferable to mere multi-judge scrutiny at appellate stage which, while useful, is flawed insofar as it does not embrace seeing the witness give his evidence and because of the further delay involved. Depleting the small senior bar in Northern Ireland is some obstacle to a plural court; "a two judge court would require three more judges, and three judge courts, six more."[90] Elevating county court judges or resident magistrates

[85] Baker, para. 172.

[86] Baker, paras. 107-108.

[87] Baker, paras. 127-129.

[88] A two judge court was the model favoured by the Alliance Party of Northern Ireland. The Democratic Unionists under Dr. Ian Paisley supported three judge courts (Baker, para. 112). So did the SACHR in their *post* Baker submissions to the Secretary of State. They further noted that if trial by judge alone remained, some requirement of corroboration, falling short of the present technical legal concept, ought to be introduced in supergrass cases (see SACHR, *Press Notice*, December 17, 1984, paras. 10-13).

[89] Baker, paras. 114-115. See also M. Robinson, *The Special Criminal Court* (1974).

[90] Baker, para. 117.

might provide further manpower. The importation of judicial manpower is another option. Indeed, Professor Twining suggested a model whereby emergency courts should positively *not* be composed of members of the extant judiciary, in order to preserve them from the attacks on their independence which might result from involvement with special procedures. He recommended special courts (multi-judge, or judge plus lay-assessors), independent of the executive, to try such cases as could not be dealt with by the ordinary courts. The special courts would approximate so far as possible to the procedures and powers of ordinary courts, for example, by only being able to convict for specific past offences and having no power to hand out sentences of indefinite duration. In these courts, "the extent of derogation from ordinary rules and procedures and from article 6 of the European Convention would be determined by the special court in the circumstances of each case."[91] Baker thought the importation of judicial manpower from Great Britain to try scheduled offences would cause "massive reaction by both Republicans and nationalists."[92] Perhaps imported judges could be used to try civil cases, freeing the extant judiciary to deal with scheduled cases. It is hoped, however, that the multi-judge court option will be re-examined most carefully, as maintaining public confidence in the court system is vital.

There remains a final issue: to which offences ought the Diplock system apply? It should be confined to those cases connected with the paramilitaries or security forces' action against them likely to result in intimidation of jurors, or the fear of it, and/or in the danger of partisan verdicts. One option, which would better emphasise the abnormality of the process, would be to require positive certification by the Attorney General that the case required Diplock trial ("certification-in").[93] Until he so certified the case would proceed in the ordinary judicial processes, thus alleviating one bail problem noted earlier (*supra*, pp. 106, 133). "Certification-in" would, no doubt be common, and require re-organisation of the Attorney General's workload, manpower and timetable of operation. Baker considered this impractical[94] and recommended extending the power to "certify-out" to a wider range of scheduled offences. On his proposal, as well as those

[91] Twining, *loc. cit.* n. 8 (quotation from p. 416).

[92] Baker, para. 118.

[93] Walsh, *The Use and Abuse of Emergency Legislation in Northern Ireland* (1983), p. 100.

[94] Baker, paras. 132, 145.

offences presently certifiable out, all scheduled offences carrying a maximum penalty of five years or less would be capable of being certified out. So would kidnapping and false imprisonment (which are sometimes offences of a domestic nature), robbery and aggravated burglary, and all scheduled offences under the Firearms (NI) Order 1981.[95] To reduce delays inherent in having to send cases to the Attorney General in London for certification approval, Baker proposed that the DPP (NI) also be given power to make such decisions, the way in which that power is to be exercised remaining subject to direction by the Attorney General.[96] Concerned lest his proposals be thought too radical, Baker also suggested that the trial judge have power to discharge the jury in cases of intimidation, harassment or of interference with its members amounting to interference with the course of justice. He could then continue the trial sitting alone, or direct it to be heard by another judge sitting without a jury.[97] Baker rejected as most undesirable (but without giving reasons) the provision of an independent check on certification decisions (leaving the case in the Diplock process) through a right of appeal to the courts.[98] It would be unusual to have such a direct check on a Law Officer's decision, but these are unusual powers.

9. *Executive or Non-Court-Oriented Processes*

(1) *Internment or detention without trial*

As President Nyerere of Tanzania has noted, such processes mean

> "that you are imprisoning a man when he has not broken any written law, when you cannot be sure of proving beyond reasonable doubt that he has done so. You are restricting his liberty, and making him suffer materially and spiritually, for what you think he intends to do, or is trying to do, or for what you believe he has done. Few things are more dangerous to the freedom of a society than that."[99]

[95] Baker, paras. 134, 135, 143, 144.

[96] Baker, paras. 145-150.

[97] Baker, para. 151.

[98] Baker, para. 139.

[99] Cited in T. M. Franck, *Comparative Constitutional Process: Cases and Materials: Fundamental Rights in the Common Law Nations* (1968) p. 231.

Internment and detention without trial have been deployed in both parts of Ireland at various times since 1916.[1] During the current emergency, three statute-based systems have authorised their use in the Province.

The Special Powers Acts and Regulations permitted detention (reg. 11) and internment (reg. 12) of persons suspected of acting or of having acted or of being about to act in a manner prejudicial to the preservation of the peace or the maintenance of order. The invocation of these powers on August 9, 1971, coupled with ill-treatment of many of those arrested, set the seal on the estrangement of the Catholic community from the regime, led the Irish Government to bring proceedings under the European Convention, and was followed by a dramatic escalation of violence. Its effects may have contributed to the Westminster Government undertaking Direct Rule. As part of a package designed to promote security and produce a political settlement, the above system was replaced by the Detention of Terrorists Order 1972, subsequently embodied in NIEPA 1973 (Sched. 1), which authorised the detention without trial of suspected terrorists where necessary for the protection of the public.[2] The third system, based on the recommendations of the Gardiner Committee, first embodied in NIEPA 1975, and now contained in Schedule 1 to NIEPA 1978, has never been operated to detain persons, only to secure their release.[3] It authorises the detention without trial of a person where the Secretary of State is satisfied

> "(*a*) that that person has been concerned in the commission or attempted commission of any act of terrorism, or in directing, organising or training persons for the purpose of terrorism; and
>
> (*b*) that his detention is necessary for the protection of the public."[4]

The last detainee was released in December 1975. This part of NIEPA 1978 is not now in force, not being renewed in July 1980. It could, however, be quickly resurrected, if the government so

[1] See, generally, J. McGuffin, *Internment* (1973); D.R. Lowry, "Internment in Northern Ireland" (1976) 8 U. Toledo L. Rev. 169. and "Internment: Detention Without Trial in Northern Ireland" (1976) 5 *Human Rights* 261.

[2] On systems one and two see K. Boyle, T. Hadden and P. Hillyard, *Law and State: The Case of Northern Ireland* (1975), Chaps. 4 and 5.

[3] Baker, para. 225.

[4] NIEPA 1978, Sched. 1, para. 8. For a useful critique see R.J. Spjut, "Executive Detention in Northern Ireland" (1975) 10 *Irish Jurist* 272.

desired, by executive order subject usually to prior parliamentary approval through laying in draft but, in cases of urgency, to subsequent ratification by the legislature (*supra*, p. 42). It is useful to examine detention without trial in operation to stress why it is unlikely to prove a practical option in the future. Furthermore, it affords a useful case-study of aspects of derogation under the European Convention on Human Rights (*supra*, pp. 83-90).

Three specific inter-related justifications were advanced for resort to such a process in the Northern Ireland context: the inability of the ordinary courts to restore peace and order; the widespread intimidation of the population which made it difficult to find witnesses willing to testify in open court and rendered jury trial problematic; and the existence of a land frontier with the Republic allowing ready escape to a "safe haven."[5] It was, moreover, perceived as having been a successful weapon in earlier IRA campaigns.[6]

Several problems can be identified. A number of inappropriate people were detained on inadequate grounds.[7] Although preventative in conception, it proved punitive in execution.[8] The process appeared to operate on a discriminatory basis; far more Republicans than Loyalists were detained. It has been suggested, however, that while cases of discrimination may have occurred and while the introduction of the initial system had a highly political element about it, its differential application was due not so much to conscious discrimination but is rather explicable in terms of the more acute nature of the IRA threat, of the particular problems it posed to the use of the ordinary courts to process terrorists, and to the effects of practical constraints on policing which meant that the Army "policed" in Republican areas employing a "military security" approach, aimed at removing terrorists from circulation in the community, while the police were confined to Loyalist areas and deployed a more traditional criminal prosecution approach.[9] Loyalist paramilitaries were processed through the courts and, where necessary, interned. Allegations of a practice of politico-religious discrimination in its operation were not upheld by Commission or Court in *Ireland*

5 *Ireland* v. *United Kingdom* (1978) 2 E.H.R.R. 25, at p. 37 (para. 36).

6 The *Sunday Times* Insight Team, *Ulster*, p. 260.

7 Diplock, para. 32.

8 W.L. Twining, "Emergency Powers and Criminal Process: The Diplock Report," [1973] Crim.L.R. 406, at p. 415.

9 Boyle, Hadden and Hillyard, *op. cit.* n. 2, pp. 41-43.

v. *United Kingdom:* Article 14 of the European Convention, as normally applicable, had not been breached, so there was no need to rely on the right of derogation on that particular issue.[10] There were also difficulties in finding an effectively credible system of reviewing the executive decision to detain. The Special Powers Act regime was most unsatisfactory in this regard. Detainees had no right of review at all. Internees could only make representation to an Advisory Committee, but could obtain legal advice to help them do so. The Committee's decision was not binding on the executive.[11] Under the second system, a person's release could be ordered, either by a quasi-judicial commissioner, after a process employing quite sophisticated adversary procedures involving the provision for the internee of State-financed legal representation, or by the Appeal Tribunal empowered to review a commissioner's decision to detain.[12]

Lord Gardiner concluded that:

> "[t]he most cogent criticism was that the procedures are unsatisfactory, or even farcical, if considered as judicial. The adversarial method of trial is reduced to impotence by the needs of security. The use of screens and voice scramblers [to protect witnesses], the overwhelming amount of hearsay evidence and the in camera sessions are totally alien to ordinary trial procedures. The quasi-judicial procedures are a veneer to an enquiry which, to be effective, inevitably has no relationship to common law procedures.
>
> The introduction of the quasi-judicial procedures was well-intentioned. Its object was to give the person suspected of terrorism every opportunity consistent with security to challenge and test the allegations made against him. Its apparent similarity to the ordinary judicial process has had the side effect of tending to bring the ordinary processes of law in Northern Ireland into disrepute.
>
> Strong criticism was made of the nature of the evidence before the commissioners. This criticism is valid to the extent that the adversarial quasi-judicial procedures are unsatisfactory for testing the reliability of evidence from paid informers and accomplices of terrorists. The most effective

[10] (1978) 2 E.H.R.R. 25, at pp. 98-100 (paras. 225-232).

[11] (1978) 2 E.H.R.R. 25, at pp. 51-54 (paras. 80-84).

[12] Boyle, Hadden and Hillyard, *op. cit.* n. 2, pp. 58-74.

testing of such evidence can only with safety be conducted in a situation of the utmost confidentiality."[13]

Six month delays were endemic in the system.[14] Throughout, redress in the courts, other than on procedural and technical grounds, was not a practical proposition.[15] The third system (under NIEPA 1975 and 1978) provided review by an Adviser.[16]

Whether internment or, later, detention increased or reduced the paramilitaries' potential for violence is a highly debatable matter.[17] Lord Gardiner thought that it might be effective in the short term but not as a long-term strategy because

> "the prolonged effects of the use of detention are ultimately inimical to community life, fan a widespread sense of grievance and injustice, and obstruct those elements in Northern Ireland society which could lead to reconciliation."[18]

The issue of internment or detention without trial has arisen under the European Convention on Human Rights in *Lawless* v. *Ireland*[19] (internment under the Republic's Offences Against the State (Amendment) Act 1940) and in *Ireland* v. *United Kingdom*[20] where the first and second systems deployed in Northern Ireland were under challenge. Such a process is clearly only supportable during war or other public emergency threatening the life of the nation. It cannot be supported by any of the heads of permissible deprivation of liberty set out in Article 5 of the Convention. It might seem at first glance to be covered by Article 5(1)(*c*) which permits

> "the lawful arrest or detention of a person effected for the purpose of bringing him before the competent legal authority on reasonable suspicion of having committed an offence or when it is reasonably considered necessary to prevent his committing an offence or fleeing after having done so."

[13] Gardiner, paras. 152-154.

[14] *Ibid.* para. 155.

[15] (1978) 2 E.H.R.R. 25, at pp. 52-54 (paras. 81-84), 90 (para. 201).

[16] Spjut, *loc. cit.* n. 4.

[17] Compare Boyle, Hadden and Hillyard, *op. cit.* n. 2, pp. 74-77, with P. Wilkinson, *Terrorism and the Liberal State* (1977), pp. 150-58.

[18] Gardiner, para. 148.

[19] (1961) 1 E.H.R.R. 15.

[20] (1978) 2 E.H.R.R. 25.

This, however, has to be read subject to Article 5(3) which mandates that persons so arrested and detained

> "shall be brought promptly before a judge or other officer authorised by law to exercise judicial power and shall be entitled to trial within a reasonable time or to release pending trial. Release may be conditioned by guarantees to appear for trial."

In short, these two provisions require that the detained person be arrested for the purpose of deploying some form of criminal trial process againt him and that any such trial take place within a reasonable time. Internment and detention did not comply since their rationale and purpose was to by-pass the criminal trial process. Nor did the review bodies in Northern Ireland constitute the agencies contemplated by these Convention provisions because (in the Special Powers Act case only) of a lack of power of binding decision and (in the case of all the measures) the failure to bring the internee promptly before them.[21] For similar reasons the bodies did not constitute the "court" contemplated by Article 5(4) which requires that a person be entitled to "take proceedings by which the lawfulness of his detention shall be decided speedily . . . and his release ordered if the detention is not lawful." Nor did review by the courts in habeas corpus applications satisfy that paragraph since, being limited to technical defects only, it "was not sufficiently wide in scope taking into account the purpose and object" of that paragraph which seems to demand binding review of the substance of the relevant decision.[22]

In both *Lawless* and *Ireland* v. *United Kingdom* internment or detention without trial was upheld as being a measure not going beyond what was required by the exigencies of the situation. Ultimately a question of fact in each case the matter involved two sub-issues: (i) whether any less draconian methods than those adopted would have been sufficient to deal with the situation; (ii) whether the method employed (and justified under (i)) was subject, so far as the situation allowed, to adequate safeguards to protect personal liberty?[23] With regard to the first sub-issue, in both cases it was held that such processes were a reasonable response to the circumstances, given the "margin of appreciation." The Court in *Lawless* considered that the ordinary processes of the

[21] (1978) 2 E.H.R.R. 25, at p. 89 (para. 199).

[22] (1978) 2 E.H.R.R. 25, at pp. 89-90 (para. 200).

[23] (1961) 1 E.H.R.R. 15, at pp. 32-34 (paras. 31-38); (1978) 2 E.H.R.R. 25, at pp. 93-95 (paras. 212-14).

criminal law were inadequate to deal with the mounting danger to the State. In particular the Court was struck by the difficulties of gathering sufficient evidence to secure conviction, difficulties which stemmed from the IRA intimidation of witnesses, its secret, terrorist nature, and which were exacerbated because its primary arena of operations lay in Ulster. As regards alternatives to internment without trial, the Court rejected any notion of sealing the border on the Republic side, to prevent trans-border attacks, on the ground that it would have had serious socio-economic repercussions on the population as a whole which would have gone beyond what was required by the situation. The possibility of overcoming the problems by setting up special criminal courts was rejected cursorily on grounds of inability to restore peace and order.[24] In *Ireland* v. *United Kingdom* similar problems posed to the use of the ordinary courts were stressed by the Commission. The Court's judgment contains little reasoning on the point.[25] Both bodies can be criticised for failure to examine alternatives, to canvass, for instance, why even a modified criminal process or special criminal courts were incapable of dealing with the situation as efficaciously as internment or detention. Surely such an approach can be expected of bodies charged with the protection of human rights. Indeed does not the term "*strictly* required" in Article 15 mandate exploration of alternatives even if, at the end of the day, they are rejected on rational grounds? That this approach was not taken seems attributable to the "margin of appreciation"; the Court noted that

> "it is certainly not the Court's function to substitute for the British Government's assessment any other assessment of what might be the most prudent or most expedient policy to combat terrorism . . . the Court accepts that the limits of the margin of appreciation . . . were not overstepped by the United Kingdom . . ."[26]

But while internment in some form might well have been required, was the system hedged around with sufficient safeguards against abuse? In *Ireland* v. *United Kingdom* the Court held that even the Special Powers Act regime, backed up by technicality-oriented, limited judicial review, fulfilled the

[24] (1961) 1 E.H.R.R. 15, at p. 33. Difficulty in gathering evidence was cited (para. 36).

[25] (1978) 2 E.H.R.R. 25, at pp. 93-95 (paras. 212-14).

[26] (1978) 2 E.H.R.R. 25, at p. 95 (para. 214).

Convention requirements in the circumstances then prevailing in Ulster. The later more sophisticated system was also satisfactory from this perspective.[27] The Court declared that

> "an overall examination of the legislation and practice at issue reveal that they evolved in the direction of increasing respect for individual liberty. The incorporation right from the start of more satisfactory judicial, or at least administrative guarantees would certainly have been desirable, especially as the Special Powers Act regime dated back to 1956-57 . . . but it would be unrealistic to isolate the first from the later phases. Where a State is struggling against a public emergency threatening the life of the nation, it would be rendered defenceless if it were required to accomplish everything at once, to furnish from the outset each of its chosen means of action with each of the safeguards reconcilable with the priority requirements for the proper functioning of the authorities and for restoring peace within the community. The interpretation of Article 15 must leave room for progressive adaptations."[28]

Once again, the role of the margin of appreciation seems an important decision-making factor.

The decision with respect to the Special Powers Act system, however, is clearly out of line with the Court's approach to the same issue in *Lawless* where it stressed the importance as safeguards of the binding decision of the Detention Commission and an element of supervision by Parliament which received regular and precise information on the operation of the scheme.[29] The Convention does not dictate any system of binding precedent. Nor, given the different scale of the emergencies, could every single factor in *Lawless* be applicable to *Ireland* v. *United Kingdom*. But the difference in scale must surely go to the question of what strategy was required in the situation rather than to the matter of safeguards since the protection of human rights demands the maintenance of some minimum due process guarantees even in an emergency situation such as that in Ulster. To say otherwise seems to deny the Convention provisions any meaningful application in that context. One minimum guarantee must be a requirement that the review body be empowered to make binding decisions. A

[27] (1978) 2 E.H.R.R. 25, at pp. 95-97 (paras. 217-220).

[28] (1978) 2 E.H.R.R. 25, p. 96 (para. 220).

[29] (1961) 1 E.H.R.R. 15, at p. 33 (para. 37).

process of review by an independent body, if only advisory, could be abused by merely going through the sham process of a reference to it knowing full well that its advice would not be implemented. Since the Court saw its role as giving guidance to decision-makers in the Member States,[30] it is the point of principle and not the fact that in Ulster the process was not so abused that is important. *Lawless* should have been strictly followed on this point and the Court ought to have held that use of the Special Powers regime of internment violated the Convention.[31] Merely to say that better safeguards were "desirable" is not enough. If the Court's decisions are to be regarded as giving guidance to decision-makers in other States (and the Court so perceives them) then surely it was up to the United Kingdom to have secured such modification of the Special Powers regime as was required by the Convention as interpreted in *Lawless.* The Court appears to regard only the more general aspects of that case to be relevant for the future; each new case is to be treated on its own facts within the framework of relevant questions dictated by *Lawless.* This is hardly laying down meaningful human rights' standards for States to follow.

In December 1975, the Secretary of State, Merlyn Rees, justified his discontinuance of detention as a practical option for dealing with terrorism in the Province:

> "From the outset detention has been a real and continuing cause of resentment, particularly in the minority community. It was a fertile ground for recruitment to the paramilitary organisations."[32]

In July 1980, a Conservative spokesman told the House of Commons that its reintroduction at that time would make matters worse.[33] It has been reported, however, that the Army favours its re-introduction on a selective basis to remove from circulation in the community the organisers and key "hit-men" of the terrorist movements.[34] It is submitted that its reinvocation would be a retrograde step. To paraphrase the SACHR: detention is anathema to the rule of law; would be a serious obstacle to claims that human rights are as fully protected in Northern Ireland as they

30 (1978) 2 E.H.R.R. 25, at p. 75 (para. 154).

31 *Cf.* Judge O'Donoghue's dissent (1978) 2 E.H.R.R. 25, at pp. 118-19.

32 Cited in SACHR, *Annual Report for 1975-76*, H.C. 130 (1976-77), at pp. 9-10 (para. 22).

33 H.C. Deb, Vol. 989, col. 435 (July 23, 1980).

34 Boyle, Hadden and Hillyard, *op cit.* n. 50, at p. 101.

ought to be in current circumstances; and would invite criticism and engender suspicion in responsible quarters at home and abroad.[35] Its reintroduction—even on a limited basis—is likely to prove counter productive, in the Catholic community at least where it would increase support for Sinn Fein and the politics of violence. A new notice of derogation from the European Convention would be required, and it might prove more difficult to convince the European Convention organs that detention is now warranted by the exigencies of the situation given its non-use since 1975, a declining rate of terrorist violence, and an increasing charge rate in the criminal prosecution process. Its reintroduction would re-open the divisive special category status debate; detainees would surely have to receive better treatment than convicted prisoners.[36] There would also remain the pervasive problem of a credible and effective review process.

Even if it is not reactivated, there remains the further question: should it remain on the statute book, ready for rapid reinvocation if necessary. The SACHR suggests not.[37] Baker recommended its total repeal.[38] On this view reintroduction should require legislation. While this emphasises the care with which one should consider resort to such a process, the possibility of a drastic escalation in the level of violence suggests that, as a last resort, detention might be necessary to restore a modicum of order. The time taken to pass legislation would give warning to those likely to be affected to go into hiding. Security might dictate the need to make provision for rapid reintroduction subject to prompt, probing Parliamentary ratification. Any reintroduction ought to be accompanied by a binding review process. A possible "model" is considered in Chapter 4 in the context of exclusion orders (*infra*, pp. 204-207).

(2) *Exclusion orders*

The powers of the Secretary of State for Northern Ireland to exclude terrorist suspects from the Province or from the United

[35] SACHR, *Annual Report for 1978-79*, H.C. 433 (1979-80), para. 10.

[36] On special category status, see Gardiner, paras. 105-108. On the campaigns for political status, see: Boyle, Hadden and Hillyard, *op. cit.* n. 50, pp. 88-97; K. Kelley, *The Longest War: Northern Ireland and the IRA* (1982), pp. 324-349; T.P. Coogan, *On the Blanket: The H-Block Story* (1980).

[37] *Annual Report for 1982-83*, H.C. 262 (1983-84), p. 19 (para. 34); *cf.* Alliance Party Baker Submission, para. 33.

[38] Baker, para. 236.

Kingdom are now contained in the PTA 1984. The former was first embodied in the PTA 1976. The mechanism for making and reviewing orders is similar to that operated in Great Britain (*infra*, pp. 191-200). The process has been little used in Northern Ireland. To December 31, 1984, 30 orders had been made: most excluding persons from the United Kingdom, resulted in the return of suspects to the Republic of Ireland. Some British citizens have been excluded from the Province. None had their home there. Some excluded to the mainland may have been suspected of involvement in acquiring arms and explosives for Loyalist paramilitaries.[39] The indigenous provenance of most terrorism in Northern Ireland means that the process is of limited use. Most suspected terrorists would fall within the exempt categories. Northern Ireland has rather been the repository for suspected terrorists excluded from the mainland (245 to December 31, 1984).[40] This has given rise to feelings of devalued citizenship and complaints that Ulster is treated as a "terrorist dustbin"[41] and fears that by emphasising the disunity of the United Kingdom, by implying that Ulster is not an equal part thereof, it plays into the hands of those who seek to change its status through violent means.[42] Such complaints are unlikely to be assuaged by claims that those returned "belong" to Northern Ireland or that there is consultation on both sides of the Irish Sea before exclusion; the "second-class Ulster" argument is not confined to objections to someone else's terrorists being dumped there but also embraces the contention that, if certain persons are not suitable to be at large in Great Britain, they ought not to be at liberty in Ulster.[43] There is evidence that moderate opinion there views it as counter productive.[44]

[39] Jellicoe, paras. 167, 178; Mrs. M. Thatcher, MP, Prime Minister, H.C. Debs, Vol. 33, col. 981; letter to the author from the Permanent Under-Secretary of State, Northern Ireland Office, January, 31, 1983; Northern Ireland Information Service, *Statistics on the PTAs. Fourth Quarter 1984 (January 24, 1985).*

[40] Home Office Statistical Bulletin, *Statistics on the Prevention of Terrorism (Temporary Provisions) Acts 1974, 1976 and 1984—Fourth Quarter 1984*, Table 5.

[41] Jellicoe, paras. 180-184.

[42] See, *e.g.* Mr. E. Powell, MP, H.C. Deb. Vol. 882, col. 670; *Official Report*, Standing Committee D (1983-84), col. 112.

[43] See, *e.g. The Times*, December 9, 1982, p. 1.

[44] SACHR, *Annual Report for 1982-83*, H.C. 262 (1983-84), p. 7.

10. A Note on the Use of Force

The use of force by soldiers and policemen in the exercise of their powers in Northern Ireland has proved controversial in a number of contexts (*e.g.* search of premises, the physical abuse of suspects), but particularly so in connection with the use of PVC baton rounds (plastic bullets) and of lethal force. Latterly, there have been allegations of a "shoot to kill" or "summary execution" policy and calls for public inquiries. A number of civil actions have been brought and some prosecutions, most resulting in acquittals. Unless justified the use of force will constitute a tort or a criminal offence. There must be a right to deploy force flowing from statute or common law, and the force must not be excessive.[45] Generally, section 3(1) of the Criminal Law Act (Northern Ireland) 1967 (substantially the same as its mainland equivalent) provides:

> "A person may use such force as is reasonable in the circumstances in the prevention of crime, or in effecting or assisting in the lawful arrest of offenders or suspected offenders, or of persons unlawfully at large."

Additionally, at common law, reasonable force may be used to defend oneself and, in certain circumstances, another person.[46] Section 3(1) can afford a defence to the person who used force but not to the person planning the security operation in which it was contemplated that force might be used.[47] When force will be "reasonable in the circumstances" is not further elaborated in the Act. The Criminal Law Revision Committee, on whose Report the provision is based, stated that

> "the court, in considering what was reasonable force, would take into account all the circumstances, including in particular the nature and degree of force used, the seriousness of the evil to be prevented and the possibility of preventing it by other means; but there is no need to specify in the [provision] the criteria for deciding the question."[48]

[45] SACHR, *Annual Report for 1982-83*, H.C. 262 (1983-84), pp. 21-23, and 36-41 (App. B) for a fuller treatment.

[46] *Ibid.* p. 36.

[47] *Farrel* v. *Secretary of State for Defence* [1980] 1 W.L.R. 172, at p. 179 *per* Viscount Dilhorne.

[48] Criminal Law Revision Committee, Seventh Report, *Felonies and Misdemeanours*, Cmnd. 2659 (1965), para. 23.

In *Attorney General for Northern Ireland's Reference (No. 1 of 1975)*,[49] the House of Lords held it to be an issue of fact not of law. Lord Diplock there proffered the following guidance for the arbiter of fact in a criminal trial (and the approach would be adaptable to civil trial):

> "The form in which the jury would have to ask themselves the question . . . would be: Are we satisfied that no reasonable man (a) with knowledge of such facts as were known to the accused or reasonably believed by him to exist (b) in the circumstances and time available to him for reflection (c) could be of opinion that the prevention of risk of harm to which others might be exposed if the suspect were allowed to escape justified exposing the suspect to the risk of harm to him that might result from the kind of force that the accused contemplated using? . . .
>
> . . . The jury would have also to consider how the circumstances in which the accused had to make his decision whether or not to use force and the shortness of time available to him for reflection, might affect the judgment of a reasonable man . . . the jury in approaching the final part of the question should remind themselves that the postulated balancing of risk against risk, harm against harm, by the reasonable man is not undertaken in the calm analytical atmosphere of the court-room after counsel with the benefit of hindsight have expounded at length the reasons for and against the kind and degree of force that was used by the accused; but in the brief second or two which the accused had to decide whether to shoot or not and under all the stresses to which he was exposed."[50]

Here D, acquitted at trial, shot and killed P, whom he believed to be an unarmed terrorist who had to be stopped and questioned or arrested, when P ran off after being called upon to halt during an army search, in a hostile area known for ambushes, of a farm where terrorists might be hiding. Here

> "the only options open to the accused were either to let the deceased escape or to shoot at him with a service rifle. A reasonable man would know that a bullet from a self-loading rifle if it hit a human being, at any rate at the range at which the accused fired, would be likely to kill him or injure him

[49] [1977] A.C. 105. Civil trial may produce a different result.
[50] [1977] A.C. 105, at pp. 137-138.

> seriously. So in one scale of the balance the harm to which the deceased would be exposed if the accused aimed to hit him was predictable and grave and the risk of its occurrence high. In the other scale of the balance it would be open to the jury to take the view that it would not be unreasonable to assess the kind of harm to be averted by preventing the [deceased's] escape as even graver—the killing or wounding of the members of the patrol by terrorists in ambush and the effect of this success by members of the Provisional IRA in encouraging the continuance of the armed insurrection and all the misery and destruction of life and property that terrorist activity in Northern Ireland has entailed."[51]

The facts and circumstances set out in the reference were declared sufficient to raise an issue for the arbiter of fact whether the Crown had established beyond reasonable doubt that D shooting P constituted, in those circumstances, unreasonable force. The decision has been criticised as abdicating the courts' responsibility to control actions of the security forces,[52] and the law castigated for failing to give clear enough guidance to the man on the spot.[53]

In practical terms, a degree of guidance and control is afforded by administrative directions enforceable as a matter of police and military discipline. The Yellow Card, issued to soldiers, contains instructions on opening fire. There are "Army Rules of Engagement for PVC Baton Rounds." Similar rules for the police are contained in the RUC Force Instructions. It is not current practice to make these detailed operational instructions public, but extracts and earlier versions have appeared in official and unofficial reports of inquiries and in the Press.[54] The rules inevitably afford scope for subjective interpretation by the man on the spot. They do not, however, define, add to or restrict his legal rights and obligations.[55] The SACHR were impressed by the strictness of the instructions to the security forces and commented that "if obeyed by the security forces no member of the law-abiding public need be concerned for his safety and neither

[51] [1977] A.C. 105, at p. 138.

[52] D.R. Lowry, "Terrorism and Human Rights: Counter-Insurgency and Necessity at Common Law" (1977) 53 *Notre Dame Law* 49, at p. 66.

[53] R. Evelegh, *Peace-Keeping in a Democratic Society: The Lessons of Northern Ireland* (1978), p. 77.

[54] See *Report of the Tribunal Appointed to Enquire into the Events on Sunday 30th January 1972 which led to Loss of Life in Connection with the Procession in Londonderry on that day*, H.C. 220 (1971-72); *The Times*, February 1, 1972, p. 1.

[55] *R.* v. *MacNaughton* (1975) N.I. 203, at p. 206 (*per* Lord Lowry C.J.).

need members of the security forces equally fear breaking the law."[56] Perhaps, at least in the special circumstances of Northern Ireland, additional criteria, drawing on and amplifying these operational instructions should be incorporated in section 3 of the Criminal Law Act (NI) 1967 as a guide to the courts. The SACHR suggest that the following are particularly relevant factors for consideration in such legislation:

> "(*a*) the necessity (or reasonable belief of necessity) to use force, particularly lethal force;
> (*b*) the seriousness of the crime to be prevented by the use of such force;
> (*c*) the possibility of preventing that crime by other means;
> (*d*) whether the person to be arrested can be identified if he escapes;
> (*e*) whether lethal force should wherever practicable only be used after prior clear warning, and calling upon the suspect to halt; and
> (*f*) whether there is substantial risk of injury to innocent persons."[57]

It was, further

> "in principle . . . of the opinion that a police officer or soldier should be entitled to open fire only where it is immediately necessary, or it appears on reasonable grounds to the person using such force to be necessary, either to protect life or prevent serious injury to himself or to some other person, or where there is a substantial risk that the person to be arrested will cause death or serious injury if his arrest is not effected without delay."[58]

The use of lethal force by the Army, particularly on "Bloody Sunday" (January 30, 1972) was challenged in *Ireland* v. *United Kingdom* but ruled inadmissible for non-exhaustion of domestic remedies.[59] The case of a man shot dead by troops in Newry in 1971 was admitted for consideration on the merits by the European Commission of Human Rights, but was the subject of a

[56] *Annual Report for 1982-83*, H.C. 262 (1983-84), p. 22 (para. 24).
[57] *Ibid.* p. 23 (para. 26).
[58] *Ibid.* p. 23 (para. 27).
[59] Council of Europe, European Commission of Human Rights, *Collection of Decisions* 41, pp. 12-13, 32-41, 85.

friendly settlement.[60] Another concerning plastic bullets was declared inadmissible.[61] The cases focussed on the right to life (non-derogable in this context)[62] in Article 2 of the Convention, which appears to provide a more stringent test than the 1967 Act:

> "Deprivation of life shall not be regarded as inflicted in contravention of this Article when it results from the use of force which is no more than *absolutely necessary:*
> (*a*) in defence of any person from unlawful violence;
> (*b*) in order to effect a lawful arrest or to prevent the escape of a person lawfully detained;
> (*c*) in action lawfully taken for the purpose of quelling a riot or insurrection." (Art. 2(2)) (emphasis supplied)

In the plastic bullets case, which in the particular circumstances, the Commission rejected as disclosing no possible violation of the Convention, it stated that

> " . . . Art.2(2) permits the use of force for the purposes enumerated in sub-paragraphs (a), (b) and (c) subject to the requirement that the force used is strictly proportionate to the achievement of the permitted purpose. In assessing whether the use of force is strictly proportionate, regard must be had to the nature of the aim pursued, the dangers to life and limb inherent in the situation and the degree of risk that the force employed might result in loss of life. The Commission's examination must have due regard to all the relevant circumstances surrounding the deprivation of life."[63]

[60] *Farrell* v. *United Kingdom* (App. No. 9013/80), Council of Europe Document DH(82)6, at pp. 13-14. BBC TV, "Panorama," "Justice Under Fire," November 12, 1984.

[61] *Keesing's Contemporary Archives* (1982), p. 31789; (1983) p. 32195; Council of Europe, European Commission of Human Rights, *Stewart* v. *United Kingdom (App. No. 10044/82)*, (July 10, 1984; reasons delivered September 1984).

[62] Art. 15(2).

[63] *Stewart* v. *United Kingdom, op. cit.* n. 61, para. 19.

Chapter 4

EMERGENCY POWERS TO COMBAT TERRORISM IN GREAT BRITAIN

1. Background and Overview

The violent struggle to free Ireland from British control has historically not been confined to the island, but has spread to the mainland with significant effects on its laws, both permanent and emergency, and on its institutions of law enforcement. The activities of the Fenians (Irish Republic Brotherhood) 1867-1872 were met by the CID at Scotland Yard.[1] The conviction of the perpetrator of the Clerkenwell Explosion led to one of the last public executions in England.[2] Fenian activities 1883-86 saw the rapid passage of the Explosive Substances Act 1883 which widened the arrest powers of the police. They led to the formation of the Special (Irish) Branch from members of Scotland Yard's CID; it developed into the present Special Branch.[3] The failure of the Easter Rising 1916 saw the internment of Irish rebels in the Frongoch camps in Wales.[4] In 1923 100 members of the Irish Self-Determination League were unlawfully deported to Ireland under the auspices of the Restoration of Order in Ireland Act 1920, and interned there.[5]

The IRA campaign which began in January 1939 led to the passage of the Prevention of Violence (Temporary Provisions) Act 1939 (hereinafter "PVA 1939").[6] It conferred extra powers on

[1] T. Bunyan, *The History and Practice of the Political Police in Britain* (1976), p. 103.

[2] P. Quinlivan and P. Rose, *The Fenians in England 1865-1872: a Sense of Insecurity* (1982), Chap. 9.

[3] Bunyan, *op. cit.* n. 1, pp. 104-105.

[4] J. McGuffin, *Internment* (1973), p. 27.

[5] *Ibid.* p. 35.

[6] For an assessment of the campaign see T.P. Coogan, *The I.R.A.* (revised ed., 1980), Chap. 5. On the making of the Act see O. Lomas "The Executive and the Anti-Terrorist Legislation of 1939" [1980] P.L. 16, and discussion *supra*, pp. 27-28.

the executive to prevent the commission in Great Britain of acts of violence designed to influence public opinion or Government policy with respect to Irish affairs (s.1(1)). Where reasonably satisfied that a person was engaged in the preparation or instigation of such acts of violence, or was knowingly harbouring such a person, the Home Secretary could issue an expulsion order requiring him to leave Great Britain (s.1(2)). If so satisfied that a person was trying or might try to enter Great Britain with a view to being so engaged, he could issue a prohibition order to keep him out (s.1(4)). Persons subject to such orders could make representations to Advisers (s.2(1)). Those ordinarily resident in Great Britain throughout their lives or the last 20 years were exempt (ss.1(2), (4)). The Home Secretary also had power to issue registration orders requiring people to register with and report to the police (s.1(3)). Breach of any of these orders was punishable with up to two years imprisonment (ss.3(1), (3)). The police were empowered to arrest persons reasonably suspected of an offence under the Act, of being subject to an expulsion or prohibition order, or of being concerned in the preparation or instigation of acts of violence to which the Act was directed. Those arrested could be held for up to 48 hours, a period extendible for up to a further five days on express direction of the Secretary of State (s.4(1)). Wider powers of search pursuant to a magistrates', or in emergencies a police superintendent's, warrant were also granted (ss.4(3), (4)). These powers supplemented recourse to the normal criminal process. They were in turn supplemented by internment powers under wartime legislation.[7] Persons returned to Northern Ireland or to the Republic might face internment there.[8] The PVA 1939 lapsed in 1954. Incidents in the 1956-62 IRA campaign were met on the mainland by the ordinary law.[9]

When the current IRA campaign spread to the mainland in 1972, it too was initially combated with ordinary powers. The Special Branch and the Bomb Squad (now the Anti-Terrorist Squad) were deployed to deal with it. They appeared initially to be against emergency powers, in part because of fears of their heavy drain on manpower.[10] The tragedy of the Birmingham pub bombings of

[7] McGuffin, *op. cit.* n. 4, p. 37.

[8] *Ibid.*

[9] For an assessment of that campaign see Coogan, *op. cit.* n. 6, Chaps. 12-14.

[10] B. Rose-Smith, "Police Powers and Terrorism Legislation" in P. Hain (Ed.), *Policing the Police*, Vol. I (1979) pp. 114-115, 119-120.

November 1974 precipitated the speedy passage of the Prevention of Terrorism (Temporary Provisions) Act 1974 (hereinafter "PTA 1974"), very much based on the PVA 1939.[11] It brought into British law the definition of "terrorism" deployed in the NIEPAs: "the use of violence for political ends, and includes any use of violence for the purpose of putting the public or any section of the public in fear" (s.14(1)), but required no express definition of terrorist. It was replaced in 1976 by another Act of the same name (hereinafter "PTA 1976") which further strengthened powers of the police and the executive, while making some small steps towards the better protection of the civil liberties of those affected by it.[12] It, in its turn, has been replaced, on the recommendations of Lord Jellicoe,[13] by the Prevention of Terrorism (Temporary Provisions) Act 1984 (hereinafter "PTA 1984") which extended the scope of some powers and reduced that of others.[13a]

Throughout the essential features of the 1974 legislation have remained intact. The PTAs have equipped the police with wider powers of arrest, detention, search seizure and ancillary powers to deal with terrorist suspects. The authorities have a choice of process to deploy against them: criminal prosecution and trial for general offences and/or offences created by the PTAs; or the extra-judicial Exclusion Order (EO) process whereby terrorist suspects can be excluded from Northern Ireland, from Great Britain or from the United Kingdom as a whole. The processes are not mutually exclusive; those tried and acquitted can be excluded, as can those persons convicted who have served their sentences.[14] Unlike Northern Ireland, the ordinary provisions on judicial admission to bail, on committal and on criminal trial apply to terrorist offenders.

[11] For comment see Leigh [1975] P.L. 1; Street [1975] Crim. L.R. 192.

[12] For comment on the 1974 and 1976 Acts, see Rose-Smith, *op. cit.* n. 10; C. Scorer, *The Prevention of Terrorism Acts 1974 and 1976: A Report on the Operation of the Law* (NCCL, 1976); C. Scorer and P. Hewitt, *The Prevention of Terrorism Act: The Case for Repeal* (NCCL, 1981); D.R. Lowry, "Draconian Powers: The New British Approach to Pre-Trial Detention of Suspected Terrorists" (1976-77) 8-9 Colum. Human Rights L.R. 185.

[13] *Review of the Operation of the Prevention of Terrorism (Temporary Provisions) Act 1976*, Cmnd. 8803 (1983) (hereinafter cited as "Jellicoe").

[13a] For comment on the PTA 1984 see D.S. Greer, *Current Law Statutes Annotated 1984*; C.P. Walker (1984) 47 M.L.R. 704; A. Samuels [1984] P.L. 365.

[14] Scorer, *op. cit.* n. 12, p. 19; Lord Elton, H.L. Debs., Vol. 448, col. 904.

2. Additional Police Powers to Deal with Terrorist Suspects

Powers of arrest provided by the PTA 1984 and related subordinate legislation supplement rather than replace existing powers under statute or at common law (ss.12(7), 13(4)). Most serious offences committed by terrorists will remain arrestable under section 24 of the Police and Criminal Evidence Act 1984 (hereinafter "PCEA 1984"). The usual battery of statutory and common law offences are available to deal with meetings and demonstrations; most carry powers of arrest with them. Of course, persons arrested under existing powers must be brought before a magistrates' court within a reasonable time.[15] In this respect, section 2(2) of the PTA 1984, which grants a constable a power of arrest in connection with display of support in public for a proscribed organisation, is merely an addition to the general pattern. It will cease to have effect when Part III of the PCEA enters into force.[15a]

By contrast, the other arrest powers created by and under the PTA 1984 have certain advantages for the police over existing powers. The person arresting does not necessarily need to suspect a specific offence; section 12(1) empowers a constable to arrest without warrant someone he has reasonable grounds for suspecting to be a person guilty of an offence under section 1, 9 or 10 of the Act, a person subject to an exclusion order excluding him from Great Britain, or a person who is or has been concerned in the commission, preparation or instigation of acts of terrorism connected with the affairs of Northern Ireland or of acts of terrorism of any other description apart from acts solely connected with the affairs of the United Kingdom or any part thereof other than Northern Ireland.[16] The Act and the Prevention of Terrorism (Supplemental Temporary Provisions) Order 1984

[15] Magistrates' Courts Act 1980, s.43; Children and Young Persons Act 1969, s.29. Under the PCEA 1984, persons arrested must be charged within 24 hours and brought before a magistrates' court as soon as practicable thereafter. Where, however, an offence under investigation is a serious arrestable offence, a senior police officer may authorise continued detention without charge up to 36 hours after the person's arrival at the police station. If the police wish to hold a suspect without charge beyond 36 hours, they must make an *inter partes* application to a magistrates' court which can grant extensions of detention for periods not exceeding 36 hours at a time or ending later than 96 hours after the person's arrival at the police station (ss.34-45).

[15a] PCEA 1984, s.26(1).

[16] On the interpretation of s.12(1)(*b*) of the PTA 1976, see *Ex p. Lynch* [1980] N.I.L.R. 126.

(hereinafter "STPO")[17] continue the immigration-type security control at designated ports and airports. Under these port powers examining officers (that is constables, immigration officers and officers of customs and excise), in practice until now Special Branch police officers, may

> "examine any persons who have arrived in or are seeking to leave Great Britain by ship or aircraft for the purpose of determining–
> (*a*) whether any such person appears to be a person who is or has been concerned in the commission, preparation or instigation of acts of terrorism to which this article applies; or
> (*b*) whether any such person is subject to an exclusion order; or
> (*c*) whether there are grounds for suspecting that any such person has committed an offence under section 9 of the Act." (art. 4)

The article applies to the same types of terrorism as section 12 (*supra*). Arrest and detention pending examination or consideration of whether to make an exclusion order are also permitted (arts. 9 and 10). Persons examined are under a duty to supply such information and/or documentation in their possession as the examiner may require for the purpose of his functions under article 4, for example, a passport or some other document satisfactorily establishing identity and nationality or citizenship (art. 5). Travellers may be required to complete embarkation cards (art. 7).

These arrest powers have the additional advantage of permitting an extended period of judicially unsupervised detention in custody; legislative provisions requiring an early appearance in court do not apply (s.12(6)). A person may be held in right of the original arrest for up to 48 hours, although persons held under article 4 of the STPO cannot be detained beyond 12 hours unless by then the examining officer has reasonable grounds for suspecting that the person is or has been concerned in the commission, preparation or instigation of an act of terrorism within the scope of the STPO (art. 4(2)). The 48 hour period may be extended by the Secretary of State in any particular case for a

[17] Prevention of Terrorism (Supplemental Temporary Provisions) Order 1984 (S.I. 1984 No. 418). *Mutatis mutandis*, an identical order applies in respect of Northern Ireland: Prevention of Terrorism (Supplemental Temporary Provisions) (Northern Ireland) Order 1984 (S.I. 1984 No. 417).

further period or periods specified by him up to a maximum of a further five days (s.12(4), (5); art. 9(2)). A person detained under the legislation is to "be deemed to be in legal custody at any time when he is so detained" (Sched. 3, para. 5(2)).

Powers ancillary to arrest and detention are also conferred. A constable may stop and search anyone he could arrest under section 12 "for the purpose of ascertaining whether he has in his possession any documents or other article which may constitute evidence that he is a person liable to arrest (Sched. 3, para. 6(1)). After a section 12 arrest he may search the person arrested for similar purposes, except where the arrest was effected on suspicion of a criminal offence in which case ordinary powers of search upon arrest would apply (Sched. 3, para. 6(2)).[17a] For the purposes of his determination, an examining officer can search persons, baggage, ships, aircraft and their contents, and may detain anything found or produced in the course of his examination for seven days, or for so long as the criminal or exclusion order processes necessitate (art. 6). Article 10(2) of the STPO permits a justice of the peace to issue a warrant authorising search of premises where a person liable to arrest and detention pending examination is reasonably suspected to be. Usually, fingerprinting a suspect requires consent or a court order. Under section 61 of the PCEA 1984, a suspect's fingerprints will be takeable: (i) with his written consent; or (ii) without consent where he has been charged with a recordable offence or informed that he will be reported for such an offence; or (iii) again without consent, on the authorisation of an officer not below the rank of superintendent who has reasonable grounds for suspecting the person's involvement in a criminal offence and that his fingerprints will tend to confirm or disprove that involvement. However, those of suspects who are acquitted or not further proceeded against in respect of the offence must be destroyed (s.64). By contrast, Schedule 3, paragraph 5(3) of the PTA 1984 permits the taking of such measures as are reasonably necessary to photograph, measure or otherwise identify a person arrested or detained under the legislation. Such power is conferred on examining officers, constables, prison officers or any other person authorised by the Secretary of State. The products of such measures are retained even where persons are released and subject to no further

[17a] Intimate searches will only be permissible under PCEA 1984, s.55.

proceedings.[18]

On application on oath by a police officer not below the rank of inspector, a justice of the peace may grant a search warrant authorising search of premises or places if he is satisfied that there is reasonable ground for suspecting that evidence is to be found there sufficient to justify the proscription of a particular organisation, or the making of an exclusion order, or which would constitute evidence of the commission of an offence under sections 1, 9 or 10 of the Act. The warrant authorises entry, search of premises, places or persons found there, and the seizure of material evidence (Sched. 3, paras. 4(1)-(3)).[18a] In cases of "great emergency" where "in the interests of the State immediate action is [thought] necessary," police officers of the rank of superintendent or above may issue such a warrant. Particulars of any such emergency case must be given to the Secretary of State as soon as may be (Sched. 3, paras. 4(4)-(5)).[18b]

As at December 31, 1984, 4,175 people had been detained at a port or airport (port arrests) and 1,730 elsewhere (inland arrests).[19] Almost two-thirds of all detentions occurred in the police force areas of Merseyside (1,364), the Metropolitan Police (1,280) and Dumfries and Galloway (1,222).[20] Extensions of detention were granted in the case of 260 persons detained at a port or airport (6 per cent.) and 561 detained elsewhere (32 per cent.). The vast majority of applications for extension have been granted.[21] Applications are usually filtered through the National Joint Unit at Scotland Yard, staffed by Special Branch officers from provincial forces as well as the Metropolitan Police, but

[18] Scorer and Hewitt, *op. cit.* n. 12, p. 47; *McVeigh, O'Neill and Evans* v. *United Kingdom* [1981] 5 E.H.R.R. 71, paras. 135-140, 222-232. The duty to destroy in s.64 of the PCEA 1984 does not apply (s.64(7)).

[18a] The warrant may not authorise searches for items subject to legal privilege, excluded material, or special procedure material: see PCEA 1984, s.9(2). Execution of and application for warrants is regulated by ss.15, 16 of that Act.

[18b] The warrant may authorise search for excluded material and special procedure material, but not for items subject to legal privilege: see PCEA 1984, Sched. 6, para. 27.

[19] Home Office Statistical Bulletin 1/85 (hereinafter cited as H.O. 1/85), *Statistics on the Prevention of Terrorism (Temporary Provisions) Acts 1974 and 1976–Fourth Quarter* 1984, Table 1.

[20] H.O. 1/85, para. 2, p. 1, Table 4.

[21] H.O. 1/85, Table 1 (note (d)).

applications concerning, in practice, Loyalist terrorist suspects arrested in Scotland are made directly to the Scottish Office by the force concerned.[22]

At some stage in the detention, the police have to decide whether to release the subject or to proceed further by way of criminal prosecution or exclusion. Most of those against whom no further action is taken are released within 48 hours, the majority within 36 hours.[23] Two main factors appear to govern the choice of process. Successive Home Secretaries have stressed the primacy of the criminal process in the fight against terrorism and have laid emphasis on resort to exclusion orders where the crucial evidence against the suspect cannot be presented in court without jeopardising informants or security networks.[24] Recourse is also had to exclusion where the evidence against the suspect, while suggestive of involvement in terrorism, would be insufficient to meet the evidential standards of a criminal trial.[25] In Great Britain, in the period November 29, 1974 to December 31, 1984, 5,905 arrests under the legislation led to the charging of 459 people (about 8 per cent.) with criminal offences and to 275 exclusion orders (about 5 per cent.).[26] Between January 1, 1979 and December 31, 1982 those rates rose to 11 per cent. and 6 per cent. respectively.[27] In that period, 459 people had their detention extended beyond 48 hours, of whom 210 (46 per cent.) were charged or excluded.[28] Thirty per cent. of those arrested inland were charged, rising to over 60 per cent. where detention was extended. Exclusion is increasingly rare following inland arrests, but formed 7 per cent. of all port detentions and over 40 per cent. of extended port detentions in that four year period.[29] From January 1, 1983 to December 31, 1984, 350 people were detained under the legislation, 216 at a port or airport, 134 elsewhere. Fifty-four were charged (about 15 per cent.) and 14 excluded (about 4 per

22 Jellicoe, para. 40.

23 H.O. 1/85, Table 8.

24 See, *e.g.* H.C. Deb. Vol. 980, col. 408 (Mr. W. Whitelaw, MP, Home Secretary); Scorer, *op. cit.* n. 12, p. 12; Scorer and Hewitt, *op. cit.* n. 12, p. 26.

25 Scorer and Hewitt, *op. cit.* n. 12, p. 26; *Review of the Operation of the Prevention of Terrorism (Temporary Provisions) Acts 1974 and 1976 by the Rt. Hon. Lord Shackleton, K.G., O.B.E.*, Cmnd. 7324 (1978) (hereinafter cited as "Shackleton"), para. 76.

26 H.O. 1/85, Table 1.

27 Jellicoe, para. 46.

28 *Ibid.* para. 47.

29 *Ibid.* paras. 48, 127.

cent.). This 19 per cent. charge and exclusion rule was higher than in previous periods (1982–14 per cent., 1981–9 per cent.), perhaps indicating continued selectivity in the use of the powers. Twelve of the 14 EOs were made against persons detained at a port or airport.[30]

The port powers and those in section 12 raise issues of compliance with the European Convention on Human Rights. The former were upheld by the Commission in *McVeigh* v. *United Kingdom* as permissible within article 5(1)(*b*) which sanctions "the lawful arrest and detention of a person . . . in order to secure the fulfilment of any obligation prescribed by law," in this case the obligation to submit to examination at the ports.[31] The Commission took into account that the obligations arose only in the limited circumstances of travel across a clear geographical or political boundary, and that "the purpose of examination is limited and directed towards an end of evident public importance in the context of a serious and continuing threat from organised terrorism."[32] The security check was important to control the movement of terrorists and it was legitimate to resort to detention where suspicions were aroused requiring examination in a depth not practicable at the port.[33] The search, questioning, fingerprinting and photographing of the applicants were legitimate interferences with their right to private life, justified under article 8(2) as measures in accordance with law which were necessary in a democratic society for the prevention of crime.[34] The retention of fingerprints, photographs and information obtained from the suspects, kept separate from criminal records where the arrestee did not have a criminal record, and reserved exclusively for use in the fight against terrorism, was similarly held necessary in the interest of public safety and for the prevention of crime, since intelligence material and forensic evidence may be of critical importance in the detection of terrorist offenders.[35] Section 12 cannot be justified pursuant to article 5(1)(*b*). Rather it raises issues under paragraphs 1(*c*) and (3) of that article, already discussed in Chapter 3 (*supra*, pp. 122-124).

[30] H.O. 1/85, Tables 1 and 5.

[31] [1981] 5 E.H.R.R. 71, paras. 168-196.

[32] [1981] 5 E.H.R.R. 71, para. 188.

[33] [1981] 5 E.H.R.R. 71, para. 195.

[34] [1981] 5 E.H.R.R. 71, paras. 222-232. Refusal to allow two of the applicants to contact their wives was, however, a breach of Art. 8(1) not justified within Art. 8(2) (paras. 233-240).

[35] [1981] 5 E.H.R.R. 71, para. 230.

In some cases involving foreign nationals its use for purposes of exclusion might be justifiable as a step to prevent unauthorised entry to the country or to secure deportation permissible under article 5(1)(*f*), a matter discussed below as part of the exclusion process (pp. 200-202).

Critics of the powers, drawing some support from the low rate of charge and exclusion when compared to initial arrests, suggest a flimsy basis for arrest in many cases; that arrest and detention are effected for purposes of harassment of particular political groups; that questioning focuses on political opinions and affiliations; and that, as in Ulster, the powers are deployed as a means of constructing a low-level intelligence dossier on particular sectors of the community as part of counter-insurgency tactics developed by military theoreticians, such as Brigadier Frank Kitson,[36] on the basis of experience in colonial emergencies, which tactics depend for their success on a significant degree of population surveillance and on encouraging informers within and defectors from the ranks of the terrorist groups and their sympathisers, in the hope of "isolating and identifying the urban guerillas and then detaching them from the supportive or ambivalent community."[37] The retention of the fingerprints, photographs and record of arrest of those released may lend some support to this view.

The primary purpose of the port powers, accepted in *McVeigh*, is said to be to deter terrorists from trying to enter the territory in question by demonstrating that they are likely to be caught.[38] The powers are selectively used—even at the main ports for travel to Ireland only one passenger in 25,000 was detained in 1981[39] —but apparently deployed on the basis of rather crude stereotypes.[40] The new rule (no detention beyond 12 hours unless on reasonable suspicion of involvement in terrorism) is a welcome addition to further encourage selective use.[41] The SACHR proposed a four hour maximum.[42] The powers do, however, arouse resentment in

[36] Frank Kitson, *Low Intensity Operations: Subversion, Insurgency and Peace-keeping* (1971): *cf.* R. Evelegh, *Peace-keeping in a Democratic Society: The Lessons of Northern Ireland* (1978), esp. Chaps. 6 and 7.

[37] For these criticisms see: D.R. Lowry, *loc. cit.* n. 12, at pp. 209-217 (the quotation is taken from p. 210); Scorer, *op. cit.* n. 12, pp. 3, 25-26; Scorer and Hewitt, *op. cit.* n. 12, p. 53.

[38] Jellicoe, para. 139.

[39] *Ibid.* para. 129.

[40] *Ibid.* para. 134.

[41] *Ibid.* para. 142.

[42] SACHR, *Annual Report for 1982-83*, H.C. 262 (1983-84), pp. 12-13. Detention

Ulster as reinforcing notions of second-class citizenship.[43] It is more difficult to make out a convincing case for wider powers of arrest and extended detention in Great Britain than in the Province, given less straitened circumstances of policing on the mainland. Justification for the width of the arrest power in section 12 (and by implication that at the ports beyond 12 hours) is founded on a "better safe than sorry" principle, customarily invoked in emergency contexts. Lord Shackleton thought

> "the primary purpose of the Act is to prevent acts of terrorism, and for this reason the police are bound to follow up any information or suspicion about involvement in terrorism although, of course, it must in every case be sufficient to justify the arrest. The difficulty for the police is that when their questioning starts they do not know the extent to which the suspect may be involved in terrorism. It is easy to argue that, if the enquiries lead nowhere, the initial grounds for detention were inadequate. But this ignores both the preventive nature of the legislation in its widest aspects and the response the police have to make to information suggesting involvement in terrorism. . . .
>
> Let us take, as an example, the case where the police receive information that a person is concerned in terrorism, be it past incidents or terrorist attacks either imminent or planned for the future. In such a case there may be little or no information to connect that person with a specific offence, such as would justify arrest under the normal provisions of the law, but the police may consider, after careful assessment of the information, that it has such serious implications for the detection either of past offences or of offences in preparation, and such potential consequences in terms of death and serious injury, that immediate action to detain the person concerned is necessary."[44]

Justification for extended detention centres on the need to give the police adequate time to interview suspected terrorists in a context where terrorist groups, increasingly conscious of their internal security, have taken steps to ensure that their activists are well trained in remaining silent during prolonged questioning,[45] a

beyond four hours on this model would require an arrest under s.12 which the Commission would limit to reasonable suspicion of a specific terrorist-type offence (*ibid.* p. 9).

[43] *Ibid.* pp. 7-11.

[44] Shackleton, paras. 84, 71.

[45] Jellicoe, para. 57; Shackleton, para. 72.

justification which would have profound implications for the suspect's right of silence if the police applied a general presumption that silence gave further grounds to suspect involvement in terrorism. Lord Shackleton suggested that the police have the necessary training to distinguish between the trained terrorist and those with "legitimate" reasons, unconnected with terrorism, for keeping silent, but did not specify how the distinction would be made.[46] It also takes time to complete forensic inquiries, check out identities and statements against existing intelligence, verify alibis through the RUC or the police in the Republic, follow up new lines of inquiry, and gather intelligence vital to the fight against terrorism.[47] Lord Jellicoe thought that the port powers had a deterrent effect "not demonstrated by the numbers apprehended."[48] He concluded that inland arrests have "led to the charging and subsequent conviction of a large number of people guilty of very serious criminal offences connected with terrorism *which in many cases would not and could not have resulted from arrest under ordinary powers*" (emphasis supplied).[49] The statistics do not prove this last assertion. It would have been useful to have been told how many, based on a close analysis of police files. It is, however, a view endorsed by Lord Shackleton's Review.[50]

The statistics do not shine as a beacon proclaiming the effectiveness of those powers. One approach is to assert that the Government has failed to establish that they are absolutely necessary and unquestionably effective, to maintain that ordinary powers of arrest would suffice, and to reject entirely the need for those special powers. That approach is taken by NCCL[51] and by the Labour Party.[52] The author prefers a more cautious approach, based on the premise that it is difficult for anyone without access to the security information presented to the reviews to judge accurately the need for and extent of effectiveness of such powers, which accepts that they may be necessary in some cases, seeks

[46] Shackleton, para. 72.

[47] Jellicoe, para. 60; Shackleton, paras. 72-76.

[48] Jellicoe, para. 139.

[49] *Ibid.* para. 56.

[50] Shackleton, para. 136.

[51] Scorer and Hewitt, *op. cit.* n. 12, *passim.*

[52] Mr. R. Hattersley, MP, then Shadow Home Secretary, H.C. Deb., Vol. 38, cols. 571-576.

methods of confining the use of such extraordinary powers to those cases which warrant it, and aims to provide enhanced safeguards against abuse.

The explicit extension of the arrest powers to cover international terrorism has proved controversial.[53] It is apt to render them *de facto* permanent features of our law. The wording of the previous legislation did not preclude such use, not being confined explicitly to terrorism connected with Northern Irish affairs.[54] That it was intended to be so limited was conveyed in guidance in a circular to the police,[55] and extended detention would only be authorised in such cases.[56] Not including the limitation in the legislation seemed sensible; at the arrest stage the constable or examining officer might be justifiably suspicious of the person before him, but not know for sure at that stage with which terrorist cause the suspect was linked.[57] The present formulation, excluding domestic terrorism unconnected with Northern Ireland, defeats that end, and is clumsy and odd; the rationale of the powers in the wider context of terrorism seems just as applicable to the domestic context, and enabling a power of arrest to cover them is hardly likely to assist "such groups to gain a coherence and identity which they currently lack," the reason proffered for their exclusion by Lord Jellicoe.[58] It has been suggested that immigration officers already possess adequate powers to deal with suspected terrorists, passing through the ports, who require leave to enter.[59] This is true up to a point. Difficulties may arise, however, over terrorist use of the Republic of Ireland as a "spring

[53] In particular, concern focused (a) on whether the extension was necessary given police successes with ordinary powers in international terrorist cases, and (b) on the position of liberation groups (*e.g.* SWAPO), legitimately resident in the UK, but involved in "terrorism" abroad. In strict law, the arrest powers in PTAs 1974 and 1976 similarly covered (a) and (b). The Home Office has issued a circular (26/1984) to the police on the proper use of s.12 of the PTA 1984, as it applies to international terrorism, which makes it clear that as regards acts of such terrorism abroad, s.12 should only be used where, in consequence, there is the prospect of deportation from the UK or a criminal charge before its courts; that it is directed primarily against international terrorist acts in the UK (Lord Elton, H.L.Deb., Vol. 449, col. 867).

[54] See s.12. Prevention of Terrorism (Temporary Provisions) Acts 1974 and 1976.

[55] Jellicoe, paras. 77, 144.

[56] *Ibid.* para. 75.

[57] Mr. W. Whitelaw, MP, Home Secretary, H.C. Deb., Vol. 1, col. 393.

[58] Jellicoe, para. 77.

[59] *Official Report*, Standing Committee D (1983-84), cols. 342-350.

board" for entry into the United Kingdom; the existence of the Common Travel Area (CTA), formed by the United Kingdom, the Republic of Ireland, the Isle of Man, and the Channel Islands, means that passengers on local journeys to the United Kingdom do not need to present themselves to an immigration officer for examination,[60] and so that officer's ordinary powers of arrest and extended detention under the Immigration Act 1971 are inapplicable to them.[61] Such passengers are, of course, subject to the filter of immigration control in the other CTA entities. Many of the groups into which international terrorists might fall come within exceptions to the CTA provisions, thereby falling within the ambit of the Immigration Act powers.[62] Closing the small gap that remained was probably sensible, but the port power, which in form applies also to those having the right of abode in the United Kingdom, should be subject to adequate safeguards. Proper training of examining officers is essential.[63] The practicalities of manpower and of securing rapid disembarkation at international ports and airports should be conducive to selective use of such powers. Where they are deployed against those not having the right of abode, it would have been preferable to have precluded supplemental recourse to the detention powers under the Immigration Act.

It is important that such wide powers of arrest and detention be used selectively and not as a matter of routine. In this respect the limitation on examination beyond 12 hours at a port is welcome, although it might usefully apply at an earlier stage (*e.g.* four hours) (*supra*, pp. 171,176). Under the PTA 1976, the section 12 powers also applied to persons reasonably suspected of withholding information about terrorism, the offence under section 11. That section 12 of the PTA 1984 does not so apply is welcome. The offence remains intact and continues to be arrestable under the PCEA 1984. However, unless section 12(1)(*b*) is narrowed, it is possible that many persons reasonably suspected of the section 11 offence would in any event come within the phrase "concerned in the commission, preparation or instigation of acts of terrorism." It may be that one will see little change in practice. It is submitted that further limitation of the section 12(1)(*b*) power to discourage

[60] On the CTA in general, see L. Grant and I. Martin, *Immigration Law and Practice* (1982), Chap. 4; J.M. Evans, *Immigration Law* (2nd ed., 1983), pp. 118-119.

[61] Mr. D. Waddington, MP, H.C. Deb. Vol. 38, col. 638.

[62] On the exceptions, see Grant and Martin, *op. cit.* n. 60, pp. 55-57.

[63] *Cf.* Jellicoe, paras. 150, 154.

speculative fishing expeditions would be valuable. This might be effected by confining the power to cases of reasonable suspicion of specific terrorist crimes, or at the very least of involvement in specific terrorist incidents (see Chap. 3, *supra*, pp. 128-129). The section 12 power is only to be used where no other power will suffice to attain the end sought, a limitation embodied in Circular advice to the police.[64] That wider powers of arrest and extended detention will be available in England and Wales under the PCEA 1984 ought to mean less recourse to section 12. The burden of ensuring adherence to the limitation ought not to rest solely on Ministers and senior police officers, important as their role is. The limitation should be included in the legislation itself as a condition of the legality of the arrest and detention, opening up the possibility of a civil action for damages as a further incentive to selective use of extraordinary powers. An exclusionary evidence rule, sufficiently sensitive to context, could also help.[65] One safeguard against abuse would be to confer a right to compensation, without the need for separate litigation, on persons improperly detained under emergency legislation and released without charge or subjection to an exclusion order, where a formal complaint against the police has been lodged and upheld.[66] A special compensation tribunal might also be considered.[67]

Adequate supervision to prevent abuse of such powers is crucial if public confidence in them is to be preserved. Hierarchical review within the police and ministries concerned provides some safeguard; not all requests for extended detention are granted.[68] Increased ministerial supervision and the opportunity to be more flexible about the periods to be granted within the five day maximum are to be welcomed. It would be preferable, however, to adopt in Great Britain the judicial supervision proposed in Chapter 3 for Northern Ireland (*supra*, pp. 130-131). In England and Wales the legal rules and the codes on treatment of suspects under the PCEA 1984 will apply with some modifications to those detained under the PTA 1984.[69] Similar provision should be made

[64] Jellicoe, para. 68; *Official Report*, Standing Committee D, (1983-84), cols. 242, 298.

[65] *Cf.* examples cited in Chap. 3, n. 80, p. 147.

[66] SACHR, *Annual Report for 1982-83*, H.C. 262 (1983-84), pp. 10-11.

[67] As was recommended in W.L. Twining, *Emergency Powers: A Fresh Start* (Fabian Tract 416, 1972), p. 27.

[68] Jellicoe, Annex D, Table 1 (note (e)), p. 129; H.O. 1/85, Table 1.

[69] Police and Criminal Evidence Act 1984, ss.56-58, 66-67.

in force orders elsewhere.[70] It is submitted that the code proposed in Chapter 3 for Northern Ireland would be preferable as regards methods of enforcement (*supra*, pp. 147-148).

3. Criminal Offences and Prosecutions

A significant number of terrorist suspects in Great Britain have been charged with and convicted of offences under the general criminal law, although not so many nor of so serious offences as in Northern Ireland.[71] Not all were arrested under powers conferred by the PTAs. Using ordinary powers the police had a number of successes in relation to the conviction of those responsible for the bombings of 1973 and 1974, including the Birmingham pub bombings. Published statistics are, however, limited to the disposition of those detained under the PTAs. As at December 31, 1984, 254 persons so detained had been charged in Great Britain with non-PTA offences only, of whom 182 were convicted, 30 acquitted or the charge "not proven," 16 still awaited trial, and 26 charges were not proceeded with Common charges, were: causing or conspiracy to cause explosions (61); firearms offences (30); Theft Act offences (75); unlawful possession or conspiracy to possess explosives with intent to endanger life (23); and conspiracy to commit offences under the PTAs (13). The few prosecutions for murder were not successful.[72] Fifty-three persons were returned to Northern Ireland under the backing of warrants' procedure, to be charged there with serious non-PTA offences only, of whom 45 were convicted, two awaited trial and six cases were not proceeded with.[73] These statistics, however, understate the numbers charged with non-PTA offences; those detained under the PTAs who were charged with offences under them as well as with ordinary offences are included in the statistics on PTA offences.[74] The nature, scope, implications and incidence of use of the offences created by the PTAs must now be examined.

[70] Jellicoe, para. 103.

[71] *Ibid.* para. 53.

[72] *Ibid.* Annex D, Table 5, p. 134. H.O. 1/85, Table 7.

[73] *Ibid.* The backing of warrants procedure is one designed to enable the detention of a fugitive offender from one legal jurisdiction of the UK (*e.g.* Northern Ireland) who is found in another legal jurisdiction of the UK (*e.g.* England and Wales), and to secure his return to the first mentioned legal jurisdiction. A warrant issued in that jurisdiction must be indorsed ("backed") by a justice of the peace in the "refuge" jurisdiction. See, generally, *Halsbury's Laws of England* (4th ed.), Vol. 29, para. 229.

[74] Jellicoe, Annex D, Table 4, p. 133; H.O. 1/85, Tables 6 and 7.

These offences are, with the exception of that in section 2 (display of support in public for a proscribed organisation), indictable in the sense of being triable either way. On conviction on indictment, persons are liable to imprisonment for a term not exceeding five years, an unlimited fine, or both (ss.1(2), 9(4), 10(3), 11(2)). On summary conviction, persons may be imprisoned for a term not exceeding six months, be subject to a fine up to the statutory maximum, or both (*ibid.*). Conviction under section 2 renders a person liable to a maximum six months imprisonment, to a fine not exceeding level five on the standard scale, or to both (s.2(1)). All proceedings, apart from those concerning regulatory offences under the travel control powers, require in England and Wales the consent of the Attorney General (Sched. 3, para. 3). Unless otherwise indicated, statistics are to December 31, 1984.

(1) *Proscribed Organisations and related offences (ss.1, 2)*

These offences do not extend to Northern Ireland (s.19(2)). Any Secretary of State (in practice the Home Secretary) may proscribe "any organisation that appears to him to be concerned in terrorism occurring in the United Kingdom and connected with Northern Irish affairs, or in promoting it or encouraging it" (s.1(4)). He does so by statutory instrument adding its name to the list in Schedule 1. He may by statutory instrument delete it from the list (deproscription) (s.1(5)). To date, only the IRA (from the inception of the legislation—November 29, 1974) and the Irish National Liberation Army (INLA) (from July 3, 1979) are Proscribed Organisations (POs) in Great Britain.

A person belonging or professing to belong to a PO is guilty of an offence (s.1(1)(*a*)). He has a defence to a membership charge if he shows that the only or last occasion on which he became a member antedates proscription and that he has not taken part in any of its post-proscription activities (s.1(7), (9)). Unlike NIEPA 1978 (*supra*, pp. 107-108), the PTAs have afforded no special help to the prosecution in proving membership. It is criminal to solicit or invite financial or other support for a PO, or knowingly to make or receive any monetary or other contribution to its resources (s.1(1)(*b*)). To arrange, manage or assist in the arrangement or management of a public or private meeting of three or more persons, or to address the same, in the knowledge that it is to be addressed by a person belonging or professing to belong to a PO or that the meeting is to support a PO or further its activities, is likewise criminal (s.1(1)(*c*)). Conviction of any of these offences may result in the court ordering forfeiture of any money or other property in the possession or under the control of the defendant at the time of the offence which was for the use or benefit of the PO (s.1(10)). No one has been charged in Great Britain with membership or professed membership of a PO, or with making contributions towards its resources or with arranging a meeting in its support.[75] Seven people have been charged with soliciting or receiving support. Only two were convicted, one for offering posters for sale, the other for soliciting or receiving money.[76] Both received prison sentences of less than one year.[77]

Display of support in public for a PO is a summary offence only. A person displays such support, if in a public place, he wears any item of dress, or wears, carries or displays any article in a way or in circumstances which arouse reasonable apprehension that he is a member or supporter of a PO (s.2(1)). Public place includes any highway and any other premises or place to which at the material time the public have, or are permitted to have, access whether on payment or otherwise (s.2(3)). Only two people have been charged with this offence. Both were convicted and fined.[78]

Proscribing an organisation is not a step to be lightly taken in a liberal democracy because of its impact on freedom of association, of assembly and of expression. Proscription powers in Northern Ireland under the NIEPAs (*supra*, pp. 107-108) and in Great Britain under the PTA cover only groups advocating violence, the power is rightly subject to parliamentary scrutiny, and it has arguably been sparingly used, given the legitimacy of the political wings of terrorist groups connected with Northern Ireland, which are not, as in the Republic, legally debarred from access to the broadcasting media.[79] Its principal rationale lies in enshrining in statutory form public aversion to such organisations to avoid, particularly in Great Britain, public outrage being expressed in public disorder; indeed it has been suggested that prompt proscription of the IRA in 1974 went some way to preventing a "backlash" against the Irish community in Great Britain. It may have some deterrent

[75] H.O. 1/85, Table 6.

[76] Scorer and Hewitt, *op. cit.* n. 12, p. 17.

[77] Jellicoe, para. 205.

[78] *Ibid.* but *cf.* H.O. 1/85, Table 6, which indicates only one conviction.

[79] See P. Wilkinson, *Terrorism and the Liberal State* (1977), pp. 168-170; *Review of the Operation of the Northern Ireland (Emergency Provisions) Act 1978 by the Rt. Hon. Sir George Baker O.B.E.*, Cmnd. 9222 (1984), para. 415 (hereinafter cited as "Baker").

value in terms of the flow of funds to POs. There have been few open demonstrations of support for POs in Great Britain since its enactment.[80] Not so in Northern Ireland. Its operational value seems limited. It is difficult to see that many cases would in practice be caught by section 2 of the PTA 1984 which would not also constitute an offence under either section 1 (political uniforms) or 5 (threatening, abusive or insulting behaviour or displays) of the Public Order Act 1936. The wearing of badges or small emblems in circumstances unlikely to give rise to disorder would be an example. Section 2 also avoids possible difficulties over the meaning of "uniform" in section 1 of the Public Order Act 1936.[81]

Proscription of organisations seeking change through non-democratic violent means is unlikely to breach the European Convention. Guarantees of freedom of conscience, expression and association are subject to legal limitation where necessary in a democratic society in the interest *inter alia* of national security, public safety, the prevention of disorder and the protection of the rights and freedoms of others.[82] The State has a "margin of appreciation" in applying limitations, a margin likely to be more widely interpreted by the Convention organs in a context of terrorism.[83] Article 17 is also relevant:

> "Nothing in this Convention may be interpreted as implying for any State, group or person any right to engage in any activity or perform any act aimed at the destruction of any of the rights and freedoms set forth herein or at their limitation to a greater extent than is provided for in the Convention."

West Germany was able to rely on this to justify its ban on the

80 Jellicoe, paras. 207-208.

81 In *O'Moran* v. *DPP; Whelan* v. *DPP* [1975] Q.B. 864, at p. 873 Lord Widgery C.J. stated: "Subject always to the de minimis rule, I see no reason why the article or articles should cover the whole of the body or a major part of the body . . . or indeed should go beyond the existence of the beret itself. In this case the articles did go beyond the beret. They extended to the pullover, the dark glasses and the dark clothing. . . . " This might achieve most of the object of s.2 of the PTA 1984, but it is purely dicta and presumably the Government wants to ensure plenary coverage of modes of public support.

82 See, *e.g.* Arts. 8(2), 9(2), 10(2), 11(2) of the Convention.

83 *McVeigh* v. *United Kingdom* [1981] 5 E.H.R.R. 71; C. Warbrick, "The European Convention on Human Rights and the Prevention of Terrorism" (1983) 32 I.C.L.Q. 82, at pp. 99-101.

German Communist Party.[84] It does not operate so as to deprive groups coming under it of all rights under the Convention, but only those directly enabling them to engage in Article 17 activity, *i.e.* Articles 8 (privacy and correspondence), 9 (conscience), 10 (expression) and 11 (assembly and association). Much depends on the aims of the organisation; those with totalitarian aims will be caught.[85] Proscription in Northern Ireland under NIEPA 1978 would in any event be justifiable pursuant to the Article 15 derogation in force until August 22, 1984.

It is unlikely that the lists of POs in either legislation will be further reduced unless the organisations concerned clearly renounce violence.[86] The lists have, however, been criticised for their underinclusive nature: not all organisations engaged in violence in the Province are banned (the Ulster Defence Association is an oft-cited example) and at present only Republican organisations are banned in Great Britain. It has been argued that if proscription's main rationale is public condemnation the list of POs ought to be uniform throughout the United Kingdom.[87]

Concern has been expressed that even pacifist or non-violent Irish Republicanism is not tolerated in Great Britain, that the PTA renders its supporters liable to prosecution or exclusion.[88] Assurances have been given by the Home Secretary that its provisions are "not intended to hamper the expression of political views about Northern Ireland."[89] It has been claimed that proscription and related offences have had "a chilling effect on the

[84] [1956-57] 1 Y.B.E.C.H.R. 222.

[85] Warbrick, *loc. cit.* n.83, at pp. 91-93.

[86] Jellicoe, para. 210.

[87] Jellicoe, para. 211. He was not prepared to recommend an addition to the PTA list "in the absence of a clear and demonstrable need for this." But, as he admits earlier in the report (paras. 177, 178), Loyalist paramilitaries have links with Scotland, and, in any event, the test for proscription in s.1 refers to "any organisation that appears [to the Secretary of State] to be concerned in terrorism occurring in the United Kingdom and connected with Northern Irish Affairs, or in promoting or encouraging it." Attempts, at committee stage in the Commons, to have the Ulster Volunteer Force (UVF) and the Ulster Freedom Fighters added to Sched. 1 to the PTA 1984 failed: *Official Report*, Standing Committee D (1983-84), cols. 55-61. Baker, para. 407, supported Jellicoe's view that symmetry alone was not a reason for extending the PTA list, nor was he prepared to recommend proscription under NIEPA of Sinn Fein or the Ulster Defence Association (para. 121).

[88] Lowry, *loc. cit.* n. 12, at p. 202.

[89] H.C. Deb., Vol. 1, cols. 341-342 (Mr. W. Whitelaw, MP); *Official Report*, Standing Committee D (1983-84), cols. 50-52 (Mr. L. Brittan MP).

media"[90]; have drastically reduced the access of groups concerned with matters Irish to television, radio, the Press, meeting rooms and other places of public debate, discussion and demonstration; and have otherwise penalised the activities of groups holding unpopular views on Northern Ireland policy.[91] It is difficult to know whether one can properly totally ascribe this to the Acts as distinct from a more general expression of anti-Irish public feeling in the wake of terrorist atrocities, but suppression of unpopular political views surely cannot aid a political solution.[92] In part, however, problems are likely to flow from the vagueness and uncertainty of these offences. Those concerned with meetings represent a dangerous slide towards guilt by association, arguably unnecessary given the law on sedition.[93] The notion of "other support" in section 1(1)(*b*) does not appear to be limited to donations in kind: "financial or other support" would not be read *ejusdem generis* and other provisions in the Act refer specifically to "money or other property."[94] It seems elastic enough to catch non-member workers for a PO, persons who distribute its literature for free, persons who advocate its aims and methods without naming it, or the drunk in the street who cries: "Support the IRA!"[95] No doubt the penumbra of uncertainty is controllable by prosecutorial discretion, but the offences fall far short of the *desideratum* of certainty in the criminal law. In any event their impact is not confined to the stage of considering whether to prosecute. It is at the arrest stage that the potentialities for harassment, produced in part by those uncertainties, present themselves.

This said, it is difficult to know how the PTA could be altered to solve the problem if one accepts the legitimacy of the public condemnation rationale. It seems difficult to more closely define "support" without missing legitimate targets. The matter is primarily one of appropriate supervision of the arrest and detention process. In this regard the Government's acceptance of Lord Jellicoe's recommendation, that the police be given appropriate guidance by way of Circular on the proper use of

90 Lowry, *loc. cit.* n. 12, at p. 201.

91 Scorer, *op. cit.* n. 12, pp. 7-8; Scorer and Hewitt, *op. cit.* n. 12, pp. 18-20.

92 D.N. Schiff [1978] P.L. 352, at pp. 355-56.

93 L.H. Leigh, *loc. cit.* n. 11, at p. 2.

94 s.1(1)(*b*) ("money or otherwise"); s.1(7) ("money or other property"); s.10(1)(*a*),(*b*), (2) ("money or other property"); Mr. D. Waddington, MP, *Official Report*, Standing Committee D (1983-84), col. 19.

95 See, generally, *Official Report*, Standing Committee D (1983-84), cols. 5-61.

sections 1 and 2, is welcome.[96] A statutory declaration along the lines of the Home Secretary's assurance could also help.

(2) *Contributions towards acts of terrorism (s.10)*

This also applies to Northern Ireland (s.19(1)). It is an offence to solicit or invite another to give or lend, whether or not for consideration, money or other property, or to receive or accept from any other person the same, intending it to be applied or used for or in connection with the commission, preparation or instigation of acts of terrorism connected with Northern Irish affairs (s.10(1), (5)). "Property" includes both real and personal property (s.10(6)). The donor, lender or person who makes the same available (whether for consideration or not) likewise commits an offence if he knows or suspects that it will or may be so used (s.10(2)). Someone convicted of soliciting, inviting or receiving may find that the court orders the forfeiture of money or other property in his possession or under his control at the time of the offence which was then intended to be used for or in connection with such ends (s.10(4)). In Great Britain, 54 persons have been charged with these offences, 35 of whom were convicted, all of whom received a prison sentence, 32 for longer than a year.[97] As at December 31, 1982, there had been seven persons charged in Northern Ireland, two of whom awaited trial. The other five were convicted, one being fined, another given a suspended sentence, and the others immediate imprisonment.[98]

These offences seem a sensible addition to the armoury of the PTA and the general criminal law, in particular by dealing with payments to "front" organisations.[99] Any impact on legitimate political groups is an issue of supervision of the arrest process.

[96] Jellicoe, para. 212. See Home Office Circular No. 90/1983, paras. 7,8.

[97] Jellicoe, para. 205; H.O. 1/85, Table 6.

[98] Jellicoe, para. 206.

[99] *Ibid.* para. 213: "I was particularly struck by the evidence which I received in Northern Ireland of the means by which terrorist activities are funded. I was told of large sums paid out, particularly in the construction industry, to bogus "security firms" which are in reality no more than front organisations for terrorist groups from both the Republican and Loyalist sides. Equivalent practices exist in the field of gaming machines in Northern Ireland. It seems to me vitally important that the police have adequate powers to deal with this problem."

(3) *Withholding information about terrorism (s.11)*

This applies throughout the United Kingdom (s.19). It is more narrowly formulated in the PTA 1984 than previously.[1] It remains confined to acts of terrorism connected with Northern Irish affairs (s.10(5)). A person commits an offence if, having information which he knows or believes might be of material assistance in preventing the commission by another person of an act of such terrorism, or in securing the apprehension, prosecution or conviction of another person for an offence involving the commission, preparation or instigation of an act of such terrorism, he fails without reasonable excuse to disclose that information to the appropriate law enforcement authorities as soon as is reasonably practicable (s.11(1)). Fifteen people have been charged under it in Great Britain, of whom 10 were convicted. Most received a non-custodial sentence.[2] In Northern Ireland to November 1, 1982, 62 people had been charged. Of the 30 cases dealt with by the courts by that date, 22 were convicted. Only three received a custodial sentence.[3]

The section attaches criminal sanctions to what is otherwise only the moral and social imperative of helping the police. Its closest parallel in England and Wales is section 5(1) of the Criminal Law Act 1967 which renders it an offence to accept a bribe in return for not giving relevant information to the police; but there it is the element of corruption which criminalises.[4] The equivalent section in the Criminal Law Act (NI) 1967 is wider in not requiring a bribe, but is confined to cases where an arrestable offence has been committed.[5]

[1] The PTA 1976 did not limit s.11 to information about "another person"—see Jellicoe, para. 233.

[2] Jellicoe, para. 218; Annex D, Table 4; H.O. 1/85, Table 6.

[3] Jellicoe, Table 12.

[4] s.5(1) provides (*re* England and Wales): "Where a person has committed an arrestable offence, any other person who, knowing or believing that the offence or some other arrestable offence has been committed, and that he has information which might be of material assistance in securing the prosecution or conviction of an offender for it, accepts or agrees to accept for not disclosing that information any consideration other than the making good of loss or injury caused by the offence, or the making of reasonable compensation for that loss or injury, shall be liable on conviction on indictment to imprisonment for not more than two years."

[5] s.5 of the Northern Ireland legislation provides that
"where a person has committed an arrestable offence, it shall be the duty of every other person who knows or believes—

The justification for section 11 is open to question. A number of police forces, particularly the RUC, informed Lord Jellicoe that the existence of the offence had persuaded persons to give vital information they would otherwise have been unwilling to divulge. He considered it to be of "significant value" to the police who could, however, operate without it if necessary.[6] The provision presents problems of vagueness and uncertainty: would fear of terrorist reprisals constitute "reasonable excuse" for non-disclosure? The role of prosecutorial discretion looms large. A legal duty to inform has grave implications for a suspect's right of silence. That it is now limited to information about a third party's activities is a step forward, as is Circular guidance that it should only be used in serious cases.[7] It could still produce disturbing conflicts in close personal relationships.[8] The pressures it might exert in the interrogation context could arguably induce detainees to lay false information against another to avoid prosecution, with detrimental results to the third party in question.[9] It may have an undesirable limiting effect on investigative journalism.[10] It no longer attracts the special powers of arrest and extended detention; Lord Jellicoe considered these ought only to apply to those suspected of personal involvement in terrorism.[11] As Lord Shackleton noted, "it has an unpleasant ring

(*a*) that the offence or some other arrestable offence has been committed; and

(*b*) that he has information which is likely to secure, or to be of material assistance in securing, the apprehension, prosecution or conviction of any person for that offence;

to give that information, within a reasonable time, to a constable and if, without reasonable excuse, he fails to do so he shall be guilty of an offence

The penalty varies "according to the gravity of the offence about which the accused does not give information" (Baker, para. 245).

6 Jellicoe, paras. 221-222. Baker (paras. 252-253) endorsed the former view and recommended the creation in a new NIEPA of a composite offence combining s.5 of the CLA(NI) 1967 and s.11 of the PTA 1984.

7 On Circular guidance see Mr. D. Waddington, MP, *Official Report*, Standing Committee D (1983-84), cols. 240-250; Home Office Circulars Nos. 90/1983 and 26/1984.

8 An attempt to limit the subject area of the information to that re. any other person "other than a spouse, child or any other relative" of D was defeated. The Government suggested that the matter be left to the discretion of the authorities, in the light of guidance in circular form, and noted that s.11 had never been used against a spouse or relative—*ibid.* cols. 239-250.

9 Scorer, *op. cit.* n. 12, pp. 36-37.

10 Mr. C. Soley, MP, *Official Report*, Standing Committee D (1983-84), col. 261. *Cf.* Att. Gen. Havers, H.C. Deb., Vol. 987, col. 1009.

11 Jellicoe, para. 232. However, it remains an arrestable offence under s.2 of the Criminal Law Act 1967; s.24 of the PCEA 1984.

about it in terms of civil liberties."[12] It ought to be dropped.

(4) *Offences ancillary to the Exclusion Order process and to travel control*

These apply throughout the United Kingdom (s.19). Failure to comply with an Exclusion Order (EO) is an offence (s.9(1)). So is knowingly harbouring the non-compliant subject of an EO, or being knowingly concerned in arrangements to secure his entry to the prohibited jurisdiction (s.9(2)). Knowing non-compliance with provisions in subordinate legislation regulating travel and examination at ports is a summary offence punishable with not more than three months imprisonment, or a fine not exceeding level four on the standard scale, or both. Twelve people have been convicted of EO offences in Great Britain, and 53 of offences connected with travel control.[13] Such offences are a logical back-up to the processes concerned. It would be preferable to employ traditional concepts of aiding and abetting rather than the width of "concerned."

4. Exclusion Orders

Part II of the PTA 1984 empowers any Secretary of State to exclude terrorist suspects from the United Kingdom (s.6), from Great Britain (s.4), and from Northern Ireland (s.5). In practice, such powers are exercised principally by the Home Secretary who is also responsible in this matter for Scotland.[14] Little use has been made of the process in Northern Ireland where policies of "Ulsterisation" and "criminalisation" are the order of the day (Chap. 3, *supra*, pp. 99-100, 161-162).

The Home Secretary makes a personal decision on the basis of evidence gathered by the police and processed at New Scotland Yard by a team of officers from the Special Branches of provincial police forces and the Metropolitan Special Branch. Careful consideration of applications for EOs by senior police officers and by civil servants up to deputy secretary level in the Home Office provides a *de facto* filter. The submission is presented through a junior Minister.[15]

[12] Shackleton, para. 133.
[13] H.O. 1/85, Table 6.
[14] Jellicoe, para. 156.
[15] *Ibid.* para. 162; Shackleton, paras. 38 and 78.

The Secretary of State may only exercise these powers "in such a way as appears to him expedient to prevent acts of terrorism . . . designed to influence public opinion or Government policy with respect to affairs in Northern Ireland" (s.3(1), (6)). An EO may be made only where the Secretary of State is satisfied that its subject "is or has been concerned . . . in the commission, preparation or instigation of acts of terrorism . . . or is attempting or may attempt to enter [the jurisdiction from which it is desired to exclude him] with a view to being concerned [in such activities]" (ss.4(1), 5(1), 6(1)). For convenience, this condition is hereinafter referred to as "involvement in terrorism." Whether an EO is made against a person thought to be involved, or an order made is later revoked, may depend on wider political considerations, for example, as in the case of the Sinn Fein President, Gerry Adams, where the EO made seemed in part to reflect public outrage that his entry to Great Britain might cause in the wake of a terrorist atrocity, and its revocation on his election as MP for West Belfast appeared designed to deny Sinn Fein a propaganda victory if entry was sought and refused.[16]

Other limits on the exercise of these powers are framed in objective language. They are concerned with matters of citizenship and residence. No British citizen may be excluded from the United Kingdom (s.6(4)). Nor may such a citizen be excluded from one part of the United Kingdom (Great Britain or Northern Ireland as the case may be) if:

(a) he is at the time ordinarily resident in that part and has been so resident there throughout the last three years; or
(b) he is at the time subject to an order excluding him from the part of the United Kingdom to which it is proposed to send him, that is Great Britain or Northern Ireland, as the case may be (ss.4(4), 5(4)).

The Secretary of State is required, in relation to any person ordinarily resident in Great Britain, "to have regard to the question whether that person's connection with any territory outside Great Britain is such as to make it appropriate that . . . an [EO] is made" (s.4(3)). *Mutatis mutandis*, corresponding duties are imposed where the issue is exclusion from Northern Ireland or the United Kingdom (ss.5(3), 6(3)).

[16] C.P. Walker, "Members of Parliament and Executive Security Measures" [1983] P.L. 537.

Up to December 31, 1984, 245 excludees had been removed from Great Britain to Northern Ireland and 40 from Great Britain to the Republic of Ireland. Thirteen others were outside Great Britain when the EO was made. Very few exclusions now result from inland arrests.[17] Its use is increasingly rare in Great Britain and rarer still against persons settled there.[18] This reflects a change in the nature of the terrorist threat on the mainland. Reliance is no longer placed on supporters and activists among long-standing residents; those responsible for attacks in recent years "probably operated as small, self-contained and independent units."[19] Recent exclusions concerned those thought to be couriers, or setting up "active service units," and those seeking arms and explosives in Scotland for extreme Loyalist groups.[20]

Very limited opportunities are available to an individual to challenge an EO in an independent forum. The supervisory jurisdiction of the High Court has not been excluded, but there is no reported case of its invocation in this context. If the Secretary of State contravened one of the objective limitations on his power—for example, by seeking to exclude from Great Britain a British citizen exempt on grounds of residence—no doubt his decision could be successfully impugned. Moreover, the High Court could probably compel him to have due regard to the issue of sufficient connection with the destination territory.[21] In practical terms, however, the crucial question concerns the suspect's alleged involvement in terrorism. The Act merely requires the Secretary of State to be satisfied on that score. The courts in recent years have not allowed the use of subjective language in statutes to negate their powers to review ministerial action. The wartime cases, which marked the nadir of judicial review, have been distinguished. It is submitted, however, that given the nature of the subject-matter, the wording of the power, the identity of its wielder, and the prevailing political context, the judiciary will only be willing to interfere with a decision on this issue where the suspect could establish that the Secretary of State acted in bad faith, a burden impossible to discharge in practice (see Chap. 2, *supra*, pp. 50-72). To contest a decision on this key issue,

[17] Jellicoe, para. 165; H.O. 1/85, Table 5.

[18] Jellicoe, para. 164.

[19] *Ibid.* para. 177.

[20] *Ibid.* para. 178.

[21] Street [1975] Crim.L.R. 192, at p. 194; *cf.* the courts' approach to analogous issues under the Housing (Homeless Persons) Act 1977 (*e.g. De Falco* v. *Crawley B.C.* [1980] 1 All E.R. 913) for the minimal protection this gives.

the individual is in effect relegated to the process of review contained in section 7 of the PTA 1984. Notice of the making of the EO must be served on its subject as soon as may be, and must set out his rights under section 7 and the manner in which those rights are to be exercised (s.7(1)).

Section 7(4) now permits a person served with an EO to make representations to the Secretary of State within seven days of service. Where he has been removed by consent from the relevant territory before that period is up, he has 14 days from his removal in which to exercise the right (s.7(5)). Under the PTA 1974 and the PTA 1976 the relevant period in both cases was 48 hours (PTA 1974) and 96 hours (PTA 1976), although in practice representations made shortly after the expiry of the period were considered. He may request a personal interview with the adviser appointed to assist the Secretary of State and this must be granted (s.7(3)(*b*), (6), (7)). Persons removed with their consent to Northern Ireland or the Republic can now have the interview there if the Secretary of State considers it reasonably practicable (s.7(8)-(10)). Persons so removed elsewhere forfeit their right to an interview.[22] The Secretary of State must reconsider the case in the light of the individual's representations and any adviser's report and advice and everything else that appears to him to be relevant (s.7(11), (12)). If reasonably practicable, he must notify the individual of his final decision, but he is not bound to give reasons (s.7(13)). Nor, it must be stressed, is he in any way bound to follow the adviser's recommendations. The time period between initial decision, interview and final decision remains unclear, but it may be in excess of four weeks.[23] The Home Secretary has powers to give effect to EOs by giving directions to carriers to secure the individual's removal to the appropriate destination.[24]

22 Under the PTA 1976 anyone removed with consent, no matter where removed, forfeited the privilege of an interview: see s.7(5) of the PTA 1976. There was no explicit right to an interview in the 1974 Act.

23 C. Scorer, *The Prevention of Terrorism Acts 1974 and 1976: A Report on the Operation of the Law* (NCCL, 1976), p. 20; see also H.C. Deb., Vol. 980, cols. 435-436 (March 4, 1980) where the Home Secretary was unable to give an exact time.

24 PTA 1984, ss.8 and 13; Prevention of Terrorism (Supplemental Temporary Provisions) Order 1984 (S.I. 1984 No. 418), art. 8. Note, in particular, that art. 8(4), insofar as it purports to sanction the non-consensual exclusion from the UK of a British citizen possessing dual nationality would appear to be *ultra vires* the Act in that it contradicts an express prohibition in s.6(4).

An EO can be revoked at any time by the Secretary of State (s.3(3)). Unless revoked earlier, it will automatically expire after three years without prejudice to the making of a new order under the powers and procedures set out above (ss.3(4), (5)). Prior to the PTA 1984 as a matter of administrative practice, in use since March 1979, an individual could apply to have his EO revoked after three years. The matter would be considered personally by the Home Secretary. Where possible the Home Office informed the individual of this right.[25] As at December 31, 1984, 97 persons had applied: 43 orders were revoked, 48 confirmed and six awaited a final decision.[26]

The Act does not specify any procedures to be followed by, nor impose any duties on, the advisers in the execution of their responsibilities. Lord Shackleton reported that the Home Office had given guidance on some particular points (not further elaborated in the report) but had not laid down any set procedure:

> "The Adviser system is not a judicial proceeding and is not intended as such. It is an independent review of the decision of the Secretary of State. . . . It is . . . a means of taking account of any points the subject of the order may wish to make (at his own instigation) and of obtaining a second opinion of the case, based upon a personal interview . . . [and] all the material which the Secretary of State has seen. . . . Both the Advisers [who sit separately] thought that the material they saw was adequate for their purpose . . . [and] sufficient as a basis on which the Secretary of State could make his judgment. There is, however, a difficulty as to whether the Adviser should see the material before or after the interview. In some cases, an Adviser decided that he should not see the police submission on the case until after he had carried out the interview, the reason being his desire to afford the person concerned an unprejudiced hearing. While there is a danger that the subject of an [EO] may seek to use the interview to identify the source of intelligence information, the Adviser may be at some disadvantage if he is not at that stage aware of the case against the subject, although it was made clear to me that if necessary he would arrange to have another interview with the subject after he had considered the police report. . . .
>
> The object of the system . . . is to enable the Adviser to form

[25] Jellicoe, paras. 171-173; H.C. Deb., Vol. 1, col. 343.

[26] H.O. 1/85, Table 5, note (*c*).

> a first-hand impression of the subject. The Home Office makes available to each Adviser, whenever a new case arises, a file containing all his earlier reports to which he can refer if he wishes."[27]

The individual has no express right to legal representation. He is given scant information as to the case against him by the Secretary of State or the Advisers because of security considerations and the need to protect informants.

It is thought unlikely that the courts would supply the omission of the legislature and lay down procedural requirements by way of review for failure to comply with natural justice or the duty to act fairly imposed at common law. In the analogous context of the adviser system operating to consider representations in national security deportation cases, the Court of Appeal held that they would interfere only where the advisers refused to hear representations: otherwise the balance between national security considerations and the interest in a fair hearing was to be struck by a Home Secretary responsible to Parliament (*supra*, pp. 71-72).

The Home Secretary views the safeguards against abuse and error described above as "real not cosmetic."[28] Certainly the interaction of internal scrutiny in the police and Home Office, the personal attention by the Secretary of State and the supervisory role of the advisers cannot be dismissed lightly. The Home Secretary rejects about one-eighth of applications.[29] Representations to Advisers have had a one-third success rate.[30] The Home Secretary, however, does not invariably follow the advice given. As at December 31, 1984, representations had only been made in 44 cases, becoming "rarer in recent years, both in absolute terms and relative to the use of the exclusion power."[31]

Several factors combine to explain this small take-up of the remedy which the increased time limits and interview outside Great Britain are designed to increase.[32] Misrepresentation by the police has been cited by the National Council for Civil Liberties as a factor in at least one case.[33] That same body also attributes individuals' reluctance to "an unwillingness to remain imprisoned

[27] Shackleton, paras. 47-49.

[28] Mr. W. Whitelaw, MP, H.C. Deb., Vol. 1, col. 346.

[29] Jellicoe, para. 166. H.O. 1/85, Table 5.

[30] Jellicoe, paras. 169, 193. H.O. 1/85, Table 5.

[31] Jellicoe, para. 169.

[32] *Ibid.* paras. 195, 196.

[33] Scorer, *op. cit.* n. 23, p. 13.

for several weeks awaiting the final decision and a reluctance to submit themselves to the farcical procedures involved."[34] Lowry, who interviewed leaders of the Irish community in the Midlands, reports "a deep mistrust of the role of the Adviser, who is regarded as an attempt to disguise unfettered executive discretion."[35] Criticism has been levelled at the way in which the advisers carry out their task and their lack of knowledge of the Irish political scene.[36] The most difficult question remains that of access to the relevant evidence. The authorities clearly have a legitimate interest in protecting intelligence networks and sources of information which may be prejudiced if full disclosure were made to the suspect. Successive Home Secretaries have refused to adopt the analogy of the *in camera* trial available for sensitive cases under the Official Secrets Acts. Attempts to judicialise the review process have been resisted on the spurious ground that this would involve as a corollary "open proceedings or public presentation of the evidence" and would "increase risks."[37] The net result, that the individual receives little information about the case against him and therefore no real opportunity to refute it, reveals the importance of thorough scrutiny of the case by the advisers. This may well occur, but a perception of the process as a sham is understandable and heightened by its inability to bind the Home Secretary. Binding review was categorically rejected by Lord Jellicoe:

> "Exclusion is a matter of public policy. It is based not merely on the conduct of the excluded person but also once his terrorist involvement is established—on matters such as the security situation at the time exclusion is considered and the danger the person poses to the public at large. Neither the courts nor any form of tribunal could properly be expected to carry out an examination of all these issues and to reach a binding decision. The Secretary of State is and should remain accountable to Parliament for the way he discharges this onerous responsibility. It is the duty of Parliament to ensure

[34] *Ibid.* p. 20.

[35] D.R. Lowry, "Draconian Powers: The New British Approach to Pre-Trial Detention of Suspected Terrorists" (1976-77) 8-9 Colum. Human Rights L.R. 185 at p. 206.

[36] C. Scorer and P. Hewitt, *The Prevention of Terrorism Act: The Case for Repeal* (NCCL, 1981), pp. 30-32; B. Rose-Smith. "Police Powers and Terrorism Legislation" in P. Hain (Ed.), *Policing the Police,* Vol. 1 (1979), pp. 147-150.

[37] Mr. R. Jenkins, MP, Home Secretary, H.C. Deb., Vol. 901, cols. 886-887.

that this accountability has real meaning."[38]

In this Lord Jellicoe remains true to a British and Commonwealth tradition on security matters.[39]

For several reasons such problems connected with the supervisory process give grounds for concern. The nature of much of the evidence on which an EO has to be based, while highly relevant to the issue of involvement in terrorism, is such as to warrant close independent scrutiny. Statements from informants may have been actuated by malice, pressure or prospects of financial or other gain.[40] According to Lord Shackleton, the information available to the Secretary of State is composed of

> " . . . first of all, the material the police prepare. This consists of information obtained from intelligence sources about the person concerned. It is sensitive and highly classified. . . . Secondly, there is other information about the person concerned—for example details about any past convictions for terrorist offences. Thirdly, there is the report of the questioning of the person which the police have carried out while he has been detained. Fourthly, there are the results of any forensic tests."[41]

There is clearly a risk that some of the evidence may be unreliable. Certainly, concern has been expressed that exclusion involves a dragnet approach which is over-inclusive in operation; that is, as well as catching hard-core terrorists, it also sweeps up persons on the periphery of terrorism and subversion, legitimate political activists and others totally uninvolved in terrorism.[42] However, Lord Jellicoe reported that in no case that he had seen had an

[38] Jellicoe, para. 191.

[39] See, *inter alia*, C. Palley, "Detention without Trial and Proper Safeguards" *The Times*, November 23, 1971; T.M. Franck, *Comparative Constitutional Process—Cases and Materials: Fundamental Rights in the Common Law Nations* (1968), pp. 206-236; Y.P. Ghai and J.P.W.B. McAuslan, *Public Law and Political Change in Kenya* (1970) pp. 430-440; International Commission of Jurists, *States of Emergency: Their Impact on Human Rights* (1983), pp. 204 (Malaysia), 223-224 (Northern Ireland); *Second Report of the Commission of Inquiry Concerning Certain Activities of the Royal Canadian Mounted Police: Freedom and Security under the Law*, Vol. 2 (1981) (Macdonald Report), pp. 801-912 (Public Service Employment), 825-828 (Deportation), 837-838 (Citizenship).

[40] Scorer, *op. cit.* n. 23, p. 12; Scorer and Hewitt, *op. cit.* n. 36, pp. 27-28.

[41] Shackleton, para. 39.

[42] See, *e.g.* Mr. G. Fitt, MP (now Lord Fitt), H.C. Deb., Vol. 1, col. 386.

order been made other than on the specified grounds; that the system was administered with fairness and integrity; and that in all the examined cases there were grounds on which the Secretary of State could be satisfied of the suspect's involvement in terrrorism.[43] Nonetheless, one ought not to be complacent about the supervisory process; these draconian powers have an impact on the individual and his family markedly similar to that of imprisonment following conviction, and it is pedantic to say that exclusion is not a punishment.[44] Exclusion to Northern Ireland, in particular, may involve the individual in loss of employment; marked problems of accommodation; separation from friends and loved ones, or at least heightened pressures on family life; transfer to a potentially hostile, if not lethal, environment; and the stigma of involvement in terrorism.[45] The gravity of the impact on families has been poignantly illustrated by Lord Fitt, former MP for West Belfast; to cite one example:

> "Nineteen years ago, a fellow from Belfast came to live in Southampton. He met a Southampton girl and married her. He has four or five children, who all speak with delicious Southampton accents. He was suspected of having done something although he was not charged. The authorities told him to go back to Belfast. He had been away from Belfast for years and had never been there on holiday. However, the Home Secretary signed an exclusion order. It broke up his marriage.
>
> The Southampton girl and her children tried to live in Belfast. They tried to live in a completely alien environment. She took the children and returned to Southampton. Her husband is still in Belfast."[46]

That three years ordinary residence prior to exclusion now suffices to exempt British citizens from the process means that such hard cases are unlikely to arise in the future. However, existing orders unless revoked earlier will only lapse three years after the passage of the PTA 1984 (s.18(2)), and fresh orders could be issued pursuant to it, so the change may do little to ease the plight of excluded individuals of longer-standing residence and

[43] Jellicoe, paras. 186-189.

[44] *Pace* Shackleton, para. 122.

[45] *Ibid.* paras. 35 and 55; Jellicoe, paras. 175, 178, 185. See, in general on sectarian assassination, M. Dillon and D. Lehane, *Political Murder in Northern Ireland* (1973).

[46] H.C. Deb., Vol. 1, col. 386.

their families. Other MPs have voiced concern over the return to Ulster of families trying to escape the troubles.[47] It is arguable, moreover, that EOs violate the European Convention on Human Rights, an issue not explored by Lord Jellicoe. The matter raises several complex issues: (1) Has there been deprivation of liberty and security of person sufficient to attract the operation of Article 5? (2) If so, is it permitted by the Convention? (3) Has the right of access to a court guaranteed by Article 5(4) been secured? (4) Has there been a violation of the guarantee of private and family life protected by Article 8?

Article 5, in protecting liberty and security of person, prohibits arbitrary interference with the physical liberty of the person in the classic sense.[48] The European Court of Human Rights has held that not every restriction on liberty amounts to a deprivation of liberty as understood in Article 5. In particular, deprivation of liberty has to be distinguished from mere restrictions on freedom of movement; the latter fall to be judged by Article 2 of Protocol 4 to the Convention, to which the United Kingdom has not subscribed: "Everyone lawfully within the territory of a State shall, within that territory, have the right to liberty of movement and freedom to choose his residence." In *Guzzardi* v. *Italy*, [49] a mafioso was removed from the mainland and confined to one part of a small island. The Court focused on the confinement and framed the relevant test as follows:

> " . . . the starting point must be his concrete situation and account must be taken of a whole range of criteria such as the type, duration, effects and manner of implementation of the measure in question. . . .
>
> "The difference between deprivation of liberty and restriction upon liberty is nonetheless merely one of degree and intensity, and not one of nature and substance. . . ."[50]

It was held that the Convention had been breached. Guzzardi's enforced residence was a deprivation of liberty which attracted Article 5 because of the combined operation of a number of factors: the very limited area of residence; close supervision by the police; the need to get permission to do such things as leave his house between certain hours, or telephone or visit the

[47] Mr. B. Cryer, MP, H.C. Deb., Vol. 1, col. 391.

[48] Z.M. Nedjati, *Human Rights under the European Convention* (1978), pp. 85-87.

[49] [1981] 3 E.H.R.R. 333.

[50] *Ibid.* paras. 92-94.

neighbouring islands or the mainland.[51] Clearly even exclusion to Northern Ireland does not involve as strict a restriction on movement; it may thus not attract the operation of Article 5. There are, however, inevitably periods of custody pending consideration of whether to make an order and pending removal after an order has been made. Indeed, if the matter is referred to the advisers, the period of detention may last in excess of four weeks. No such point was raised in *Guzzardi*, but those detentions surely constitute deprivation of liberty sufficient to invoke Article 5. The key issue, then, is whether it is permitted by any of the heads in paragraph (1) of that Article:

> "No one shall be deprived of his liberty save in the following cases and in accordance with a procedure prescribed by law:
> (*a*) the lawful detention of a person after conviction by a competent court;
> (*b*) the lawful arrest and detention of a person for non-compliance with the lawful order of a court or in order to secure the fulfilment of any obligation prescribed by law;
> (*c*) the lawful arrest or detention of a person effected for the purpose of bringing him before the competent legal authority on reasonable suspicion of having committed an offence or when it is reasonably considered necessary to prevent his committing an offence or fleeing after having done so;
> (*d*) the detention of a minor by lawful order for the purpose of educational supervision or his lawful detention for the purpose of bringing him before the competent legal authority;
> (*e*) the lawful detention of persons for the prevention of the spreading of infectious diseases, of persons of unsound mind, alcoholics or drug addicts or vagrants;
> (*f*) the lawful arrest or detention of a person to prevent his effecting an unauthorised entry into the country or of a person against whom action is being taken with a view to deportation or extradition."

Sub-paragraphs (*a*), (*d*) and (*e*) are irrelevant here. Nor can sub-paragraph (*b*) be relied on: "obligations prescribed by law" envisages specific obligations, not nebulous notions of loyalty or

51 *Ibid.* para. 95.

good citizenship.[52] Sub-paragraph (*c*), with its reference to prevention, would at first sight appear to offer justification, but it has to be read in conjunction with paragraph (3):

> "Everyone arrested or detained in accordance with the provisions of paragraph 1(*c*) . . . shall be brought promptly before a judge or other officer authorised by law to exercise judicial power and shall be entitled to trial within a reasonable time or to release pending trial. Release may be conditioned by guarantees to appear for trial."

In other words, these two provisions require that the detainee be confined for the purpose of deploying some form of criminal trial process against him, and that any such trial take place within a reasonable time.[53] EOs do not conform to the dictates of these provisions; like internment without trial, held to be incompatible with Article 5 in both *Lawless* v. *Ireland*[54] and *Ireland* v. *United Kingdom*,[55] their purpose is to by-pass the criminal process. Nor can the advisers constitute the agencies contemplated by these provisions; they lack the power of binding decision regarded as necessary by the court in the latter case.[56] Sub-paragraph (*f*) was invoked by the United Kingdom before the Commission in *McVeigh and others* v. *United Kingdom*, but the Commission found it unnecessary to offer an opinion on the issue.[57] It is thought that it might support the detention pending exclusion of non-British citizens, as persons held "with a view to deportation." It is more difficult to regard that phrase, set as it is alongside notions of entry to a country and extradition which evoke "State to State" movement, as flexible enough to cover the exclusion of nationals from one part of the national territory to another.[58] Significantly, perhaps, no reliance was placed on this provision in *Guzzardi*.

[52] *Lawless* v. *Ireland* (Merits) (1961) [1979-80] 1 E.H.R.R. 15, paras. 9 and 12; *Engel Case* [1979-80] 1 E.H.R.R. 647, para. 69; *Guzzardi* v. *Italy* [1981] 3 E.H.R.R. 333, para. 101; *McVeigh* v. *United Kingdom* [1981] 5 E.H.R.R. 71, paras. 168-196.

[53] *Ireland* v. *United Kingdom* [1979-80] 2 E.H.R.R. 25, para. 199.

[54] [1979-80] 1 E.H.R.R. 15, paras. 8-15.

[55] [1979-80] 2 E.H.R.R. 25, para. 199.

[56] *Ibid.* para. 200.

[57] [1981] 5 E.H.R.R. 333, paras. 197-200.

[58] *Cf.* the argument of counsel for the applicants in *McVeigh* [1981] 5 E.H.R.R. 333, paras. 106-109.

Article 5(4) mandates that: "Everyone who is deprived of his liberty by arrest or detention shall be entitled to take proceedings by which the lawfulness of his detention shall be decided speedily by a court and his release ordered if the detention is not lawful." In *Ireland* v. *United Kingdom*, the court held that this required consideration of the substance of the decision on which deprivation of liberty was based; the ability of the High Court of Northern Ireland to review decisions on essentially technical and ancillary points was not sufficiently far-reaching.[59] It is, therefore, submitted that the availability of the courts' supervisory jurisdiction to excludees would not satisfy Article 5(4). Moreover, nor would the adviser system; the scrutinising body must be a "court," that is, a body sufficiently independent of the executive, empowered to make binding decisions.[60] Insofar as exclusion might be compatible with Article 5(1)(*f*), however, review would perhaps only need to extend to the necessity for detention pending deportation rather than to the merits of the decision to exclude itself.[61]

The effect of EOs on the excludee and his family raises issues of compliance with Article 8(1), which states: "Everyone has the right to respect for his private and family life. . . . " Subject to requirements of proportionality, Article 8(2) permits legal restriction of these rights where necessary in a democratic society to safeguard national security, to prevent crime, or to protect the rights and freedoms of others. It is uncertain whether the disruptive effect of exclusion on family life of the type referred to above is sufficient to violate Article 8. The jurisprudence of the Convention is not so clearly developed in this area as to permit the formulation of a clear opinion. Certainly the Convention does not guarantee a family's right to live in any particular country but only the provision of an effective family life as such no matter where. In several cases concerning the deportation of husbands, however, the Commission has examined the possibilities of the family moving to the destination State and whether either spouse has a connection with it.[62] Clearly, much will depend on the

[59] [1979-80] 2 E.H.R.R. 25, para. 200.

[60] *Ibid.* paras. 199-200.

[61] *Caprino* v. *United Kingdom* [1982] 4 E.H.R.R. 97.

[62] Nedjati, *op. cit.* n. 48, pp. 157-159; A.C. Evans, "Expulsion under the 1971 Immigration Act" (1983) 46 M.L.R. 433, esp. at pp. 436-437, and "United Kingdom Immigration Policy and the European Convention of Human Rights" [1983] P.L. 91, esp. at pp. 100-103.

detailed facts of individual cases, and, in any event, in the present context the Convention organs are liable to give broad scope to the permissible restrictions on the rights.[63]

It is submitted that changes should be implemented to tighten up the grounds on which EOs can be made and to provide a speedier system of review by an independent judicial body with power to make binding decisions. It is thought that such reforms would ensure compliance with Article 5(4) of the European Convention on Human Rights; improve the quality of the decision-making process by subjecting it to more thoroughgoing review; help to promote community confidence in so far as the provision of better safeguards against error and abuse might allay perceptions of the review process as a sham; and support legitimate State interests in the preservation of vital intelligence networks and sources of information on which the authorities depend in the fight against terrorism.

The decision to exclude ought to be contained in a Provisional Exclusion Order (PEO) to emphasise the individual's merely suspect status and the lack of finality at this stage.[64] It should remain the non-delegable personal responsibility of a Secretary of State directly accountable to Parliament. In practice, it ought to be in the hands of the Home Secretary (responsible for the United Kingdom and Great Britain) and the Northern Ireland Secretary (responsible for Ulster) to ensure some sort of consistency of approach and experienced decision making. The grounds on which an order can be made ought to be formulated more specifically. The recommendation of the Gardiner Report on detention without trial in Ulster affords a useful model; a PEO should be made only where:

[63] See *McVeigh* v. *United Kingdom* [1981] 5 E.H.R.R. 333, para. 157.

[64] For the germ of ideas here, the writer is indebted to Mr. A. Holley, MP, H.C. Deb, Vol. 882, col. 875 (November 28, 1975); R.J. Spjut, *Executive Detention in Northern Ireland* (1975) 10 Ir.Jur. 272; and to the *Report of a Committee to consider, in the context of civil liberties and human rights, measures to deal with terrorism in Northern Ireland*, Cmnd. 5847 (1975) (hereinafter cited as "Gardiner"). *Cf.* Leigh, [1975] P.L. 1, at p. 4. There was an unsuccessful attempt during the passage of the PTA 1984 to insert into the legislation a right of appeal against exclusion to an Exclusion Tribunal with power to revoke or confirm the EO. The Tribunal would have been composed of three High Court judges. The individual would have had rights to legal aid and legal representation. The Secretary of State would have had to give the individual notice of the reasons for exclusion and of the evidence against him. This Labour proposal was defeated 250-112 with the Liberals voting against—see H.C. Debs, Vol. 52, cols. 942-962.

(1) the Secretary of State is satisfied that a person is or has been concerned in the commission, or attempted commission of any act of terrorism, or in directing, organising, recruiting or training persons for the purpose of terrorism, or is seeking to enter the relevant jurisdiction to engage in such activities;
and
(2) the Secretary of State considers that that person's freedom in the relevant jurisdiction would seriously endanger the general security of the public.[65]

The second requirement does little more than translate into law the Home Secretary's stated practice[66] but is nonetheless valuable for that. Since the suspect may already have been in custody for up to seven days, it is imperative that the process operates as speedily as is consonant with considered decision making; experience in Ulster revealed undue delays as a factor in community dissatisfaction with detention without trial.[67] The evidence, because of its nature, ought to be subjected to the closest scrutiny to establish that the criteria are met at that stage. A PEO ought not to be made to enable the police to build up their case; the extended period of detention following arrest was designed for that purpose. So far as is compatible with the need to protect informants and intelligence networks, the Secretary of State should be obliged to annex to the PEO a written statement as to the specific nature of the terrorist activities on which his decision is based,[68] and a copy given to the suspect.

The issue should then be automatically referred to an Exclusion Review Board (ERB) with power to translate the PEO into a Confirmed Exclusion Order (CEO) or to refuse to do so. The ERB's decision on refusal must be binding on the Secretary of State if it is to achieve wider credibility. It is unlikely to detract from his responsibility to Parliament for the process and policy as a whole, while his accountability to that body in respect of individual cases is more apparent than real given that "security"

[65] Gardiner, para. 166, App. G.

[66] The Home Secretary stated in Parliament during the 1980 renewal debate on the PTA 1976 that he must be "absolutely satisfied in each application that the person concerned has been involved in terrorism and that the safety of this country requires his exclusion": see H.C. Deb, Vol. 980, col. 406 (March 4, 1980). See also Home Office Circular No. 26/1984, paras. 78-81.

[67] Gardiner, para. 145.

[68] *Ibid.* App. G, para. 6(2); Spjut, *loc. cit.* n. 64.

considerations prevent adequate disclosure to Parliament.[69] In any event, the remainder of the proposals are readily adaptable to an advisory system. It would be sensible, however, to allow him to retain his power to revoke an order whenever he wishes, for example, to enable him progressively to phase out the system as part of moves towards a political settlement or in response to a diminishing level of violence, or the like, as happened with detention without trial in Ulster (*supra*, pp. 152-161).[70] The ERB should be obliged to satisfy itself that the criteria for an EO were clearly fulfilled. Additionally, where satisfied that a prosecution could have been brought, it should have powers to recommend that that be done rather than issue a CEO; the process ought to operate in a manner consonant with the Government's view of the primacy of the criminal process in the range of legal responses to terrorism.

The ERB should have power to examine any person it considers able to help it in the discharge of its task. No Executive Privilege bar should be placed in its way. The suspect should have the right to make written and oral representations, to legal advice and representation, and to call witnesses. The proceedings should be primarily inquisitorial rather than adversarial. As the Gardiner Report noted, too close resemblance to the ordinary judicial process may have a detrimental effect on public confidence in the ordinary processes of law, and, in any event, adversarial procedures contribute little to the individual's ability to challenge the police case, given the nature of much of the evidence against him.[71] The Board should be obliged, however, to disclose to the suspect and his representative as much of the case against him as it considers consonant with countervailing security interests.[72] In the nature of things, the Board might be expected to be cautious here, but its duty to probe deeply into the police case would go some way to protecting the suspect's interests. Its interview with the suspect ought to take place no more than seven days after service of the PEO, and its decision delivered within seven days thereafter. In short, the aim would be for a maximum 21 days detention between arrest and exclusion or release. The ERB might usefully be equipped with powers to award compensation where it considered there was no foundation in the case against the

[69] But *cf.* Jellicoe, para. 191.

[70] K. Boyle, T. Hadden and P. Hillyard, *Law and State: The Case of Northern Ireland* (1975), pp. 73-74.

[71] Gardiner, paras. 145, 153 (*supra*, pp. 154-155).

[72] *Cf.* MacDonald Report, *loc. cit.* n. 39 (same pages).

suspect,[73] and to draw the attention of the appropriate disciplinary authorities to irregularities. Non-compliance with time limits ought to entitle the suspect to automatic release.[74]

The ERB should be composed of persons qualified for judicial office but not members of the existing judiciary, who should be seen to stand aloof from such extraordinary procedures.[75] Its members should familiarise themselves with the intricacies of the Irish scene. The Board should sit in panels of three:

> "the deprivation of a citizen's liberty by executive action and extra-judicial process is such a grave step that the responsibility for investigating a case . . . merits consideration by more than one person, however carefully selected. It would be impossible for an individual at the same time to probe in depth by questioning a witness, to take a note of the questions and answers, and to evaluate the evidence in the context of other information and documents. To ensure thorough investigation of each case in private and a consistency of approach a plural board is necessary."[76]

With relatively small numbers caught up in the exclusion process, it is thought that a plural board would create few logistical difficulties.

It is submitted that the drastic effect of EOs on an individual against whom no crime has been proved and on his family warrants the provision of financial assistance with resettlement, or, at the very least, for visiting purposes in cases of separation, on a basis complementary to that provided to the families of convicted prisoners.[77] If certain persons engaged in visits to excludees are thought to be couriers,[78] the powers in the Act are surely sufficient to cope.

[73] *Cf.* Gardiner, App. G., para. 15; SACHR, *Annual Report for 1982-83,* H.C. 262 (1983-84), pp. 10-11; W.L. Twining *Emergency Powers: A Fresh Start* (Fabian Tract 416, 1972), p.27.

[74] Gardiner, para. 165.

[75] Thus giving effect to Professor Twining's "Sterilisation" principle: see "Emergency Powers and Criminal Process: the Diplock Report" [1973] Crim.L.R. 406, at p. 409.

[76] Gardiner, para. 163; but *cf.* Shackleton, para. 125.

[77] *Cf.* Gardiner paras. 177-178, App. H.; Shackleton, para. 128.

[78] This was the official reason for refusing to implement Lord Shackleton's recommendations on this score: see Mr. M. Rees, MP, Home Secretary, H.C. Deb., Vol. 964, col. 1515 (March 21, 1979).

These proposals assume that exclusion will continue as a policy for dealing with terrorism. It is, however, debatable whether it should do so. Lord Jellicoe considered that

> "the exclusion of some people . . . has materially contributed to public safety in the United Kingdom and that this could not have been achieved through the normal criminal process."[79]

In some instances, it had rid Great Britain of dangerous terrorists; substantially impaired terrorist effectiveness by rendering illegal their travel between Ulster and the mainland and between the Republic and the United Kingdom; and had provided a process for dealing with undoubted terrorists where the form and sensitivity of the case against them was such as to preclude any other process.[80] He did not suggest, however,

> "that the benefits of every exclusion order have outweighed its costs in terms of civil liberties and of hardship to the excluded person and his family."[81]

He concluded that exclusion should remain available in extreme cases, but that the possibility of its abolition should be kept under review without prejudice to the continuance of the other powers in the legislation.[82] Within the United Kingdom, exclusion is primarily a matter of one-way traffic to Ulster. There is evidence that moderate opinion there views it as counter-productive.[83] It exhibits many of the disadvantages of internment without trial without the benefit of secure confinement of the individual concerned. Under Lord Jellicoe's proposals as embodied in the PTA 1984, the criminal process will be the only available process in an increasing number of cases, as it has been to date with Loyalist terrorist suspects in Great Britain and most terrorist suspects in Northern Ireland.[84] Is it not time to let the power lapse and rely solely on that criminal process to deal with all terrorist suspects who are either British citizens or have the right of abode in the United Kingdom? Consideration could be given to holding part of the trial *in camera* as in Official Secrets Acts' cases. Existing

[79] Jellicoe, para. 176.

[80] *Ibid.*

[81] *Ibid.*

[82] *Ibid.* paras. 178, 200.

[83] *Supra*, pp. 161-162; SACHR, *Annual Report for 1981-82*, H.C. 230 (1982-83), pp. 12-13.

[84] Jellicoe, para. 177.

deportation powers would provide an alternative or supplemental process for many suspects without the right of abode, although the fact that Commonwealth citizens and Irish citizens ordinarily resident here on January 1, 1973 and continuously so throughout the last five years are exempt,[85] would arguably be a ground for retaining intact the powers in section 6 of the PTA 1984 to exclude non-British citizens and persons not having the right of abode from the United Kingdom.

[85] Immigration Act 1971 (c.77), ss.3, 7.

Chapter 5

EMERGENCY POWERS TO ASSIST IN THE MAINTENANCE OF ESSENTIAL SUPPLIES AND SERVICES

1. Introduction, Background and Overview

Disruption of supplies and services regarded as essential to the community, whether caused by war, civil commotion, industrial action, natural or man-made disaster, constitutes one area in which written constitutions sanction resort to emergency powers.[1] The legitimacy of resort to such powers in such circumstances is also recognised in international law, which, furthermore, permits the prohibition of or restrictions on industrial action by groups of public services workers–typically, the armed forces and the police–and regards as permissible, in circumstances of emergency or calamity threatening the life or well-being of the community, the exactment of community service.[2] Inevitably, systems for dealing with threats to or disruption of essential supplies and services vary among nations, and it may be unwise to assume that a method, operated in the context of written constitution and a more legalised industrial relations' system, can be transplanted successfully to the very different constitutional and industrial relations context of the United Kingdom, as experience with the Industrial Relations Act 1971 arguably bears witness.

[1] Chap. 1, *supra*, pp. 2-6. See, *e.g.* the Constitutions of Antigua and Barbuda (Art. 21), Barbados (Art. 25), Bangladesh (Art. 141A). The Republic of Ireland has a Protection of the Community (Special Powers) Act 1926 which enables a Proclamation of Emergency by the Government "if at any time [it] is of opinion that a national emergency has arisen of such a character that it is expedient in the public interest that extraordinary measures should be taken to ensure the due supply and distribution of the essentials of life to the community" (s.1(1)). Apparently it has never been invoked: J.M. Kelly, *The Irish Constitution* (1980), pp. 140-141. Jamaica's Emergency Powers Law 1961 is in similar terms to the United Kingdom Emergency Powers Act 1920; Lloyd G. Barnett, *The Constitutional Law of Jamaica* (1977), pp. 425-428.

[2] Chap. 2, *supra*, pp. 91-93. See, in particular, on the last point: Art. 4(3)(*d*), European Convention on Human Rights; Art. 8(3)(*c*)(iii), UN Covenant on Civil and Political Rights 1966. For texts see I. Brownlie, *Basic Documents on Human Rights* (2nd ed., 1981).

The concept of essential supplies and services is, however, by no means clearly or uniformly defined.[3] Jeffery and Hennessy suggest that:

> "the supply of food and water can indisputably be declared vital, as, for the most part, can that of fuel and power. Such is the dependence of modern Britain on the continuous supply of oil fuel and electric power, that even a localised stoppage in either of these industries can have a disproportionately damaging effect on all other sectors of the economy and the day to day life of the community. The wide-spread adoption of continuous processes in many industries has increased their reliance on a number of crucial supplies. In the late 1970s, for example, the CCU [Civil Contingencies Unit] took the threat of stoppage at British Oxygen very seriously indeed because of the severely disruptive 'knock-on' effect this would have had. . . .
>
> Food, water and fuel are unequivocally essential. So too are fire and ambulance services. But governments have at times also to decide whether to implement emergency arrangements in less clear-cut cases, such as public transport and communications."[4]

The emergency provisions of the United States' Taft-Hartley Act, whereby the Attorney General can seek a court-ordered cooling-off period in respect of industrial action, can be set in motion where the President considers that a strike affecting the whole or part of any industry will, if permitted to go ahead or continue, "imperil the national health or safety."[5] Similar provisions in the ill-fated and short-lived Industrial Relations Act 1971 in Great Britain were invocable in respect of "industrial action which is gravely injurious to the national economy, imperils national security, creates a serious risk of disorder, endangers the life of a substantial number of people or exposes a substantial number to serious risk of disease or personal injury."[6] The Centre for Policy Studies brings within the concept of essential service "the ambulance service, the fire brigade, the hospital nurses and all

[3] See A. Pankert, "Settlement of Labour Disputes in Essential Services" (1980) 119 *Int'l.Lab.Rev.* 723.

[4] K. Jeffery and P. Hennessy, *States of Emergency: British Governments and Strikebreaking since 1919* (1983), p. 265.

[5] Green Paper, *Trade Union Immunities*, Cmnd. 8128, para. 316.

[6] *Ibid*, para. 322.

medical staff, gas, water, electricity, nuclear power and sewerage services" and also those auxiliary services in which a withdrawal of labour could have the effect of paralysing one of those essential services.[7] The TUC *Guide to the Conduct of Disputes* (1979) recommends that

> "the union(s) involved should, where necessary, make arrangements in advance and with due notice, in consultation and preferably by agreement with the employer, for the maintenance by their members of supplies and services essential to the health or safety of the community or otherwise required to avoid causing exceptional hardship or serious pollution."[8]

As Gillian Morris has noted with respect to essential services, "a service whose disruption would endanger public health or safety seems to be a 'lowest common denominator' definition."[9]

Currently in the United Kingdom, three statutory regimes permit recourse to quite wide ranging emergency powers to combat, or to mitigate the effects of, actual or potential disruption to a broad range of supplies and services falling within the above definitions. The first such regime, the Drought Act 1976, applies only to England and Wales. The emergency powers in the Energy Act 1976, the second regime, are applicable throughout the United Kingdom. The third regime is embodied in the Emergency Powers Act 1920 (hereinafter "EPA 1920"), in its Northern Ireland equivalent (the Emergency Powers Act (NI) 1926), and in the Emergency Powers Act 1964 (hereinafter "EPA 1964"). This regime, applicable throughout the United Kingdom, has been the most extensively used of the three, and examination of it and its use, with the emphasis on Great Britain, represents the major portion of this chapter. Before examining these regimes, however, it is useful, for a proper appreciation of them, to consider briefly a number of permanent legal provisions relevant to this sphere, to set a context in which the emergency powers operate. It is also of interest to note ad hoc legislative responses of government and Parliament to particular situations in which key services have been disrupted by industrial action, or there has been need to clear up after a natural disaster. The ill-fated attempt of the Heath

[7] Centre for Policy Studies, *The Right to Strike in a Free Society* (March 1983), pp. 7-8.

[8] TUC Guide, *Conduct of Industrial Disputes* (1979), para. 6, pp. 11-12.

[9] G.S. Morris, "The Regulation of Industrial Action in Essential Services" (1983) 12 I.L.J. 69, at p. 69.

Administration to create a more permanent legal structure to inhibit industrial action in key sectors through the Industrial Relations Act 1971 ought also to be recalled. An ad hoc legislative response to particular events or the creation of a more permanent structure constitute alternative or supplementary responses to the problem with which the emergency provisions attempt to deal.

In terms of permanent provisions, current labour law, with its limitations on secondary sympathetic or supportive action and on secondary picketing (*i.e.* other than at one's place of work), and its provisions for injunctive relief and for actions for damages against union funds in respect of action outside union immunities, may yet be shown to have as inhibiting an effect in the sphere of industrial action affecting essential supplies and services as in any other sphere, although so far management in nationalised industries has proved reluctant to have resort to it, perhaps for fear of exacerbating particular disputes.[10] Criminalisation of incitement to disaffection effectively renders unlawful industrial action by the police and the armed forces. The former may not join a trade union,[11] and industrial action by either group could constitute, respectively, disciplinary offences or offences under military law.[12] Moreover a number of specialised criminal offences could be committed by certain groups of workers, for example, merchant seamen and postal and telecommunications workers, merely by taking industrial action.[13] Action by firemen, health service employees, gas, electricity and water workers, and public health employees could fall foul of section 5 of the Conspiracy and Protection of Property Act 1875 which criminalises the wilful and malicious breach of a contract of service or hiring where the person breaking it knows, or has reasonable cause to believe, that the probable consequences of the

[10] See, generally on immunities, civil actions, secondary action and secondary picketing, D.R. Newell, *The New Employment Law Legislation: A Guide to the Employment Acts 1980 and 1982* (1983), Chaps. 1-3. On secondary picketing see R. Lewis and B. Simpson, *Striking a Balance? Employment Law after the 1980 Act* (1981), Chap. 8.

[11] Police Act 1964, s.53(1); Incitement to Mutiny Act 1797 and Incitement to Disaffection Act 1934. The armed forces, police and police associations do not fall within the definitions of "worker" and "trade union" in the Trade Union and Labour Relations Act 1974, ss.28 and 30.

[12] Police Act 1919, s.2(1), Police Act 1964, s.47(1); Morris, *loc. cit.* n. 9, at pp. 71-72; G.S. Morris, *A Study of the Protection of Public and Essential Services in Labour Disputes 1920-1976* (unpublished Ph.D. thesis, University of Cambridge, 1978), pp. 9-19.

[13] Morris, *loc. cit.* n. 9, at pp. 72-75.

breach will be to endanger human life, to cause serious bodily injury, or to expose valuable property to serious injury or destruction.[14] Such offences have rarely been invoked. As Gillian Morris has noted, British practice has rather focused on using alternative means to secure supplies and/or services once disrupted rather than relying on the deterrent effect of the criminal law.[15]

A local authority, where an emergency or disaster involving destruction of or a danger to life or property occurs, or is imminent, or there is reasonable ground for apprehending such an emergency or disaster, if of the opinion that it is likely to affect the whole or part of its area or all or some of the inhabitants of that area, may take certain steps. It may incur such expenditure as it considers necessary in taking action itself (alone or jointly with someone else) which is calculated to avert, alleviate or eradicate in its area, or among those inhabitants, the effect or potential effects of the event, or it may make grants or loans to other persons or bodies on conditions determined by the council in respect of any such action taken by those persons or bodies.[16] Water authorities have a similar duty to render aid to the local authorities concerned.[17] Urgent needs payments can be made under the supplementary benefits scheme to persons affected by such disasters, even though they are not otherwise in receipt of benefit, but only very much as a last resort.[18]

On several occasions, Parliament has enacted ad hoc statutes to help ameliorate the effect of industrial action in the public sector or to assist in clearing up in the aftermath of a natural disaster and in preventing its recurrence. Thus, "the Imprisonment (Temporary Provisions) Act was passed to alleviate the consequences of industrial action by prison officers in 1980 and the Administration of Justice (Emergency Provisions) (Scotland) Act in 1979 to deal with the impact of the civil service dispute on the Scottish legal system."[19] The Coastal Flooding (Emergency

[14] *Ibid.* at p. 75.

[15] Morris, *op. cit.* n. 12, p. 558.

[16] Local Government Act 1972, s.138.

[17] Water Act 1973, s.28.

[18] A. Ogus and E. Barendt, *The Law of Social Security* (2nd ed., 1982), pp. 493-494; M.S. Rowell and A.M. Wilton, *The Law of Supplementary Benefits* (1982), Chap. 7.

[19] Morris, *loc. cit.* n. 9, at p. 70. The 1980 Act gave the Secretary of State power to approve accommodation for the detention of persons and to otherwise alleviate the position in prisons by directing the release of persons on remand, increasing powers of early release and giving directions to

Powers) Act 1953, a response to the floods of January that year, made special provision for works of defence against sea-water, for the rehabilitation of agricultural land damaged by sea-water, and for connected purposes.

Ad hoc emergency legislation may have a role in the resolution of disputes between central and local government, enabling central government to send in commissioners to run a local authority where, for example, because of a local authority's actual or imminent financial collapse, actual or threatened disruption to services is, or is likely to be, on such a scale as could not adequately be met by use of existing statutory default powers. The Government reportedly had such legislation ready as an option in its dispute with Liverpool City Council which failed to set a rate for some weeks in 1984.[20]

The Industrial Relations Act 1971 attempted to deal with the problem of disputes affecting essential supplies and/or services by making provision for a statutory cooling-off period on the American model of the Taft-Hartley Act. The Secretary of State for Employment was empowered to seek an order from the National Industrial Relations Court to restrain a union, employer or any other named person from calling, inducing or financing industrial action where the action in question had:

> "caused or . . . would cause an interruption in the supply of goods or in the provision of services of such a nature, or on such a scale, as to be likely—
>
> (*a*) to be gravely injurious to the national economy, to imperil national security or to create a risk of serious public disorder,
>
> or
>
> (*b*) to endanger the lives of a substantial number of persons or to expose a substantial number of persons to serious risk of disease or personal injury." (s.138)

A court-ordered cooling-off period could last for up to 60 days (s.139(2)(*c*)). The Act also empowered the Secretary of State to seek a court-ordered ballot of the workers involved (ss.141, 142).

magistrates in respect of fine defaulters. To the same end, magistrates were given increased powers to remand a person in his absence. The 1979 Act modified applicable time limits on detention and in legal proceedings during the emergency period.

20 See David Lipsey and Roger Ratcliffe, "Rebellion at City Hall" *The Sunday Times*, March 25, 1984, pp. 15, 18; *ibid*, p. 1; *The Sunday Times*, April 29, p. 2; *The Sunday Times*, June 10, 1984, p. 3. A compromise was reached and a rate fixed.

If no settlement was reached, however, action could resume. The Government would have to look elsewhere (*e.g.* the EPAs 1920 and 1964) for powers to mitigate the effects of the action on the community. As the Government Green Paper on Trade Union Immunities (1981) noted:

> "the principle behind the provision was not that the Government should have power to ban strikes, but that it should be given a delaying power during which there could be further negotiations to find a settlement. The provision was used only once: in the 1972 national rail dispute. The Secretary of State for Employment successfully sought orders for a cooling-off period during which industrial action was suspended, and then, for a ballot. The result of the ballot was, however, an endorsement of the industrial action which was then resumed."[21]

Apparently, resumption of the action after the cooling-off period and ballot has also been the typical experience of resort to the Taft-Hartley Act in the United States.[22] Such experience suggests that such mechanisms are of limited value in this field.[23]

The three emergency powers regimes must now be examined.

(1) *The Drought Act 1976*

This Act was a response to the severe water shortage which occurred in some localities during the hot dry summer of 1976. Existing powers were thought inadequate as being too inflexible. Hosepipe bans could be imposed to save water, but otherwise water authorities could only resort to a complete shut-off with standpipes erected in the streets. The 1976 Act provides the necessary flexibility.[24] If, on due application by a water authority to him, the Secretary of State "is satisfied that, *by reason of an exceptional shortage of rain*, a serious deficiency of supplies of water in any area exists or is threatened" (emphasis supplied), he may by order make such provision as is authorised by section 1 of the Act "as appears to him to be expedient with a view to meeting the

[21] *Op. cit.* n. 5, para. 315.

[22] *Ibid.* para. 317.

[23] For an analysis and assessment of the Industrial Relations Act 1971, see A.W.J. Thomson and S.R. Engleman, *The Industrial Relations Act: A Review and Analysis* (1975), esp. Pt. III; O. Kahn-Freund, "The Industrial Relations Act 1971—Some Retrospective Reflections" (1974) 3 I.L.J. 186.

[24] *1976 Scottish Current Law Statutes Annotated.* Emergency powers in the Water Act 1958 continue to apply in Scotland.

deficiency." Section 1 orders may permit water authorities or persons authorised by them to take water from, or discharge it to, a specified source; may restrict the taking of water from a specified source if taking it from there would seriously affect available supplies; may suspend, vary or attach conditions to consents given with respect to the discharge of sewage or trade effluent; may suspend or vary obligations with respect to the taking or discharge of water, its treatment or its supply, whether with respect to quantity, pressure, quality, means of supply or otherwise; and may restrict the use of water for one or more specified purposes (s.1(3)). Orders prohibiting or limiting the use of water may apply to particular consumers, specified classes of consumer, or consumers generally (s.1(4)). Typical orders may thus ban such things as the hosepipe watering of gardens, the topping-up of pools or ponds not containing fish, the use of mechanical or automatic car washes, water-cleaning of the outside of buildings, the use of ornamental fountains or cascades (save where the water used was recycled), automatic cistern flushing in low occupation or unoccupied buildings, car-washing, and the like.[25] Orders may be effective for up to six months, but may be extended by further order up to a maximum of one year from the first order's commencement (ss.1(8), 5(6)). If, however, the Secretary of State "is further satisfied that the deficiency is such as to be likely to impair the economic or social well-being of persons in the area," section 2 gives him more extensive powers to be applied as appears necessary to meet the deficiency. An order under the section may authorise most of the things that can be done under section 1, but, further, may authorise the water authority to prohibit or limit the use of water for such purposes as the authority shall think fit, and may allow the authority to supply water in their area, or in any place within that area, by means of standpipes or watertanks, and to erect, set up and maintain standpipes or watertanks in any street in that area (s.2(3)). Such an order may also contain such supplemental provisions as appear to the Secretary of State to be expedient (*ibid.*). The Secretary of State is further empowered to give directions to water authorities on which such powers have been conferred, as to the manner in which and the circumstances in which any power is, or is not, to be exercised (s.2(4)). Orders empowering the authority to prohibit or limit the use of water

[25] Mr. J. Silkin, MP, Minister for Planning and Local Government, H.C. Deb., Vol. 916, col. 1747. See, *e.g.* the South-West Water Authority (Prescribed Uses: No. 6) (Drought) Order 1976 (S.I. 1976 No. 1483).

may permit the power to be exercised in relation to consumers generally, a class of consumer, or a particular consumer (s.2(5)). A section 2 order may remain in force for up to three months. It can be extended from time to time but not for more than five months from the day it came into operation (s.2(10)). Orders under both sections are made by way of statutory instrument, but are not subject to laying before Parliament and are not published in the annual volumes of Statutory Instruments. Public notice provisions apply both to applications for orders and to their coming into force (ss.1(9), 2(11), Sched. 1). The Secretary of State may require the authority or company concerned to keep him sufficiently informed to enable him to exercise a supervisory role and, if necessary, revoke an instrument (ss.3(6), 5(5)). The subjective formulation of the power to issue orders renders judicial review unlikely (*supra*, pp. 50-72).

The majority of orders made under the Act have been section 1 orders, most of which appear to have dealt with variations as to sources of supply of water. A number have banned non-essential uses of water to conserve stocks. Until 1984, 1976 had seen the most severe restrictions, being the year in which eight section 2 orders (the total to June 27, 1984) were made. Parts of the country served by the South-West Water Authority, the North-West Water Authority, and the Welsh Water Authority (and its predecessors) have been the most severely affected. The summer of 1984 apparently had more severe shortages than ever before, at least in some regions. By July 20, over 21 million people in the areas served by the Severn Trent, North-West, Welsh, South-West, Wessex, Yorkshire and Thames water authorities were subject to hosepipe bans under section 16 of the Water Act 1945. Bans on the non-essential use of water under section 1 of the Drought Act 1976 were in force in parts of the Welsh, South-West and North-West water authorities' areas, and, in the first two areas, water supplies were being taken from old mineworkings. Cut offs in supplies for up to 17 hours a day were anticipated from August 9 in the South-West area and from early September in South-East Wales. Calls for a "national water grid" to prevent or alleviate future crises by enabling deficiencies in one area to be met by transfers from areas with more plentiful supplies, were rejected as impractical or too expensive. Careful management, consumer economies and timely rainfall rendered unnecessary cut offs in supply.[26]

[26] The information in this paragraph has been compiled from a variety of sources: material kindly supplied by the Department of the Environment; a

Orders under the Drought Act are backed up by criminal sanctions, but obviously effective water conservation is dependent on a common sense response by consumers and a shared perception of a situation of crisis. It must be stressed, however, that the Act only applies to deficiencies brought about through exceptional shortages of rain. Serious disruptions in supply from other causes (*e.g.* industrial disputes, or severe damage to reservoirs, supply stations or pipes through man-made or natural disaster, or threat of the same), could, however, be met, if only in part, by resort to a proclamation of emergency under EPA 1920, provided that a sufficiently substantial portion of the national community was affected (*infra*, pp. 223-228).

(2) *The Energy Act 1976*

This Act replaced the Fuel and Electricity Control Act 1973, which had required periodic renewal by order approved by both Houses of Parliament, as the legal response to energy crises and consciousness. It implements international obligations of the United Kingdom as a member of the European Communities, of the International Energy Authority and as a signatory to the International Energy Program.[27] It contains permanently applicable powers to regulate the production, supply, acquisition and use of crude liquid petroleum, natural gas and petroleum products, any substance whether solid, liquid or gaseous, used as fuel, and electricity (hereinafter referred to as "section 1 substances"). It also contains more far-reaching powers to achieve these ends which are exercisable only in circumstances of emergency. The "permanent" powers permit such steps as the setting of maximum prices for petroleum products (s.1(4)), giving directions as to the maintenance of fuel stocks at specified levels (ss.6, 7),[28] and as to the flaring of natural gas (s.12), while section

statement in the Commons by the Secretary of State for Wales, Mr. N. Edwards, MP (H.C. Deb, Vol. 64, col. 1243); *The Sunday Times*, July 15, 1984, p. 7, July 29, 1984, p. 2; *The Times*, July 10, 1984, p. 2, July 24, 1984, p. 1, July 26, p. 1, January 31, 1985, p. 5.

[27] Dr. J. Dickson Mabon, H.C. Deb, Vol. 913, col. 323.

[28] s.6 gives the Secretary of State power to give directions to producers, suppliers and users of crude liquid petroleum or petroleum products with respect to the maintenance of stocks at certain levels, including specifying that a certain level be maintained in Northern Ireland. The section implements EEC obligations under Dir. 68/414/EEC (J.O. 1968, L.308/14) as amended by Dir. 72/425/EEC (J.O. 1972, L.291/154). For the current position on maintenance of stocks see the Petroleum Stocks Order 1976 (S.I. 1976 No. 2162), as amended by S.I. 1980 No. 1609, S.I. 1982 No. 968, S.I. 1983 No. 909.

4(3) allows Her Majesty by Order in Council to make provision for modifying or excluding obligations or restrictions imposed, or extending any power conferred by or under, an enactment which directly or indirectly affects the use of a section 1 substance. The last power would, *inter alia*, permit the imposition of lower speed limits as a fuel-saving measure.[29] The "emergency" or "reserve" powers are exercisable only when an Order in Council has been made pursuant to section 3. Such an order may be issued where the reserve powers are required for the implementation of obligations incumbent on the United Kingdom, as a member of the European Communities or the International Energy Authority or as a party to the International Energy Agreement, to take emergency measures in connection with the reduction, or threatened reduction, of fuel supplies (s.3(1)(*a*)). A section 3 order may also be issued where there exists, or is imminent, in the United Kingdom an actual or threatened emergency affecting fuel or electricity supplies which makes it necessary in Her Majesty's opinion that the government should temporarily have at its disposal exceptional powers for controlling the sources and availability of energy (s.3(1)(*b*)). In either case, some measure of control over its issue is afforded by the need to lay the order before Parliament after it is made, in the former case, for information only, in the latter case requiring affirmative approval (*supra*, p. 43). An order under section 3(1)(*b*) lapses after 12 months unless both Houses resolve that it should be continued. Judicial review of the necessity for such an order is likely to be perfunctory (*supra*, pp. 63-65).

What can be done when a section 3 order is in force? In the first place, the power to set maximum prices, otherwise confined to petroleum products, then extends to crude liquid petroleum and natural gas (s.1(4)). Secondly, the order makes available a reserve power, contained in section 2(1), of control by government directions to undertakings as to their production, supply or use of section 1 substances. Without prejudice to the generality of section 2(1), section 2(2) specifies that (a) directions to producers as to production and/or use may prohibit or restrict the use of any material for the production of a section 1 substance and may extend to the disposal of stocks of such a substance or of any such material; (b) directions to suppliers may prohibit or restrict the

[29] By virtue of ss.4(3), 22 of and Sched. 3, Pt. II to the Energy Act 1976, the Fuel Control (Modification of Enactments) (Speed limits) Order 1973 (S.I. 1973 No. 2051), made under FECA 1973, was continued in force. It was revoked, and not replaced, by S.I. 1977 No. 1870.

supply (anywhere in the world) of any section 1 substance to specified persons, and may require the supply of any such substance (anywhere in the world) to specified persons in accordance with specified requirements including, in the case of crude liquid petroleum, natural gas or petroleum products, requirements as to price; and (c) directions as to the use by undertakings of any section 1 substance may prohibit or restrict its use for specified purposes or during specified periods. Thirdly, section 4(1) permits the Secretary of State to authorise a supplier or user of any section 1 substance to "disregard or fall short in discharging any obligation imposed by or under any enactment or any contractual obligation relating to or involving the supply or use of that substance." Fourthly, section 4(2) empowers the Secretary of State, or a person acting on his behalf, to relax certain road traffic and transport laws set out in Schedule 1 to the Act to enable the use of vehicles as public carriage vehicles without the requisite licences; to permit persons to be employed as or to act as drivers or conductors of public service vehicles without the requisite licences; to relax rules as to drivers' hours; and to provide a defence to certain offences concerned with driving whilst uninsured. Fifthly, the existence in force of a section 3 Order in Council, extends the power to modify enactments (s.4(3), *supra*, pp. 220-221) to those enactments which relate to the supply or use of a section 1 substance.

Non-compliance with the Act, or with orders or directions made under it, is an offence (s.18). Schedule Two to the Act sets out powers to request information, call for documents, and to enter premises for inspection and enforcement purposes. As with the Drought Act 1976, a shared perception of emergency among suppliers and consumers, and a common sense response by them, are doubtless required if these powers are to be fully effective in conserving energy.

A section 3 Order in Council has yet to be issued. However, under the Energy Act's precursor, the Fuel and Electricity Control Act 1973, which contained similar powers, a number of regulations were issued during the period of the industrial disputes involving miners and electrical power workers in late 1973 to early 1974, at a time when oil supplies had been reduced by the Arab oil producers. These regulations, which aimed to conserve fuel and to stabilise its price, and which regulated the use of electricity, in particular through a three day week for industry, in part replaced somewhat similar regulations issued pursuant to a proclamation of emergency under the EPA 1920. Both sets of regulations are examined below (pp. 258-265) in the context of an analysis of the taking and use of powers under that 1920 Act. Should a similar emergency arise, of course, regulations of that type could be issued under the Energy Act 1976, without the need to issue a royal proclamation of emergency, although one might be required if, for example, vehicles had to be requisitioned to move fuel. Some idea of the likely efficacy of restrictions under the Energy Act 1976 can perhaps be gleaned from reflection on that experience with similar restrictions in the early 1970s.

(3) *The Emergency Powers Acts 1920 and 1964*

Section 1(1) of the EPA 1920 (as amended by the EPA 1964) permits the proclamation of a state of emergency when events deprive, or seem likely to deprive, the community of the essentials of life, by interfering with the supply and distribution of food, water, fuel or light or with the means of locomotion. It gives access to a power to make regulations to enable, *inter alia*, the maintenance of the essentials of life to the community. Section 2 of the EPA 1964 renders permanent a power enabling members of Her Majesty's forces to be used on agricultural or other work of urgent national importance.

The invocation and use of these powers is examined in the second section of this chapter, while the third section of this chapter deals with the nature of the regulations made during proclamations of emergency.

2. *The Scope, Invocation and Use of the Emergency Powers Acts 1920 and 1964*

Chapter 2 examined how a decision to proclaim an emergency or to use troops was reached (*supra*, pp. 29-34). This section of this chapter examines the situations in which the powers have been and could legitimately be used.

(1) *Proclamations of emergency under the Emergency Powers Act 1920*

As amended by the EPA 1964, section 1(1) of the EPA 1920 states:

> "If at any time it appears to Her Majesty that *there have occurred, or are about to occur, events of such a nature* as to be calculated, by interfering with the supply and distribution of food, water, fuel or light, or with the means of locomotion, to

deprive the community, or any substantial portion of the community, of the essentials of life, Her Majesty may, by proclamation (hereinafter referred to as a proclamation of emergency), declare that a state of emergency exists." (italics supplied)

A proclamation cannot remain in force for longer than a month, but another proclamation may be issued at or before the end of that period (s.1(1)). During the currency of a proclamation, Her Majesty in Council is given rule-making power of significant proportions (s.2(1)). The nature of that power, the limits on it, and the nature of the regulations made pursuant to it, will be examined in section three of this chapter. This part of this section examines the occasions on which proclamations have been made and potential limits on their issue. It will be recalled that the occasion of the proclamation must be communicated to Parliament, and the regulations made laid before that body subject to the affirmative resolution of both Houses which may add to, alter or revoke them by resolution (*supra*, pp. 42-43, 45).[30] Judicial review of the necessity for a proclamation has been non-existent and is likely, at best, to be very limited (*supra*, pp. 63-65).

The words in italics in section 1(1) (*supra*) represent the amendment made in 1964. As enacted in 1920, the section read: "any action has been taken or is immediately threatened by any person or body of persons of such a nature and on so extensive a scale as to be calculated," etc. This reflected the "mischief" at which the Act was aimed, namely, industrial disputes. In particular, the government was concerned to have powers to combat, or mitigate the effects of, action by the "Triple Alliance" of coalminers, railwaymen and transport workers, who had formed a loose confederation "to co-ordinate industrial action on 'matters of a national character or vitally affecting a principle.' "[31] It may well be that government and employers overestimated the Alliance's potential power to bring the country to a standstill through a general strike,[32] but the Alliance's embodiment of the threat of revolutionary syndicalism and the fear that "industrial unrest might be the tip of a revolutionary iceberg" were potent factors behind the legislation and the creation of a strike breaking machine, the Supply and Transport Organisation (STO), the

[30] For the somewhat less stringent requirements in otherwise equivalent Northern Ireland legislation see Chap. 1, n. 41.

[31] Jeffery and Hennessy, *op. cit.* n. 4, p. 2.

[32] *Ibid.*

ancestor of today's Civil Contingencies Unit (CCU).[33] The broadening of the section in 1964 may owe much to the bad winter of 1962-63, and "was simply to enable the government to proclaim an emergency to meet disruption caused by abnormal weather, natural disasters or 'interference from abroad.' "[34] No doubt it would also embrace man-made technological disasters at nuclear power plants or chemical installations, provided that they interfered with one or more of the items mentioned in section 1(1). The Home Secretary of the day viewed the extension of the proclamation power, and the rendering permanent by the EPA 1964 of the former wartime power to employ services' personnel on agricultural work or work of urgent national importance (*infra*, pp. 229-233), as "a wise exercise in foresight . . . an insurance policy against contingencies—remote contingencies perhaps, but real ones nevertheless."[35]

The actual use of the proclamation power in Great Britain has been confined to industrial disputes involving six groups of workers[36]: Miners (1921, 1926, 1972, 1973-74); dockers (1948, 1949, 1970, 1972); transport workers (the London Bus and Tramways strike, 1924); railwaymen (1955, 1973-74); electricity workers (1970, 1973-74); and merchant seamen (1966). These disputes have been predominantly national or widespread. Three—the London bus and tram strike, 1924, the docks' disputes, 1948 and 1949—have been localised. Emergencies have thus been proclaimed on 12 separate occasions, nine since 1945 and five during the Conservatives' period of office under Mr. Edward Heath, 1970-74. The power was last invoked in Great Britain in the period November 13, 1973 to March 11, 1974. It has been invoked by Governments of varying political complexion: once by a Liberal-Unionist coalition (1921); five times by a Labour Government (1924, 1948, 1949, 1966 and March 4-11, 1974); and seven times by a Conservative Administration (1926, 1955, 1970 (twice), 1972 (twice), and 1973-74). The periods during which proclamations have been in force during such disputes have varied in length: from four days in 1924, to seven and a half months during the General Strike (May 4-12) and continuing coal stoppage in 1926. One month is about average. Essential supplies

[33] *Ibid.* p. 9.

[34] *Ibid.* p. 228.

[35] *Ibid.* p. 229.

[36] The information on pp. 225-226 is taken from Jeffery and Hennessy, *op. cit.* n. 4, App. II, pp. 274-275, and from G.S. Morris, "The Emergency Powers Act 1920" [1979] P.L. 317, Table 1 (p. 320), Table 2 (p. 335).

and services emergencies have thus been of relatively short duration compared with anti-terrorism emergencies. Most proclamations have been issued shortly after the commencement of the industrial dispute, usually within its first week. There is, of course, no requirement that the dispute or other relevant event referred to in section 1 precede the proclamation; anticipatory invocation falls within the scope of the power granted, and in 1926 the issue of the proclamation antedated the coal stoppage and the General Strike. In the miners' dispute in 1972, by contrast, the proclamation was issued one month after the strike began, some three months after an overtime ban had commenced. In some instances resort to the power has been regarded essentially as a precautionary measure "in case the disruption caused by the industrial action should increase."[37] However, although extensive use of the powers made available by the proclamation of emergency is a feature principally of the four coal stoppages (1921, 1926, 1972, 1973-74), in most instances powers have been taken "with the purported intention of putting at least some of them to immediate use."[38] There have been a number of similar proclamations in Northern Ireland.[39]

Potential use of the section 1 power is clearly not limited to industrial disputes. Nor are all industrial disputes within its purview. So what types of disruptive events *are* covered? Involving and affecting which supplies and services? As to the former issue, the neutral term "events," inserted in 1964, is wide enough to cover a variety of actions by individuals and/or groups at home and abroad, the effects of abnormal weather, and disasters, whether natural, manmade or technological. As to the latter issue, the difficulty of defining "essential supplies and services" has already been noted (*supra*, pp. 212-213). What is clear, however, is that the section 1 power to proclaim a state of emergency is not so widely drawn as to encompass all of the entities within those definitions examined earlier in this chapter. The scope of the section 1 power is limited in three ways. First, in terms of the supplies and/or services that the events or apprehended events must interfere or be likely to interfere with, namely, the supply and distribution of food, water, fuel or light, or with the means of locomotion. Secondly, it is limited in terms of the proportion of the community which must feel the impact of the interference or likely interference with these things; the events, by so interfering,

[37] Morris, *loc. cit.* n. 36, at p. 335.
[38] *Ibid.*
[39] See sources cited in Chap. 1, n. 53.

must be calculated "to deprive the community, or any substantial portion of the community, of the essentials of life." Apparently, this was intended to convey the notion that the aim of the legislation was to deal with "national" emergencies. The "substantial portion" reference was merely designed to make it clear that the power could be invoked where, although the entire community was not affected, the greater part were.[40] It is thus arguable that a purely localised emergency, albeit interfering with one of the specified supplies and/or services, is not within the scope of the section 1 power. Indeed, Gillian Morris appears to regard its invocation in the 1924 London Bus and Tramways dispute as questionable in this regard,[41] although the fact that the disruption involved the capital, the seat of government and centre of national commercial importance is, no doubt, an argument in favour of the propriety of the proclamation. Local transport disputes in other centres of population would probably not fall within the proclamation power. As Jeffery and Hennessy have noted, however, local disputes in the "oil fuel and electric power" industries can damage other sectors of industry. Localised disputes involving the supply of energy may now be dealt with under the Energy Act 1976 (*supra*, pp. 220-223) without the necessity for a proclamation of emergency. Local water shortages brought about by exceptional shortage of rain, but not by industrial action or other disruptive occurrences, can, as has been seen, be met with powers conferred by the Drought Act 1976 (*supra*, pp. 217-220).

The third limitation on the section 1 power lies in the concept "the essentials of life," which is nowhere defined in the EPA 1920, although one presumes that it includes the supplies and/or services mentioned in the section, and medicines appear to be regarded as within the necessities referred to in the rule-making power (s.2, *infra*, pp. 233-236).[42] Damage to the economy as a result of disruption to the supplies and/or services specified in section 1, has sometimes been stated as one ground for the issue of particular proclamations.[43]

[40] Attorney General, Sir Gordon Hewart, H.C. Deb., Vol. 133, cols. 1663-1664 (October 26, 1920), noted in Morris, *loc. cit.* n. 36, at p. 322, n. 17.

[41] *Loc. cit.* n. 36, at p. 322.

[42] See, *e.g.* a typical regulation dealing with the supply of medicines: reg. 25 of the Emergency Regulations 1973 (S.I. 1973 No. 1881).

[43] Gillian Morris records: "Whilst Government spokesmen made frequent reference during other 'emergency disputes' to the economic and, in some cases, political repercussions, in 1948 and 1949 the Government justified the proclamation by the need to protect external trade as well as essential food

Industrial action by any of the six groups of workers in whose disputes the EPA 1920 has been invoked is covered, at least prima facie, by the provisions of section 1.[44] So too would be a national waterworkers' dispute.[45] However, groups such as firemen, ambulancemen, doctors, nurses and health-service ancillary workers, commonly embraced by the notion of "essential service personnel," cannot readily be brought within its scope. Their actions are not such as to interfere with one of the specified supplies and/or services. Nor might the typical industrial action of health service employees interfere with a sufficiently broad class of persons as to satisfy the substantial portion of the community element. Postal and telecommunications workers' industrial action might affect enough people, and "communication" perhaps be regarded, on a broad approach, as an essential of life, but such workers cannot readily be said to interfere with one of the specified supplies and/or services. A police strike, subject of course to criminal penalties under non-emergency law (*supra*, pp. 214-215), would also be difficult to fit within the terms of the section 1 power as it does not of itself interfere with one of those specified supplies and/or services. Gillian Morris has suggested, however, that "it may be strongly argued that the state of lawlessness and consequential interference with the designated supplies and services this would probably, sooner or later, entail would be an event of such a nature"[46] as to come within the section. In any event, the work of all or any of these groups of workers could properly be described as "urgent work of national importance," and thus come within the terms of an emergency power rendered permanent by section 2 of the EPA 1964. The scope and use of that power must now be examined.

supplies, and in 1966 the need for powers was based on economic grounds alone. On each occasion, the (Conservative) Opposition supported the resort to emergency powers, although maintaining during the 1966 debate that the Act as it stood did not permit regard to economic circumstances in declaring a state of emergency and urging a broadening of its terms to include such considerations." (*loc. cit.* n. 36, at p. 322.)

44 *Ibid.* at p. 321.

45 *The Times*, January 25, 1983, p. 2, reported that the CCU had met once the water strike began and draft regulations were ready to go before Parliament.

46 Morris, *op. cit.* n. 12, p. 36.

(2) *Use of Her Majesty's forces under the EPA 1964 and its predecessor*

In 1964, section 2 of the EPA 1964 rendered permanent a power enshrined originally as Regulation 6 of the Defence (Armed Forces) Regulations 1939[47] which had been continued in force temporarily since the end of the Second World War.[48] Prior to Regulation 6, the use of troops on civilian work had been sanctioned during proclamations of emergency under the EPA 1920 by a regulation made under section 2 of that Act. For example, regulation 24 of the Emergency Regulations (No. 2) 1926 read:

> "Where a Secretary of State by order has declared that any service is a service of vital importance to the community, it shall be the duty of every person subject to the Naval Discipline Act, or to military law, or to the Air Force Act, to obey any command given by any superior officer in relation to employment upon or in connection with such service and every command shall be deemed to be a lawful command within the meaning and for the purposes of those Acts and that law."[49]

As rendered permanent in 1964, Defence Regulation 6 allows the Defence Council, by order, to:

> "authorise officers and men of Her Majesty's naval, military or air forces under their respective control to be temporarily employed in agricultural work or such other work as may be approved in accordance with instructions issued by the Defence Council as being urgent work of national importance, and thereupon it shall be the duty of every person subject to the Naval Discipline Act, military law or airforce law to obey any command given by his superior officer in relation to such employment, and every such command shall be deemed to be a lawful command within the meaning of the Naval Discipline Act, the Army Act, 1955, or the Air Force Act, 1955, as the case may be."[50]

[47] S.R. & O. 1939 No. 1304.

[48] By the Emergency Laws (Transitional Provisions) Act 1946, the Emergency Laws (Miscellaneous Provisions) Act 1947, various Continuance Orders under s.7 of the 1947 Act, and the Emergency Laws (Repeal) Act 1959.

[49] S.R. & O. 1926 No. 556.

[50] This was the form set out in Sched. 2, Pt. C to the Emergency Laws (Repeal) Act 1959, as modified by the formation of the Defence Council under the Defence (Transfer of Functions) Act 1964.

As with regulation 24 of the Emergency Regulations (No. 2) 1926 (and the equivalent regulation in the 1921 emergency),[51] the power rendered permanent in 1964 removed any doubt as to the legality of such orders given when servicemen were performing such non-military tasks. No proclamation is required to invoke it, only a decision of the Defence Council (*supra*, pp. 33-34). No special procedure exists, as in proclamation cases, for parliamentary oversight of the decision to employ servicemen on such tasks on which it has been thought wise to use them.[52] It may be that the provision does no more than legalise such orders and brings them within the legal regime of military discipline, and that the first portion of Defence Regulation 6 (to "national importance") merely restates, without limiting, a prerogative power to deploy troops at will, a view taken by the Ministry of Defence.[52a]

Rendering the power permanent in 1964 was justified to Parliament particularly in terms of the humanitarian work servicemen could do.[53] It would appear that, since 1945, servicemen have been used pursuant to this power on more than 20 occasions, predominantly in industrial disputes. Sometimes their use has coincided with or overlapped with the deployment of powers under the EPA 1920. However, in the post-war period, none of the Codes of Regulations issued under that Act has contained an equivalent of regulation 24 of the Emergency Regulations 1926. Servicemen have been used to do the work of dockers (1945, 1947, 1948, 1949, 1950), meat-handlers (1946, 1947, 1950), petrol distribution workers (1953), seamen (1960, 1966), dustmen and sewage workers (Tower Hamlets 1970, Glasgow 1975), firemen (Glasgow 1973, nationwide 1978), electricity manual workers (1949), ambulancemen (1979) prison officers (1980) and gas-maintenance workers (1950). During the 1972 docker's strike, the RAF airlifted fuel to the Scottish islands. RAF personnel operated some air traffic control during the civilian

[51] Reg. 22 of the Emergency Regulations 1921, *The Board of Trade Journal*, April 7, 1921.

[52] See generally on the use of troops, C.J. Whelan, "Military Intervention in Industrial Disputes" [1979] I.L.J. 222; S. Peak, *Troops in Strikes* (1984). The latter work was published too late to deal with its arguments in the text. Peak questions whether s.2 of the Emergency Powers Act 1964 can authorise use of troops in industrial disputes (see esp. pp. 51-62). Assuming (as is the position argued herein) that it can, he queries whether particular disputes fell within its ambit.

[52a] Peak, *op. cit.* n. 52, pp. 51-62.

[53] Jeffery and Hennessy, *op. cit.* n. 4, p. 228.

controllers' dispute in 1977. The severe winter of 1946-47, when the national transport system was paralysed, saw troops and prisoners of war used to move coal supplies. Service aircraft and lorries helped to move post during the dispute on the railways in 1955. On June 28-29, 1982, when National Union of Railwaymen members stopped work simultaneously on the railways and London underground, troops laid wirenetting on wet London parks to provide free parking for the increased number of vehicles brought into the capital. Troops stood by, ready to step in to help, in the transport dispute (1947), the docks' strike (1970), the nuclear power workers' dispute (1977), the petrol-tanker drivers' industrial action (1978), and the road haulage dispute (1978-79).[54] Their use was thought possible in the waterworkers' dispute (1982-83) and the strike in the docks in 1984.[55]

Section 2 of the EPA 1964 and Defence Regulation 6 do not contain or give rise to powers to requisition land or chattels. Accordingly, where disputes arise which do not or cannot result in a proclamation of emergency under the EPA 1920, which would enable requisition powers to be taken (*infra*, pp. 236-237), servicemen must rely on services' premises, vehicles and equipment or such non-services' premises, vehicles and equipment as are voluntarily made available by their owners. Thus, in the ambulance drivers' dispute (1979), army ambulances were used, while in the national firemen's strike (1978), army "Green Goddess" fire engines, retained in readiness for possible civil defence deployment, were used, rather than existing fire services' appliances, ostensibly to avoid provocation by having to cross picket lines at fire stations.[56] "During the three months stoppage in order to replace 32,000 strikers, over 20,000 troops in all were used, assisted by 4,000 senior officers and large numbers of part-time firemen."[57]

The only legal limits on a duly signed order authorising the use of service personnel under section 2 of the EPA 1964 and Defence Regulation 6 appear to be its confinement to agricultural work or work deemed by the Defence Council to be of urgent national

[54] This information has been gleaned from a combination of sources: Jeffery and Hennessy, *op. cit.* n. 4, *passim* ; Whelan, *loc. cit.* n. 51, at pp. 224-225; Morris, *op. cit.* n. 12, p. 484.

[55] D. Macintyre and P. Knightley, "Nightmare in the Pipeline" *The Sunday Times*, January 30, 1983, p. 17. See also, *The Times*, January 22, 1983, p. 2; January 25, 1983, p. 2; July 16, 1984, p. 2.

[56] Whelan, *loc. cit.* n. 52 at p. 226; Jeffery and Hennessy, *op. cit.* n. 4, pp. 241-242.

[57] Jeffery and Hennessy, *op. cit.* n. 4, p. 241.

importance. Clearly that body regards local disputes in health and safety related services and in the distribution of food or fuel as coming within that latter concept. At one time, indeed, Queen's Regulations mistakenly interpreted the power as applying *only* to limited and local emergencies.[58] The real limits on the use of service personnel are practical. A smaller, non-conscript services' establishment with many other commitments and calls on its time, limits the scope of their potential use. The use of Her Majesty's forces, moreover, will in reality have to be confined to tasks for which their service training fits them well (*e.g.* driving vehicles, airlifting mail or supplies, transporting fuel or supplies by sea) or to relatively unskilled labour intensive tasks (*e.g.* dustmen and, to a lesser extent through containerisation, dockers). As Christopher Whelan has noted:

> "Not all disputes are susceptible to effective intervention by the military. . . . While the development of technological and industrial skills increases the likelihood of dire effects on the community in the event of industrial action, it also takes several jobs beyond the range of military skills. Many public services jobs require little technological skill, and remain labour intensive. Occasionally, the military possess a special skill that can be utilised such as the use of the R.A.F. to supply a strategic radar station during a strike by civil air traffic control assistants in 1977, on the grounds of national security. In the firemen's dispute, 1978, service personnel were trained to use their own and other old equipment, since using modern equipment such as hydraulic platforms, turntable ladders, pump escapes and, in particular, breathing equipment would be too complex or unsafe. Where the level of technological skill required in an industry is high, troops may have a more limited role. The possibility of military intervention in industries such as petrochemicals, aerospace, atomic energy, and the power industry is accordingly difficult to assess. There is some evidence that during a 'secret military foray' into the Ballylumford power station in Northern Ireland during the Ulster Workers' Council strike [*infra*, p. 266], the Army found it could not man the station without the assistance of middle management which was not forthcoming."[59]

[58] Whelan, *loc. cit.* n. 52 at p. 224, n. 18.

[59] *Ibid.* at p. 233.

Jeffery and Hennessy record that "during a railways' strike in the 1960s it was found that less than twenty soldiers in the entire army were able to drive railway locomotives,"[60] and further note that "certainly by the 1970s the Civil Contingencies Unit harboured no illusions about the possibility of either volunteers or troops keeping British Rail in motion should the NUR or ASLEF close down the network in a national strike."[61] Government must also consider most carefully whether the introduction of service labour would aggravate rather than help in the dispute.[62] It is arguable that subjecting the decision to use troops to prompt parliamentary review might prove beneficial in concentrating minds on the question.[63]

3. Powers Taken During the Currency of a Proclamation Under the Emergency Powers Act 1920

When a proclamation of emergency is in force, Her Majesty in Council is empowered by order

> "to make regulations for securing the essentials of life to the community, and these regulations may confer or impose on a Secretary of State or other Government department, or any other persons in Her Majesty's service or acting on Her Majesty's behalf, such powers and duties as Her Majesty may deem necessary for the preservation of the peace, for securing and regulating the supply and distribution of food, water, fuel, light and other necessities, for maintaining the means of transit or locomotion, and for any other purposes essential to the public safety and the life of the community, and may make such provisions incidental to the powers aforesaid as may appear to Her Majesty to be required for making the exercise of those powers effective." (s.2(1))

[60] Jeffery and Hennessy, *op. cit.* n. 4, p. 225.

[61] *Ibid.*

[62] This appeared to be a factor influencing contingency planners during the 1984-85 coal stoppage. It was reported in *The Times* (April 18, 1984, p. 30) that the Government, in the event of an all-out strike, would ask major construction companies (*e.g.* Taylor Woodrow) for the loan of 30 tonne trucks to be used as "lorry trains" to break any blockade of coal stocks at pitheads. Civilian drivers might have been used.

[63] *Cf.* Morris, *op. cit.* n. 12, p. 485. It does not seem necessary to go as far as requiring the whole panoply of a proclamation of emergency under the EPA 1920 before the use of troops could be sanctioned.

The Regulations made under this power require prompt parliamentary affirmation to continue in force (s.2(2), *supra*, pp. 42-43).[64] Judicial review of the necessity for the Regulations or whether they further the prescribed purposes is unlikely to be more than perfunctory (*supra*, pp. 65-67).[65] Although the section confers wide powers indeed, the Act explicitly provides three limitations (arguably the only substantive limitations on rules otherwise relatable to the purposes prescribed in s.2(1))[66] which the courts would doubtless be willing to enforce (*supra*, pp. 66-67). First, the rule-making power does not extend to the imposition of any form of compulsory military service or industrial conscription (s.2(1)).

Secondly, nor may a regulation be made under the Act which criminalises participation in a strike or peacefully persuading others to participate (s.2(1)). That prohibition has been reiterated in those Regulations rendering contravention of or failure to comply with any of the other Regulations in the Emergency Regulations issued a summary offence; such Regulations usually contain the proviso:

> "that a person shall not be guilty of an offence against any of these Regulations by reason only of his taking part in, or peacefully persuading any other person or persons to take part in, a strike."[67]

Indeed, the Emergency Regulations in 1974 went further in an attempt to comply with the spirit of this limitation in section 2(1) by making it clear, where it had not been so before, that the offence of sabotage did not apply to industrial action short of a strike. In previous Emergency Regulations that offence was constituted where any person did any act:

> "with intent to impair the efficiency or impede the working or movement of any vessel, aircraft, hovercraft, vehicle, machinery, apparatus or other thing used or intended to be used in the performance of essential services, or to impair the usefulness of any work, structure or premises used or intended to be used as aforesaid."[68]

[64] For much weaker procedures in Northern Ireland legislation see Chap. 1, n. 41.

[65] Morris, *loc. cit.* n. 36, at p. 324.

[66] *Ibid.*

[67] The Emergency (No. 2) Regulations 1973 (S.I. 1973 No. 2089), reg. 38(1).

[68] *Ibid.* reg. 32(1).

And it was further stated that this prohibition applied:

> "in relation to any omission on the part of any person to do anything which he is under a duty, either to the public or to any person to do, as they apply in relation to the doing of any act by a person."[69]

That this might penalise industrial action short of a strike was noted by the Standing Joint Committee of both Houses on Statutory Instruments, and was drawn to the attention of both Houses.[70] The revised provision in 1974 instead provided, in respect of omissions, that the offence of sabotage would cover failure to perform a "relevant duty," that is, a duty imposed by virtue of any enactment, rule of law or contract, not being a duty to work periods of duty (however described) determined by or in accordance with a contract.[71]

The third limitation on the rule-making power in the EPA 1920 prevents its use to alter existing procedure in criminal cases or to confer any right to punish by fine or imprisonment without trial (s.2(3)). As thus worded, it would probably not preclude the making of a regulation authorising internment without trial, since preventative detention for the public good might well not be regarded as punishment but merely preventive action, and, in extreme circumstances at least, is relatable to the prescribed purposes in section 2(1) viz. "preservation of the peace" and/or "any other purposes essential to the public safety and the life of the community."[72] No regulation authorising internment without trial has been made under the Act, and one suspects it would prove politically impossible to do so save in a most extreme crisis.

Section 2(1) authorises the conferment and imposition of powers and/or duties on "a Secretary of State or other Government department or any persons in Her Majesty's service or acting on Her Majesty's behalf." It is by no means clear that this enables their imposition and conferment on local authorities as was done in the 1921 and 1926 emergencies (*infra*, pp. 244-249). Occasionally concern was expressed within Whitehall over the

[69] *Ibid.* reg. 32(2).

[70] Mr. A. Booth, MP, H.C. Deb., Vol. 866, cols. 1282-1283. *Fifth Report from the Joint Committee on Statutory Instruments*, HC13-v (1973-74), para. 6.

[71] The Emergency Regulations 1974 (S.I. 1974 No. 33), reg. 30(2), (3).

[72] *Cf. R.* v. *Halliday, ex p. Zadig* [1917] A.C. 260 (power to issue regulations for "securing the public safety and defence of the realm" authorised internment); C.K. Allen, *Law and Orders* (3rd ed., 1965), p. 378; Morris, *loc. cit.* n. 36, at p. 322; De Smith, *Constitutional and Administrative Law* (4th ed., 1981), p. 517; (3rd ed., 1977), p. 507.

questionable legality of this.[73] That no steps were taken in 1964, when amending the EPA 1920, to clarify the position may well mean that the Civil Contingencies Unit "had shelved any plans to involve local authorities in the emergency machine."[74]

The powers taken and used under the Act have varied with the nature of the dispute (*infra*, pp. 243-265). It has, however, been the usual practice to bring forward a much more extensive Code of Regulations than the particular dispute occasioning the proclamation of emergency would seem to warrant.[75] Only in the 1949 and 1955 emergencies were much reduced codes promulgated.[76] This is not to say that the precise provisions of each code have been identical; although the general structure and purport of the codes have been similar over the years, there has been a process of adaptation, amendment, addition and removal in the light of experience with differing emergencies and changes in the general law. Bringing forward more extensive codes, rather than ones limited to the exigencies of the particular situation, has tended to be justified by government as a wise exercise in foresight; the powers might be needed should the dispute spread to other industries or develop in an unusual manner.[77]

The nature of the precise powers used in particular emergencies is examined in some detail below (pp. 243-265). But what of their general nature over the years? Gillian Morris has analysed the contents of the regulations as falling into five main groups.[78] First, those authorising interference with and control of property and the production, disposition and use of goods and supplies. Of particular importance are powers of requisition, subject to compensation, of land and chattels, and of fixing maximum prices of certain commodities, confined since 1945 to foodstuffs (including animal feedstuff).[79] Regulations in 1926, 1949, 1966 and 1970 permitted the billeting of servicemen.[80] Secondly, Regulations have provided for central control of public services,

[73] Jeffery and Hennessy, *op. cit.* n. 4, p. 140. s.2(1) of the Emergency Powers Act (NI) 1926 gives an express power with respect to local authorities.

[74] *Ibid.* p. 229.

[75] Morris, *loc. cit.* n. 36, at p. 325.

[76] *Ibid.*

[77] *Ibid.* at pp. 325, 335.

[78] *Ibid.* at pp. 326-331.

[79] See, *e.g.* regs. 23, 30, 31 of the Emergency (No. 2) Regulations 1973 (S.I. 1973, No. 2089).

[80] Morris, *loc. cit.* n. 36, at p. 326. See, *e.g.* reg. 25 of the Emergency Regulations (No. 2) 1926 (S.R. & O. 1926 No. 556).

other than transport, thus enabling control, direction and regulation of the supply and consumption of gas, electricity and water.[81] Thirdly, Regulations have usually sanctioned extensive central control of transport and ports, the latter often through local port committees under the direction of the Secretary of State.[82] Fourthly, pre-1945 Regulations contained quite extensive public order powers.[83] For example, regulation 22(1) of the Emergency Regulations (No. 2) 1926 provided:

> "Where there appears to be reason to apprehend that the assembly of any persons for the purpose of the holding of any meeting or procession will conduce to a breach of the peace and will thereby cause undue demands to be made upon the police, or will promote disaffection, it shall be lawful for the Secretary of State, or for any mayor, magistrate or chief officer of police who is duly authorised by a Secretary of State, or for two or more of such persons so authorised, to make an order prohibiting the holding of the meeting or procession, and if a meeting or procession is held or attempted to be held in contravention of any such prohibition, it shall be lawful to take such steps as may be necessary to disperse the meeting or procession or prevent the holding thereof."[84]

The demise of this type of provision no doubt in part reflects the availability of permanent (if less extensive) powers to ban processions (but not meetings) on anticipation of serious public disorder provided by section 3 of the Public Order Act 1936,[85] and of the other provisions of that Act which in their turn supplement quite extensive, if less specific, common law powers to prevent a

[81] Morris, *loc. cit.* n. 36, at pp. 327-328. See, *e.g.* regs. 17-20 of the Emergency (No. 2) Regulations 1973 (S.I. 1973 No. 2089).

[82] Morris, *loc. cit.* n. 36, at pp. 328-329. See, *e.g.* regs. 3-16, 26-29 (S.I. 1973 No. 2089).

[83] Morris, *loc. cit.* n. 36, at pp. 329-331.

[84] S.R. & O. 1926 No. 556.

[85] The power to ban processions contained in s.3(2) (outside London) and s.3(3) (within London) is only exercisable where the chief officer of police (outside London) or the appropriate Commissioner of police (within London) is of opinion that the powers available to him in s.3(1) (directions as to route etc.) are insufficient to prevent serious public disorder. Under s.3(2), applications for a ban have to be approved by the district council and the Home Secretary. Under s.3(3) they require the Home Secretary's approval.

breach of the peace.[86] Indeed the uncertainty of the common law powers may prove advantageous to the authorities.[87] Once extensive powers of control in the regulations over firearms, ammunition and explosives have similarly been abandoned in consequence, presumably, of sufficient provision in permanent enactments dealing with those matters.[88]

Finally, although now not so extensive as in the pre-1950 codes, the Regulations have created criminal offences and have equipped the police with coercive powers to seek out and to deal with suspected offenders. It is useful to contrast the modern with the older and wider offences and police powers so as to indicate the potentially very wide interferences with liberty which can be authorised under the EPA 1920. Supplemental police powers of entry and search, much wider than those available at common law or under the PCEA 1984,[89] were found in the codes up to 1949. Thus regulation 33(2) of the Emergency Regulations (No. 2) 1926 stated:

[86] See, *e.g.* *O'Kelly* v. *Harvey* (1883) 15 Cox C.C.435; *Humphries* v. *Connor* (1864) 17 I.C.L.R. 1; *Duncan* v. *Jones* [1936] 1 K.B. 218.

[87] As, arguably, in the 1984-85 coal-stoppage where miners, on their way to picket mines in Nottinghamshire were stopped by police, using common law powers, in S. Yorkshire, Derbyshire and even the Dartford Tunnel in Kent—see *The Times*, March 17, 1984, p. 1 (A.G. Haver's statement on the common law power), March 19, p. 1 (Nottinghamshire road blocks), March 24, p. 1 (Kent action), and p. 9 (leader comment on preventive policing), and H.C. Deb, Vol. 58, cols. 203-247 (April 10, 1984). The High Court refused Kent miners an injunction against police action, but on procedural rather than substantive grounds (*The Times*, March 24,, 1984 p. 9). Police action was coordinated through the National Reporting Centre at Scotland Yard, which centre was set up after the Bristol riots in 1981 (*The Sunday Times*, March 25, 1984, p. 4). The Civil Contingencies Unit was not involved (*The Times*, March 19, 1984, pp. 1, 32). In *Moss* v. *McLachlan*, preventing a convoy of miners proceeding beyond a motorway junction within five miles of several pits was upheld as a reasonable step to prevent a reasonably apprehended breach of the peace (*The Times*, November 29, 1984).

[88] Morris, *loc. cit.* n. 36, at p. 329. See, *e.g.* reg. 19 of the Emergency Reg. (No. 2) 1926 (S.R. & O. 1926 No. 556). Compare the Firearms Act 1968, ss.6, 19.

[89] For powers available at common law and under statute prior to the Police and Criminal Evidence Act 1984 see L.H. Leigh, *Police Powers in England and Wales* (1975) Chaps. VII and IX; Royal Commission on Criminal Procedure, *The Investigation and Prosecution of Criminal Offences in England and Wales: The Law and Procedure*, Cmnd. 8092-1 (1981), paras. 20-41. For powers of stop and search, entry search and seizure in the Police and Criminal Evidence Act 1984, see ss.1-3, 8-19. Note, in particular, that those powers of seizure, unlike reg. 33(2) of the 1926 Regulations, do not generally extend to seizure of items intended for use in the commission of a future offence. However, similarly

> "Any police constable may, if authorised by order of a chief officer of police, enter, if need be by force, any premises or place suspected of having been, or being, used for any purpose endangering the public safety or otherwise contrary to these regulations, and may search any part of such premises or place and may seize or detain anything found therein which is suspected of having been, or being used, *or of being intended for use*, for any such purpose as aforesaid, or the keeping of which in such premises or place involves the commission of any offence against these regulations:
>
> Provided that when the alleged offence is an offence in connection with a registered newspaper, the powers conferred by this paragraph of this regulation shall not be exercised except with the consent of a Secretary of State, and any copies of the newspaper, and any printing press or other plant, or part thereof, which is used for the purpose of printing and producing the newspaper, seized or detained in pursuance of such powers, shall be disposed of in such manner as the Secretary of State may determine." (emphasis added)

Regulation 33(3) gave a constable power to search "any person whom he *believes* to be in possession of, or to be using or carrying any article, the possession of which by such person is an offence against these regulations, and may seize and detain any such article found on such person." A constable could stop and search any vehicle where he had reason to suspect it to be used for any purpose prejudicial to the public safety, or contrary to the regulations, or to be carrying any article the possession of which contravened the Regulations, and could seize and detain any such vehicle or any such article found in it (*ibid.* reg. 33(4)). All the codes have conferred on constables a power to arrest without warrant; for example, regulation 36 of the Emergency (No. 2) Regulations 1973 provided that:

> "where a constable, with reasonable cause, suspects that an offence against any of those Regulations has been committed, he may arrest without warrant anyone whom he, with reasonable cause, suspects to be guilty of the offence."

Criminal offences under the regulations can only be summary in nature (EPA 1920, s.2(3)). The offence of sabotage as contained in more recent codes has already been referred to (pp. 234-235). The

extensive powers of seizure are to be found in NIEPA 1978 (*supra*, pp. 112-115).

equivalent offences in the 1921 and 1926 regulations were much more widely drawn and criminalised any act "calculated to injure a number of properties used in connection with the maintenance of essential services."[90] Pre-war regulations also embodied widely drawn offences of inciting disaffection or of obstructing or impeding action taken under the regulations. Thus, regulation 21(1) of the Emergency Regulations (No. 2) 1926 provided that:

> "If any person attempts or does any act calculated or likely to cause mutiny, sedition or disaffection among any of Her Majesty's forces, or among the members of any police force, or any fire brigade, or to cause sedition or disaffection among the civilian population, or to impede, delay or restrict the supply or distribution of food, water, fuel, light or other necessities, or the means of transit or locomotion, or any other service essential to the public safety or the life of the community, he shall be guilty of an offence against the regulations."[91]

This provision was subject to the usual express proviso that a person could not be guilty of such an offence by reason only of participation in a strike or the peaceful persuasion of another to participate in it. Regulation 21(*b*) further provided that:

> "If any person prints, produces, publishes or distributes any document containing any report or statement the publication of which would be a contravention of the foregoing provisions of this regulation, or if any person without lawful authority or excuse has in his possession, or on premises in his occupation or under his control, any such document, he shall be guilty of an offence against these regulations, unless he proves that he did not know and had no reason to suspect that the document contained any such report or statement, or that he had no intention of transmitting or circulating the document or distributing copies thereof to or amongst other persons."

Regulation 28 of that 1926 Code made it an offence to obstruct, knowingly mislead, or otherwise interfere with or impede, or withhold any information which one may reasonably be required to furnish, from any officer or other person carrying out the orders of any government department or otherwise acting within his

[90] Morris, *loc. cit.* n. 36, at p. 330. See, *e.g.* reg. 20, of the Emergency Regulations (No. 2) 1926 (S.R. & O. 1926 No. 556).

[91] S.R. & O. 1926 No. 556.

duty under the regulations. By contrast, the 1973 and 1974 Codes of Emergency Regulations, which might be thought more likely models for the future, provided that

> "No person shall–
> (*a*) do any act calculated to induce any member of Her Majesty's forces or constables to withhold his services or commit breaches of discipline; or
> (*b*) with intent to contravene, or to aid, abet, counsel or procure a contravention of, paragraph (a) of this Regulation, have in his possession or under his control any document of such a nature that the dissemination of copies thereof among members of Her Majesty's forces or constables would constitute such a contravention."[92]

and, further, stated that

> "no person shall do any act having reasonable cause to believe that it would be likely to endanger the safety of any member of Her Majesty's forces or of any constable or of any person who is charged with the exercise or performance of any power or duty under any of these Regulations or is performing essential services."[93]

It was also made criminal to wilfully obstruct any person acting in the course of his duty as a constable, or exercising or performing any power or duty under the Regulations or performing any service essential to the community, or to do any act with reasonable cause to believe that the act would be likely to prevent any person from, or mislead or interfere with any person in, exercising or performing any such duty, power or service.[94] Those 1973 and 1974 Codes criminalised trespass on, or on premises in the vicinity of, any premises used or appropriated for the purposes of services essential to the community. A person so trespassing might, without prejudice to any other proceedings which could be taken against him, be removed from such premises by the "appropriate person," namely, any person acting on behalf of Her Majesty, any constable, or the occupier of the premises or

[92] The Emergency (No. 2) Regulations 1973 (S.I. 1973 No. 2089), reg. 35; the Emergency Regulations 1974 (S.I. 1974 No. 33), reg. 33; the Emergency (No. 2) Regulations 1974 (S.I. 1974 No. 175), reg. 33; the Emergency (No. 3) Regulations 1974 (S.I. 1974 No. 350), reg. 33.

[93] *Ibid.* regs. 34(1) (1973 Code), 32(1) (1974 Codes).

[94] *Ibid.* regs. 34(2) (1973 Code), 32(2) (1974 Codes).

any person authorised by the occupier.[95] To loiter, for any purpose prejudicial to the public safety, in, or in the vicinity of, any premises used or appropriated for essential services, was likewise criminal.[96] Moreover,

> "where in any proceedings taken against a person [for such loitering], it [was] proved that at the material time he was present in, or in the vicinity of, the premises concerned, the prosecution [might] thereupon adduce such evidence of the character of that person (including evidence of his having been previously convicted of any offence) as tends to show that he was so present for a purpose prejudicial to the public safety."[97]

Those who loitered in the vicinity of any such premises for any purpose committed an offence if, having been requested by the appropriate person to leave, they continued so to loiter.[98] An attempt to commit, a conspiracy to commit, or the doing of any act preparatory to the commission of an offence under the Regulations, were likewise all offences against the Regulation in question.[99] So was the giving of any assistance to any person whom one knew or had reasonable cause to suspect to be guilty of an offence against the Regulations, so long as the assistance was rendered with intent to prevent, hinder or interfere with the apprehension, trial or punishment of that person for that offence.[1]

As has been implied, contravention of or failure to comply with any of the Regulations constituted an offence against the Regulations. So did contravention of or failure to comply with any order made, direction given or requirement imposed under any of the Regulations. Maximum penalties for contravention or non-compliance were imprisonment for a term not exceeding three months, a fine not in excess of £100, or both, but a person could not be guilty of an offence against any of the Regulations solely because of participation in a strike or the peaceful persuasion of another to participate in it.[2] Criminal penalties as an enforcement mechanism thus supplemented powers of entry, disconnection of utilities, execution of works in default,

[95] *Ibid.* regs. 33 (1973 Code), 31 (1974 Codes).

[96] *Ibid.*

[97] *Ibid.* regs. 34(2) (1973 Code), 31(2) (1974 Codes).

[98] *Ibid.* regs. 33(3), (4), 38(1) (1973 Code), 31(3), (4), 36(1) (1974 Codes).

[99] *Ibid.* regs. 37(1) (1973 Code), 35(1) (1974 Codes).

[1] *Ibid.* regs. 37(2) (1973 Code), 35(2) (1974 Codes).

[2] *Ibid.* regs. 38(1) (1973 Code), 36(1) (1974 Codes).

inspection of books and records, and the imposition of requirements to keep records which were contained in some of the directions in schemes regulating the use of commodities and utilities (gas, water, electricity) made pursuant to the Act and the Regulations.[3]

Inevitably, as has been said, the precise nature of the powers actually used, as distinct from merely promulgated, varies with the nature of the events occasioning the proclamation of emergency. Thus, a transport dispute would principally necessitate measures to increase and to maximise the use of available transport; a dockers' or seamen's dispute, measures to ensure as smooth running of the ports as possible to avoid congestion and to enable the unloading of essential supplies, in particular perishable cargoes; while disputes in the coal, electrical and other fuel-supply industries would typically involve measures to conserve fuel and power supplies. A waterworkers' dispute would involve use of powers, similar to those contained in the Drought Act 1976 (*supra*, pp. 217-220), as to the conservation and regulation of the water supply. Measures might have to be taken in respect of such disputes to prevent hoarding and profiteering. In order to give some indication of the powers taken and used, the rationale of their invocation, and the matching of the measures used to suit the changing exigencies of the situation, the remainder of this section of this chapter examines in more detail a number of disputes which have led to a proclamation of emergency: the General Strike and coal-stoppage 1926 (the only full scale operational use of the Government's Supply and Transport Organisation, the precursor of the Civil Contingencies Unit (*supra*, pp. 29-33)) and the post-1945 emergencies resulting from industrial disputes in the docks, on the railways, amongst merchant seamen, and affecting the supply of energy. Examination of the response to the 1973-74 energy crisis is particularly useful because it involved the use of regulatory powers under the Fuel and Electricity Control Act 1973, the precursor of the Energy Act 1976 (*supra*, pp. 220-223). It thus affords an indication of the types of measure which could be adopted under the latter enactment in any future "energy emergency" without the need to resort to a proclamation of emergency under the EPA 1920. Greater emphasis is placed on the post-1945 disputes as better befitting a modern legal study. The 1926 experience, although atypical of resort to the EPA 1920 is, however, instructive in terms of the use of that Act to combat a

[3] See, *e.g.* regs. 17, 20 (S.I. 1973 No. 2089).

perceived threat to the established constitutional order, and cannot be ignored.

(1) *The coal stoppage and General Strike 1926*

On March 10, 1926, the Royal Commission on the Coal Industry issued its report. Neither miners nor employers accepted it. The miners refused to accept a reduction in pay or an increase in working-hours and were "locked out" as from May 1. The threat of a similar stoppage in 1925 had been averted by a temporary government subsidy to the industry and the appointment of the Royal Commission. Apparently, the Government considered then either that its Supply and Transport Organisation was not ready for such a stoppage, or that the public were not ready for the type of confrontation between unions and Government that might ensue.[4] By contrast, in 1926 the Government's preparations were "extensive and well publicised."[5] The TUC, as co-ordinator of union support for the miners, faced with a general strike it did not particularly desire, was much less well prepared.[6] A state of emergency was proclaimed on April 30 in consequence of the apprehended coal stoppage.[7] The General Strike, which hit railways and docks hardest, began at midnight on May 3-4. It lasted nine days. By May 15-16 there had been a general return to work. The coal-stoppage, however, continued into December. The state of emergency ended on December 19.

The Government, probably mistakenly, viewed the General Strike as a direct challenge to its constitutional authority.[8] The Code of Regulations promulgated on May 1 was, accordingly, not just "coal-related." Troops were moved to Scotland, South Wales and Lancashire at the commencement of the coal stoppage.[9] His Majesty's forces had several roles: as a show of force to "cow" the populace (*e.g.* troops in the East End of London); to provide emergency communications and intelligence schemes; to protect installations and volunteer labour; and to provide a labour force themselves.[10] On May 5, the Home Secretary issued four orders

[4] K. Jeffery and P. Hennessy, *States of Emergency: British Governments and Strikebreaking since 1919* (1983), pp. 91-94.

[5] *Ibid.* p. 104.

[6] *Ibid.* pp. 103-104.

[7] S.R. & O. 1926 No. 450.

[8] Morris, *loc. cit.* n. 36, at pp. 338-339.

[9] *Ibid.* at p. 338.

[10] Jeffery and Hennessy, *op. cit.* n. 4, pp. 112-122.

under regulation 24[11] (*supra*, pp. 229-230) authorising the use of service personnel on essential tasks with regard to the maintenance of the electricity supply (naval ratings were deployed as stokers in power stations)[12] ; the maintenance of power for the electrical and mechanical plant of the Port of London (submarines moored in the Thames were used to provide power)[13]; the transport of petrol; and the continuance of railway services, although in fact no service personnel were used in this latter task.[14] Regulation 26 sanctioned the movement of police from one force area to another,[15] increased numbers of special constables were recruited and the Cabinet authorised the establishment of a "Civil Constabulary Reserve."[16] On May 1, the Explosive Substances Order 1926 required such substances to be kept in secure places approved by chief constables. The Order applied to the coalfield counties.[17] On May 3, regulation 13A was added to the emergency code. It empowered the Secretary of State to restrict the application of finance coming from abroad, and was designed to prevent Soviet funding of the stoppages.[18] It provided that:

> "Where a Secretary of State [had] reason to believe that any monies, securities or credits [had] been or [were] about to be transmitted from outside the United Kingdom to the United Kingdom, or [were] about to be applied in the United Kingdom on instructions from outside the United Kingdom, for any purpose prejudicial to the public safety or the life of the community, he [could] by order prohibit the bank or person to or with whom the monies, securities or credits [were] or [were] about to be transmitted, deposited or

[11] G.S. Morris, *A Study of the Protection of Public and Essential Services in Labour Disputes 1920-1976* (unpublished Ph.D. thesis, University of Cambridge, 1978), p. 176.

[12] Jeffery and Hennessy, *op. cit.* n. 4, p. 113.

[13] *Ibid.*

[14] Morris, *op. cit.* n. 11, p. 176.

[15] S.R. & O. 1926 No. 556. There is now a permanent power permitting this in the Police Act 1964, ss.13, 14; and the Police Act 1969, s.1.

[16] Morris, *loc. cit.* n. 36, at p. 335.

[17] S.R. & O. 1926 No. 460. It applied to the counties of Northumberland, Durham, Cumberland, Lancashire, the West Riding of Yorkshire, Derbyshire, Nottinghamshire, Staffordshire, Monmouthshire, Denbigh, Glamorgan and Camarthen, and to the boroughs therein. S.R. & O. Nos. 523 and 527 brought in Brecknock county(including Brecon), Leicestershire, Warwickshire and the boroughs therein.

[18] Morris, *loc. cit.* n. 36, at p. 340.

> established, from paying, transferring or otherwise dealing with any [of the same] without a licence in writing from the Secretary of State."

Orders made under regulation 13A could remain in force for seven days. Banks and other persons so requested by the Secretary of State, were under a duty to furnish such information as he might require to further the purposes of regulation 13A.[19]

Gillian Morris records that:

> "Considerable use was made . . . of regulations concerned with the maintenance of law and order and political stability. . . . During the period that the emergency regulations were in force a total of 7,960 persons were prosecuted for offences connected with the General Strike and coal stoppage, 4,656 for offences under the ordinary law and 3,404 for breaches of the regulations. The majority of charges for contravention of the regulations concerned offences of injuring property used to produce or maintain essential supplies and services, acts likely to cause mutiny, sedition, or disaffection, and obstruction of officers acting in accordance with their duty under the regulations. A high proportion of such proceedings were brought as a consequence of the General Strike. The conduct of the strike was on the whole peaceful, although there were disturbances in certain mining areas and in London, and 1,389 of the 1,760 charges brought under the regulations during this period were for violence and disorder. 150 charges of incitement were preferred. Police made several raids on local offices of the Communist Party and the left-wing Minority Movement and a number of charges were brought for the production, distribution, or possession of militant strike bulletins. . . .
>
> The power to prohibit the holding of meetings and processions was exercised on 18 occasions up to September 22 (most of them during the General Strike). The Home Secretary by an order of October 19, empowered Chief Constables to prohibit meetings without reference to him if they considered that they would lead to a breach of the peace in order to counter a campaign by members of the Communist Party to prevent a return to work, and 63 meetings were prohibited in England and Wales in the period between the making of the order and November 14."[20]

[19] For full text, see S.R. & O. 1926 No. 556.

[20] Morris, *loc. cit.* n. 36, at pp. 339, 340-341.

The Emergency Code contained extensive powers to regulate the supply and distribution of essential commodities (*e.g.* food, fuel and coal).[21] Apparently, the extensive use of volunteers and voluntarist arrangements meant that no great reliance had to be placed on those powers other than in regard to milk and coal. Volunteers were recruited through local Voluntary Service Committees and such private organisations as Chambers of Commerce, and the Organisation for the Maintenance of Supplies. Supply of volunteers far exceeded demand. They were used to man transport and to unload food supplies at the docks. There was no food rationing.[22] In London, however, milk distribution was regulated through the London Milk Pool Committee, based in Hyde Park, operating pursuant to the Milk Distribution (Emergency) Orders 1926.[23] TUC offers of cooperation in the distribution of food were firmly rejected by the Government which presented the TUC in the role of an "alternative government" with which it could not legitimately deal.[24] Local strike committees did, however, issue permits which assisted in moving essential supplies. The TUC was also anxious to maintain other essential services such as sanitation, health, and supplies of power for hospitals and homes. The nature of the power supply system inevitably meant that this maintenance of supplies also protected industries on the same power circuits. Such union co-operation, the successful working of the voluntarist arrangement, high fuel stocks in a period of warm weather, the failure of oil tanker drivers and the white-collar power union to join the strike, all contributed to its failure.[25] Perhaps as Thomas Jones has suggested

> "The General Strike could not succeed because some of those who led it did not wholly believe in it and because few, if any, were prepared to go through with it to its logical conclusion, violence and revolution."[26]

Coal conservation measures under regulation 14 of the

[21] S.R. & O. 1926 No. 556, regs. 2, 13, 17.

[22] Morris, *loc. cit.* n. 36, at p. 340; Jeffery and Hennessy, *op. cit.* n. 4, at pp. 97-98, 108-110, 112-114, 124-125.

[23] S.R. & O. 1926, Nos. 530, 531, 541, 551, 553.

[24] Jeffery and Hennessy, *op. cit.* n. 4, p. 108.

[25] *Ibid.* pp. 111-114.

[26] Cited, *ibid.* p. 122.

Emergency Powers (No. 2) Regulations 1926,[27] and the importation of foreign coal were obviously very important during the coal stoppage. The Coal (Emergency) Directions 1926,[28] made under regulation 14, placed in the hands of local authorities, their officers and committees[29] the regulation of a conservation system in which domestic consumers were restricted initially to obtaining only one hundredweight of coal per week and maintaining stocks of no more than five hundredweights, and business and industrial consumers had to halve their consumption.[30] Local authorities could modify these restrictions through exemptions granted in appropriate cases.[31] Domestic restrictions became tighter (one hundredweight per fortnight) but were later relaxed to enable purchase of a greater amount when foreign coal became available.[32] Coal Emergency Committees were established to take charge of coal distribution under the direction of the Secretary for Mines.[33] Its export or movement coastwise or inland from ports required ministerial approval.[34] Gas manufacturers were required to produce gas from substances other than coal, when possible, but, where coal had to be used, to produce it in such a manner as to effect the greatest possible saving in coal.[35] Gas suppliers were required to supply gas at the lowest possible pressure during off-peak periods to enable its supply at the correct pressure in periods of highest demand.[36] Doing this constituted compliance with any statutory and contractual obligations as to supply.[37] Public lighting was to be reduced to a minimum (other than those lights required for safety),[38] and lighting for advertising and display purposes was prohibited.[39] Industrial and business users had to halve their gas and electricity consumption, unless local authorities permitted higher

[27] S.R. & O. 1926 No. 556.

[28] S.R. & O. 1926 No. 452.

[29] *Ibid.* Art. 2; S.R. & O. 1926 No. 453 (power of local authority to delegate to committee).

[30] *Ibid.* Arts. 4, 7.

[31] *Ibid.* Arts. 4, 8.

[32] S.R. & O. 1926 Nos. 554, 930, 1369.

[33] S.R. & O. 1926 No. 452, Pts. IV, V, Sched. 1.

[34] *Ibid.* Pt. VI.

[35] *Ibid.* Arts. 23-28.

[36] *Ibid.* Art. 27.

[37] *Ibid.* Art. 29.

[38] *Ibid.* Art. 31.

[39] *Ibid.* Art. 30.

consumption in the public interest.[40] Use of coal for pleasure boats (including passenger steamers) but not public ferries was also banned for a period.[41] Restrictions were progressively relaxed in November and December as the miners drifted back to work.[42] During the coal stoppage and General Strike, 361 people were convicted for offences against the Coal Directions.[43]

(2) *Industrial disputes in the docks (1948, 1949, 1970 and 1972)*

In May-June 1948 there was an almost complete stoppage of work in the London docks. The dispute centred on the disciplining of men who had refused to handle an "obnoxious cargo," zinc oxide, at the ordinary rate of pay. There was little evidence of communist fomentation although one trade union leader saw the unofficial strike as "political." Troops were sent in to unload perishable cargoes at Poplar Docks. When the strike spread to Merseyside, the Cabinet agreed on June 28 to proclaim a state of emergency, enabling troops to be deployed to best advantage by making available a power to requisition buildings and equipment. The Emergencies Committee of the Cabinet considered the Home Office's draft Code of Regulations. Public order, safety, sedition and disaffection regulations were included against official advice as to their necessity.[44] A radio broadcast to the nation by Prime Minister Attlee, appealing to patriotism, was instrumental in securing a return to work the next day, June 29. As he had promised, no Regulations were in fact made. The state of emergency lapsed on July 27.[45]

During the two months, May-June 1949, there were a series of unofficial dock strikes, particularly affecting Avonmouth and Liverpool, over the "blacking" of Canadian ships organised in conjunction with the striking Canadian Seamen's Union. Late in May, troops moved into Avonmouth docks to handle perishable cargoes. The dispute escalated in Liverpool.[46] A broadcast to the nation by the Minister of Labour procured a return to work by

40 *Ibid.* Arts. 32, 33.

41 Coal (Emergency) (No. 2) Directions 1926 (S.R. & O. 1926 No. 587).

42 S.R. & O. 1926 Nos. 1478, 1561.

43 Morris, *op. cit.* n. 11, p. 179.

44 Jeffery and Hennessy, *op. cit.* n. 4, pp. 190-194.

45 *Keesing's Contemporary Archives* (hereinafter "Keesing") (1948-50), pp. 9365A, 9366.

46 Jeffery and Hennessy, *op. cit.* n. 4, pp. 206-208.

June 15. The "blacking" dispute, however, closed two London docks by the end of June. A state of emergency was proclaimed with effect from midnight on July 10-11. The Regulations issued authorised the Minister of Transport to establish an emergencies committee to run any port and to suspend the dock labour scheme at any such port so as to enable the employment of any workers, a measure designed to legitimate fully the use of troops on dock work. The Committee established on July 12 was largely composed of ex-senior civil servants, members of the Prime Minister's Advisory Board on purging the Civil Service of communists, thus reflecting governmental perception of the political provenance of the stoppages. Other powers included one to permit police to be used outside their own area and another to sanction the billeting of troops.[47] The state of emergency ended on July 26, after intervention by the Canadian Minister of Labour and the Canadian Seamen's Union procured a return to work in the docks.[48]

A pay dispute led to an official dockers' strike on July 13, 1970. On the 16th a state of emergency was proclaimed by the newly elected Heath Government, determined to stand up to inflationary pay claims, and a Court of Inquiry, under Lord Pearson, was set up. Port emergency committees were established in 12 major ports the next day. They were chaired by the port's general manager or other senior officer. Troops stood by, ready to unload perishable cargoes, but strikers agreed to do this themselves to avoid the employment of service labour. Principally, the Regulations issued covered: giving directions to port authorities, the movement of ships, the use of goods and passenger vehicles, setting maximum food prices, the provision of public services, the requisitioning of land and chattels (*e.g.* buildings and vehicles) and the maintenance of public order. The Court of Inquiry reported on July 27, recommending the award of a moderate wage increase. Three days later the strike was called off. The emergency committees were disbanded, and the state of emergency ended on August 4.[49]

Further disputes in the docks, particularly over "containerisation," resulted in an official strike from July 28, 1972. A state of emergency was proclaimed on August 3, a precautionary measure to prevent food shortages. Local port committees were set up on August 4. The RAF were involved in

[47] Keesing, p. 10105.

[48] Jeffery and Hennessy, *op. cit.* n. 4, p. 208.

[49] *Ibid*, p. 233; Keesing, p. 24220A. For text of regulations see the Emergency Regulations 1970 (S.I. 1970 No. 1042).

airlifting fuel to the Scottish Islands, while similar strikers' co-operation in moving other essential supplies obviated the need for wider military deployment as in 1970. The dispute ended in mid-August after employers had tentatively accepted some of the recommendations of the Joint Special Committee on the Ports Industry.[50]

(3) *The ASLEF disputes on the railways (1955, 1973-74)*

On May 28, 1955, 6,000 railway footplatemen, members of ASLEF, went on strike over the maintenance of pay differentials.[51] Aircraft and lorries were used to move essential mails over the longer postal trunk routes. No servicemen were deployed on the railways themselves, probably to avoid alienating the NUR drivers whose continued working enabled the maintenance of a skeleton service. There may also have been problems in finding servicemen with the necessary skills to drive locomotives and operate signalling equipment. The public were urged to conserve fuel, light and power and to limit their use of the postal and telegraphic services.[52] Steps were taken to encourage car-sharing through the conclusion of an agreement "with the insurance companies whereby the use of private cars for giving lifts (but not for hire) would be covered by an owner's existing policy, and that immediate cover should be given to owners with vehicles in mothballs who wished to use them during the emergency. Drivers would be indemnified by the government against the risk of injury or death to passengers, provided that their vehicles displayed the sign 'FREE LIFTS AT YOUR OWN RISK', and that passengers' attention had been drawn to it before boarding."[53] On May 31, a state of emergency was proclaimed, despite an increase in the number of drivers reporting for work and the number of trains running.[54] The 25 regulations promulgated in the Code aimed, in part, to maximise use of available transport. They gave effect to the insurance arrangement noted above; allowed ministers to authorise the use of goods' vehicles without the requisite carriers' licences or outside the terms of existing licences, the use of passenger vehicles without

[50] Jeffery and Hennessy, *op. cit.* n. 4, p. 237; Keesing, p. 25554. For text of regulations see the Emergency (No. 2) Regulations 1972 (S.I. 1972 No. 1164).

[51] Jeffery and Hennessy, *op. cit.* n. 4, p. 224.

[52] *Ibid.* p. 225.

[53] *Ibid.* pp. 225-226.

[54] *Ibid.* p. 226. For text of regulations see the Emergency Regulations 1955 (S.I. 1955 No. 791).

PSV licences or road service vehicle licences, and unlicensed persons to act as drivers or conductors of road passenger vehicles. The limit on the number of passengers in such vehicles could also be waived. Vehicles normally operating only within factories or on open-cast coal sites might be allowed on the road. Use of vehicles on the road without excise licences could also be sanctioned. The Minister could relieve the British Transport Commission or the London Transport Executive of their statutory obligations to carry passengers and goods, and permit them to give priority to essential goods over less urgent ones. As precautionary measures powers were taken to regulate the mails, the supply of gas, electricity and fuel, and the distribution of food and animal feedstuffs.[55] Power to requisition tipper vehicles was delegated to regional transport commissioners, but the response to appeals for their voluntary transfer rendered its implementation unnecessary.[56] Negotiations brought an end to the strike on June 14. The proclamation of emergency was revoked a week later.[57]

Another ASLEF dispute was a factor contributing to the continuation of the state of emergency during the fuel crises of 1973-74. It is examined below (pp. 262-265).

(4) *The seamen's strike (1966)*

An official strike of merchant seamen began on May 16, 1966. The dispute was over wages, but called into question the government's prices and incomes policy; a shipowners' surrender would have made nonsense of the 3½ per cent. pay norm.[58] The Prime Minister viewed the strike, in a broadcast to the nation, as "a strike against the state—against the community."[59] A state of emergency was proclaimed on May 23. Regulations promulgated were seen essentially as reserve powers "giving ministers power to fix maximum prices of specified foodstuffs, to control ports and dock labour in order to relieve congestion, to restrict postal services, to relax restrictions on road transport, to requisition ships, vehicles and aircraft, and to prevent sabotage."[60] The Prime

[55] Keesing, p. 14243.

[56] G.S. Morris, "The Emergency Powers Act 1920" [1979] P.L. 317, at p. 336.

[57] Jeffery and Hennessy, *op. cit.* n. 4, p. 226.

[58] *Ibid.* p. 230, citing R.H. Crossman, *The Diaries of a Cabinet Minister—Vol. I: Minister of Housing 1964-1966* (1975), p. 524.

[59] Jeffery and Hennessy, *op. cit.* n. 4, p. 230.

[60] *Ibid.* p. 231. For text of regulations see the Emergency Regulations 1966 (S.I.

Minister informed the House of Commons on June 20 that it had not to that time been necessary to invoke the powers; that the general level of supplies was satisfactory; and that availability of air transport lessened the impact on British exports (although emergency plans to use RAF planes to transport key exports were to be discussed with industry). Existing services to the Scottish islands might be supplemented with naval vessels.[61] His most startling revelation concerned security services' (MI5) intelligence concerning Communist orchestration of the strike, and their plans to extend it to the docks and to other workers in order to bring the country to a standstill.[62] On June 22, port emergency committees were set up in the major ports to prevent congestion if necessary by keeping out extra ships.[63] Keesing's *Contemporary Archives* record that:

> "foreign vessels had continued to enter and unload at British ports throughout the strike, as the docks were unaffected . . . special arrangements were made through the use of naval vessels to ensure supplies for outlying Scottish islands. . . . In addition, Manx shipowners and the NUS on June 5 reached agreement on a weekly service from Liverpool to the Isle of Man to ensure the delivery of foodstuffs and other commodities, including coal supplies, essential to the island's economy."[64]

It would appear that the Prime Minister's announcement encouraged moderate seamen to press for an end to the strike. On June 23 talks were held between both sides in the dispute under the chairmanship of Lord Pearson. An employers' consensus on annual leave procured a return to work on July 2. The state of emergency ended on July 6.[65]

(5) *Coal and power disputes (1970, 1972, 1973-74)*

On December 7, 1970, manual workers in the electricity supply industry began a "go slow," an official "work to rule" coupled with a ban on overtime working in support of a 25-30 per cent.

1966 No. 600), operative from May 24, 1966. On June 23 they were replaced, in the same terms, by the Emergency (No. 2) Regulations 1966 (S.I. 1966 No. 740).

61 Keesing, p. 21548.

62 Jeffery and Hennessy, *op. cit.* n. 4, pp. 232-233.

63 *Ibid.* p. 231.

64 Keesing, p. 21551.

65 *Ibid.*

pay claim, at a time when the Government was trying to avoid inflationary pay awards. The action "led to immediate voltage reductions and disconnections, and the electricity authorities took steps to maintain supplies to priority users and to spread the remainder as evenly as possible."[66] A state of emergency was proclaimed on December 12 and the usual set of regulations was promulgated.[67] The Electricity (Advertising and Display) Order 1970[68] was made under regulation 19 of the Emergency (No. 2) Regulations 1970 which enabled the Secretary of State to regulate the supply and consumption of solid and liquid fuel, refinery products, electricity and gas. The order prohibited, save under licence of the Secretary of State, the use of electricity supplied by an electricity board for purposes of advertising (including shop window and other displays) and for floodlighting. Such electricity could, however, be used to broadcast adverts on television or to project them onto screens at cinemas and theatres. Its use to illuminate traffic signs and the signs of registered pharmacists was also sanctioned, as was its use on the railways. The order became operative on December 14. The Secretary of State for Trade and Industry had told the House of Commons on December 12 that it was impracticable to use troops to man the power stations.[69] The Government capitulated to the "apparently unresistable, power of the electricity workers,"[70] and the dispute was settled with a generous and inflationary pay award on December 14.[71] The state of emergency ended on December 17.

The coalminers' national strike during January-February 1972 saw more extensive use of powers available under the EPA 1920. The strike began on January 9, but had been preceded by a 10-week overtime ban and was coupled with an intensive and successful campaign of secondary picketing (involving so-called "flying pickets") to hamper the movement of coal to power stations.[72] In consequence coal stocks at power stations were down to two weeks' supply at the normal rate of consumption. Yet a

66 Morris, *loc. cit.* n. 56, at p. 336.

67 The Emergency (No. 2) Regulations 1970 (S.I. 1970 No. 1864). A state of emergency had been proclaimed in Northern Ireland from midnight December 7-8, 1970—see Keesing, p. 24578.

68 S.I. 1970 No. 1866.

69 Jeffery and Hennessy, *op. cit.* n. 4, p. 234.

70 *Ibid.*

71 *Ibid.*

72 *Ibid.* pp. 234-235.

state of emergency was not proclaimed until February 9.[73] Jeffery and Hennessy suggest that the Government were perhaps anxious not to repeat "the precipitate proclamations of 1970."[74] The Emergency Regulations 1972 came into operation on February 10.[75]

Regulation 17(1) of this Code permitted electricity boards, so long as they were acting with the authority of the Secretary of State, to disregard or fall short in discharging obligations, imposed by statute or contract, covering the giving or continuing of supplies of electricity, or its supply in accordance with the standards laid down in the enactment or contract, "to such extent as appear[ed] to them to be necessary or expedient for maintaining or making the best use of supplies of electricity available for distribution or for conserving or making the best use of supplies of fuel or power available for the generation of electricity." Regulation 17(2) gave the Secretary of State power to issue directions (whether specific or exercised by order applicable to general classes of premises) to businesses and occupiers of premises, regulating or prohibiting the consumption of electricity on those premises, and power to cut off supplies, the power in either case to be exercisable "if and so far as it appear[ed] to [him] necessary or expedient for maintaining or making the best use of supplies of electricity available for distribution."[76] Entry to premises to check whether directions were being contravened could also be sanctioned. Regulation 21 empowered the Secretary of State to regulate the supply, acquisition, consumption and distribution of solid and liquid fuels, refinery products, electricity and gas.

Orders were made relieving electricity boards of their statutory obligation to supply electricity to all consumers, as from 6.00 a.m. on February 11. Keesing's *Contemporary Archives* record that:

> "complete power cuts were introduced throughout most of the country on a rota basis on February 11th whereby each area or part of an area was allocated a series of four hour periods each week in which there was a high likelihood of disconnection."[77]

[73] Morris, *loc. cit.* n. 56, at p. 342.

[74] Jeffery and Hennessy, *op. cit.* n. 4, p. 234. The Home Secretary gave the reason as a desire to avoid putting negotiations at risk (Mr. R. Maudling, H.C. Deb., Vol. 831, cols. 34-38).

[75] S.I. 1972 No. 157.

[76] Keesing, p. 25185.

[77] *Ibid.* p. 25186.

That same day, the Electricity (Advertising, Display and Floodlighting) (Restriction) Order 1972[78] came into operation. It banned the consumption of electricity supplied by an electricity board for advertising purposes (including shop window and other displays) or for floodlighting, except under licence of the Secretary of State or for certain purposes specified in the Order. These covered television or radio advertising, projection of advertisements onto cinema or theatre screens, and the illumination of traffic signs, public telephones and signs indicating hospitals, emergency services' premises and specified medical-related premises (*e.g.* doctors, chemists). The Order did not apply to the railways. On February 12, the Electricity (Non-Domestic Heating) (Restriction) Order 1972[79] came into effect. It prohibited the consumption of electricity supplied by an electricity board for space-heating, except under licence granted by the Secretary of State, at offices, shops, public halls, public houses, catering establishments and premises used for recreation, entertainment and sport. The premises of doctors, dentists, pharmacists, opticians and vets were excluded from the ban insofar as the premises were used for the purposes of the practice or the business. The Order also permitted the use of such electricity for such purposes as operating or controlling the use of central heating plant consuming other fuels.

Industry was effectively put on a three day week from February 14.[80] Directions under regulation 21 came into effect then which required some 20,000 industrial consumers with an estimated demand of 100 megawatts or more, not to use any electricity on Sundays and on three other days in the week. Larger users on separate circuits who operated continuous processes were required to halve their consumption. Railways, the gas and water industries, sewage and drainage works, docks, harbours, larger airports, bakeries, milk production and other major food plants, major hospitals, medical premises, oil refineries, newspapers, broadcasting and television, were all exempt from these restrictions which were relaxed on February 19 to permit consumption for operating communications equipment, including telex.[81] The effect of the restrictions on employment was drastic; on February 14, some 800,000 workers were laid off. The number

[78] S.I. 1972 No. 160.
[79] S.I. 1972 No. 169.
[80] Keesing, p. 25186.
[81] The Electricity (Directions) Order 1972 (S.I. 1972 No. 225).

had doubled by February 18.[82]

The acceptance by Government and employers of the report of the Wilberforce Inquiry into miners' pay led to the NUM calling off its pickets.[83] On February 23, further relaxations on controls were introduced. The use of electricity for space-heating was permitted between midnight and 7.00 a.m.[84] Consumption at any time in connection with computers and ancillary equipment was sanctioned. Premises affected by the "Sunday and three other days" ban could use electricity for any purpose between the hours of midnight and 7.00 a.m., and in their offices at any time except for space-heating. Continuous process users could increase consumption to 60 per cent. of normal.[85] On February 24, the use of electricity for controlling fans or blowers or burners used in connection with furnaces and kilns fired by other fuels was permitted.[86]

Restrictions on the use of electricity by industry on specified days were lifted on February 28, and continuous process users' consumption was then raised to 85 per cent. of normal.[87] The miners returned to work on that day. On February 29, the advertising, floodlighting and heating restrictions were lifted in respect of the Orkneys and Shetlands, the Outer Hebrides and Tiree.[88] All restrictions on industry and those on space heating were revoked on March 2.[89] Rota cuts had been progressively reduced and ended on that day. The ban on advertising and floodlighting ended with the expiry of the emergency powers on March 8.[90]

As Jeffery and Hennessy have noted:

> "the effectiveness of the miners' secondary pickets, enabling them to control power supplies with the passive support of their trade union colleagues, meant that one union in the

[82] Keesing, p. 25186.

[83] *Ibid.*

[84] The Electricity (Non-Domestic Heating) (Restriction) Amendment Order 1972 (S.I. 1972 No. 239).

[85] The Electricity (Directions) No. 2 Order 1972 (S.I. 1972 No. 240).

[86] The Electricity (Directions) No. 3 Order 1972 (S.I. 1972 No. 245).

[87] The Electricity (Directions) No. 4 Order 1972 (S.I. 1972 No. 265).

[88] The Electricity (Restrictions) (Amendment) Order 1972 (S.I. 1972 No. 273).

[89] The Electricity (Directions) (Revocation) Order 1972 (S.I. 1972 No. 305); the Electricity (Non-Domestic Heating) (Restriction) (Revocation) Order 1972 (S.I. 1972 No. 306).

[90] Keesing, p. 25186.

> 1970s could do what both the Triple Alliance and the general strike had failed to do in the 1920s. It is a demon still to be exorcised in the contingency planning community."[91]

The power that existed to hold the community to ransom had been amply demonstrated, with important effects on the subsequent policy of governments, contingency planners and trade unions.[92]

The state of emergency November 1973-March 1974 was more complicated than its predecessors, saw extensive use of emergency powers to regulate the use of energy under the EPA 1920, and witnessed the creation of a new legislative apparatus, the Fuel and Electricity Control Act 1973, the precursor of the Energy Act 1976, to enable far-reaching restrictions to be imposed in that field without the need to resort to a proclamation of emergency which might prove politically damaging at home and abroad. As in 1966, 1970 and 1972, the industrial disputes in question involved powerful groups of workers (miners, electrical power engineers and railwaymen) challenging a Government incomes' policy designed to combat inflation.

The aftermath of the 1973 "October War" in the Middle East saw a sudden cutback in oil supplies from that region to the West, imposed by the Arab oil-producers. In November 1973, coalminers banned overtime and weekend working, and the electrical power engineers (who effectively run the power-stations) banned out-of-hours' working. Both groups' industrial action was designed to support pay claims far in excess of those permitted under "Stage Three" of the Heath Administration's statutory counter-inflation strategy, itself a species of emergency power.[93] Faced with a run-down of coal-stocks at power stations, the Government proclaimed a state of emergency on November 13 and the usual code of Regulations came into effect the next day.[94] Of particular importance were regulations 17 and 21, in the same terms as those in the miners' dispute in 1972 (*supra*, pp. 254-255), and regulation 22 which permitted the Secretary of State to give directions to suppliers as to the supply of solid or liquid fuels, and to direct refiners of liquid fuel "as to the production of any liquid fuel, or other refinery products, or as to the use, disposal or supply

[91] Jeffery and Hennessy, *op. cit.* n. 4, p. 235.

[92] *Ibid.* pp. 235-236, 239; on the government's plans to combat a miners' strike see P. Hennessy, "Striking lessons from history" *The Times*, July 24, 1984, p. 10.

[93] Jeffery and Hennessy, *op. cit.* n. 4, p. 239.

[94] The Emergency Regulations 1973 (S.I. 1973 No. 1881).

of any refinery products, including those forming part of any stock held by him for the purposes of his business." From December 11, however, the effective parent power for the restrictions lay in the Fuel and Electricity Control Act 1973 (FECA 1973) which applied to petroleum and any substance derived therefrom, to "any substance, whether solid, liquid or gaseous . . . used as fuel" and to electricity as it applied to the other substances (s.1). Section 2 empowered the Secretary of State to regulate or prohibit the supply, production, acquisition or use of these substances; to give directions to their producers about their production and use; and to give directions to their suppliers as to whom they should not supply. It enabled him to regulate prices of petrol and its derivatives. Under section 2 directions could be given to users as to the purposes for which and the period in which fuel might be used. Section 4(1) permitted suppliers and/or users to be allowed to disregard or fall short in discharging statutory or contractual obligations in connection with those substances to which the Act applied. Section 4(2) permitted the use of vehicles free of certain restrictions (*e.g.* PSV licences) and the relaxation of drivers' hours, but only when an order was in force under section 2(1). Section 4(3) empowered Her Majesty in Council to "make provision for modifying or excluding any obligation or restriction imposed, or extending any power conferred by or under an enactment which directly or indirectly affects the use of [fuel or electricity]." One justification cited for the Act was the power it gave to introduce petrol rationing. This was not actually introduced, although coupons were distributed at the end of November.[95]

On November 15, the Electricity (Heating) (Restriction) Order 1973[96] came into force. It banned the unlicensed use of electricity supplied by an electricity board for spaceheating on premises used wholly or mainly as an office or showroom, retail shop, bank or petrol station, restaurant, catering establishment, or for the sale or consumption of intoxicating liquor; as a television, film, or photographic studio, library, museum, art gallery, exhibition or other public hall; as a school, college or other place of education, church, chapel or other place of public worship or for recreation, entertainment or sport. Exemptions were provided for parts of such premises used as living accommodation; where necessary to maintain the health of someone ill, disabled or infirm, or to

[95] Morris, *loc. cit.* n. 56, at p. 344; Mr. P. Walker, Secretary of State for Trade and Industry, H.C. Deb., Vol. 865, col. 1262.

[96] S.I. 1973 No. 1900.

preserve the health of livestock; to operate controls for central heating run on other fuels; to prevent damage to central heating plant; to run heating, cooling or air-conditioning so far as necessary to prevent damage to apparatus, goods or material sensitive to changes in temperature or humidity; and on medical-related premises. On the same day, an order–in essentially the same terms as those employed in 1970 and 1972 (*supra*, pp. 254,256)–banned the use of electricity for advertisements, displays and floodlighting.[97] In addition, government departments and nationalised industries were instructed to cut their consumption of fuel and electricity by 10 per cent.[98] On November 16 schools and other places of education were exempted from the heating restrictions and all premises covered by the Heating Order were allowed to use electricity between 00.30 and 7.30.[99]

On November 19, oil company deliveries were lowered by 10 per cent., but priorities were set for the food industry, public transport and services, and the armed forces. The public were urged to use a voluntary 50 mph speed limit and to limit Sunday driving.[1] To prevent hoarding, the sale of petrol in cans was banned. Under the Motor Fuel (Restriction of Supplies) Order,[2] operative on November 21, motor fuel had to be supplied directly into the tank of a motor vehicle. Other users could only have it supplied in normal quantities by their normal suppliers who had to keep records showing the quantity so supplied, the date of supply and the identity of the user so supplied. Exemption licences could be granted by the Secretary of State.

The FECA 1973 came into force on December 6. The next day a 50 mph speed limit on all roads came into force under the Fuel Control (Modification of Enactments) (Speed Limits) Order 1973,[3] which extended the Secretary of State's power under the Road Traffic Act 1967 to impose temporary speed limits so that that power was exercisable in the interests of motor fuel conservation. Up to 50 per cent. of street lights were switched off. Motorists were encouraged to give lifts. Distributors making

[97] The Electricity (Advertising, Display etc.) (Restriction) Order 1973 (S.I. 1973 No. 1901).

[98] Keesing, p. 26296.

[99] The Electricity (Heating) (Restriction) Variation Order 1973 (S.I. 1973 No. 1913).

[1] Keesing, p. 26227.

[2] S.I. 1973 No. 1943.

[3] S.I. 1973 No. 2051 (made under s.4(3) of the FECA 1973).

commercial deliveries were urged to be fuel conscious. Fuel allocations to airlines were reduced, but Air-Sea Rescue exempted.[4] Under section 2(1) of the FECA 1973, the Fuel and Electricity (Heating) (Control) Order 1973[5] was made operative from December 11. It prohibited the heating by electricity (whether or not supplied by an electricity board), or by any fuel, of certain premises above a temperature of 63°F. The premises covered were in essence those already covered by existing heating restriction orders under the Emergency Regulations (*supra*, pp. 259-260). The list of exemptions was, however, extended to cover also the maintenance of the health of pregnant women, the under fives and the over 60s, and to permit the heating of school premises to a greater temperature during school hours. Medical related premises were, however, subject to the temperature restrictions. Heating to a higher temperature was permissible where demanded by other enactments or with a licence from the Secretary of State. On December 13, lighting restrictions were introduced under the Electricity (Lighting) (Control) Order 1973[6] which applied to those premises already covered by existing heating controls (apart from television or film studios), and to cinemas, theatres, and those parts of hotels and similar establishments open to the public or for the communal use of residents. Lighting was restricted, in the case of areas lit by tungsten lamps, to an electrical load not in excess of two watts per square foot of floor area, and in areas lit by fluorescent tubes or a mixture of both types of lighting, to 1 watt per square foot. The restrictions, waivable through licences, did not apply to rooms lit by a single fluorescent tube or 40 watt bulb, or where their effect would be to require a reduction which might endanger the safety of persons or the security of premises, or to parts of schools during school hours. Also on December 13, the advertisements, etc., heating and supply of motor fuel restrictions under the Emergency Regulations 1973 were revoked[7] and replaced by virtually identical orders under FECA 1973.[8] Nonetheless, on that

[4] Keesing, p. 26297.

[5] S.I. 1973 No. 2068.

[6] S.I. 1973 No. 2080 (made under s.2(1) of the FECA 1973).

[7] The Electricity (Restrictions) (Revocation) Order 1973 (S.I. 1973 No. 2110); the Motor Fuel (Restriction of Supplies) (Revocation) Order 1973 (S.I. 1973 No. 2111).

[8] The Motor Fuel (Restriction of Acquisition) Order 1973 (S.I. 1973 No. 2087); the Electricity (Advertising, Display etc.) (Control) Order 1973 (S.I. 1973 No. 2091); the Electricity (Heating) (Control) Order 1973 (S.I. 1973 No. 2092).

day a further proclamation of emergency was issued and a new set of Emergency Regulations promulgated, omitting regulations 21 and 22 (*supra*, pp. 258-259), now adequately covered by the FECA 1973.[9] Apparently, no further action was taken under the Emergency Regulations.[10] Orders under the FECA 1973 set maximum prices for petrol and paraffin from December 15.[11]

December 13 had seen a deepening of the industrial crises; the ASLEF ban on overtime, Sunday and rest-day working for the main drivers on the railways came into effect.[12] The ban was included as one of the grounds supporting the proclamation, and continuance of the emergency regulations was thought necessary to help with the maintenance of certain transport services.[13] The Prime Minister informed Parliament that this action would require a further 20 per cent. reduction in the use of electricity. Coal stocks at power stations were already 40 per cent. below their normal level and were being run down at the rate of one million tons per week. Drastic measures were required. There could be no immediate resort to rota cuts as in 1972; the power engineers' overtime ban precluded selective cuts, and such cuts as could be made would hit essential services, the old and children, indiscriminately. Resort to such cuts could not, however, be ruled out if other measures did not produce the requisite saving. Domestic consumers and the public generally were urged to save electricity through such measures as "switch off when not needed," "turn down thermostats," confining electric heating to one room if it had to be used at all. Television broadcasts would close down at 10.30 p.m. save over Christmas and on New Year's Eve.[14] Under the Electricity (Industrial and Commercial Use) (Control) Order 1973,[15] industrial and commercial users were restricted in their use of electricity (whether or not supplied by an electricity board) to their normal daily use for no more than five days in the period December 17-31. Large continuous process

[9] The Emergency (No. 2) Regulations 1973 (S.I. 1973 No. 2089).

[10] Morris, *loc. cit.* n. 56, at p. 344.

[11] The Paraffin (Maximum Retail Prices) Order 1973 (S.I. 1973 No. 2118); the Motor Fuel (Maximum Retail Prices) Order 1973 (S.I. 1973 No. 2119).

[12] Keesing, p. 26297.

[13] Morris, *loc. cit.* n. 56, at p. 344 (n. 94).

[14] Keesing, pp. 26297-26298.

[15] (S.I. 1973 No. 2120). Certain modifications were soon made to this to accommodate the different holiday period in Scotland: see the Electricity (Industrial and Commercial Use) (Control) (Amendment) Order 1973 (S.I. 1973 No. 2137).

users were restricted to 65 per cent. of normal consumption. Exceptions to the five day rule were made for: emergencies; emergency services; preserving the health of livestock; lifts and escalators; hospital and medical-related premises; railways; agricultural purposes; newspapers and the sale of food or animal feedstuffs. Modifications were made from December 20 to permit the use of generators using waste power or existing petroleum stocks within the user's normal allocation.[16] To combat the effect of the 50 mph speed-limit and the fuel shortage on transport, from December 20 lorry drivers were allowed to work longer hours than those specified in the Transport Act 1968.[17]

A more formal three-day week was instituted on December 31. Electricity board areas were divided up according to plans available from the boards concerned.[18] In some areas building and engineering operations, industrial and commercial premises other than shops could only use electricity supplied by an electricity board on Monday, Tuesday and Wednesday. In other areas, Thursday, Friday and Saturday were the permitted days for such concerns. Shops, too, were subject to area divisions: for some, mornings were the permitted period for electricity use, for others afternoons, and the periods would rotate each week. Sunday hours were 9.30-12.30, 14.30-17.00. The usual sorts of exemptions applied.

By January 7, some 885,000 workers were on short-time working. Special arrangements were made to permit full-time working in certain sections of banking and in those parts of the oil industry particularly connected with offshore oil development in the North Sea.[19] January saw further restrictions in street lighting, but from January 18 the full use of electricity was permitted for certain purposes in the iron and steel industry. Although the power engineers had returned to normal working at the beginning of the month, enabling rota cuts to be introduced, it was not possible to abandon the three-day week because the NUM were balloting their members on strike action and, on January 28,

[16] The Electricity (Industrial and Commercial Use) (Control) (Second Amendment) Order 1973 (S.I. 1973 No. 2146). This restricted the definition of electricity in the principal Order (S.I. 1973 No. 2120) to mean only electricity supplied by an electricity board.

[17] Keesing, p. 26299.

[18] The Electricity (Industrial and Commercial Use) (Control) (No. 2) Order 1973 (S.I. 1973 No. 2172).

[19] Keesing, p. 26299.

ASLEF announced a stepping-up in their campaign of industrial action through projected selective one day stoppages.[20] However, particularly to help those enterprises and (especially female) workforces that would not normally work on Saturdays, those concerns so far restricted to the use of electricity at that end of the week were permitted to use it on Wednesdays to Fridays instead, or opt to stay as they were.[21]

The miners' ballot showed 81 per cent. support for strike action. The strike was set to begin on February 9. On February 7, Parliament was dissolved and a General Election called, with the issue "who runs the country" much to the fore.[22] The state of emergency was further continued from February 9.[23] Restrictions on television broadcasting were lifted for the period of the election campaign, and the commercial three-day week restrictions were not to apply to premises used for election purposes. However, no exemption was granted from heating and lighting restrictions. ASLEF abandoned its selective one day stoppage tactic so as not to harm Labour's electoral chances. Not so the miners who went on strike on February 9, although their claim had been referred to the Pay Board the day before.[24] An easing of the fuel situation resulted in the demise of restrictions on the acquisition of petrol from February 22.[25] The election held on February 28 produced a House of Commons in which neither major party had an overall majority. On March 4, the Labour Government was formed.[26]

The new Government immediately exempted the miners from Stage Three of the counter-inflation policy and their dispute was settled on March 6, although the proclamation of emergency was then renewed as a precautionary measure.[27] The three day week, estimated to have cost the country £2,000 million, was lifted from

[20] *Ibid.* p. 26362.

[21] *Ibid.*; the Electricity (Industrial and Commercial Use) (Control) (Second Amendment) Order 1974 (S.I. 1974 No. 117).

[22] Keesing, p. 26363; K. Jeffery and P. Hennessy, *States of Emergency: British Governments and Strikebreaking since 1919* (1983), p. 240.

[23] The Emergency (No. 2) Regulations 1974 (S.I. 1974 No. 175).

[24] Keesing, p. 26363.

[25] The Motor Fuel (Restriction of Acquisition) (Revocation) Order 1974 (S.I. 1974 No. 245).

[26] Keesing, p. 26363.

[27] *Ibid.*; the Emergency (No. 3) Regulations 1974 (S.I. 1974 No. 350).

midnight March 8-9.[28] On March 11, a Royal Proclamation terminated the state of emergency.[29] From midnight March 23-24 other restrictions on the use of electricity were removed.[30] Supplies of petrol and aviation gasoline remained at 10 per cent. below normal for the time being. The speed limit restrictions were relaxed from March 29 to permit motorway driving at 70 mph.[31]

The emergency had seen coal stocks drop to 8.3 million tons by March 9, only 1.3 million tons above the level at which, in winter, disconnections would be necessary. The restrictions had resulted in estimated savings of 20 per cent. of normal consumption.[32] Once again, the power of industrial muscle in the coal and electricity supply industries had been amply demonstrated.

(6) *Industrial disputes and emergency powers 1974 to date*

The 1973-74 emergency was the last occasion on which the powers in the EPA 1920 were invoked in Great Britain. The reserve powers of the Energy Act 1976 (*supra*, pp. 220-223) have yet to be used. Yet the period to date has witnessed a number of disputes involving groups of workers in respect of whose industrial action the EPA 1920 could have been invoked: road-haulage workers (1978-79); a threatened strike by petrol tanker drivers (1979); seamen (1981); air-traffic controllers (1977, 1981); railwaymen (1982); and waterworkers (1982-83). A national miners' strike threatened in 1981 and a widespread stoppage occurred in 1984-85. A national waterworkers' stoppage was expected in the winter of 1980-81 when a full set of emergency regulations was prepared in readiness for a proclamation of emergency.[33] To some extent, non-invocation of the EPA 1920 has reflected the changing nature of industrial power (*e.g.* the declining importance of sea-transport, and the shift of goods from rail to road), reliance on management and/or workers taking steps to maintain essential services (*e.g.* the road-haulage dispute 1978-79, and the waterworkers' dispute 1982-83), and government

[28] An estimate given by Mr. E. Varley, MP, Secretary of State for Energy: Keesing, p. 26363. The Electricity (Industrial and Commercial Use) (Control) (Revocation) Order 1974 (S.I. 1974 No. 377).

[29] Keesing, p. 26363.

[30] The Fuel and Electricity (Control) (Revocation) Order 1974 (S.I. 1974 No. 511) revoking S.I.s 1973, Nos. 2068, 2080, 2091 and 2092.

[31] Keesing, p. 26363.

[32] *Ibid.* p. 26416.

[33] Jeffery and Hennessy, *op. cit.* n. 22, pp. 255-261.

surrender to key-workers' demands.[34] As has been seen (pp. 230-231), a number of disputes were able to be successfully met by government resistance to demands backed up with the use of service personnel under the EPA 1964 (*e.g.* firemen 1977-78, ambulancemen 1979).

A state of emergency was, however, proclaimed in May 1974 in Northern Ireland, under its equivalent of the EPA 1920, when the Province was paralysed by a general strike organised by the Ulster Workers Council in protest against the new "power-sharing" Executive, established under the Northern Ireland Constitution Act 1973, and the proposed Council of Ireland, both of which could be said to have been repudiated by Ulster voters in terms of the results in the February 1974 general election.[35] Concentration on restricting electricity output by the Province's power stations reduced it to 10 per cent. of normal. Although troops were used to distribute fuel, it soon became obvious that they could not be used to man power stations since the civilian operators would not afford the necessary co-operation. The threat of a complete electrical shutdown was all too real; by May 19, the date of the proclamation, only one power station was operating. Milk had to be poured away down drains for lack of transport and dockers refused to unload vegetables and fruit. The strike was called off when the Executive resigned on May 28. As Jeffery and Hennessy have noted, whatever its other implications for the future of government in Northern Ireland, "the whole affair constituted a sombre lesson in the ability of the armed services to break a large-scale strike."[36]

4. Assessment, Future Prospects and Reform

Ronald Kidd, while conceding that "any Government is entitled to be armed with certain reasonable powers to deal with a widespread upheaval which may dislocate the entire machinery of the State,"[37] appears to regard the EPA 1920 as a significant threat to freedom in that "the Regulations can be so drawn as to suspend

[34] *Ibid.* See also A. King, "Precision Instrument" *The Sunday Times*, April 15, 1984, p. 17.

[35] For an excellent detailed account of the strike see R. Fisk, *The Point of No Return: The Strike which Broke the British in Ulster* (1975). For an analysis of the election results and their significance see R. Rose, *Northern Ireland: A Time of Choice* (1976), p. 31.

[36] Jeffery and Hennessy, *op. cit.* n. 22, p. 241, from which the above summary is précised.

[37] R. Kidd, *British Liberty in Danger* (1940), p. 51.

practically all our civil liberties and to weight the scales heavily against those who may be in active opposition to the government of the day."[38] Governments have preferred to present emergency powers in this field as a vital insurance policy against contingencies which may threaten essential supplies and services and constitute a threat to the life of the community, rather than as a strike-breaking mechanism.[39] It cannot, however, be gainsaid that resort to such powers inevitably blunts the impact of the strike weapon, rendering it, at the least, less quickly effective.[40] Nor can it be said, with government as effective employer in several disputes and with its concern for the effective management of the economy at stake in others, that government deploys such powers from a wholly disinterested position.[41] The use of the powers in the coal stoppage and General Strike (1926) illustrates their potential for interference with liberty. That experience is, however, atypical of their use. Their more typical use appears less spectacular, much more a common sense response to preserve the essentials of life for the community, although it may be queried whether the cost of resort to them in the miners' disputes (1972, 1973-74), rather than conceding to the wage demands as an exceptional case, did not outweigh any benefits to be gained by their use. Invocation in some disputes might be viewed as over-prompt (*e.g.* 1966), but in others the Government might equally be criticised for acting too late (*e.g.* the miners' dispute 1972). Some may question whether it is right to use such powers to prop up incomes policies, statutory or otherwise,[42] but the resolution of that issue perhaps turns on the appropriateness of incomes policies themselves and is thus far beyond the capabilities or the scope of this book. There does, however, seem little necessity to bring forward a full Code of Regulations each time. The mechanism for creating new powers and securing parliamentary approval of them is surely flexible and speedy enough to permit additions to much reduced codes if and when exigencies demand.[43]

[38] *Ibid.*
[39] See, *e.g.* on the EPA 1964, *supra*, pp. 225-230.
[40] Jeffery and Hennessy, *op. cit.* n. 22, p. 263.
[41] Morris, *loc. cit.* n. 56, at p. 352.
[42] *Ibid.* at pp. 348-352.
[43] *Cf.* G.S. Morris, *A Study of the Protection of Public and Essential Services in Labour Disputes* (Unpublished Ph.D. thesis, University of Cambridge, 1978), p. 246.

It would clearly be inappropriate to dispense with such powers as are available under the emergency legislation examined in this chapter. Other methods might, however, be used to reduce the necessity for resort to them in industrial disputes. A harsher economic climate, fear of unemployment and the changing socio-economic circumstances of key workers and industries may well reduce resort to strike action. A restricted entitlement to social security benefits for strikers and their families may have an inhibitive effect.[44] Maintaining high stocks of coal at power stations and making more use of stations fuelled by oil or nuclear power, while costly, might reduce the impact of a miners' strike, at least where the Midland's coalfields remain in production.[45] It still remains to be shown that current labour law works to inhibit secondary supportive action by one key group in favour of another (*e.g.* by railwaymen and dockers in support of miners), or whether it will successfully inhibit stoppages brought about by so-called "flying pickets," although experience in the miners' strike (1984-85) gives little cause to be sanguine.[46] It is, no doubt, hoped that a statutory requirement to ballot members before taking strike action[47] will inhibit resort to that weapon. A non-statutory ballot requirement has worked in that fashion in recent years with the miners but did not preclude the "rolling

[44] On the restrictions, see A. Ogus and E. Barendt, *The Law of Social Security* (2nd ed., 1982), pp. 120-129, 501-507. For a comment on implications in the miners' strike, see P. Paterson, "The soup-kitchen sanction" *The Sunday Times*, April 29, 1984, p. 15.

[45] P. Beresford, "Coal: danger point eight months away" *The Sunday Times*, July 29, 1984, p. 49.

[46] Although the NCB won a High Court injunction against the Yorkshire miners' executive with respect to "flying pickets" (*The Times*, March 25, 1984, p. 1), no action was taken in respect of breaches of it, on the basis that it would not be constructive in finding a settlement (*ibid.* March 20, 1984, pp. 1, 28; D. MacIntyre, "Why it is still not time to bring in flying judges" *The Sunday Times*, June 3, 1984, p. 65). The British Steel Corporation were reportedly considering court action in respect of the coal blockade (*The Times*, June 21, 1984, p. 1) but no action was taken as coal continued to be moved. While official policy of the transport and railway unions was to support the miners through refusal to move coal, union members appeared less keen to operate that policy. The South-Wales Area of the NUM was fined £50,000 for breach of an injunction against secondary picketing obtained by two haulage firms, and its assets were sequestrated. Sequestration of the assets of the NUM itself was ordered because of contempt committed by ignoring court orders as to the unofficial nature of the strike, which orders were made in challenges by some members of the NUM in terms of the union rulebook.

[47] Trade Union Act 1984, ss.10, 11.

strike" of 1984-85. However, the Industrial Relations Act experience, and the experience in the United States with the Taft-Hartley Act, (*supra*, pp. 214, 218-219) cannot make one over-sanguine about the prospects for success, particularly if the economic climate changes. It may yet prove possible to conclude effective binding no-strike agreements in key sectors of industry and the public service, to buy out the right to strike and replace it with compulsory arbitration, or to ban strikes in essential supplies and services' industries. The Government is reportedly re-examining these options, but other reviews and inquiries have seemed sceptical about their feasibility or utility.[48] Privatisation and localised bargaining might reduce the possibility for concerted action to cripple vital supplies and services[49] as might the de-unionisation of key installations (*e.g.* GCHQ).[50] Of course, where strike action is taken, some reliance can be placed on worker maintenance of such supplies and services through agreed codes of conduct (*e.g.* in the National Health Service, or in safety work in mines). Indeed, Gillian Morris rightly reminds us that particularly in such key sectors as power supplies, but "in essential services in general, consensus among the workers involved that supplies should not be severed, is ultimately the only guarantee of their maintenance."[51] Experience, however, has shown such arrangements to be of varying reliability with, for example, in the Health Service, problems of differing interpretation of emergency cases.[52] Moreover, as none of these measures could provide an absolute guarantee against paralysing industrial action, retention of emergency powers as a fall-back is obviously necessary. Such powers could not be abandoned, in any event, because of the need to be able to respond quickly to disruptions in essential supplies and/or services caused other than through industrial action, for example, through terrorist action, events overseas, technological or natural disasters, or abnormal weather conditions.

A more pertinent issue, then, is how the powers might be usefully reformed. All would profit from greater parliamentary oversight (*supra*, pp. 48-50) and more open discussion of their

[48] See G.S. Morris, "The Regulation of Industrial Action in Essential Services" (1983) 12 I.L.J. 69, at pp. 70-71, 82-83 for a concise summary of these options, their protagonists, and doubts cast on their utility.

[49] *Ibid.* at p. 32.

[50] For a concise summary of action taken at GCHQ see *Council of Civil Service Unions* v. *Minister for the Civil Service* [1984] 3 W.L.R. 1174.

[51] *Op. cit.* n. 43, p. 560.

[52] See, generally, Morris, *loc. cit.* n. 48, at pp. 80-82.

rationale and mode of operation. It would be dangerous to extend the scope of the EPA 1920 to cover serious damage to the economy as a result of disruption to any supplies and/or services. To do so "would probably enable the executive to assume emergency powers on a permanent basis."[53] Extending the EPA 1920 powers to embrace very localised disputes arguably could have the same effect, and ought to be avoided. A prohibition on regulations authorising internment ought to be inserted in the EPA 1920. Such draconian schemes ought in this context to remain the prerogative of statute. That powers *can* be conferred on local authorities ought to be made clear. Finally, it is arguable that provision ought to be made for some alternative organisation to supplement the work done in emergencies by service personnel. Using the police for some tasks, as in the disputes involving ambulancemen and social workers, is possible, but threatens their impartiality, and has traditionally been avoided by emergency planners. Civilian volunteers are another possibility, but could prove divisive. Moreover, as Jeffery and Hennessy have noted:

> "Trained and disciplined pairs of hands, under tight government control, are infinitely preferable. But the introduction of troops is in itself an emotive step. It may well escalate a dispute and will certainly throw the forces into the thick of political controversy. . . . As an alternative to the armed forces, the civil defence corps, which was disbanded in 1968, might be reconstituted. . . . A civil defence corps, under civilian Home Office control would be well placed, for example, to decontaminate water-supplies at street and household level should a power or water strike create widespread health hazards. Locally recruited men . . . well-known in their neighbourhoods, could protect individuals from danger and distress without the stigma of 'strike-breaking' necessarily being attached to their actions. It would be for the police and army to handle affairs at picketed installations, not civil defence volunteers. Such a force would be a national and not a sectional asset, indispensable when the necessities of life are cut off by act of God or man."[54]

[53] Morris, *loc. cit.* n. 56, at p. 322.

[54] *States of Emergency: British Governments and Strikebreaking since 1919* (1983), p. 267.

Chapter 6

ENHANCED CONTROL AND ACCOUNTABILITY

It has been seen that emergency powers to combat terrorism and to assist in the maintenance of essential supplies and services confer wide-ranging authority and discretion on the executive subject to limited parliamentary surveillance and minimal judicial supervision. These powers also effect often substantial inroads into accepted civil liberties and rights of citizens. A number of suggestions for reform in the powers themselves, in accompanying safeguards and in mechanisms of control and accountability, have been advanced for consideration as improvements on the present position. It now remains to examine two more general issues of reform in terms of enhanced control and accountability of decision-makers:

(a) whether extant emergency powers should be gathered into a statutory code with enhanced parliamentary and possibly judicial supervision;

(b) whether, as an alternative or a supplement to such a code, the existence of a Bill of Rights in the United Kingdom might make some difference to decision-making, and to the control and accountability of decision-makers, in respect of emergency powers, in particular in terms of enhanced consideration of civil liberties' issues.

1. Should There be a Statutory Code of Emergency Powers?

In 1972, Professor William Twining called for the enactment of an Emergency Powers (Security) Act for the United Kingdom as a whole which

> "should contain provision for all the powers which the authorities may reasonably require to deal with an outbreak of violent subversion, but any derogation from the ordinary rights of the individual should be balanced by the provision

of additional safeguards against abuse and of procedures for dealing with complaints and for the compensation of those who suffer loss or injury as a result."[1]

To implement the powers in any particular area would require an executive proclamation of a state of emergency therein, which proclamation would require parliamentary approval.[2] Similar suggestions have been made by others.[3] The suggested mechanism for invocation is an extension of that embodied in the EPA 1920, although in the security context the "meat" of the substantive powers would be set out in the Act itself rather than created through regulations, and the suggestion has a parallel in the Republic of Ireland's Offences Against the State Act 1939.[4]

It is suggested here that the idea might usefully be broadened, and that consideration be given to enacting a statutory code of emergency powers gathering together, in line with some of the specific reforms canvassed in this book, the types of emergency powers now contained in NIEPA 1978, the PTA 1984, the EPA 1920 and 1964 (including a typical code of regulations under the EPA 1920), the Energy Act 1976 and, perhaps, the Drought Act 1976, although the much less controversial situations in which this last Act is invocable could constitute a good reason for retaining it separately. The code could also put into statutory form such common law emergency powers as were thought valuable and abolish others, thereby clarifying the legal position on available powers to meet emergencies. Each of the above Acts could form a separate part of the code.

1 W.L. Twining *et al*, *Emergency Powers: A Fresh Start*, Fabian Tract 416 (1972), p. 29. In "Emergency Powers and Criminal Process: The Diplock Report" [1973] Crim. L.R. 406, at p. 408, n. 6, he stated that he no longer favoured its enactment in the near future mainly because the political climate was such that it was unlikely that its enactment would comply with the principles set out in the Tract.

2 Fabian Tract 416, *ibid.*

3 Lord MacDermott, "Law and Order in Times of Emergency" [1972] *Jur. Rev.* 1, at pp. 20-21; R. Evelegh, *Peace-Keeping in a Democratic Society: The Lessons of Northern Ireland* (1975), at pp. 117-118. Dr. C.P. Walker also seems to be in favour of the enactment of some such legislation to replace NIEPA 1978 and the PTA 1984, although he may have in mind something more permanent, rather than legislation invocable only by proclamation: "The Jellicoe Report on the Prevention of Terrorism (Temporary Provisions) Act 1976" (1983) 46 M.L.R. 484, at p. 486.

4 See M. Robinson, "The Protection of Human Rights in the Republic of Ireland" in C. Campbell (Ed.), *Do We Need a Bill of Rights?* (1980), pp. 50-77; J.M. Kelly, *Fundamental Rights in the Irish Law and Constitution* (2nd ed., 1967), pp. 77-88.

Parts of the code or specific provisions within parts could be invoked throughout the United Kingdom or in specified parts (but not very small parts) by means of an executive proclamation of emergency subject to prompt and periodic parliamentary approval. The interval at which further parliamentary sanction would be required might vary according to the particular power (*e.g.* EPA 1920 emergencies tend to be of shorter duration than anti-terrorist emergencies) but should not be greater than one year. Following the example of Commonwealth Constitutions (*e.g.* Zimbabwe, *supra*, pp. 4-6), one might require the approval of a two-thirds majority in each House so as to emphasise the gravity of the step to be taken but without making it impossible to introduce emergency powers where clearly needed. This would, of course, run contrary to the British way of doing things, and could be circumvented by a sufficiently determined executive procuring the enactment of the powers it wanted in another statute. Resort to this would, however, attract criticism and public attention.

Whenever the code (or a provision thereof) was invoked, the operation of the powers taken could be subjected to scrutiny by a Select Committee of both Houses of Parliament and/or by an independent body set up to monitor human rights' protection, for example, as part of a Bill of Rights (*infra*, pp. 275-277). The Standing Advisory Commission on Human Rights (SACHR) in Northern Ireland (*supra*, pp. 77-78) provides some precedent here. In order to make resort to emergency powers as politically vulnerable an act as possible (thus making it a step not to be lightly taken), a provision could be contemplated for judicial review of their invocation. A proposal to this end was advanced by the Canadian Civil Liberties Association to the Commission of Inquiry Concerning Certain Activities of the Royal Canadian Mounted Police.[5] The courts' approval of the necessity for invocation and their judgment that the measures taken did not go beyond what the exigencies of the situation demanded could be made a condition of the proclamation of emergency or of the questionable measure continuing in force beyond a certain period, and, if required to be laid before Parliament, could enhance that body's consideration of the matter. The suggestion by the Canadian Civil Liberties Association contemplated securing the

[5] A.A. Borovoy, *Submissions to Commission of Inquiry Concerning Certain Activities of the Royal Canadian Mounted Police, re Emergency Powers and the War Measures Act, from Canadian Civil Liberties Association* (1970), pp. 5-6. A copy was kindly supplied to the author by a member of the delegation, Professor W.S. Tarnopolsky, Director, Human Rights Research and Education Centre, University of Ottawa.

approval of the Supreme Court of Canada by means of an executive request for an advisory opinion.[6] Provision could be made here for the request to be made to the appellate committee of the House of Lords, a novel departure and one, like having such judicial review in this situation at all, inevitably controversial. The value of judicial review, and the difficulties and disadvantages of it in this context, to some extent mirror those in connection with a Bill of Rights, and are more fully explored below.

The statutory code as a whole could be subject to periodic review by Parliament, following a review by a Select Committee or independent body, through, for example, a requirement of quinquennial re-enactment as is now required for the PTA 1984, and has been recommended for NIEPA 1978 or its replacement (*supra*, pp. 48-50). As well as furthering parliamentary scrutiny and executive accountability, it might also afford an opportunity to consider the necessity for at least some of the provisions in a period of calm, divorced from the distorting glare and pressing concerns of a current emergency. It could also enable periodic additions to the powers in the light of experience and bring what in some contexts (*e.g.* the EPA 1920) is an area very much regulated by Whitehall and surrounded by secrecy, into public scrutiny.

2. Might a Bill of Rights Enhance Protection of Civil Liberties in Times of Emergency?

A Bill of Rights is a document setting out human rights and freedoms, regarded as important by a society, which empowers judges to declare invalid or inoperative to the extent of the inconsistency other laws (including statutes) found to infringe the protected rights and/or freedoms.[7] A Bill of Rights in this sense constitutes some inroad into usual notions of parliamentary sovereignty. There have been several proposals for such a Bill, either for the United Kingdom as a whole or for Northern Ireland alone.[8] The leading contender for the text of the protected rights

6 *Ibid.*

7 *Cf.* Lord Lloyd, "Do We Need a Bill of Rights?" (1976) 39 M.L.R. 121, at pp. 122-123.

8 For a list to 1976 see P. Wallington and J. McBride, *Civil Liberties and a Bill of Rights* (1976), App. 5, p. 146. Since then see Lord Wade's Bills (H.L. 11 (1976-77), H.L. 54, H.C. 100 (1979-80), H.L. 54, H.C. 60 (1980-81)); Lord Brockway's Bill of Rights (Northern Ireland), H.L. 80 (1976-77). Wallington and McBride advanced a model of their own: *ibid.* App. 1. A European

and freedoms in such a Bill is that of the European Convention on Human Rights (*supra*, pp. 83-90).[9] Judicial review could be supplemented by scrutiny of legislative proposals by a Human Rights' Commission reporting to Parliament.[10] Additionally, a Commission could have roles in education and in assisting litigants.[11] The sponsoring department could also be obliged to lay before Parliament its opinion on whether its particular legislative proposal was compatible with the Bill of Rights.[12]

The general merits and demerits of such a device to protect human rights have been well canvassed elsewhere.[13] It is by no means clear that a constitutional mechanism which may work well enough in the different context of a "written," "higher law" constitution (*e.g.* in federal states such as the USA and Canada with its new Charter of Rights embodied in its now patriated constitution), could successfully be transplanted into a unitary state, possessing no "written" constitution and with a strong judicial adherence to the legal doctrine of parliamentary sovereignty.

The benefits of a Bill of Rights in the sphere of emergency powers would inevitably be more limited than in normal times. The benefits might be said to centre on its provision of another public forum in which government could be required to justify its resort to emergency powers, in a context in which the decision-maker, an independent court applying the Bill of Rights, was duty bound to consider the matter, not only in terms of state necessity, but also of the human rights' values embodied in the text of the Bill of Rights. In short, it provides one more mechanism of accountability. Such research as has been done on executive decision-making with respect to past emergency powers (*supra*, pp. 25-29) suggests that the executive may not adequately consider the impact of such powers on these fundamental values, and parliamentary consideration might be thought somewhat

Human Rights Convention Bill (H.C. 73) received a first reading in the Commons under the Ten Minute Rule on December 13, 1983. The SACHR in its *post*-Baker submissions to the Secretary of State renewed its call for the adoption of a Bill of Rights: *Press Release*, December 17, 1984, para. 5(a).

9 Wallington and McBride, *op. cit.* n. 8, Chap. 3; Bills noted in n. 8.

10 Wallington and McBride, *op. cit.* n. 8, pp. 108-111.

11 *Ibid.*

12 *Cf.* Canadian Bill of Rights 1960, s.3; see W.S. Tarnopolsky, *The Canadian Bill of Rights* (2nd revised ed., 1975), pp. 125-128.

13 Wallington and McBride, *op. cit.* n. 8; C. Campbell (Ed.), *op. cit.* n. 4; M. Zander, *A Bill of Rights?* (2nd ed., 1980).

perfunctory, given the context in which speedy enactment of the powers is sought and granted. It might be expected that the existence of a Bill of Rights, raising the prospect of judicial challenge in a more far-reaching form, could do something to alter that position within the executive by pushing the civil liberties' issues more to the forefront, although it must be conceded that the matter might tend to become more one of so framing the legislation as not to invite judicial criticism, in much the same way as parliamentary tactics were much to the fore in executive consideration of the Prevention of Violence Act 1939 as detailed in Owen Lomas' study (*supra*, pp. 27-28). A detailed report on the compatability of the proposed powers with the Bill of Rights, required to be laid before Parliament by the sponsoring department and/or a Human Rights Commission established by the Bill of Rights, might promote more careful and meaningful consideration of the powers by the legislature.

Proponents of judicial review in this context, whether as part of a Bill of Rights or as a condition for the continuance in force beyond a certain period of a proclamation of emergency invoking all or part of a statutory code of emergency powers (*supra*, pp. 271-274), see its value as rendering resort to emergency powers as politically vulnerable an act as possible, so that although a government could still act swiftly and decisively when faced with a clearly genuine threat to the state, it might be less likely to brave the obstacle course of enhanced parliamentary scrutiny and judicial review in those more questionable situations of less moment where an argument that ordinary powers would suffice might have more weight.[14] Invocation of judicial review might be achieved by requiring the executive, when it proclaims an emergency or seeks the enactment of emergency powers, to seek from the Constitutional Court interpreting the Bill of Rights (*e.g.* the House of Lords) an advisory opinion on the propriety of the invocation and of the measures proposed to be taken, which opinion would have to be laid before Parliament to enhance its consideration of the matter. Judicial review might also be invoked by allowing Bill of Rights' issues concerning the invocation and use of emergency powers to be challenged by affected individuals and groups in the ordinary course of judicial business.[15] As Kevin Boyle has noted, a Bill of Rights could have a further valuable effect:

[14] Borovoy, *op. cit.* n. 5, at p. 6.

[15] Wallington and McBride, *op. cit.* n. 8, pp. 99-101.

"the existence of a fundamental statement of rights combined with human rights' education would help to sensitise the legal profession (and the public) to the vulnerability of individual's rights under emergency conditions."[16]

Whether a Bill of Rights could work in the United Kingdom so as to enhance the role of judicial review in emergencies and so to aid the better protection of civil liberties, is dependent on three interacting matters. First of all, on the relationship between the Bill of Rights and emergency powers; in other words on the nature of the derogation clause, if any, included in the Bill of Rights which would reflect how much power government was willing to leave to judges. Secondly, its ability to be of value in the United Kingdom legal context turns in great part on whether entrenchment is legally possible and, if so, the nature and degree of entrenchment adopted. Thirdly, much would depend on the attitude of the judiciary to the tasks a Bill of Rights would set for them in general and particularly in emergency contexts. It must be stressed at the outset that the prognosis on all three is not encouraging for the prospects for success of a Bill of Rights in this area.

What form might a derogation clause take? How much power might government be prepared to concede to the judiciary? Those countries with Bills of Rights as part of their constitutional system have varying provisions with regard to the existence and/or scope of judicial review in emergency contexts. They tend to preclude or severely limit it. Thus, the Canadian Bill of Rights 1960, an ordinary statute of the Federal Parliament applicable only to matters within federal jurisdiction, precluded judicial challenge pursuant to its provisions of anything done under the authority of the War Measures Act 1914, which gave to the executive extensive rule-making powers consequent upon an executive proclamation of emergency.[17] When it was last invoked in the apprehended insurrection that was the October crisis in Quebec in 1970,[18] the judiciary were accordingly powerless to

[16] K. Boyle, "Emergency Conditions," in C. Campbell (Ed.), *op. cit.* n. 4, 84 at p. 87.

[17] s.6(5).

[18] Tarnopolsky, *op. cit.* n. 12, pp. 331-348; *Second Report of the Commission of Inquiry Concerning Certain Activities of the Royal Canadian Mounted Police: Freedom and Security Under the Law—Vol. 2,* (1981, Canadian Govt. Publishing Centre), pp. 915-920. The crisis was precipitated by the kidnapping of James Cross, the British Trade Commissioner, and Pierre Laporte, a minister in the provincial government in Quebec, by the Front de liberation du Quebec

apply to the measures the standards enunciated by the Bill of Rights. Similarly, Article 150 of the Malaysian Constitution enables the proclamation of an emergency where the Monarch is satisfied that there exists a grave emergency threatening the security or economic life of the Federation or part thereof. Such a proclamation, which the courts appear to be disinclined to question, enables Parliament, notwithstanding anything in the Constitution, to make laws with respect to any matter if it appears to Parliament that the law is required because of the emergency.[19] The emergency provisions of the Indian constitution similarly enable suspension of many of the fundamental provisions of the Constitution on civil liberties and have led to an attenuated judicial review.[20] Under the Constitution of the Republic of Ireland, no law enacted by Parliament expressly for the purpose of the public safety and the preservation of the State in time of war or armed rebellion can be challenged as to its constitutional validity.[21] "Time of war" is given an extended meaning. It includes a time when each House of the legislature resolves that there exists a national emergency affecting the vital interests of the State because of the existence of an armed conflict in which the State is not a participant. Moreover, "time of war or armed rebellion" continues beyond the end of the war, armed conflict or armed rebellion and covers the period thereafter until such time as each House resolves that the national emergency occasioned by such occurrences has ended. The Irish Supreme Court has held, however, that all judicial review is not thereby excluded. To take a recent example: the Emergency Powers Act 1976 was enacted during the currency in force of a resolution of the legislature that a national emergency existed because of the armed conflict in Northern Ireland. The 1976 Act was to continue in force for a year, according to its own provisions, renewable by parliamentary resolution. The provision noted below is not now in force, but the national emergency resolution remains so and a government order

(FLQ). The Minister was later murdered. The FLQ was banned and many arrests were made under the special powers made available by the War Measures Act, and later under the Public Order (Temporary Provisions) Act 1970.

[19] R. Cumaraswany, "States of Emergency in Malaysia" in International Commission of Jurists, *States of Emergency: Their Impact on Human Rights* (1983), p. 193, at pp. 201-202.

[20] A.G. Noorani and F.S. Nariman, "The State of Emergency in India" *ibid.* p. 169, at pp. 185-188.

[21] Robinson, *op. cit.* n. 4, pp. 55-69; J.M. Kelly, *The Irish Constitution* (1980), pp. 132-142 (annotations to Art. 28.3).

could resurrect the provision.[22] Section 2 of the 1976 Act enabled persons suspected of terrorist-type offences to be held in custody without charge for up to seven days. The Supreme Court, which upheld its constitutional validity when a Bill on a reference to it by the President, also ruled that a person detained under it

> "may not only question the legality of his detention if there has been non-compliance with the express requirements of section 2, but may also rely on provisions of the Constitution for the purposes of construing that section and of testing the legality of what has been done in purported operation of it. A statutory provision of this nature which makes such inroads upon the liberty of the person must be strictly construed . . . the section is not to be read as an abnegation of the arrested person's rights, constitutional or otherwise, in respect of matters such as the right of communication, the right to have legal and medical assistance, and the right of access to the Courts. If the section were used in breach of such rights the High Court might grant an order for release under the provisions for *habeas corpus* contained in the Constitution."[23]

The remedy of habeas corpus may not, however, be invoked to prohibit, control or interfere with any act of the Defence Forces during the existence of a state of war or armed rebellion, but here "state of war" does not bear the extended meaning noted above.[24] The Jamaican Constitution proclaims, in respect of freedom from arbitrary arrest or detention, that

> "nothing contained in or done under the authority of any law shall be held to be inconsistent with or in contravention of this section to the extent that the law in question authorises the taking during a period of public emergency of measures that are reasonably justifiable for the purpose of dealing with the situation that exists during that period of public emergency."[25]

By contrast, although under the Constitution of the United States habeas corpus can be suspended where in cases of rebellion or invasion the public safety may require it,[26] Bill of Rights' protection is not expressly suspended, and, in theory at least, the

[22] Kelly, *ibid.* at p. 401.

[23] *Re Article 26 and the Emergency Powers Bill 1976* [1977] I.R. 159, at p. 173.

[24] Art.40.4.6; Kelly, *op. cit.* n. 21, p. 436.

[25] Lloyd G. Barnett, *The Constitutional Law of Jamaica* (1977), pp. 425-428.

[26] United States' Constitution, Art. I, s.9.

necessary accommodation between the need to permit action to be taken to meet grave situations and the need to protect civil liberties, can be made by the Supreme Court, so that

> "through the use of the 'executive' and 'commander in chief' powers and presidential initiative the presidents of the United States were able to conduct wars through administrative measures which could never be justified in normal peacetime conditions. Similarly, congress, through its war power, was able to intrude upon the jurisdiction of the states, and upon the civil liberties of individuals, to an extent which would not be permitted during peace-time."[27]

In 1982, the United Kingdom Parliament passed the Canada Act patriating to Canada the power to amend its own constitution through the terms of the Constitution Act 1982 embodied as Schedule B to the United Kingdom Statute.[28] Part 1 of that Constitution Act contains the Canadian Charter of Rights and Freedoms which, like the rest of the constitution, constitutes the supreme law of Canada, alterable through the special process set out in section 52 to the Act.[29] The Charter contains no specific emergency clause, but "guarantees the rights and freedoms set out in it subject only to such reasonable limits prescribed by law as can be demonstrably justified in a free and democratic society."[30] Ostensibly, the task of balancing civil liberties against the need for prompt, effective action in emergencies is remitted to the judiciary.[31] However, section 33(1) of the Charter allows Parliament expressly to declare in an enactment that it, or a provision in it, shall operate notwithstanding certain specified provisions in the Charter. Such a clause is called a *non obstante* clause. An enactment containing such a declaration is to have such operation as it would have but for the provision of the Charter referred to in the declaration. Declarations have a maximum duration of five years but may be re-enacted for further periods

[27] W.S. Tarnopolsky, "Emergency Powers and Civil Liberties" (1971) 15 Can. Pub. Admin. 194, at p. 202.

[28] Canada Act 1982, c. 11. For comment see (1983) 61 Can. Bar Rev. 1-442.

[29] See P.W. Hogg, "Supremacy of the Canadian Charter of Rights and Freedoms" (1983) 61 Can. Bar Rev. 69.

[30] s.1 of the Charter.

[31] B. Hovius and R. Martin, "The Canadian Charter of Rights and Freedoms in the Supreme Court of Canada" (1983) 61 Can. Bar Rev. 354; A. Morel, "La Clause Limitative de l'Article de la Charte Canadienne des Droit et Libertes: Une Assurance Contre le Gouvernement des Juges" (1983) 61 Can. Bar Rev. 81.

not exceeding five years each time.[32] Inclusion of a *non obstante* clause in future Canadian emergency legislation could thus remove it or parts of it from judicial scrutiny under certain provisions of the Charter, in much the same way as the government was able to exempt the Public Order (Temporary Provisions) Act 1970, which replaced use of the War Measures Act 1914 during the October crisis in Quebec in 1970, from key provisions of the Canadian Bill of Rights 1960.[33]

Comparative constitutional experience thus reveals a variety of models for a derogation clause. Michael O'Boyle put forward one based on Article 15 of the European Convention on Human Rights (as interpreted by the Court and Commission; *supra*, pp. 83-90, 155-159) to form part of a Bill of Rights' for Northern Ireland. On this model, judicial review would focus: (a) on whether there existed an actual or imminent emergency, whose effects involved the whole Province and threatened the continuance of the organised life of the community, which plainly could not adequately be met by the normal methods of restriction envisaged by the Bill of Rights (*e.g.* restricting freedom of assembly to protect public order); (b) on whether the measures taken went beyond what was required by the exigencies of the situation; (c) on whether any of the rights and freedoms declared to be non-derogable had been infringed.[34] Most other Bills of Rights advanced for the United Kingdom have not, as such, contained a derogation clause giving the courts power to review in emergencies. In so far as emergencies have been mentioned at all, indeed, the relevant clauses have instead exempted the EPA 1920 from the scope of the bill,[35] or have given the government the right to take derogating measures in time of war or other public emergency and have made conclusive a declaration by Her Majesty in Council that such a situation exists.[36] Failure to include a clause enabling derogation subject to judicial scrutiny no doubt reflects views on the propriety of judicial review in such a sensitive context. It also reflects the difficulties of legally entrenching any Bill of Rights in the United Kingdom.

32 s.33(3)-(5) of the Charter.

33 See Tarnopolsky, *op. cit.* n. 12, p. 346.

34 M.P. O'Boyle, "Emergency Situations and the Protection of Human Rights: A Model Derogation Provision for a Northern Ireland Bill of Rights" (1977) 28 N.I.L.Q. 160, at pp. 185-187.

35 See cl. 7 of Lord Arran's Bill H.L. 19 (1970-71).

36 See Lord Wade's Bills cl. 4 H.L. 54, H.C. 100 (1979-80); H.L. 54 (1980-81). For the text of the 1979 Bill, see C. Campbell (Ed.), *op. cit.* n. 4, pp. 20-22.

Derogation clauses affording the courts a measure of review can, legally speaking, constitute a fetter on executive and legislative action when part of a written constitution having a higher legal sanctity than other laws, or if embodied in a devolutionary instrument setting out the powers of a subordinate legislature; the subordinate legislature would act *ultra vires* if it exceeded the limits on its powers (including the Bill of Rights) embodied in its constituent instrument. Such a clause as O'Boyle's could thus be effective as a fetter on a Northern Ireland executive and legislature enjoying devolved powers similar to those in the Government of Ireland Act 1920 which regulated the powers of Stormont until 1972. It would, however, have very little impact if, as seems likely, law, order and security measures remained the exclusive responsibility of the United Kingdom Parliament. Were that Parliament ever to extinguish its powers as part of a new constitutional settlement creating, through a Constitutional Convention, a new "written," higher law constitution, accepted by the electorate at a referendum, no doubt such a clause would be similarly effective as part of the new constitutional order. Such a prospect is most unlikely. Whether a clause such as that suggested by O'Boyle could work if embodied in a Bill of Rights contained in an Act of Parliament is, rather, the heart of the matter, and would depend (a) on whether some form of entrenchment is legally possible under the present constitutional system in the United Kingdom, and (b) if so, on the form and degree of entrenchment actually adopted. By entrenchment is here understood a process whereby one Act of Parliament is given a higher status than other Acts of Parliament in the sense that it cannot be repealed or amended by the ordinary enacting process but instead requires the amending or repealing Act to be passed according to some special manner and form, for example, necessitating a two-thirds majority in each House of Parliament, or requiring the insertion of a special clause into an Act passed by ordinary procedure.[37]

At present, parliamentary sovereignty is regarded by the courts as meaning that Parliament can make or unmake any law whatsoever, and that a later statute impliedly repeals an earlier one to the extent of any inconsistency.[38] Legal opinion differs on whether, faced with a purported entrenchment, the courts would modify that view. The House of Lords Select Committee on a Bill

[37] On the difficulties of entrenchment see Wallington and McBride, *op. cit.* n. 8, pp. 83-93; J. Jaconelli, *Enacting a Bill of Rights* (1980), esp. Chap. VI.

[38] S.A. De Smith, *Constitutional and Administrative Law* (4th ed., 1981), pp. 73, 83.

of Rights took the view that they would not, that entrenchment, even to the limited extent of requiring in a statute an express declaration of intent to override the Bill of Rights, was not legally possible.[39] Others take the view that Parliament can bind its successors as to manner and form, that an entrenchment might constitute a redefinition of Parliament for the particular purpose of overriding the Bill of Rights.[40] This is not the place to attempt to resolve the conundrum. What is clear, however, is that, in the context of a Bill of Rights, the implied repeal rule, if not modified, would have two effects in terms of the relationship of the Bill of Rights to existing and future statutes. As regards existing statutes, the Bill of Rights would impliedly repeal those provisions inconsistent with the provisions in the Bill of Rights. Thus, provisions, for example in NIEPA 1978 or in the PTA 1984 would be invalidated unless (a) something akin to O'Boyle's derogation clause were included and the courts were to hold the provisions justified pursuant to it (*i.e.* in effect saying that because of the derogation clause there was no inconsistency between the two sets of provisions), or (b) such provisions were specifically exempted from the operation of the Bill of Rights through a clause in the Bill itself. The latter course was favoured by the Whitehall inter-departmental Working Group Concerning Legislation on Human Rights with particular reference to the European Convention.[41] It was also the device used in Lord Arran's 1970 proposal in order to preserve fully intact the rule-making power in the EPA 1920.[42] As regards statutes passed subsequent to the Bill of Rights, if no entrenchment is possible or, if possible, none was adopted, the later statute would prevail. If, for example, Lord Wade's 1979 and 1981 Bills had been enacted, the role of the judges would only have been to construe the enactment (*e.g.* another NIEPA or PTA) so far as possible so as to conform with the Bill of Rights and, where that proved impossible, to give effect to that

[39] *Report of the Select Committee on a Bill of Rights*, H.L. 176 (1977-78), paras. 14, 17. See also the advice to the Committee from its Special Adviser, D. Rippengal, "The Question of Entrenchment" in *Minutes of Evidence taken before the Select Committee on a Bill of Rights*, H.L. 81 (1977-78), esp. p. 10.

[40] R.F.V. Heuston, *Essays in Constitutional Law* (2nd ed., 1984), Chap. 1: "Sovereignty": W.S. Tarnopolsky, *op. cit.* n. 12, pp. 92-112; M.A. Fazal, "Entrenched Rights and Parliamentary Sovereignty" [1974] P.L. 289.

[41] *Report of a Working Group of Certain Government Departments Concerning Legislation on Human Rights, With Particular Reference to the European Convention on Human Rights* (1976), para. 3.47, reproduced in *Minutes of Evidence*, *op. cit.* n. 39, pp. 28-63.

[42] cl. 7, H.L. 19 (1970-71).

subsequent enactment.[43] On that model, there is little role for a derogation clause since, that clause having no higher status than any other provision in an Act of Parliament, the later statute would prevail even if inconsistent with the terms of the clause. There, Lord Wade's further provision denying the courts jurisdiction to challenge an executive declaration of emergency was superfluous.[44] Similarly, even if the minimal entrenchment constituted by a section stating that the Bill of Rights would prevail over a later statute not containing an express clause stating that it was to apply notwithstanding the Bill of Rights, were possible and adopted, any derogation clause, having no higher status than any other provision in the Bill of Rights, could be circumvented by inclusion of the "notwithstanding clause" in the later statute. Granted, its inclusion, when the Bill of Rights made express provision for derogation, would require public and parliamentary justification, but such justification might be afforded in such terms as the emergency requiring very extreme measures and raising issues much too sensitive for judicial scrutiny. Even if entrenchment were to consist in requiring a two-thirds majority in each House to override the Bill of Rights, voting patterns on emergency legislation suggest that such majorities might be readily obtainable.[45] Only if the derogation clause itself could not legally be overriden at all (and, in the absence of a written constitution, this is probably not feasible), or if the required majority for circumvention were not obtained, or if the government and legislature were willing to refrain from circumventing it, thus leaving it to the courts to uphold the enactment as a legitimate exercise of the right to derogate, would a derogation clause open the way to judicial review of the existence of the emergency and the need for the particular measures taken to combat it.

[43] cl. 3, H.L. 54, H.C. 100 (1979-80), H.L. 54 (1980-81).

[44] cl. 4, *ibid.*; see: P. Wallington, "What does a Bill of Rights mean in practice?" in C. Campbell (Ed.), *op. cit.* n. 4, 38, at pp. 42-43; NCCL evidence to Select Committee, *Minutes of Evidence, op. cit.* n. 39, p. 166 (para. 39).

[45] For example, the PTA 1974 was approved by both Houses without a division: see C. Scorer, *The Prevention of Terrorism Acts 1974 and 1976: A Report on the Operation of the Law* (1976). Its successor, the PTA 1976, attracted only 11 votes against in the Commons (H.C. Deb., Vol. 904, cols. 592-594). The third reading of NIEPA 1975 was approved without a division in the Commons (H.C. Deb., Vol. 895, col. 1202). The third reading of the Energy Act 1976 similarly did not require a division (H.C. Deb., Vol. 917, col. 1822).

It is very unlikely that government would be willing to subject its actions and chosen measures in such a sensitive area to the degree of judicial scrutiny such a clause might involve. The SACHR (*supra*, pp. 77-78) recommended that such matters not be left to courts,[46] a view shared by the House of Lords Select Committee on a Bill of Rights[47] and the report of the inter-departmental Working Group noted above.[48] Nor do senior members of the judiciary, perhaps antipathetical to the general role a Bill of Rights would demand of them, seem keen to have any such task thrust upon them. Several judges, albeit extrajudicially, have publicly doubted the possibility of entrenchment.[49] Lord Diplock once noted in respect of judicial scrutiny of the derogation issue:

> "It lies upon judges to decide whether a derogation satisfies the requirement of being strictly required by the exigencies of the situation. First, let me say that judges, by their training, by their experience, by the comparative isolation in which, by reason of their office, they are bound to live, are ill-fitted, compared with commoners, to decide in an emergency what the exigencies of the situation require. Secondly, it has to be decided by judges applying the judicial process, and the judicial process requires judges to act on evidence and not upon their own notions.
>
> In emergencies, Governments act upon intelligence which very often cannot be disclosed and put in evidence at all, so as to preserve the secrecy of sources, or, it may be, in order to avoid exacerbating the situation. Is it right that in an emergency the decision as to what is necessary should be left to me rather than to Government? Power hungry as I may be, I would hesitate to regard myself as fit to make that decision."[50]

But even if it were left to the courts—for example, if an Emergency Powers Code, invocable by executive proclamation, subject to parliamentary approval, provided that the propriety of

[46] SACHR, *The Protection of Human Rights by Law in Northern Ireland*, Cmnd. 7009 (1977), para. 7.12, pp. 68-69.

[47] *Op. cit.* n. 39, para. 44.

[48] *Op. cit.* n. 41, para. 3.47.

[49] See Lord Hailsham, *Minutes of Evidence*, *op. cit.* n. 39, p. 25, and Lord Scarman, *ibid.* pp. 367-368.

[50] Cited by Lord Boston of Faversham in "Arguments Against a Bill of Rights" in C. Campbell (Ed.), *op. cit.* n. 4, 23, at pp. 27-28.

the proclamation and the necessity for measures taken under it were subject to judicial scrutiny as a condition for their continuance in force (*supra*, pp. 273-274)–one cannot be over sanguine about the practical difference this would make to the end result in particular cases. Judges might continue to display a marked deference to executive opinion, and would be reluctant to substitute their view for that of the executive branch of government on matters more within its own knowledge than that of the judges. One would expect the courts to adopt something like the "margin of appreciation" test used by the European Court of Human Rights in applying the derogation provision in the European Convention on Human Rights (Art. 15; *supra*, pp. 83-90), giving the government "a permitted range of honest judgment" as to the existence of the emergency and the measures required to be taken.[51] The approach of the European Court of Human Rights is hardly stringent or individual-oriented. Although the Canadian experience in 1970 is not exactly in point because Bill of Rights issues were precluded by an express clause in the Bill of Rights itself, it is noteworthy that in upholding executive action under the regulations, the Quebec Courts attracted criticism for failing to deal with a constitutional issue under the Canadian constitution, then solely the British North America Acts.[52] Even in the United States, where the accommodation between Bill of Rights' values and necessity in emergencies may rest squarely with the courts, the latter were not slow to uphold as valid the enforced movement inland of Japanese-Americans from the West-Coast in the Second World War, which movement was challenged as a denial of the constitutional right to equal protection of the laws.[53] Nor is the Supreme Court's approach in the McCarthy era an encouraging precedent.[54]

[51] *Cf.* Borovoy, *op. cit.* n. 5, at p. 6: the test proposed by the Canadian Civil Liberties Association was such as not to necessarily require the Court to substitute its own opinion, but rather a narrower one–in all the circumstances are there reasonable and persuasive grounds to justify the conclusion that the situation fell within the definition required by the emergency powers statute.

[52] H. Marx, "The 'Apprehended Insurrection' of October 1970 and the Judicial Function" (1972) 7 U.B.C.L. Rev. 55.

[53] See, *e.g.* E. Hudon, "The status of persons of Japanese ancestry in the United States and Canada during World War II: a tragedy in three parts" (1977) *Les Cahiers de droit* 61, esp. at pp. 75-81.

[54] Wallington and McBride, *op. cit.* n, 8, p. 34.

Opening up emergencies to judicial review might well provide another forum of public accountability, and on that score constitute a valuable step forward. It is unlikely to be taken.

INDEX